Y0-BCQ-796

The Recovery of the Anabaptist Vision

Harold S Gender

THE RECOVERY
of the
ANABAPTIST VISION

A Sixtieth Anniversary Tribute

To Harold S. Bender

Edited by Guy F. Hershberger

HERALD PRESS
SCOTTDALE, PENNSYLVANIA

THE RECOVERY OF THE ANABAPTIST VISION
Copyright © 1957 by Mennonite Publishing House, Scottdale, Pa. 15683
Library of Congress Catalog Card Number: 57-10214
International Standard Book Number: 0-8361-1421-3
Third Printing, 1972
Printed in the United States

Preface

This volume of essays is published in recognition of nearly thirty-five years of service to Anabaptist-Mennonite historiography. Several of the younger scholars whose essays appear in the group first suggested the project as an expression of appreciation for their mentor whose labors have made a significant contribution to an understanding of Anabaptism, its origins, its character, its history, and its meaning.

In planning the project the most promising design seemed to be a series of essays co-ordinated in such a way as to summarize succinctly in one volume the more significant findings of recent scholarship concerning the rise of Anabaptism, its theological concepts, and its course in history. Since many scholars, both European and American, some members of churches within the Anabaptist tradition and some not, have made their contribution to this chapter in historiography, it was felt that these varied contributions should in some way be represented in the summary volume. Inasmuch as what is here presented was so dramatically epitomized in *The Anabaptist Vision,* Harold S. Bender's own incisive presidential address before the American Society of Church History, it seemed altogether fitting that this address should be included and that the entire volume should be entitled *The Recovery of the Anabaptist Vision.*

The project was planned chiefly by Paul Peachey, John C. Wenger, John H. Yoder, and the editor. Robert Friedmann read a number of the manuscripts. Elizabeth Bender and John C. Wenger read all of them. The latter also prepared the index. The first copy of the book was presented to Harold S. Bender on July 19, 1957, the sixtieth anniversary of his birth.

Contents

✠ GUY F. HERSHBERGER ✠

Introduction

Anabaptist historiography[1] was formerly the prerogative of its enemies, typified by Christoph Andreas Fischer's polemic, *Von der Wiedertauffer verfluchtem Ursprung, gottlosen Lehre und derselben gründliche Widerlegung,* published in 1603. For a long time indictments such as these were generally accepted by historians, who failed to consult Anabaptist confessional writings and other sources, so that until well into the nineteenth century Anabaptism was uncritically identified with the Peasants' War of 1525 and the Münster incident of 1534-35.

Eventually, however, historical scholarship was bound to correct these views. Once the voluntary church, the separation of church and state, and religious liberty—ideas for which the Anabaptists had striven so valiantly in the sixteenth century—came to be widely accepted, the despised movement began to draw the attention of scholars. The result has been a remarkable reversal of opinion within the world of scholarship regarding the nature and the goals of Anabaptism.

During the sixteenth and seventeenth centuries the Anabaptists themselves produced valuable source materials for the study of their history. One of the first sources was the old hymnal, the *Ausbund,* begun in 1535 by the prisoners in the castle at Passau, the first edition of which appeared in 1564. Certain writings of Menno Simons and Dirk Philips were also

* Guy F. Hershberger is Professor of History and Sociology at Goshen College, and author of *War, Peace, and Nonresistance* (Scottdale, 1944, revised, 1953), and *The Mennonite Church in the Second World War* (Scottdale, 1951).

1 For an extended treatment of Anabaptist-Mennonite historiography see the comprehensive article "Historiography" by Harold S. Bender and Cornelius Krahn in *The Mennonite Encyclopedia* (Scottdale, 1956) 2:751-69.

available, and in 1562 the Dutch martyrbook *Het Offer des Heeren* was published containing a collection of martyr testimonials. This was later expanded by Tieleman Jansz van Braght into his *Martyrs' Mirror,* printed at Dordrecht in 1660. The first historical treatise produced by the Mennonites appeared at Amsterdam in 1615 with the title, *Het beginsel en voortganck der geschillen, scheuringen, en verdeeltheden onder de gene die Doopsgesinden genoemt worden.*

The use of these and other sources, including German and Swiss productions, made it possible for Gottfried Arnold to emerge at the close of the seventeenth century as the first church historian to depart from the hitherto accepted interpretation of Anabaptism in his *Unparteyische Kirchen- und Ketzer-Historie,*[2] in which he corrected a number of false assertions concerning the character of the movement, although obviously not removing its classification as heretical. During the eighteenth century further Anabaptist sources were made available, among the most important being a mass of historical notices, council protocols, orders, and provisions of the Swiss government concerning the earliest Anabaptists included in J. C. Füsslin's Swiss Reformation sources, *Beyträge zur Erläuterung der Kirchen-Reformations-Geschichten des Schweitzerlandes.*[3]

A new chapter in Anabaptist historiography was opened in the mid-nineteenth century when Carl Adolf Cornelius published his *Geschichte des Münsterischen Aufruhrs.*[4] Basing his work on careful research in original sources, Cornelius broke completely from the traditional state-church treatment of the subject. Although Walther Köhler as late as 1925 was able to say, "At the time when the older men of our generation were students we scarcely heard anything mentioned [about the Anabaptists], and if it did happen, a judgment was passed upon it in advance by the use of the word 'fanat-

2 First published in Frankfurt, 1699; enlarged third edition (Schaffhausen, 1740-42).
3 Five volumes (Zürich and Leipzig, 1741-53).
4 Leipzig, 1855-60.

ics,' "[5] it was C. A. Cornelius nevertheless who at long last had paved the way for an objective and trustworthy Anabaptist historiography, in which Köhler himself later played an important role. From Cornelius onward a succession of Dutch, German, and Swiss historians continued the work, eventually to be joined by their American colaborers.

Among the Mennonites themselves the Dutch were the first to develop a historiography of high quality. Even prior to the work of Cornelius the Mennonite Theological Seminary together with the library and archives of the Mennonite Church in Amsterdam had become a center of historical research. The outstanding nineteenth-century works on Dutch Mennonite history were Samuel Muller's *Jaarboekje voor de Doopsgezinde Gemeenten in Nederland;*[6] A. M. Cramer's *Het leven en de verrigtingen van Menno Simons,*[7] the first comprehensive biography of Menno; and S. Blaupot ten Cate's *Geschiedenis der Doopsgezinden in Friesland,*[8] *Geschiedenis der Doopsgezinden in Groningen, Overijssel en Oost-Friesland,*[9] and *Geschiedenis der Doopsgezinden in Holland, Zeeland, Utrecht en Gelderland.*[10] The *Doopsgezinde Bijdragen,*[11] a Dutch Mennonite yearbook, also published much historical material. From 1870 to 1893 it was edited by J. G. de Hoop Scheffer. In the twentieth century Dutch Mennonite historical scholarship was continued by Karel Vos, W. J. Kühler, A. F. Mellink, and N. van der Zijpp. Vos is the author of *Menno Simons, 1496-1561, Zijn leven en zijne reformatorische denkbeelden.*[12] In 1952 van der Zijpp wrote *Geschiedenis der Doopsgezinden in Nederland,*[13] the first modern thorough history of the Dutch Mennonites.

Volumes II, V, VII, and X of the *Bibliotheca Reformatoria Neerlandica,*[14] edited by Samuel Cramer and F. Pijper, contain much valuable Anabaptist source material, including

5 Cf. *ME*, 2:753.
6 Amsterdam, 1837-50.
7 Amsterdam, 1837.
11 Amsterdam, Leeuwarden, and Leiden, 1861-1919.
12 Leiden, 1914.
14 The Hague, 1903-14.

8 Leeuwarden, 1839.
9 Leeuwarden, 1842.
10 Amsterdam, 1847.
13 Arnhem, 1952.

martyr letters and hymns, records of disputations, and writings of Melchior Hofmann, Michael Sattler, Dirk Philips, and other sixteenth-century leaders.

Important Swiss publications appearing in the last quarter of the nineteenth century were Emil Egli's *Aktensammlung zur Geschichte der Züricher Reformation in den Jahren 1519-1532*,[15] *Die Züricher Wiedertäufer zur Reformationszeit*,[16] and *Die St. Galler Taufer*;[17] Ernst Müller's *Geschichte der Bernischen Täufer*;[18] and Paul Burckhardt's *Die Basler Täufer*.[19] The first sociological treatment of the Swiss Mennonites was Ernst Correll's *Das Schweizerische Täufermennonitentum, Ein soziologischer Bericht*.[20] Another twentieth-century Swiss publication by a Swiss author is Samuel Geiser's *Die Taufgesinnten-Gemeinden*, a work not limited to the Swiss Mennonites.[21] *Brüder in Christo*[22] by Fritz Blanke of the University of Zürich tells the story of the first Anabaptist congregation at Zollikon. Swiss Anabaptist sources are now being published in the *Quellen zur Geschichte der Täufer in der Schweiz*, the first volume of which, edited by L. von Muralt and Walter Schmid, appeared in Zürich in 1952.

An outstanding nineteenth-century German contribution to Mennonite historiography was made by Max Goebel, whose *Geschichte des christlichen Lebens in der rheinisch-westfälischen evangelischen Kirche*[23] is a sympathetic treatment and an important source for the study of Anabaptism in the Rhineland. Ludwig Keller, the author of *Die Geschichte der Widertäufer und ihres Reichs zu Münster*,[24] of *Ein Apostel der Wiedertäufer*,[25] a biography of Hans Denk, and of *Die Reformation und die älteren Reformparteien*,[26] was a German historian who had a great influence on those who followed him, including John Horsch, the American Mennonite historian. Another outstanding contribution was that of Gustav Bossert, who concentrated on the history of the

15 Zürich, 1879.
16 Zürich, 1878.
17 Zürich, 1887.
18 Frauenfeld, 1895.
19 Basel, 1898.
20 Tübingen, 1925.
21 Karlsruhe, 1931.
22 Zürich, 1955.
23 Coblenz, 1849-60.
24 Münster, 1880.
25 Leipzig, 1885.
26 Leipzig, 1885.

Reformation in Württemberg. His *Das Blutgericht in Rottenburg am Neckar*[27] is an account of the trial and death of Michael Sattler, the greatest leader of the South German Anabaptists. In his writings, all based on careful research, Bossert, even though a Lutheran, rejected completely the traditional state church interpretation of the Anabaptist movement. Many of his articles appeared in periodicals and encyclopedias. Perhaps his most valuable contribution was his work as editor of *Quellen zur Geschichte der Wiedertäufer, I: Herzogtum Württemberg*.[28] This is the first of a series of three volumes, known as the *Täufer-Akten*, published prior to World War II by the Verein für Reformationsgeschichte. Since the war this publication project has been continued by a Täufer Akten-Kommission made up of representatives of the VRG and of the Mennonitischer Geschichtsverein, with support from American Mennonite historical societies. Several volumes of the *Quellen zur Geschichte der Täufer,* as the new series is called, have made their appearance. Eventually, it is hoped, all of the documents bearing on the history of the Anabaptist movement will be published.

Most significant for their treatment of Anabaptism were the standard religio-sociological works of Ernst Troeltsch, *Protestantisches Christentum und Kirche in der Neuzeit*[29] and *Die Soziallehren der christlichen Kirchen und Gruppen,*[30] and Max Weber's *Gesammelte Aufsätze zur Religionssoziologie I,*[31] and "Wirtschaft und Gesellschaft" in *Grundriss der Sozialökonomie*.[32] With the publication of these works during the first quarter of the century the foundation for an objective Anabaptist historiography was finally complete. The next quarter century was now in a position to reap the fruits of generations of painstaking scholarship.

A noteworthy contribution to German Mennonite historiography was that of Christian Hege (1869-1943) **and**

---

[27] Barmen, 1892.   [28] Leipzig, 1930.   [29] Berlin, 1909.
[30] Third edition, 1923. Translated into English as *The Social Teaching of the Christian Churches* (London, 1931).
[31] Tübingen, 1920.   [32] 1922.

Christian Neff (1863-1946), who founded the Mennonitischer Geschichtsverein in 1933 and its publication, the *Mennonitische Geschichtsblätter*.[33] Their greatest work was the *Mennonitisches Lexikon*,[34] whose first installment was published in 1913, and which had been published to the letter "O" in 1942 when the work was suspended because of the war. Publication was resumed in 1951 under the editorship of Ernst Crous and Harold S. Bender. Hege and Neff themselves wrote more than half of the material in the *Lexikon*, while outstanding contributions were made by Bossert of Württemberg, Vos of the Netherlands, and Johann Loserth of Graz.

In recent German Mennonite historiography, the more significant contributions have been made by Walther Köhler, whose "Die Zürcher Täufer" appeared in *Gedenkschrift zum 400-jährigen Jubiläum der Mennoniten oder Taufgesinnten*;[35] by W. Wiswedel in *Bilder und Führergestalten aus dem Täufertum*;[36] by Ethelbert Stauffer's "Märtyrertheologie und Täuferbewegung";[37] by Cornelius Krahn's *Menno Simons (1496-1561), Ein Beitrag zur Geschichte und Theologie der Taufgesinnten*;[38] by Abraham Fast in *Die Kulturleistungen der Mennoniten in Ostfriesland und Münsterland*;[39] by Horst Penner in *Weltweite Bruderschaft*;[40] and by Ernst Crous, the present director of the Mennonitische Forschungsstelle, Göttingen, and the German editor both of the *Mennonitisches Lexikon* and of *The Mennonite Encyclopedia*.[41]

The Russian phase of Mennonite history has been told by a number of their own historians including P. M. Friesen, whose *Die Alt-Evangelische Mennonitische Brüderschaft in Russland 1789-1910*[42] presents a valuable collection of source material. Among the more important studies treat-

---

[33] Karlsruhe, 1936 ff.   [34] Frankfurt, Weierhof, and Karlsruhe, 1913 ff.
[35] Ludwigshafen, 1925.
[36] Three volumes (Kassel, 1928, 1930, 1952).
[37] This appeared in the *Zeitschrift für Kirchengeschichte* (Stuttgart, 1933) 15:545-98 and in English in the *Mennonite Quarterly Review* (Goshen, 1945) 19:179-214.
[38] Karlsruhe, 1936.   [39] Emden, 1947.   [40] Karlsruhe, 1955.
[41] To be published in four volumes (Scottdale, 1955 ff.).
[42] Halbstadt, 1911.

ing the Russian Mennonites who migrated to the United States and Canada are C. Henry Smith, *The Coming of the Russian Mennonites;*[43] Cornelius Krahn, ed., *From the Steppes to the Prairies;*[44] Gustav E. Reimer and G. R. Gaeddert, *Exiled by the Czar: Cornelius Jansen and the Great Mennonite Migration, 1874;*[45] and E. K. Francis, who features the Mennonites of Manitoba in a sociological study, *In Search of Utopia.*[46] The emigration following the Russian revolution of 1917 stimulated numerous studies, one of the most significant being Adolf Ehrt, *Das Mennonitentum in Russland.*[47] J. W. Fretz, *Pilgrims in Paraguay*[48] is a study of the pilgrims from Russia in their new home.

Before the end of the nineteenth century American Baptist historians were making their contribution to Anabaptist historiography. First was Henry S. Burrage's *A History of the Anabaptists in Switzerland,*[49] followed by A. H. Newman's *History of Anti-Pedobaptism . . . to 1609*[50] and Henry C. Vedder's *Balthasar Hübmaier.*[51] Although they published little on Anabaptism as such, both August and Walter Rauschenbusch were students of the movement which definitely influenced their views and their writings. Walter Rauschenbusch's publication[52] of an English translation of Conrad Grebel's letter of September 5, 1524, to Thomas Müntzer is an illustration of this interest. Excellent twentieth-century treatments by English Baptist authors are R. J. Smithson's *The Anabaptists, Their Contributions to Our Heritage,*[53] and Ernest A. Payne's *The Anabaptists of the 16th Century and Their Influence in the Modern World.*[54]

Henry E. Dosker's *The Dutch Anabaptists*[55] and A. J. F. Zieglschmid's edition of *Die älteste Chronik der Hutterischen Brüder*[56] are illustrations of a growing interest in Anabaptism

43 Berne, Ind., 1927. 46 Glencoe, Ill., 1955. 49 Philadelphia, 1882.
44 Newton, 1939. 47 Langensalza, 1932. 50 Philadelphia, 1897.
45 Newton, 1956. 48 Scottdale, 1953. 51 New York, 1905.
52 In the *American Journal of Theology* (Chicago, January 1905).
53 London, 1935. 54 London, 1949. 55 Philadelphia, 1921.
56 Philadelphia, 1943. Also *Das Klein-Geschichtsbuch der Hutterischen Brüder* (Philadelphia, 1947). Zieglschmid's work was preceded by Josef Beck's *Die Geschichts-*

on the part of American historians. Most significant of all is Roland H. Bainton's deep interest and objective treatment of the left wing of the Reformation as found in his *David Joris, Wiedertäufer und Kämpfer für Toleranz im 16. Jahrhundert*,[57] *The Travail of Religious Liberty*,[58] and *The Reformation of the Sixteenth Century*,[59] the latter including the best treatment of the Anabaptists to be found in any general church history or history of the Reformation. The true character of Anabaptism is at last being reported by the best modern church historians, whose graduate students are continuing the work, an example being Franklin H. Littell's *The Anabaptist View of the Church*.[60]

Although the early American Mennonites had little opportunity or training for historical scholarship, the Anabaptist tradition was kept alive among them, nevertheless, through continued republication of certain important sources. From 1727, the date of the first American Mennonite imprint, to 1890, the date of the first publication by John Horsch, the American Mennonites, who by now had a flourishing publication center at Elkhart, Indiana, had published no less than eight editions of the *Dordrecht Confession of Faith,* ten of the *Ausbund,* six of the *Martyrs' Mirror,* and two editions of the works of Menno Simons, besides at least nine editions of portions of Menno's writings. Portions of the writings of Dirk Philips appear in at least six imprints and of P. J. Twisck in two imprints. For a generation after its founding in 1864 the *Herald of Truth* was the principal organ for the expression of Anabaptist-Mennonite ideals in America. The very first issue set forth the doctrine of nonresistance, an emphasis which remained a permanent feature of this periodical.

The first American Mennonite historian was D. K. Cassel, whose *History of the Mennonites*[61] and *Geschichte der*

Bücher der Wiedertäufer (Vienna, 1883) and Rudolf Wolkan's *Geschicht-Buch der Hutterischen Brüder* (Vienna, 1923).

57 Leipzig, 1937.   59 Boston, 1952.
58 Philadelphia, 1951.   60 Philadelphia, 1952.   61 Philadelphia, 1888.

Mennoniten,[62] although compilations more than histories, contained much valuable material gathered from primary sources. These works were followed by C. H. A. van der Smissen's *Kurzgefasste Geschichte und Glaubenslehre der Altevangelischen Taufgesinnten oder Mennoniten,*[63] based on secondary sources, and C. H. Wedel's *Abriss der Geschichte der Mennoniten.*[64] The first and to date the only scholarly general history of the American Mennonites is C. Henry Smith's *The Mennonites of America.*[65] This material in revised form was included in Smith's general histories (European and American), *The Mennonites*[66] and *The Story of the Mennonites.*[67] Another work by Smith is *The Mennonite Immigration to Pennsylvania.*[68] Smith's first work appeared while he was on the faculty of Goshen College, during which time the first beginnings of a Mennonite historical library at this place were made. It was only a beginning, however, when in 1913 Smith transferred to Bluffton College, where the remainder of his work was done.

The above provides the general background and setting for the chapter in Anabaptist-Mennonite historiography to which the present volume is dedicated. This chapter begins with the immigration in 1887 of a twenty-year-old youth named John Horsch[69] who had left his home in Germany in search of freedom to practice the nonresistant faith which was denied him in his native country, and who came with a sense of mission to revive within American Mennonitism the spirit of original Anabaptism. Beginning in 1885 when he was but eighteen years of age, and continuing for more than eight years, Horsch maintained a correspondence with Ludwig Keller, the Münster archivist, historian, and author of *Ein Apostel der Wiedertäufer.* Urged by Keller to "arouse among

62 Philadelphia, 1890.
63 Summerfield, Ill., 1895.
64 Four volumes, total 756 pages (Newton, 1900-4).
65 Goshen, 1909.
66 Berne, Ind., 1920.
67 Berne, 1941; revised (Newton, 1950).
68 Norristown, Pa., 1929.
69 Cf. the John Horsch memorial number of the *Mennonite Quarterly Review* (July 1947) 21:129-232.

9

your brotherhoods the genius of the old Anabaptists," the twenty-year-old Horsch began his fifty-four years of historical and theological writing with an article, "Nachfolge Christi," in John F. Funk's *Herold der Wahrheit* (June, 1887), and indicated his intention to publish future articles based on the older writings and the history of the church.

Within three years 125 or more brief articles had been published. On Keller's advice these articles were used as the basis for Horsch's first book, *Kurzgefasste Geschichte der Mennoniten Gemeinden*,[70] which contains an excellent Anabaptist bibliography. The next book to appear was *The Mennonites, Their History, Faith, and Practice*,[71] followed by *A Short History of Christianity*.[72] During the eight years while he was associated with Funk's publishing work (1887-95), and again during the thirty-three years (1908-41) that he was with the Mennonite Publishing House at Scottdale, Horsch collected a most remarkable library, rich in Dutch, German, and Swiss Anabaptist sources which were the foundation for his lifelong scholarly work. Even the Funk library was largely a Horsch collection. Eventually the Funk and the Horsch collections were acquired by the Mennonite Publishing House, and after Horsch's death much of this library was transferred to the Mennonite Historical Library of Goshen College.

The fruits of Horsch's scholarly efforts are found today in the following works, besides numerous articles in the *Mennonite Quarterly Review* and other periodicals: *Menno Simons*;[73] *Die Biblische Lehre von der Wehrlosigkeit*;[74] *Modern Religious Liberalism*;[75] *The Principle of Nonresistance as Held by the Mennonite Church, An Historical Survey*;[76] *The Hutterian Brethren; A Story of Martyrdom and Loyalty, 1528-1931*;[77] and *Mennonites in Europe,* published posthumously.[78]

70 Elkhart, 1890.
71 Elkhart, 1893.
72 Cleveland, 1903.
73 Scottdale, 1916.
74 Scottdale, 1920.
75 Scottdale, 1921.
76 Scottdale, 1927.
77 Goshen, 1931.
78 Scottdale, 1942.

Anabaptist Research and Interpretation

Harold S. Bender and Anabaptist Research

Harold Stauffer Bender, eldest son of George L. and Elsie Kolb Bender, was born at Elkhart, Indiana, in 1897. In 1918 he earned the B.A. degree at Goshen College, in 1922 the B.D. at Garrett Biblical Institute, and in 1923 the M.A. at Princeton University and the Th.M. at Princeton Theological Seminary. In 1923 he married Elizabeth Horsch, daughter of John and Christine Funck Horsch, who accompanied him to Europe for a year of study at Tübingen on a George S. Green Traveling Fellowship. During this year he became thoroughly acquainted with Anabaptist historiography, its sources and their depositories, as well as with the scholars in the field. It was here that the present writer, who was just completing his doctorate at Munich, learned to know the Benders and then accompanied them to the United States in the autumn of 1924 where with Bender he joined the faculty of Goshen College.

One of Bender's first undertakings following his new appointment was the organization of the Mennonite Historical Society of which he has served as president from the beginning. *The Goshen College Record*[1] reports an enthusiastic organization meeting on October 15, 1924, at which time "the way was cleared for active work," including "research and publication." During the academic year 1924-25 the new society held five meetings. Ernst Correll presented the work of the *Mennonitisches Lexikon*[2] at one, and John F. Funk, ninety-year-old pioneer publisher, twice spoke on the beginnings of Mennonite publication work in America.

* Ernst H. Correll, Professor of Economic History in the American Uuniversity, Washington, D.C., is a member of the editorial board of the *Mennonite Quarterly Review* and of *Studies in Anabaptist and Mennonite History*, and is author of *Das Schweizerische Täufermennonitentum: Ein Soziologischer Bericht* (Tübingen, 1925).

1 *The Goshen College Record* (October 1924) 5-6.
2 For the significance of the *Lexikon* see above, p. 6.

At the time of the June commencement, 1925, the Mennonite Historical Society, in co-operation with the college, sponsored a quadricentennial program, celebrating the four hundredth anniversary of Anabaptist beginnings in Zürich. To this writer's knowledge this was the only quadricentennial service held in the western hemisphere. The principal speakers were John Horsch and Albert H. Newman, the Baptist church historian, who gave two addresses each. Horsch spoke on "The Origin and Faith of the Swiss Brethren" and "The Origin of the Dutch Mennonites." Newman's subjects were "Hubmaier and the Moravian Anabaptists" and "The Significance of the Anabaptist Movement in the History of the Christian Church." The presence of Horsch and Newman, then the two leading American authorities on sixteenth-century Anabaptism, presaged the comprehensiveness of approach and the quality of work which the Mennonite Historical Society was to perform in the decades that followed.

In January, 1926, the Mennonite Historical Society's promise of active work in research and publication began its fulfillment in the appearance of *The Goshen College Record Review Supplement,* with 48 pages of solid scholarly articles, book reviews, and research notes. The two leading articles were papers of Horsch and Newman read at the quadricentennial. Bender presented "A Survey of Mennonite Historical Literature for 1925" which listed 25 books, pamphlets, and dissertations in German, Dutch, and English, and a similar number of significant scholarly articles in the three languages. Bender and Correll also presented a translation of "Conrad Grebel's Petition of Protest and Defense to the Zürich Council in 1523," with notes, an introduction, and an appendix. This article was the beginning of continued studies destined to culminate in Bender's biographical study, *Conrad Grebel, the Founder of the Swiss Brethren.*[3] During 1926 two more issues of the *Review Supplement* appeared, featuring among other materials the remaining quadricenten-

3 Goshen, 1950.

nial papers of Horsch and Newman; an article by Correll on "Gustav Bossert's Contribution to Mennonite History," with a bibliography; and more letters and papers of Conrad Grebel translated by Edward Yoder with annotations by Correll, Bender, and Yoder.

The Goshen College Record's report of the founding of the Mennonite Historical Society in October, 1924, also said: "The Society is taking special interest in the Mennonite Historical Library . . . . It expects to purchase books and materials to constantly enlarge and improve the library . . . . A drive for old books from the churches throughout the country will soon be undertaken . . . ." The significance of this statement can be appreciated only by realizing how small was the meager collection of titles in what was called the Mennonite Historical Library in 1924, located on three shelves in a not easily accessible or even visible niche in the college library then housed in the administration building.

While this proved to be the beginning of larger things to come, the scholar circumscribed by its narrow limits was overcome by a nostalgia for the Mennonite library in Amsterdam, the *Mennonitisches Lexikon* collections of Neff and Hege at Weierhof and Frankfurt, Germany, and the Horsch collection at Scottdale, all of them rich depositories of source materials. Whatever research and writing was done in those early years at Goshen depended almost exclusively on materials supplied by Scottdale, besides libraries in Chicago, Princeton, and Columbia, supplemented by the Library of Congress and other depositories. Except for the Horsch collection at Scottdale, however, little of the material required by the Anabaptist scholar was available in America. And rich as it was in the history of the Anabaptists and European Mennonites, even this collection, said Bender in 1929, "contained but a portion of American Mennonite literature, and the few private collections [of American materials] of any note were either narrow in scope or slight in extent. A prime necessity for the Mennonite historian, the collection and cataloguing

15

of the literature of the American Mennonites, was still to be supplied.

"This task I undertook in the autumn of 1924. The Mennonite Historical Society of Goshen College, established at that time, was the vehicle for much of the work, and furnished slender but essential resources. Since most of the literature of earlier days was out of print, and not to be had even in the shops of antiquarians, it was necessary to make a personal search in the only places where this literature was to be found, namely, in the homes of Mennonites. So the search proceeded. In these five years, through the gracious consent and aid of innumerable kind friends, I have sought the desired volumes in hundreds of homes in the more populous Mennonite centers of Pennsylvania, Maryland, Ontario, Ohio, and Indiana. It has been on the whole a pleasant and even delightful search. Often fruitless, yet occasionally it has been richly rewarded, to the joy of seeker and friend alike. The tragedies of book-collecting have pursued me likewise. It has been my lot to hear many times the doleful story of recent selling of old papers and books to the junk dealer, or of burning as rubbish at the last house cleaning. At places too, other seekers had preceded me, especially in Pennsylvania. Governor Pennypacker and A. H. Cassell of Harleysville had been everywhere, yet even they had not found everything. The most pleasant side of the experience was the almost uniform generosity. Seldom was any opposition met, but rarely was a price asked, and occasionally I was thanked and almost paid for taking the old books away. One kindly old lady in Lancaster County had been puzzled almost to distraction by the problem of her old German religious books. She could no longer read them; to throw them away was a sin; none of her friends wanted them; to sell them would have been a sacrilege. Out of a full heart she thanked me kindly for having been so kind as to relieve her of her books."[4]

4 Harold S. Bender, *Two Centuries of American Mennonite Literature: A Bibliography of Mennonitica Americana, 1727-1928* (Goshen, 1929) vii.

From time to time *The Goshen College Record* reported Bender's book-hunting travels and the fruits of his labors as he visited home after home (assisted at times by S. C. Yoder), from Bucks and Montgomery counties in Pennsylvania and Waterloo County, Ontario, westward to Johnson and Henry counties in Iowa. During 1925-26 the collection was augmented by 73 titles (80 volumes) of duplicates from the Horsch collection at Scottdale. By March 1928, Bender was able to report almost complete files of *The Herald of Truth* and other periodicals and serials from their beginnings in 1864. Following the death of John F. Funk in 1930 the Mennonite Historical Library acquired that portion of his private library which had not been sold to Scottdale, besides Funk's correspondence and personal papers, described by the present curator of the Mennonite Historical Library as "a valuable and extensive collection of personal and official records which reflect Funk's activities and interests as a minister and bishop in the Mennonite congregation in Elkhart, as a leader in the wider activities of the (old) Mennonite Church, as a promoter of Mennonite emigration from Russia to the western plains, as a businessman, and as the father of a family."[5]

By 1931 the accessioned holdings of the Mennonite Historical Library amounted to 2,000 volumes plus a large number of pamphlets, manuscripts, and other materials.[6] Following the death of John Horsch in 1941 that portion of the Scottdale collection most useful for research purposes, approximately 900 volumes, was transferred to Goshen. It was at this point that Robert Friedmann, well-known Anabaptist scholar who had migrated from Vienna in 1940, came to Goshen to assist in the merging of the Horsch collection with the Mennonite Historical Library. In 1945 Friedmann in a letter to the writer referred to the Horsch collection, stating that many of its items "are exceedingly valuable or rare. Most of these books are German, some are Dutch, only a few Eng-

5 Nelson P. Springer, "The Mennonite Historical Library at Goshen College," *Mennonite Quarterly Review* (October 1951) 25:302.
6 *Ibid.*, 302.

lish, but important are all, making Goshen College a real research center in Mennonite studies. One has to admire Father Horsch for his scholarship and being a connoisseur in rare books."

In 1943 the Mennonite Historical Library reported holdings of 2,500 volumes. In 1945 the figure was 2,900; and in 1948 over 3,500.[7] From 1947 to 1949 extensive purchases were made of historical materials in Europe, including important portions of the libraries of two outstanding historians, the late W. J. Kühler of Amsterdam and Christian Hege of Germany, the late coeditor of the *Mennonitisches Lexikon*. In August, 1951, the curator reported a shelf list of 4,800 catalogued volumes, with "1,450 volumes awaiting cataloguing and at least 3,200 bound volumes of a serial nature—a total of 9,450 volumes," over half of which were in German, one third in English, one eighth in Dutch, and the remaining two per cent in ten other languages and dialects.[8] Finally, by early 1957 the Mennonite Historical Library contained over 13,000 volumes of books, pamphlets, and serials; more than twenty-seven file drawers of photostats, manuscripts, seminars, term papers, photographs, uncatalogued pamphlets, tracts, and other non-book materials; more than 150 microfilms, and 100 maps. It currently receives 230 periodicals, appearing quarterly or more frequently.[9]

The Goshen and the Bethel College historical libraries are now the largest collections of Anabaptist-Mennonite materials in the world, the former being especially rich in sixteenth- and seventeenth-century Anabaptistica, as well as in Mennonitica Americana. The Bethel College Mennonite Historical Library was established by A. Warkentin in 1935, although the collection was begun earlier by C. H. Wedel. Cornelius Krahn has directed the library since 1944 and under his leadership it has grown steadily until by 1956 it contained over 12,000 volumes including serials. The hold-

7 *Ibid.*, 302-3.
8 *Ibid.*, 303-4.
9 Statement of Curator, April 9, 1957.

18

ings of the Bethel College library are most complete in the area of Dutch, Prussian, Polish, and Russian Mennonitica. Third in size of Mennonite historical collections is the Amsterdam Mennonite library which is especially rich in Dutch materials.

Other important European collections are found in the Prussian State Library (now at the University of Marburg), in the University of Munich, in the libraries of Zürich, and in the Mennonitische Forschungsstelle at Göttingen. In the United States the Union Theological Seminary Library in New York has the greatest general collection of Anabaptist materials outside the Mennonite libraries. The Crozer, Colgate-Rochester, and Southern Baptist Seminary libraries also have collections of Anabaptist materials. Other Mennonite libraries in the United States are: Bluffton College with 4,000 volumes; Mennonite Biblical Seminary, 1,600; and Eastern Mennonite College, 1,000 volumes. Only the Bethel and Goshen College libraries are attempting exhaustive collections in all fields, languages, and groups. They have established a union catalog.[10]

Obviously, the growing Mennonite Historical Library at Goshen College could not long be confined to its three shelves in an inaccessible nook of the college library. In 1927 the collection was moved to a small room on the third floor of the administration building and a little more than a year later to a larger and more accessible room on the first floor, where it remained until it was moved into the new fireproof Memorial Library building in 1940. In the meantime the Mennonite General Conference had established the Archives of the Mennonite Church in 1939 under the administration of its historical committee, the same to be housed with the Mennonite Historical Library on the basement floor of the new building. In June, 1940, appropriate dedication services were held for the new Mennonite Historical Library quarters, featuring an address by C. Henry Smith on "Progress in Men-

10 Cf. article "Historical Libraries" in *Mennonite Encyclopedia*, 2:749-51.

nonite History in America." The dedication ceremony was in charge of President S. C. Yoder, who said: "When I first came here, H. S. Bender pushed for two things: a society to study the life, faith, traditions, and practices of our ancestors, and a Mennonite journal. These efforts resulted in the Mennonite Historical Society of Goshen College and *The Mennonite Quarterly Review*. In this new building we have set aside space where all this material can be gathered up for convenience in use, where it will be readily accessible to students, faculty, and research scholars. It is for the use of all who may be interested."[11]

Ample as these facilities seemed in 1940, they were soon too small to care for the expanding library, archives, and research program, so that in 1957 plans were under way for a new Mennonite Historical Library quarters to be located in the Goshen College Biblical Seminary building soon to be erected on the campus. In a setting such as this, scholarship and the publication of its fruits, the standard for which had been set by the *Review Supplement* of 1926, must continue. In the year following this preliminary effort *The Mennonite Quarterly Review* was founded with Harold S. Bender as editor and John Umble, Guy F. Hershberger, and Edward Yoder as associate editors. Beginning with January, 1927, this journal of Anabaptist-Mennonite history, theology, thought, life, and affairs has appeared once each quarter throughout the years. These thirty volumes of scholarly articles, research notes, documents, and book reviews constitute one of the most significant contributions to Mennonite historiography during this period.

As the source material for American Mennonite historiography was being gathered it was also evident that such a mine of materials would be useful only to the extent that it was organized systematically in the best bibliographical tradition. This task was assumed with the same characteristic vigor as the collection itself and the result was a comprehen-

11 *Goshen College Bulletin: Alumni News Letter* (July 1940) 2.

sive, analytical bibliography of Mennonitica Americana, classified chronologically within periods and according to the varied Mennonite groups producing the items, and done in a manner ever since most helpful to scores of searchers, national and international, bibliophiles and historians. The widely comprehensive tasks of collection and comparison were a fitting apprenticeship for one who, with no other anticipatory knowledge, would twenty years later be found at the helm of *The Mennonite Encyclopedia.*

Promisingly, publication of the bibliography was begun in the initial issue of *The Mennonite Quarterly Review* (January, 1927). Subsequent to six installments the series matured into a manual and guidebook without parallel in the American field. It became No. 1 of *The Studies in Anabaptist and Mennonite History,* entitled *Two Centuries of American Mennonite Literature, A Bibliography of Mennonitica Americana, 1727-1928.*[12] In the light of developments during recent decades, a few words from this writer's appraisal of the work are restated here: "This bibliography is indeed more than a useful product of painstaking compilation. What we have in reality before us is the framework of American Mennonite history starting from the first settled period which allowed production activities, and reaching into the modern era with its various groups, all of them faithfully reflected in their literary documents. American Mennonite history is made to reveal its own religious development."[13] To numerous scholars and libraries since its appearance, this volume has seemed indeed "as a very promising nucleus for further research and publication."

Since the publication of the *Two Centuries of American Mennonite Literature,* seven additional titles have appeared in the *Studies in Anabaptist and Mennonite History,* as follows: John Horsch, *The Hutterian Brethren 1528-1931* (1931); Harry F. Weber, *Centennial History of the Mennon-*

---

12 Published by the Mennonite Historical Society (Goshen, 1929).
13 *MQR* (October 1930) 4:291.

ites of Illinois (1931); Sanford C. Yoder, *For Conscience Sake: A Study of Mennonite Migrations Resulting from the World War* (1940); John Umble, *Ohio Mennonite Sunday Schools* (1941); Robert Friedmann, *Mennonite Piety Through the Centuries, Its Genius and Its Literature* (1949); H. S. Bender, *Conrad Grebel, Founder of the Swiss Brethren* (1950); and Delbert L. Gratz, *Bernese Anabaptists and Their American Descendants* (1953).

During these years Harold S. Bender also found time for numerous other literary productions. Besides articles appearing in the learned journals, not to mention numerous pamphlets and popular articles in Mennonite periodicals, he completed the work for the doctorate in church history at Heidelberg in 1935, with a dissertation on Conrad Grebel.

The Grebel biography was the product of a program of research inspired by the quadricentennial year, and first announced at the time the Mennonite Historical Society was founded in 1924. As originally conceived the plan called for an English translation with technical annotations of the Grebel-Vadian correspondence and of other German, Greek, and Latin materials, and the early publications of a two-volume work, the first of which should be the Grebel biography and the second the correspondence and other papers of Grebel. This task as conceived in 1924 was to be a co-operative venture with Bender, Correll, and Edward Yoder as participants. The founding of the *Mennonite Quarterly Review* in 1927, however, and the numerous tasks associated with that project, together with Correll's transfer to the American University and absorption with other responsibilities, caused the completion of the Grebel study to be delayed. Bender eventually wrote the biography as his doctoral dissertation, which, as mentioned above, was published in revised and expanded form in 1950 as No. 6 of the *Studies in Anabaptist and Mennonite History*. Even before this Yoder had completed the translation of the letters and had written the philological annotations. Correll had also done further research in European archives in 1926, but the historical and theological annotations for the Grebel documents still remain to be completed. It is hoped, however, that this task will not be delayed much longer and that the publication of the second volume will soon be accomplished.

While for most of us the admixture of scholarship with administrative work is a frustrating experience, the editor of the *Mennonite Quarterly Review* has taken even this in his stride. From 1931 to 1944 he was dean of Goshen College, during which time he played a major role in raising the academic standards of the school and obtaining its accreditation by the regional accrediting association. Since 1944 he has been serving as dean of the Goshen College Biblical Seminary, which under his leadership has become a full seminary with a three-year curriculum, admission to which presupposes the baccalaureate degree. All of this has been accompanied by active membership on a variety of church committees and boards including the executive committee of the Mennonite Central Committee and the chairmanship of its peace section.

The latter responsibility has called for leadership in a number of extended missions to Europe, occasional appearances before congressional hearings concerned with legislation affecting the Christian peace testimony, as well as the promotion of conferences and related work. One of the conferences sponsored by the peace section was held at Winona Lake, Indiana, in 1950, at which time a most significant statement, *A Declaration of Christian Faith and Commitment,* was adopted setting forth the Anabaptist-Mennonite peace position and its meaning for our time. In 1930 Dean Bender served as special commissioner for the MCC in Europe to supervise the migration of 1,700 Russian Mennonite refugees from Germany to Paraguay, including the necessary negotiations with the German government. This was followed eight years later with a visit to the Paraguayan settlement. With the recent opening of Russia to western visitors, Dean Bender was a member of the MCC delegation which went to Russia in December, 1956, for the renewal of contacts with the dispersed Mennonite settlements, with whom there had been little communication for a quarter of a century.

In the meantime the most ambitious scholarly undertaking of Harold S. Bender's career was launched some ten years ago when plans were laid for the publication of *The Mennonite Encyclopedia*. At that time C. Henry Smith and Bender presented to the three major American Mennonite publication boards a proposal to publish an English edition of the *Mennonitisches Lexikon*, revised and brought up-to-date, particularly with respect to the American scene. The plan was approved, publication rights were obtained from the owners of the *Lexikon*, an editorial and publication organization was set up, and the work was begun; but few persons at the time, if any, realized the magnitude of the task which they had undertaken. The *Lexikon* itself had been completed only to the letter "O," although since then extended to "R" through the efforts of Ernst and Rosa Crous. It was also discovered that only about one-third of the old German text would be usable. The remainder of the material for the *Encyclopedia* would need to be produced afresh. Many new areas of information and much new research by hundreds of writers had to be done before the completion of this monumental project could be realized.

The publishing committee representing the three boards appointed Smith and Bender as coeditors of the *Encyclopedia*, with Cornelius Krahn and Melvin Gingerich as associate and managing editors respectively, besides ten assistant editors and a much larger editorial council. Following Smith's death in 1948, when the groundwork for the project had barely been laid, the top responsibility was placed on Bender alone. In the division of the editorial work Cornelius Krahn has had chief responsibility for materials on the Russian Mennonites and the American Mennonites of Russian background. N. van der Zijpp has chief responsibility for the Dutch, and Ernst Crous for the German sections. As editor,

Bender is chiefly responsible for the remaining American Mennonite sections and for the co-ordination and execution of the entire project which required the co-operation of 470 different writers for the first volume alone.

The scene for the map making, translations, and processing of manuscripts, the final editorial work and proofreading is the Mennonite Historical Library. A major portion of the work, especially in translations, copy editing, and proofreading, has been done by Elizabeth Horsch Bender as assistant editor, who in addition to her thorough knowledge of the German language and long and arduous labors on the *Encyclopedia,* as well as on the *Mennonite Quarterly Review,* has become something of an Anabaptist-Mennonite authority in her own right. Volumes I and II of the *Encyclopedia* appeared in 1955 and 1956 respectively, carrying the work through the letter "H." Most of the articles for volumes III and IV, scheduled to appear in 1957 and 1958, have been written, although the processing of the material and attention to details will need to continue for months to come. Absorption with these details is the daily fare of Elizabeth Bender, while in constant consultation with her husband, who in addition to his supervision of the *Encyclopedia* project is at present also engaged in work on his proposed new book, a history of the Mennonite Church in America.

The era in which this most recent chapter in Anabaptist-Mennonite historiography is being written is a significant one. Anabaptism, like every important movement in history, has had its succession of eras, its vicissitudes of fortune and misfortune, its periods of rise and decline, of dormancy, of confusion, and of awakening. Harold S. Bender himself has, for good reasons, designated the era of John F. Funk and his contemporaries following the American Civil War as the age of the Great Awakening. There are equally good reasons why the first two decades of the twentieth century, especially the period of World War I and the years immediately following, may be characterized as an era of confusion, of uncertainty, of an absence of co-ordination and purpose, and of a lack of vision within Mennonitism as a whole.

In 1917 the communist revolution had struck at the heart of the Russian communities and had set in motion a chain of tragic events which permanently changed the order of life for tens of thousands of Mennonites. In Germany Mennonitism had been modified by Pietism on the one hand and by rationalism on the other to such an extent that the vision of the Anabaptist fathers seemed hopelessly dimmed. During the war the way of the cross had given way to that of the sword to such an extent that military service was everywhere taken for granted by a once nonresistant people; and the church was not at all prepared to resist the devastating influence of national socialism when it came a decade later. Among the Dutch Mennonites a century or more of rationalism had reached its zenith and the first signs of a renewed Anabaptism were beginning to be seen. In America the Mennonites were just beginning to emerge from their cultural isolation only to find themselves in the midst of the fundamentalist-modernist controversy which served merely to confuse the basic issues with which Anabaptism is concerned and to obscure the vision which the leaders of the earlier awakening had sought to bring.

It was at this juncture in world Mennonitism that the most recent chapter in its historiography began. Certainly many forces were at work to shape the character of the era which followed. Not the least of these, however, was the sound historical scholarship which led the church to a basic understanding of its heritage, of the meaning of Anabaptism, and of the New Testament Christianity of which it seeks to be a faithful exponent. Conscious of the place which Anabaptism must rightfully hold within Christendom as a whole, the founders of the *Mennonite Quarterly Review,* and of all that has been associated with it these thirty-odd years, have given themselves unsparingly to this task so that an impact of no mean proportions has been made on historical scholarship and religious thought beyond its circle, while the church within the circle has experienced a second Great Awakening, having found anew the meaning of its own faith, through having rediscovered the vision of its sixteenth-century founders.

In this era the Mennonites of the world have come to know each other for the first time in centuries, symbolized by the Mennonite World Conference of whose preparatory commission Harold S. Bender is currently chairman. In 1957 Anabaptist-Mennonite historical scholarship is an international enterprise. Lines of communication keep Newton, Goshen, and other American centers of research in living touch with Amsterdam and Göttingen. Mennonite colleges are marshaling their forces for the promotion of an integrated Christian education with a truly Anabaptist orientation. The crisis of World War II, instead of scattering the forces of Anabaptism, dissipating its energies, and dissolving its principles, served rather to draw the Mennonites of the western hemisphere together in a unified approach to the challenge of the hour, an experience which has made its impact on the world and which in the end has left the churches with a clearer vision of the meaning of Anabaptism and of New Testament Christianity than in the beginning. As soon as the guns were silenced Mennonites from every part of the globe found each other and since then have labored together as never before in the proclamation of the Word, in the ministry of Christian service, and in the fellowship of love. It is this world of history and scholarship, of missions and service, and of Christian fellowship across international boundaries which has enabled Harold S. Bender to distill the essence of Anabaptism as he has come to understand it, and as he has formulated it in an article entitled "The Anabaptist Vision," the recovery of which vision is the theme of the present volume.

"The Anabaptist Vision" in its original form was Bender's presidential address before the American Society of Church History in New York in December, 1943. This presentation saw the essence of Anabaptism as gathered in two foci. The first focus finds the essential nature of Christianity as discipleship. The second focus sees the church as a voluntary brotherhood of love and nonresistance, with nonconformity and suffering as corollary concepts. While Dean Bender would be the first to insist that the interpretation of Anabaptism is an ever continuing process, it was nevertheless clear from the beginning that "The Anabaptist Vision" was a fresh interpretation, a brilliant synthesis, which has since come to be recognized as a classic statement to be reckoned with for years to come. First published in *Church History*,[14] then in the *Mennonite Quarterly Review*,[15] it has since been reprinted in pamphlet form[16] in response to steady demands.

A Dutch edition, *De Doperse Visie*,[17] translated by C. F. Brüsewitz, has been published by the Doopsgezinde Vredesgroep, and a French edition, *La Vision Anabaptiste*,[18] translated by Marthe Ropp and John H. Yoder, has been published by the publishers of *Christ Seul*.

14 (March 1944) 13:3-24.
15 (April 1944) 18:67-88.
16 Scottdale, 1945 ff.
17 Amsterdam, 1948.
18 Grand-Charmont par Montbéliard, 1950.

✠ HAROLD S. BENDER ✠

The Anabaptist Vision[1]

"Judged by the reception it met at the hands of those in power, both in Church and State, equally in Roman Catholic and in Protestant countries, the Anabaptist movement was one of the most tragic in the history of Christianity; but, judged by the principles, which were put into play by the men who bore this reproachful nickname, it must be pronounced one of the most momentous and significant undertakings in man's eventful religious struggle after the truth. It gathered up the gains of earlier movements, it is the spiritual soil out of which all nonconformist sects have sprung, and it is the first plain announcement in modern history of a programme for a new type of Christian society which the modern world, especially in America and England, has been slowly realizing—an absolutely free and independent religious society, and a State in which every man counts as a man, and has his share in shaping both Church and State."

These words of Rufus M. Jones[2] constitute one of the best characterizations of Anabaptism and its contribution to our modern Christian culture to be found in the English language. They were brave words when they were written nearly fifty years ago, but they have been abundantly verified by a generation of Anabaptist research since that time.[3] There

1 Presidential address, the American Society of Church History, December 1943. Reprinted from *Church History* (March 1944) 13:3-24 and *Mennonite Quarterly Review* (April 1944) 18:67-88, with slight revisions in text and footnotes.

2 Rufus M. Jones, *Studies in Mystical Religion* (London, 1909) 369. Professor Walter Köhler of Heidelberg has recently expressed a similar evaluation, asserting that the historical significance of the Anabaptists "erschöpft sich nicht in dem Duldermut, der Arbeitstreue, dem kulturellen Fleiss. . . . Nein, die Mennoniten dürfen ohne Ueberhebung einen Platz in der Weltgeschichte beanspruchen als Bahnbrecher der modernen Weltanschauung mit ihrer Glaubens- und Gewissensfreiheit."

3 The results of this research are best found in: *Mennonitisches Lexikon*, edited by Christian Hege and Christian Neff (Frankfurt a. M. and Weierhof, Germany, 1913 ff.), completed to letter "N," continued since World War II by Ernst Crous and

can be no question but that the great principles of freedom of conscience, separation of church and state, and voluntarism in religion, so basic in American Protestantism, and so essential to democracy, ultimately are derived from the Anabaptists of the Reformation period, who for the first time clearly enunciated them, and challenged the Christian world to follow them in practice. The line of descent through the centuries since that time may not always be clear, and may have passed through other intermediate movements and groups, but the debt to original Anabaptism is unquestioned.

The sixteenth century reformers understood the Anabaptist position on this point all too well, and deliberately rejected it. The best witness is Heinrich Bullinger, Zwingli's successor in Zürich, whose active life span covers the first fifty years of the history of the Swiss Anabaptists and who knew them so well that he published two extensive treatises against them in 1531 and 1561.

According to Bullinger, the Swiss Brethren taught: "One cannot and should not use force to compel anyone to accept the faith, for faith is a free gift of God. It is wrong to compel anyone by force or coercion to embrace the faith, or to put to death anyone for the sake of his erring faith. It is an error that in the church any sword other than that of the divine Word should be used. The secular kingdom should be separated from the church, and no secular ruler should exercise authority in the church. The Lord has commanded simply to

H. S. Bender, now at letter "R"; Ernst Correll, *Das Schweizerische Täufermennonitentum: Ein Soziologischer Bericht* (Tübingen, 1925); *The Mennonite Quarterly Review* (Goshen, 1927 ff.); *Mennonitische Geschichtsblätter* (Weierhof, 1936 ff.); R. J. Smithson, *The Anabaptists, Their Contribution to Our Protestant Heritage* (London, 1935); John Horsch, *Mennonites in Europe* (Scottdale, 1942); C. Henry Smith, *The Story of the Mennonites* (Berne, Indiana, 1941), third edition, revised and enlarged by C. Krahn (Newton, 1950); L. von Muralt, *Glaube und Lehre der Schweizerschen Wiedertäufer in der Reformationszeit* (Zürich, 1938). Cf. also: Wilhelm Pauck "The Historiography of the German Reformation During the Past Twenty Years IV, Research in the History of the Anabaptists," *Church History* (December 1940) 9:335-361; Harold S. Bender, "Recent Progress in Research in Anabaptist History," *MQR* (January 1934) 8:3-17. *Quellen zur Geschichte der Wiedertäufer* (Leipzig, 1930 ff.), three volumes; L. von Muralt and W. Schmid, *Quellen zur Geschichte der Täufer in der Schweiz* (the first volume was published in Zürich, 1952); *Quellen zur Geschichte der Täufer* (now in process of publication under auspices of the Taufer Akten-Kommission).

preach the Gospel, not to compel anyone by force to accept it. The true church of Christ has the characteristic that it suffers and endures persecution but does not inflict persecution upon anyone."[4]

Bullinger reports these ideas, not in commendation but in condemnation urging the need of rigid suppression. He attempts a point by point refutation of the Anabaptist teaching, closing with the assertion that to put to death Anabaptists is a necessary and commendable service.

But great as is the Anabaptist contribution to the development of religious liberty, this concept not only does not exhaust but actually fails to define the true essence of Anabaptism. In the last analysis freedom of religion is a purely formal concept, barren of content; it says nothing about the faith or the way of life of those who advocate it, nor does it reveal their goals or program of action. And Anabaptism had not only clearly defined goals but also an action program of definiteness and power. In fact the more intimately one becomes acquainted with this group the more one becomes conscious of the great vision that shaped their course in history and for which they gladly gave their lives.

Before describing this vision it is well to note its attractiveness to the masses of Christians of the sixteenth century. Sebastian Franck, himself an opponent, wrote in 1531, scarcely seven years after the rise of the movement in Zurich: "The Anabaptists spread so rapidly that their teaching soon covered the land as it were. They soon gained a large following, and baptized thousands, drawing to themselves many sincere souls who had a zeal for God. . . . They increased so rapidly that the world feared an uprising by them though I have learned that this fear had no justification whatsoever."[5] In the same year Bullinger wrote that "the people were running after them as though they were living saints."[6] Another con-

4 Quoted in translation by John Horsch, *Mennonites in Europe*, 325, from Bullinger's *Der Wiedertäufferen Ursprung*, etc. (Zürich, 1560).

5 Horsch, 293, from Sebastian Franck's *Chronica, Zeytbuch und Geschychtbibel* (Strasbourg, 1531).

6 Heinrich Bullinger, *Von dem unverschampten fräfel . . . der selvsgesandten Widertouffern* (Zürich, 1531), folio 2v.

temporary writer asserts that "Anabaptism spread with such speed that there was reason to fear that the majority of the common people would unite with this sect."[7] Zwingli was so frightened by the power of the movement that he complained that the struggle with the Catholic party was "but child's play" compared to the conflict with the Anabaptists.[8]

The dreadful severity of the persecution of the Anabaptist movement in the years 1527-1560 not only in Switzerland, South Germany, and Thuringia, but in all the Austrian lands as well as in the Low Countries, testifies to the power of the movement and the desperate haste with which Catholic, Lutheran, and Zwinglian authorities alike strove to throttle it before it should be too late. The notorious decree issued in 1529 by the Diet of Spires (the same Diet which protested the restriction of evangelical liberties) summarily passed the sentence of death upon all Anabaptists, ordering that "every Anabaptist and rebaptized person of either sex should be put to death by fire, sword, or some other way."[9] Repeatedly in subsequent sessions of the imperial diet this decree was reinvoked and intensified; and as late as 1551 the Diet of Augsburg issued a decree ordering that judges and jurors who had scruples against pronouncing the death sentences on Anabaptists be removed from office and punished by heavy fines and imprisonment.

The authorities had great difficulty in executing their program of suppression, for they soon discovered that the Anabaptists feared neither torture nor death, and gladly sealed their faith with their blood. In fact the joyful testimony of the Anabaptist martyrs was a great stimulus to new

7 F. Roth, *Augsburgs Reformationsgeschichte* (Munich, 1901) 2:230.

8 Letter of Zwingli to Vadian, May 28, 1525, *Huldreich Zwinglis Sämtliche Werke*, ed. Egli, Finsler, Köhler, *et al.* (Leipzig, 1914) 7:332.

9 The full official text of the decree may be found in *Aller des Heiligen Römischen Reichs gehaltene Reichstage, Abschiede und Satzungen* (Mainz, 1666) 210, 211. It is also edited by Ludwig Keller in *Monatshefte der Comenius Gesellschaft* (Berlin, 1900), 9:55-57 and by Bossert in "Die Reichsgesetze über die Wiedertäufer" in *Quellen zur Geschichte der Wiedertäufer, I. Band Herzogtum Württemberg* (Leipzig, 1930), 1*-10*. See the excellent discussion of Anabaptist persecution by John Horsch in "The Persecution of the Evangelical Anabaptists," *MQR* (January 1938) 12:3-26.

recruits, for it stirred the imagination of the populace as nothing else could have done.

Finding therefore that the customary method of individual trials and sentences was proving totally inadequate to stem the tide, the authorities resorted to the desperate expedient of sending out through the land companies of armed executioners and mounted soldiers to hunt down the Anabaptists and kill them on the spot singly or *en masse* without trial or sentence. The most atrocious application of this policy was made in Swabia where the original four hundred special police of 1528 sent against the Anabaptists proved too small a force and had to be increased to one thousand. An imperial provost-marshal, Berthold Aichele, served as chief administrator of this bloody program in Swabia and other regions until he finally broke down in terror and dismay, and after an execution at Brixen lifted his hands to heaven and swore a solemn oath never again to put to death an Anabaptist, which vow he kept.[10] The Count of Alzey in the Palatinate, after three hundred and fifty Anabaptists had been executed there, was heard to exclaim, "What shall I do, the more I kill, the greater becomes their number!"

The extensive persecution and martyrdom of the Anabaptists testify not only of the great extent of the movement but also of the power of the vision that burned within them. This is most effectively presented in a moving account written in 1542 and taken from the ancient Hutterian chronicle where it is found at the close of a report of 2,173 brethren and sisters who gave their lives for their faith:[11]

"No human being was able to take away out of their hearts what they had experienced, such zealous lovers of God were they. The fire of God burned within them. They would die the bitterest death, yea they would die ten deaths rather than forsake the divine truth which they had espoused. . . .

10 *Geschicht-Buch der Hutterischen Brüder*, edited by Rudolf Wolkan (Macleod, Alberta, and Vienna, 1923) 142, 181.
11 *Ibid.*, 182-187. The following quotation is composed of extracts selected from this account without regard to the original order, chiefly from 186-7.

"They had drunk of the waters which had flowed from God's sanctuary, yea, the water of life. They realized that God helped them to bear the cross and to overcome the bitterness of death. The fire of God burned within them. Their tent they had pitched not here upon earth, but in eternity, and of their faith they had a foundation and assurance. Their faith blossomed as a lily, their loyalty as a rose, their piety and sincerity as the flower of the garden of God. The angel of the Lord battled for them that they could not be deprived of the helmet of salvation. Therefore they bore all torture and agony without fear. The things of this world they counted in their holy mind only as shadows, having the assurance of greater things. They were so drawn unto God that they knew nothing, sought nothing, desired nothing, loved nothing but God alone. Therefore they had more patience in their suffering than their enemies in tormenting them.

". . . The persecutors thought they could dampen and extinguish the fire of God. But the prisoners sang in their prisons and rejoiced so that the enemies outside became much more fearful than the prisoners and did not know what to do with them. . . .

"Many were talked to in wonderful ways, often day and night. They were argued with, with great cunning and cleverness, with many sweet and smooth words, by monks and priests, by doctors of theology, with much false testimony, with threats and scolding and mockery, yea, with lies and grievous slander against the brotherhood, but none of these things moved them or made them falter.

"From the shedding of such innocent blood arose Christians everywhere, brothers all, for all this persecution did not take place without fruit. . . ."

Perhaps this interpretation of the Anabaptist spirit should be discounted as too glowing, coming as it does from the group itself, but certainly it is nearer to the truth than the typical harsh nineteenth century interpretation of the movement which is well represented by the opening sentence of *Ursula,* the notable historical novel on the Anabaptists published in 1878 by the Swiss Gottfried Keller, next to Goethe perhaps the greatest of all writers in the German language: "Times of religious change are like times when the mountains open up; for then not only do all the marvelous creatures of the human spirit come forth, the great golden dragons, magic beings and crystal spirits, but there also come to light all the hateful vermin of humanity, the host of rats and mice and pestiferous creation, and so it was at the time of the Reformation in the northeast part of Switzerland."[12]

Before defining the Anabaptist vision, it is essential to state clearly who is meant by the term "Anabaptist," since the name has come to be used in modern historiography to cover a wide variety of Reformation groups, sometimes thought of as the whole "left wing of the Reformation" (Roland Bainton), "the Bolsheviks of the Reformation" (Preserved Smith). Although the definitive history of Anabaptism has not yet been written, we know enough today to draw a clear line of demarcation between original evangelical and constructive Anabaptism on the one hand, which was born in the bosom of Zwinglianism in Zürich, Switzerland, in 1525, and established in the Low Countries in 1533, and the various mystical, spiritualistic, revolutionary, or even antinomian related and unrelated groups on the other hand, which came and went like the flowers of the field in those days of the great renovation. The former, Anabaptism proper, maintained an unbroken course in Switzerland, South Germany, Austria, and Holland throughout the sixteenth century, and has continued until the present day in the Mennonite movement, now almost 500,000 baptized members strong in Europe and America.[13] There is no longer any excuse for permitting our

12 *Gottfried Keller's Werke*, ed. by Max Nussberger (Leipzig, n.d.) 6:309. See Elizabeth Horsch Bender, "The Portrayal of the Swiss Anabaptists in Gottfried Keller's *Ursula*," MQR (July 1943) 17:136-150.

13 In Switzerland, this group was called "Swiss Brethren," in Austria "Hutterites," in Holland and North Germany, "Menists." All these groups seriously objected to the name "Anabaptists" which was a term used to designate a punishable heresy and which after the tragic Münster episode (1534-35) was a name of odious opprobrium. I use the term here only for custom's sake. The term "Mennonite" came into wider use in the seventeenth century and was ultimately applied to all the groups except the Hutterites.

understanding of the distinct character of this genuine Anabaptism to be obscured by Thomas Müntzer and the Peasants War, the Münsterites, or any other aberration of Protestantism in the sixteenth century.

There may be some excuse, however, for a failure on the part of the uninformed student to see clearly what the Anabaptist vision was, because of the varying interpretations placed upon the movement even by those who mean to appreciate and approve it. There are, for instance, the socialist writers, led by Kautsky, who would make Anabaptism either "the forerunner of the modern socialism" or the "culminating effort of medieval communism," and who in reality see it only as the external religious shell of a class movement.[14] There are the sociologists with their partial socio-economic determinism as reflected in Richard Niebuhr's approach to the social origin of religious denominations. There is Albert Ritschl, who sees in Anabaptism an ascetic semi-monastic continuation of the medieval Franciscan tertiaries, and locates the seventeenth century Pietists in the same line;[15] and Ludwig Keller who finds Anabaptists throughout the pre-Reformation period in the guise of Waldenses and other similar groups whom he chooses to call "the old-evangelical brotherhood,"[16] and for whom he posits a continuity from earliest times. Related to Keller are the earlier Baptist historians (and certain Mennonites) who rejoice to find in the Anabaptists the missing link which keeps them in the apostolic succession of the true church back through the Waldenses, Bogomiles, Cathari, Paulicians, and Donatists, to Pentecost. More recently there is Rufus M. Jones who is inclined to class the Anabaptists with the mystics, and Walther Köhler who finds an Erasmian humanist origin for them.

14 Ernst H. Correll, *Das Schweizerische Täufermennonitentum* (Tübingen, 1925), "Allgemeine historisch-soziologische Kennzeichnung," 3-10, gives an excellent concise survey. See particularly 6, footnote 1. See also Karl Kautsky, *Communism in Central Europe in the Time of the Reformation* (1897). Troeltsch rejected the theory of the socio-economic origin of the Anabaptists.

15 Albrecht Ritschl, *Geschichte des Pietismus* (Bonn, 1880). Cf. R. Friedmann, "Conception of the Anabaptists," *Church History* (December 1940) 9:351.

16 Ludwig Keller, *Die Reformation und die älteren Reformparteien* (Leipzig, 1885). Cf. also Friedmann, *op. cit.*, 352.

However, there is another line of interpretation which is being increasingly accepted and which is probably destined to dominate the field. It is the one which holds that Anabaptism is the culmination of the Reformation, the fulfilment of the original vision of Luther and Zwingli, and thus makes it a consistent evangelical Protestantism seeking to recreate without compromise the original New Testament church, the vision of Christ and the Apostles. This line of interpretation begins in 1848 with Max Göbel's great *Geschichte des christlichen Lebens in der rheinisch-westfälischen . . . Kirche,* continues with the epoch-making work of C. A. Cornelius, particularly in his *Geschichte des Münsterischen Aufruhrs* (1855-1860), follows in the work of men like Johann Loserth, Karl Rembert, and John Horsch, and is represented by such contemporaries as Ernst Correll of Washington and Fritz Blanke of Zürich. A quotation from Göbel may serve to illustrate this interpretation:

"The essential and distinguishing characteristic of this church is its great emphasis upon the actual personal conversion and regeneration of every Christian through the Holy Spirit. . . . They aimed with special emphasis at carrying out and realizing the Christian doctrine and faith in the heart and life of every Christian in the whole Christian church. Their aim was the bringing together of all the true believers out of the great degenerated national churches into a true Christian church. That which the Reformation was originally intended to accomplish they aimed to bring into full immediate realization."[17]

Johann Loserth says: "More radically than any other party for church reformation the Anabaptists strove to follow

17 Max Göbel, *Geschichte des christlichen Lebens,* etc. (Coblenz, 1848) 1:134. Ritschl, *op. cit.,* 22, characterizes Göbel's views as follows: "Die Wiedertäuferei also soll nach Göbel gründlichere, entschiedenere, vollständigere Reformation sein, welche als 'Kind der Reformation' Luthers und Zwinglis zu erkennen aber von Luther seit 1522, von Zwingli seit 1524 aufgegeben worden wäre." Ritschl *(op. cit.,* 7) himself states the Anabaptist position as follows: "Nicht minder haben die Wiedertäufer sich dafür angesehen, dass sie das von Luther und Zwingli begonnene Werk der Wiederherstellung der Kirche zu seinem rechten Ziel führten."

the footsteps of the church of the first century and to renew unadulterated original Christianity."[18]

The evidence in support of this interpretation is overwhelming, and can be taken from the statements of the contemporary opponents of the Anabaptists as well as from the Anabaptists themselves. Conrad Grebel, the founder of the Swiss Brethren movement, states clearly this point of view in his letter to Thomas Müntzer of 1524, in words written on behalf of the entire group which constitute in effect the original Anabaptist pronunciamento:

"Just as our forebears [the Roman Catholic Papal Church] fell away from the true God and the knowledge of Jesus Christ and of the right faith in Him, and from the one true, common divine word, from the divine institutions, from Christian love and life, and lived without God's law and gospel in human, useless, un-Christian customs and ceremonies, and expected to attain salvation therein, yet fell far short of it, as the evangelical preachers [Luther, Zwingli, etc.] have declared, and to some extent are still declaring; so today, too, every man wants to be saved by superficial faith, without fruits of faith, without the baptism of test and probation, without love and hope, without right Christian practices, and wants to persist in all the old fashion of personal vices, and in the common ritualistic and anti-Christian customs of baptism and of the Lord's Supper, in disrespect for the divine word and in respect for the word of the pope and of the anti-papal preachers, which yet is not equal to the divine word nor in harmony with it. In respecting persons and in manifold seduction there is grosser and more pernicious error now than ever has been since the beginning of the world. In the same error we, too, lingered as long as we heard and read only the evangelical preachers who are to blame for all this, in punishment for our sins. But after we took the Scriptures in hand, too, and consulted it on many points, we have been instructed somewhat and have discovered the great and hurtful error of the shepherds, of ours too, namely that

18 Horsch, op. cit., 289.

we do not daily beseech God earnestly with constant groanings to be brought out of this destruction of all godly life and out of human abominations, and to attain to true faith and divine instruction."[19]

A similar statement was made in 1538, after fourteen years of persecution, by an Anabaptist leader who spoke on behalf of his group in the great colloquy at Berne with the leaders of the Reformed Church:

"While yet in the national church, we obtained much instruction from the writings of Luther, Zwingli, and others, concerning the mass and other papal ceremonies, that they are vain. Yet we recognized a great lack as regards repentance, conversion, and the true Christian life. Upon these things my mind was bent. I waited and hoped for a year or two, since the minister had much to say of amendment of life, of giving to the poor, loving one another, and abstaining from evil. But I could not close my eyes to the fact that the doctrine which was preached and which was based on the Word of God, was not carried out. No beginning was made toward true Christian living, and there was no unison in the teaching concerning the things that were necessary. And although the mass and the images were finally abolished, true repentance and Christian love were not in evidence. Changes were made only as concerned external things. This gave me occasion to inquire further into these matters. Then God sent His messengers, Conrad Grebel and others, with whom I conferred about the fundamental teachings of the apostles and the Christian life and practice. I found them men who had surrendered themselves to the doctrine of Christ by 'Bussfertigkeit' [repentance evidenced by fruits]. With their assistance we established a congregation in which repentance was in evidence by newness of life in Christ."[20]

19 Letter of Conrad Grebel to Thomas Müntzer, Sept. 5, 1524, *Thomas Müntzers Briefwechsel,* ed. H. Böhmer and P. Kirn (Leipzig, 1931) 92; English translation, Walter Rauschenbusch, "The Zurich Anabaptists and Thomas Münzer" *American Journal of Theology* (January 1905) 9:92.

20 Taken from an unpublished manuscript in the *Staatsarchiv des Kantons Bern, (Unnütze Papiere, Bd.* 80), entitled *Acta des Gesprächs zwüschenn predicannten und Touffbrüderenn* (1538). Copy in the Goshen College Library.

It is evident from these statements that the Anabaptists were concerned most of all about "a true Christian life," that is, a life patterned after the teaching and example of Christ. The Reformers, they believed, whatever their profession may have been, did not secure among the people true repentance, regeneration and Christian living as a result of their preaching. The Reformation emphasis on faith was good but inadequate, for without newness of life, they held, faith is hypocritical.

This Anabaptist critique of the Reformation was a sharp one, but it was not unfair. There is abundant evidence that although the original goal sought by Luther and Zwingli was "an earnest Christianity" for all, the actual outcome was far less, for the level of Christian living among the Protestant population was frequently lower than it had been before under Catholicism. Luther himself was keenly conscious of the deficiency. In April, 1522, he expressed the hope that, "We who at the present are well nigh heathen under a Christian name, may yet organize a Christian assembly."[21] In December, 1525, he had an important conversation with Caspar Schwenckfeld, concerning the establishment of the New Testament church. Schwenckfeld pointed out that the establishment of the new church had failed to result in spiritual and moral betterment of the people, a fact which Luther admitted, for Schwenckfeld states that "Luther regretted very much that no amendment of life was in evidence."[22] Between 1522 and 1527 Luther repeatedly mentioned his concern to establish a true Christian church, and his desire to provide for earnest Christians (*"Die mit Ernst Christen sein wollen"*) who would confess the gospel with their lives as well as with their tongues. He thought of entering the names of these "earnest Christians" in a special book and having them meet

---

21 Karl Holl, *Gesammelte Aufsätze zur Kirchengeschichte* (2nd and 3rd ed.) (Tübingen, 1923), 359.
22 *Corpus Schwenckfeldianorum* (Leipzig, 1911) 2:280 f. See also K. Ecke, *Schwenckfeld, Luther und der Gedanke einer apostolischen Reformation* (Berlin, 1911) 101 f. See also the discussion on this topic in J. Horsch, "The Rise of State Church Protestantism," *MQR* (July 1932) 6:189-191.

separately from the mass of nominal Christians, but concluding that he would not have sufficient of such people, he dropped the plan.[22a] Zwingli faced the same problem; he was in fact specifically challenged by the Swiss Brethren to set up such a church; but he refused and followed Luther's course.[23] Both reformers decided that it was better to include the masses within the fold of the church than to form a fellowship of true Christians only. Both certainly expected the preaching of the Word and the ministration of the sacraments to bear fruit in an earnest Christian life, at least among some, but they reckoned with a permanently large and indifferent mass. In taking this course, said the Anabaptists, the reformers surrendered their original purpose, and abandoned the divine intention. Others may say that they were wise and statesmanlike leaders.[24]

The Anabaptists, however, retained the original vision of Luther and Zwingli, enlarged it, gave it body and form, and set out to achieve it in actual experience. They proceeded to organize a church composed solely of earnest Christians, and actually found the people for it. They did not believe in any case that the size of the response should determine whether or not the truth of God should be applied, and they refused to compromise. They preferred to make a radical break with fifteen hundred years of history and culture if necessary rather than to break with the New Testament.

May it not be said that the decision of Luther and Zwingli to surrender their original vision was the tragic turning point of the Reformation? Professor Karl Müller, one of the

22a See Luther's *Deutsche Messe*, translated in *Works of Martn Luther* (ed. C. M. Jacobs *et al.* (Philadelphia, 1932) 6:172, 173.

23 "Drei Zeugenaussagen Zwinglis im Täuferprozess" in *Huldreich Zwinglis Sämtliche Werke* (Leipzig, 1927) 4:169.

24 Against this interpretation of Luther (and Zwingli) it may be argued that Luther never completely and consistently adopted the concept of a church of "earnest Christians only" which is here attributed to him, but that along with it he also retained the contradictory concept of the church functioning as a "corpus regens," that is, as an institution of social control. It may be agreed that Luther held the two concepts for a time and that he finally abandoned the former in favor of the latter, but the fact nevertheless remains that the former was for a time dominant, and that it is the implicit meaning of his whole basic theological position. The retention and eventual dominance of the second concept is an evidence of the carry-

keenest and fairest interpreters of the Reformation, evidently thinks so, for he says, "The aggressive, conquering power, which Lutheranism manifested in its first period was lost everywhere at the moment when the governments took matters in hand and established the Lutheran Creed,"[25] that is to say, when Luther's mass church concept was put into practice. Luther in his later years expressed disappointment at the final outcome of the Reformation, stating that the people had become more and more indifferent toward religion and the moral outlook was more deplorable than ever. His last years were embittered by the consciousness of partial failure, and his expressions of dejection are well known. Contrast this sense of defeat at the end of Luther's outwardly successful career with the sense of victory in the hearts of the Anabaptist martyrs who laid down their lives in what the world would call defeat, conscious of having kept faith with their vision to the end.

Having defined genuine Anabaptism in its Reformation setting, we are ready to examine its central teachings. The Anabaptist vision included three major points of emphasis; first, a new conception of the essence of Christianity as discipleship; second, a new conception of the church as a brotherhood; and third, a new ethic of love and nonresistance. We turn now to an exposition of these points.

First and fundamental in the Anabaptist vision was the conception of the essence of Christianity as discipleship. It was a concept which meant the transformation of the entire way of life of the individual believer and of society so that it should be fashioned after the teachings and example of

over of medievalism in Luther's thought. In regard to Zwingli, Wilhelm Hadorn says: "It must be admitted that not only Zwingli but also other Swiss and South German Reformers, e.g., Oecolampad and Capito, originally held views similar to the Anabaptists" (*Die Reformation in der Deutschen Schweiz*, [Leipzig, 1928], 104). Walter Köhler says: "Es ist, wie bei Luther auch, die Kapitulation der autonomen Kirchgemeinschaft vor der Obrigkeit eingetreten." *Zwinglis Werke* (Leipzig, 1927) 4:29.

25 Karl Müller, *Kirchengeschichte*, 2:1, 476. Müller describes the essential goal of the Anabaptists as follows: "Es bedeutete inmitten der Auflösung aller Verhältnisse genug, dass hier eine Gemeinschaft stand, die die Heiligung des Lebens allem anderen voranstellte und zugleich in den unteren Volksschichten wirklich Fuss gefasst, sie mit selbständiger Religiösität gefüllt hat." (*Kirchengeschichte*, 2:1, 330.)

Christ.[26] The Anabaptists could not understand a Christianity which made regeneration, holiness, and love primarily a matter of intellect, of doctrinal belief, or of subjective "experience," rather than one of the transformation of life. They demanded an outward expression of the inner experience. Repentance must be "evidenced" by newness of behaviour. "In evidence" is the keynote which rings through the testimonies and challenges of the early Swiss Brethren when they are called to give an account of themselves. The whole life was to be brought literally under the lordship of Christ in a covenant of discipleship, a covenant which the Anabaptist writers delighted to emphasize.[27] [The focus of the Christian life was to be not so much the inward experience of the grace of God, as it was for Luther, but the outward application of that grace to all human conduct and the consequent Christianization of all human relationships.] The true test of the Christian, they held, is discipleship. The great word of the Anabaptists was not "faith" as it was with the reformers, but "following" (*Nachfolge Christi*). And baptism, the greatest of the Christian symbols, was accordingly to be for them the "covenant of a good conscience toward God" (I Peter 3:21),[28] the pledge of a complete commitment to obey Christ, and not primarily the symbol of a past experience. The Anabaptists had faith, indeed, but they used it to produce a life. Theology was for them a means, not an end.

That the Anabaptists not only proclaimed the ideal of full Christian discipleship but achieved, in the eyes of their

26 Johannes Kühn, *Toleranz und Offenbarung* (Leipzig, 1923) 224, says: "With the Anabaptists everything was based on a central idea. This central idea was concretely religious. It was Jesus' command to follow Him in a holy life of fellowship." Professor Alfred Hegler of Tübingen describes the Anabaptist ideal as "liberty of conscience, rejection of all state-made Christianity, the demand for personal holiness, and a vital personal acceptance of Christian truth." Professor Paul Wernle says, "Their vital characteristic was the earnestness with which they undertook the practical fulfillment of New Te iment requirements both for the individual and for the church." These and other similar quotations are to be found in Horsch, "The Character of the Evangelical Anabaptists as reported by Contemporary Reformation Writers." *MQR* (July 1934) 8:135.

27 Pilgram Marpeck, the outstanding writer of the Swiss and South German Brethren, is an example. See J. C. Wenger, "The Theology of Pilgram Marpeck," *MQR* (October 1938) 12:247.

28 The German (Luther) translation of I Peter 3:21 calls baptism the "Bund eines guten Gewissens mit Gott."

43

contemporaries and even of their opponents, a measurably higher level of performance than the average, is fully witnessed by the sources. The early Swiss and South German reformers were keenly aware of this achievement and its attractive power. Zwingli knew it best of all, but Bullinger, Capito, Vadian, and many others confirm his judgment that the Anabaptist Brethren were unusually sincere, devoted, and effective Christians. However, since the Brethren refused to accept the state church system which the Reformers were building, and in addition made "radical" demands which might have changed the entire social order, the leaders of the Reformation were completely baffled in their understanding of the movement, and professed to believe that the Anabaptists were hypocrites of the darkest dye. Bullinger, for instance, calls them "devilish enemies and destroyers of the Church of God."[29] Nevertheless they had to admit the apparent superiority of their life. In Zwingli's last book against the Swiss Brethren (1527), for instance, the following is found: "If you investigate their life and conduct, it seems at first contact irreproachable, pious, unassuming, attractive, yea, above this world. Even those who are inclined to be critical will say that their lives are excellent."[30]

Bullinger himself, who wrote bitter diatribes against them, was compelled to admit of the early Swiss Brethren that "Those who unite with them will by their ministers be received into their church by rebaptism and repentance and newness of life. They henceforth lead their lives under a semblance of a quite spiritual conduct. They denounce covetousness, pride, profanity, the lewd conversation and immorality of the world, drinking and gluttony. In short, their hypocrisy is great and manifold."[31]

Bullinger's lament (1531) that "the people are running after them as though they were the living saints" has been reported earlier. Vadian, the reformer of St. Gall, testified

---

29 Bullinger, *Von dem unverschampten fräfel* (1531), fol. 75r.
30 S. M. Jackson, *Selected Works of Huldreich Zwingli* (Philadelphia, 1901) 127.
31 Bullinger, *Der Widertäufferen Ursprung*, fol. 15v.

44

that "none were more favorably inclined toward Anabaptism and more easily entangled with it than those who were of pious and honorable disposition."[32]

Capito, the reformer of Strasbourg, wrote in 1527 concerning the Swiss Brethren: "I frankly confess that in most [Anabaptists] there is in evidence piety and consecration and indeed a zeal which is beyond any suspicion of insincerity. For what earthly advantage could they hope to win by enduring exile, torture, and unspeakable punishment of the flesh. I testify before God that I cannot say that on account of a lack of wisdom they are somewhat indifferent toward earthly things, but rather from divine motives."[33]

The preachers of the Canton of Bern admitted in a letter of the Council of Bern in 1532 that "The Anabaptists have the semblance of outward piety to a far greater degree than we and all the churches which unitedly with us confess Christ, and they avoid offensive sins which are very common among us.[34]

Walter Klarer, the Reformed chronicler of Appenzell, Switzerland, wrote: "Most of the Anabaptists are people who at first had been the best with us in promulgating the word of God."[35]

The Roman Catholic theologian, Franz Agricola, in his book of 1582, *Against the Terrible Errors of the Anabaptists*, says, "Among the existing heretical sects there is none which in appearance leads a more modest or pious life than the Anabaptists. As concerns their outward public life they are irreproachable. No lying, deception, swearing, strife, harsh language, no intemperate eating and drinking, no outward personal display, is found among them, but humility, patience, uprightness, neatness, honesty, temperance, straightforwardness in such measure that one would suppose that they had the Holy Spirit of God."[36]

32 Joachim von Watt, *Deutsche Historische Schriften*, ed. Ernst Götzinger (St. Gall, 1879) 2:408.
33 C. A. Cornelius, *Geschichte des Münsterischen Aufruhrs* (Leipzig, 1860) 2:52.
34 W. J. McGlothlin, *Die Berner Täufer bis 1532* (Berlin, 1902) 36.
35 J. J. Simler, *Sammlung alter und neuer Urkunden* (Zürich, 1757) 1:824.
36 Karl Rembert, *Die Wiedertäufer im Herzogtum Jülich* (Berlin, 1899) 564.

A mandate against the Swiss Brethren published in 1585 by the Council of Bern states that offensive sins and views were common among the preachers and the membership of the Reformed Church, adding, "And this is the greatest reason that many pious, God-fearing people who seek Christ from their heart are offended and forsake our church [to unite with the Brethren]."[37]

One of the finest contemporary characterizations of the Anabaptists is that given in 1531 by Sebastian Franck, an objective and sympathetic witness, though an opponent of the Anabaptists, who wrote: "The Anabaptists . . . soon gained a large following, . . . drawing many sincere souls who had a zeal for God, for they taught nothing but love, faith, and the cross. They showed themselves humble, patient under much suffering; they brake bread with one another as an evidence of unity and love. They helped each other faithfully, and called each other brothers. . . . They died as martyrs, patiently and humbly enduring all persecution."[38]

A further confirmation of the above evaluation of the achievement of the Anabaptists is found in the fact that in many places those who lived a consistent Christian life were in danger of falling under the suspicion of being guilty of Anabaptist heresy. Caspar Schwenckfeld, for instance, declared, "I am being maligned, by both preachers and others, with the charge of being Anabaptist, even as all others who lead a true, pious Christian life are now almost everywhere given this name."[39] Bullinger himself complained that ". . . there are those who in reality are not Anabaptists but have a pronounced averseness to the sensuality and frivolity of the world and therefore reprove sin and vice and are consequently called or misnamed Anabaptists by petulant persons."[40]

---

37 Ernst Müller, *Geschichte der Bernischen Täufer* (Frauenfeld, 1895) 88. Müller speaks (p. 89)) of the mandate of 1585 as conceiving of "das Täuferwesen" as a just judgment of God on the church and the people of Bern.

38 Sebastian Franck, *Chronica, Zeytbuch und Geschychtbibel*, folio 444v.

39 Schwenckfeld's *Epistolar* (1564) 1:203.

40 Bullinger, *Der Widertäufferen Ursprung* (1561), fol. 170r.

The great collection of Anabaptist source materials, commonly called the *Täufer-Akten,* now being published, contains a number of specific illustrations of this. In 1562 a certain Caspar Zacher of Waiblingen in Württemberg was accused of being an Anabaptist, but the court record reports that since he was an envious man who could not get along with others, and who often started quarrels, as well as being guilty of swearing and cursing and carrying a weapon, he was not considered to be an Anabaptist.[41] On the other hand in 1570 a certain Hans Jäger of Vöhringen in Württemberg was brought before the court on suspicion of being an Anabaptist primarily because he did not curse but lived an irreproachable life.[42]

As a second major element in the Anabaptist vision, a new concept of the church was created by the central principle of newness of life and applied Christianity. Voluntary church membership based upon true conversion and involving a commitment to holy living and discipleship was the absolutely essential heart of this concept. This vision stands in sharp contrast to the church concept of the Reformers who retained the medieval idea of a mass church with membership of the entire population from birth to the grave compulsory by law and force.

It is from the standpoint of this new conception of the church that the Anabaptist opposition to infant baptism must be interpreted. Infant baptism was not the cause of their disavowal of the state church; it was only a symbol of the cause. How could infants give a commitment based upon a knowledge of what true Christianity means? They might conceivably passively experience the grace of God (though Anabaptists would question this), but they could not respond in pledging their lives to Christ. Such infant baptism would not only be meaningless, but would in fact become a serious obstacle to a true understanding of the nature of Christianity

41 *Quellen zur Geschichte der Wiedertäufer, I. Band Herzogtum Württemberg,* ed. Gustav Bossert (Leipzig, 1930) 216 ff.
42 *Ibid.,* 259 ff.

and membership in the church. Only adult baptism could signify an intelligent life commitment.

An inevitable corollary of the concept of the church as a body of committed and practicing Christians pledged to the highest standard of New Testament living was the insistence on the separation of the church from the world, that is nonconformity of the Christian to the worldly way of life. The world would not tolerate the practice of true Christian principles in society, and the church could not tolerate the practice of worldly ways among its membership. Hence, the only way out was separation ("*Absonderung*"), the gathering of true Christians into their own Christian society where Christ's way could and would be practiced. On this principle of separation Menno Simons says, "The entire evangelical Scriptures teach us that the church of Christ was and is, in doctrine, life, and worship, a people separated from the world."[43]

In the great debate of 1528 at Zofingen, spokesmen of the Swiss Brethren said, "The true church is separated from the world and is conformed to the nature of Christ. If a church is yet at one with the world we cannot recognize it as a true church."[44]

In a sense, this principle of nonconformity to the world is merely a negative expression of the positive requirement of discipleship, but it goes further in the sense that it represents a judgment on the contemporary social order, which the Anabaptists called "the world," and sets up a line of demarcation between the Christian community and worldly society.

A logical outcome of the concept of nonconformity to the world was the concept of the suffering church. Conflict with the world was inevitable for those who endeavored to live an earnest Christian life. The Anabaptists expected opposition; they took literally the words of Jesus when He said, "In the world ye shall have tribulation," but they also took literally His words of encouragement, "But be ye of good cheer, I have overcome the world."

43 *The Complete Writings of Menno Simons* (Scottdale, 1956) 679.
44 *Handlung oder Acta der Disputation gehalten zu Zofingen* (Zürich, 1532).

Conrad Grebel said in 1524, "True Christian believers are sheep among wolves, sheep for the slaughter; they must be baptized in anguish and affliction, tribulation, persecution, suffering, and death; they must be tried with fire and must reap the fatherland of eternal rest not by killing their bodily, but by mortifying their spiritual, enemies."[45]

Professor Ernest Staehelin of Basel, Switzerland, says "Anabaptism by its earnest determination to follow in life and practice the primitive Christian Church has kept alive the conviction that he who is in Christ is a new creature and that those who are identified with His cause will necessarily encounter the opposition of the world."[46]

Perhaps it was persecution that made the Anabaptists so acutely aware of the conflict between the church and the world, but this persecution was due to the fact that they refused to accept what they considered the sub-Christian way of life practiced in European Christendom. They could have avoided the persecution had they but conformed, or they could have suspended the practice of their faith to a more convenient time and sailed under false colors as did David Joris, but they chose with dauntless courage and simple honesty to live their faith, to defy the existing world order, and to suffer the consequences.

Basic to the Anabaptist vision of the church was the insistence on the practice of true brotherhood and love among the members of the church.[47] This principle was understood to mean not merely the expression of pious sentiments, but the actual practice of sharing possessions to meet the needs of others. Hans Leopold, a Swiss Brethren martyr of 1528, said of the Brethren, "If they know of any one who is in need, whether or not he is a member of their church, they believe it their duty, out of love to God, to render help and aid."[48]

---

45 Böhmer-Kirn, *op. cit.*, 97.   46 Horsch, *op. cit.*, 386.

47 P. Tschackert, *Die Entstehung der Lutherischen und reformierten Kirchenlehre* (Göttingen, 1910) 133, says of the Anabaptists that they were "a voluntary Christian fellowship, striving to conform to the Christian spirit for the practice of brotherly love."

48 Johannes Kühn, *op. cit.*, 231.

Heinrich Seiler, a Swiss Brethren martyr of 1535, said, "I do not believe it wrong that a Christian has property of his own, but yet he is nothing more than a steward."[49]

An early Hutterian book states that one of the questions addressed by the Swiss Brethren to applicants for baptism was: "Whether they would consecrate themselves with all their temporal possessions to the service of God and His people."[50] A Protestant of Strasbourg, visitor at a Swiss Brethren baptismal service in that city in 1557, reports that a question addressed to all applicants for baptism was: "Whether they, if necessity require it, would devote all their possessions to the service of the brotherhood, and would not fail any member that is in need, if they were able to render aid."[51]

Heinrich Bullinger, the bitter enemy of the Brethren, states: "They teach that every Christian is under duty before God from motives of love, to use, if need be, all his possessions to supply the necessities of life to any of the brethren who are in need."[52]

This principle of full brotherhood and stewardship was actually practiced, and not merely speculatively considered. In its absolute form of Christian communism, with the complete repudiation of private property, it became the way of life of the Hutterian Brotherhood in 1528 and has remained so to this day, for the Hutterites held that private property is the greatest enemy of Christian love. One of the inspiring stories of the sixteenth and seventeenth centuries is the successful practice of the full communal way of life by this group.[53]

49 Ernst Müller, *op. cit.*, 44. See Ernst Correll, *op. cit.*, 15 ff., on the attitude of the various Anabaptist groups on community of goods.

50 Horsch, *op. cit.*, 317.

51 A. Hulshof, *Geschiedenis van de Doopsgezinden te Straatsburg van 1525 tot 1557* (Amsterdam, 1905) 216.

52 Bullinger, *Der Widertäufferen Ursprung*, fol. 129v.

53 John Horsch, *The Hutterian Brethren 1528-1931* (Goshen, 1931), gives the only adequate account in English of the Hutterian Brethren. It is of interest to note that Erasmus, Melanchthon, and Zwingli condemned private owneship of property as a sin. See Paul Wernle, *Renaissance und Reformation* (Tübingen, 1912), 54, 55, for the citations from Erasmus and Melanchthon, and Horsch, *Hutterian Brethren*, 132, footnote 126, for the citation from Zwingli. Wilhelm Pauck says that Bucer's ideal state was that of Christian communism, "Martin Bucer's Conception of a Christian State," *Princeton Theological Review* (January 1928) 26:88.

The third great element in the Anabaptist vision was the ethic of love and nonresistance as applied to all human relationships. The Brethren understood this to mean complete abandonment of all warfare, strife, and violence, and of the taking of human life.[54]

Conrad Grebel, the Swiss leader, said in 1524: "True Christians use neither worldly sword nor engage in war, since among them taking human life has ceased entirely, for we are no longer under the Old Covenant. . . . The Gospel and those who accept it are not to be protected with the sword, neither should they thus protect themselves."[55]

Pilgram Marpeck, the South German leader, in 1544, speaking of Matthew 5, said: "All bodily, worldly, carnal, earthly fightings, conflicts, and wars are annulled and abolished among them through such law . . . which law of love Christ . . . Himself observed and thereby gave His followers a pattern to follow after."[56]

Peter Riedemann, the Hutterian leader, wrote in 1545: "Christ, the Prince of Peace, has established His Kingdom, that is, His Church, and has purchased it by His blood. In this kingdom all worldly warfare has ended. Therefore a Christian has no part in war nor does he wield the sword to execute vengeance."[57]

Menno Simons of Holland, in expounding the doctrine of the new birth, said: "These regenerated people . . . are the

---

54 Not all of the Anabaptists were completely nonresistant. Balthasar Hubmaier for instance for a brief period (1526-28) led a group of Anabaptists at Nikolsburg in Moravia who agreed to carry the sword against the Turk and pay special war taxes for this purpose. This group, which became extinct in a short time, was known as the "Schwertler" in distinction from other Moravian Anabaptists called the "Stäbler," who later became the Hutterites and have continued to the present. It is obvious that Hubmaier and the "Schwertler" represent a transient aberration from original and authentic Anabaptism. Bullinger (*Von dem unverschampten fräfel*, fol. 139v.) testifies that the Swiss Brethren considered war to be "das ergist uebel das man erdencken mag," and (*Der Widertäufferen Ursprung*, fol. 16r.) says "they do not defend themselves, therefore they do not go to war and are not obedient to the government on this point." See also, extensive compilation of evidence by John Horsch in his booklet, *The Principle of Nonresistance as Held by the Mennonite Church, A Historical Survey* (Scottdale, 1927) 60 pages.

55 Letter of Grebel to Müntzer, Böhmer-Kirn, *op. cit.*, 97.

56 Pilgram Marpeck, *Testamenterläuterung* (n.d., n.p., ca. 1544), fol. 313r.

57 Peter Riedemann, *Rechenschaft unserer Religion, Lehre und Glaubens, von den Brüdern die man die Hutterischen nennt* (Berne, Indiana, 1902) 105.

children of peace who have beaten their swords into plow-shares and their spears into pruning hooks, and know war no more. . . . Spears and swords we leave to those who, alas, regard human blood and swine's blood about alike."[58]

In this principle of nonresistance, or Biblical pacifism, which was thoroughly believed and resolutely practiced by all the original Anabaptist Brethren and their descendants throughout Europe from the beginning until the last century,[59] the Anabaptists were again creative leaders, far ahead of their times, in this antedating the Quakers by over a century and a quarter. It should also be remembered that they held this principle in a day when both Catholic and Protestant churches not only endorsed war as an instrument of state policy, but employed it in religious conflicts. It is true, of course, that occasional earlier prophets, like Peter Chelcicky, had advocated similar views, but they left no continuing practice of the principle behind them.

As we review the vision of the Anabaptists, it becomes clear that there are two foci in this vision. The first focus relates to the essential nature of Christianity. Is Christianity primarily a matter of the reception of divine grace through a sacramental-sacerdotal institution (Roman Catholicism), is it chiefly enjoyment of the inner experience of the grace of God through faith in Christ (Lutheranism), or is it most of all the transformation of life through discipleship (Anabaptism)? The Anabaptists were neither institutionalists, mystics, nor pietists, for they laid the weight of their emphasis upon following Christ in life. To them it was unthinkable for one truly to be a Christian without creating a new life on divine principles both for himself and for all men who commit themselves to the Christian way.

58 *The Complete Writings of Menno Simons*, 94, 198.

59 Mennonites of Holland, Germany, France, and Switzerland gradually abandoned nonresistance in the course of the nineteenth century. The emigrant Mennonites in Russia and North America have maintained it. The Mennonites of the United States furnished forty per cent of all conscientious objectors in Civilian Public Service in World War II, and the Mennonites of Canada a still higher per cent of the conscientious objectors in that country.

The second focus relates to the church. For the Anabaptist, the church was neither an institution (Catholicism), nor the instrument of God for the proclamation of the divine Word (Lutheranism), nor a resource group for individual piety (Pietism). It was a brotherhood of love in which the fullness of the Christian life ideal is to be expressed.

The Anabaptist vision may be further clarified by comparison of the social ethics of the four main Christian groups of the Reformation period, Catholic, Calvinist, Lutheran, and Anabaptist. Catholic and Calvinist alike were optimistic about the world, agreeing that the world can be redeemed; they held that the entire social order can be brought under the sovereignty of God and Christianized, although they used different means to attain this goal. Lutheran and Anabaptist were pessimistic about the world, denying the possibility of Christianizing the entire social order; but the consequent attitudes of these two groups toward the social order were diametrically opposed. Lutheranism said that since the Christian must live in a world order that remains sinful, he must make a compromise with it. As a citizen he cannot avoid participation in the evil of the world, for instance in making war, and for this his only recourse is to seek forgiveness by the grace of God; only within his personal private experience can the Christian truly Christianize his life. The Anabaptist rejected this view completely. Since for him no compromise dare be made with evil, the Christian may in no circumstance participate in any conduct in the existing social order which is contrary to the spirit and teaching of Christ and the apostolic practice. He must consequently withdraw from the worldly system and create a Christian social order within the fellowship of the church brotherhood. Extension of this Christian order by the conversion of individuals and their transfer out of the world into the church is the only way by which progress can be made in Christianizing the social order.

However, the Anabaptist was realistic. Down the long perspective of the future he saw little chance that the mass of humankind would enter such a brotherhood with its high ideals. Hence he anticipated a long and grievous conflict between the church and the world. Neither did he anticipate the time when the church would rule the world; the church would always be a suffering church. He agreed with the words of Jesus when He said that those who would be His disciples must deny themselves, take up their cross daily and follow Him, and that there would be few who would enter the strait gate and travel the narrow way of life. If this prospect should seem too discouraging, the Anabaptist would reply that the life within the Christian brotherhood is satisfyingly full of love and joy.

The Anabaptist vision was not a detailed blueprint for the reconstruction of human society, but the Brethren did believe that Jesus intended that the kingdom of God should be set up in the midst of earth, here and now, and this they proposed to do forthwith. We shall not believe, they said, that the Sermon on the Mount or any other vision that He had is only a heavenly vision meant but to keep His followers in tension until the last great day, but we shall practice what He taught, believing that where He walked we can by His grace follow in His steps.

The Rise of Anabaptism

✠ FRITZ BLANKE ✠

Anabaptism and the Reformation[1]

I

Beside the main channel of the Reformation there flowed three other streams: Anabaptism, spiritualism, and anti-Trinitarianism. Although there were transitions and borderline phenomena between these three streams, they can nevertheless be held to be essentially distinct. Anabaptism in turn may be divided into four branches: the Swiss Brethren; the Hutterian Brethren in Moravia; the Melchiorites, notorious for their apocalyptic kingdom in Münster 1534-35; and the Mennonites.

It is the merit of Ernst Troeltsch to have discerned as much as fifty years ago the difference between Anabaptism and spiritualism. The point at which the two streams separate is the Scripture. The Anabaptists are Biblicists. They seek to remain as close as possible to the Bible, whereas the spiritualists value the immediate illumination by the Holy Spirit higher than the revelation in the Word. The spiritualists had four leading representatives: Andreas Carlstadt, Thomas Müntzer, Sebastian Franck, and Caspar Schwenckfeld. Within sixteenth-century spiritualism there are various gradations. For instance, Carlstadt and Schwenckfeld must be considered as moderates, Müntzer and Franck as radical spiritualists; but this distinction does not concern us here. Whereas the Anabaptists, as we shall demonstrate below, were children of the Reformation, the spiritualists had their roots in late medieval Catholic mysticism, with which they mingled ideas borrowed

---

* Fritz Blanke is Professor of Church History in the University of Zürich and author of *Brüder in Christo: Die Geschichte der ältesten Täufergemeinde, Zollikon, 1525* (Zürich, 1955).

1 This paper was first given as a lecture in the Wasserkirche in Zürich on the occasion of the 425th anniversary of Zwingli's death, October 11, 1956.

from the Reformation. A third independent Protestant stream was that of the anti-Trinitarians, also known as Socinians, for Lelio and Fausto Socini, who criticized the doctrine of the Trinity on rational grounds. Stimulated partly by Reformation ideas, they really belonged within Renaissance humanism.

The following pages deal with the Anabaptists, especially with the first group, the Swiss Brethren, from whom all the other branches of the sixteenth-century movement received the practice of adult baptism. The Swiss Brethren came into existence in Zürich. Here were formed the first congregations of Anabaptists. The city on the Limmat is the cradle of the now world-wide Anabaptist-Mennonite-Baptist tradition. I shall first describe the origins of the Zürich brotherhood and then draw conclusions as to the essential nature of the movement as a whole. Only at the source of a movement do the waters run pure. It is our obligation to evaluate the Anabaptist church of the sixteenth century according to the original intentions of its founders, just as we do with respect to the churches of the Reformation.

II

Under the influence of Huldrych Zwingli the council of Zürich decreed the Reformation in January 1523. Naturally the total population of Zürich did not at one stroke become convinced evangelical Christians. In 1523-24 Zwingli himself distinguished three different groups within the population. There were people in Zürich (city and canton), he said, who were Protestant out of hatred for Catholicism. That was the category (still extant) of "negative Protestants," who are Protestant because they under no conditions wish to be Catholics. The second group is made up of libertinistic Protestants, who see in the Gospel nothing but an opportunity to lead a looser life. But there is also a third circle: those who "work in the Word of God," who seek to live according to the Word of God and to penetrate ever deeper into the Holy

58

Scriptures. This last group is Zwingli's "staff," the narrow circle of his collaborators.

The founders of Anabaptism in Zürich were Conrad Grebel and Felix Manz. It is highly significant to see that in the early stages of the Reformation they belonged to the third circle just mentioned. They were originally faithful followers of Zwingli. Conrad Grebel came from a patrician family of the city. His father was a member of the council. Conrad himself had received a humanistic education.[2] The Grebel family still exists in Zürich; a descendant of Conrad Grebel is at present pastor in Zwingli's church, the Grossmünster. Felix Manz was the son of a canon in Zürich, one of the many illegitimate sons of priests of those times, to whose number the Zürich Reformers Leo Jud and Heinrich Bullinger as well belonged. Like Grebel, Manz had been trained as a humanist.[3]

Our first major question is on what grounds these disciples of Zwingli turned away from their master. To solve the problem, we must not seek information first from Zwingli; we must ask the Anabaptists themselves. Previous research concerning Anabaptism has, with a few praiseworthy exceptions, committed the error of seeking information about the meaning of Anabaptism from its opponents, drawing a picture of the movement from antagonistic sources. That is just as if we were to seek to draw a picture of Martin Luther's lifework on the basis of documents written by his enemies. If we wish to do justice to the first Anabaptists, we must seek first to ascertain their understanding of themselves. The sources provide us with adequate information.

In September 1524, before the administration of the first "rebaptism," Conrad Grebel wrote a letter to Thomas Müntzer in Thuringia, in the name of his circle of friends in Zü-

2 We are indebted to Harold S. Bender for the definitive description of the life and work of Conrad Grebel: *Conrad Grebel, c. 1498-1526, The Founder of the Swiss Brethren, Sometimes Called Anabaptists* (Goshen, 1950). I wish on this occasion to express to Professor Bender the deep gratitude of scholars of the Zürich Reformation for this fundamental work. See my review of the book in the *MQR* (July 1957).

3 A scholarly biography of Manz by Ekkehard Krajewski has been completed in manuscript.

rich. In this letter the causes for the separation from Zwingli were set forth.[4] Grebel's thought is as follows: Zwingli put the Bible into our hands and encouraged us, even though we were not theologians, to study it. We have followed his advice, and in reading the New Testament we have found in one respect another teaching than that which Zwingli had given us. We have discovered another view of the church. In Zürich, as in the rest of the Christian world, every newborn child is baptized and is henceforth considered as a church member; as a result, church and people are identical, the church is everybody's church. But in the New Testament (Matt. 7:14) the church is a fellowship, not of the many, but of the few who truly believe and who live aright.

This was Grebel's new understanding of the church. Zwingli knew only the *Volkskirche,* and accepted it. How shall we designate what Grebel and his friends had discovered? They wanted a church free from the guardianship of the state, accepting such members as joined out of an uncoerced decision. They sought a free church in the double sense: a congregation free from the state and based upon voluntary membership. This was the first goal of Anabaptism. Their real interest was not in baptism, but in the church. They sought a fellowship of those who by God's grace had come to faith, who desired earnestly to be Christians and to testify to the Gospel in word and work. The baptism of believers was simply the most striking external manifestation of this new kind of church. Because of this external peculiarity Zwingli named Grebel and his fellows "Rebaptizers," an epithet which stuck to the movement as a whole. The "Anabaptists" themselves refused this name; they called themselves, according to primitive Christian practice, brethren and sisters.

But Grebel did not only demand withdrawal from the

---

4 The most recent printing of this letter is to be found in L. von Muralt and W. Schmid (Eds.), *Quellen zur Geschichte der Täufer in der Schweiz,* Vol. I (Zürich, 1952). The first English translation of the letter by Walter Rauschenbusch appeared in the *American Journal of Theology* (January 1905) 9:91 ff.

Volkskirche; in the same letter to Müntzer he rejected the participation of the Christian in the life of the state. In the opinion of his group the Christian should accept no civil office or military service. Grebel's letter of September 1524 is the Reformation's earliest testimony to a radical Christian *church* pacifism. Thus two new thoughts were born in Zürich in *state* 1523-24; a new vision of the church and a new understanding of the state. How did these ideas take concrete form? Grebel's wife gave birth to a son in the fall of 1524. Grebel refused to have the child baptized; an infant has no faith, and faith must precede baptism. Others of Grebel's friends also refused, in the same period, to bring their newborn children for baptism. Infant baptism was at that time not only a churchly practice, but also a civil obligation. The collision between Grebel and his companions on the one hand, and the city-state of Zürich on the other, was immediate.

To clear up the difference of opinion the council arranged for a discussion between the advocates and the opponents of infant baptism. A public debate took place on January 17, 1525. According to the judgment of the council before which the debate was held, Grebel and his companions were defeated by Zwingli. The council's decisions were made accordingly on the evening of the same day. All parents who had neglected to have their children baptized were to do so within a week, on pain of banishment. Grebel and Manz were silenced and four of their friends, Wilhelm Reublin, Ludwig Hätzer, Johannes Brötli, and Andreas Castelberg, were banished. The government hoped thus to be able to extinguish the spark.

What should the condemned group do? Should they abandon their plans? They said to themselves, "We must obey God rather than men" (Acts 5:29), and met secretly on the evening of January 21, apparently in the home of Felix Manz' mother in the Neugasse near the Grossmünster. In this meeting Grebel baptized Georg Blaurock, whereupon Blaurock baptized several of the others present. That was the birth of Anabaptism, the earliest free church. Grebel and his companions considered the baptism which they had received as infants to be invalid, and formed a congregation of those who had become Christians through belief and baptism.

The newly baptized friends withdrew from Zürich to the nearby village of Zollikon. Here Brötli, who for some time had been living in the village as vicar, had spread the group's ideas among the people. In this village the first Anabaptist congregation came into being in late January 1525.[5] From house to house the villagers celebrated the Lord's Supper in apostolic simplicity. In the cottages the farmers read the words of institution and shared the bread and wine. Such a celebration of communion was a revolution. For in January 1525 in Zürich, city and countryside, communion was still celebrated according to the Roman rite. That was the will of the Zürich council. The council had voted in January 1523 for the preaching of the Gospel, but had forbidden the modification of the forms of worship. It was feared that the populace would be disturbed by the rapid abandon of the old and familiar usage. Zwingli and his colleagues were forced to celebrate communion in the form of the Roman mass, omitting only the so-called transubstantiation formula. Not until Easter week in 1525 was the evangelical Lord's Supper introduced.

In addition to the communion services there were evangelistic meetings as well in the cottages in Zollikon. Georg Blaurock, the Romansch from the Grisons,[6] showed himself to be a powerful evangelist. The result was a spiritual awakening of soul-shaking depth. Men were inwardly moved; they confessed their sins and began to weep. In remorse they came to Blaurock and his friends and asked for baptism as the sign that God had forgiven them. The movement of repentance

---

5 Cf. Fritz Blanke, *Brüder in Christo: Die Geschichte der ältesten Täufergemeinde* (Zürich, 1955).

6 Cf. J. A. Moore, *Der starke Jörg* (Kassel, 1955); also the article "Blaurock, Georg," in *Mennonite Encyclopedia* (Scottdale, Pa., 1955) 1:354.

in Zollikon was genuine and powerful. It was a wrestling with the grace of God. Political and social motives played no part in it.

Today the founding of a free church is no longer anything extraordinary. In modern times there have been free church movements again and again. But in Zollikon we have to do with the *first* Protestant free church. That was a turning point of historic proportions. For at that time state churchdom ruled the entire Christian world. Only in the hamlet of Zollikon did a group of Spirit-moved persons dare to form a brotherhood, a Christian church, without the help of the state. But the state of that day, in which religion and the civil community formed a unity, could not tolerate such an autonomous brotherhood. The council in Zürich considered the religious independence of the peasants in Zollikon to be rebellion.

On January 30 the city police of Zürich came to Zollikon. They imprisoned all the newly baptized men, together with Blaurock and Manz. Blaurock and the men from Zollikon were released soon afterwards. The movement subsided in Zollikon but struck new roots elsewhere. Brötli worked in Hallau in the canton of Schaffhausen and formed a church there.[7] Reublin was soon in Waldshut where he was able to win the powerful reformer Balthazar Hubmaier and with him the city's church.[8] Thus the persecution of the Anabaptists disseminated their teaching.

Blaurock and Grebel, joined later in the year by Manz, preached and baptized in the Zürich Oberland with considerable success. But they had been condemned to silence, and accordingly were seized and imprisoned. Zwingli had several conversations with them, but they refused to recant. According to the barbarous practice of the times they were tortured, but in vain. Finally the authorities lost their patience. The council decided on March 7, 1526, that henceforth any-

---

7 Cf. J. A. Moore, "Johannes Brötli," *The Baptist Quarterly* (January 1953) 15:29-34.
8 Cf. article "Reublin," in *Mennonitisches Lexikon* (Karlsruhe, 1956) 3:477-80.

one guilty of rebaptizing would be drowned. Drowning was chosen as a particularly dishonorable form of punishment. On January 5, 1527, Felix Manz, the first Anabaptist martyr,[9] died the death of a confessor. He was drowned in Zürich in the middle of the Limmat (between today's Rathaus bridge and Rudolf-Brun bridge) and buried in the dump by St. Jacob's. During Zwingli's life, between 1527 and 1531, three more Anabaptists, peasants from the Oberland, were drowned in the Limmat: Jakob Falck from Gossau, Heini Reimann from the district of Grüningen, and Conrad Winckler from Wassberg near Maur. By 1531 the movement was practically eradicated from the canton.

We must ask how Zwingli could accept this bloody persecution. The Anabaptists demanded the separation of church and state, which the council refused, intending to maintain strictly the prevailing system. The council had made possible the Reformation in Zürich, for which Zwingli was indebted to the state. If Zwingli had accepted or supported the free church movement the entire Reformation would have been smothered by the state, and Zürich would have returned to Catholicism. That the Reformer had to avoid such a development is clear. In today's Protestantism the situation has changed. State-churchdom is in recession. At the 1954 Evanston Assembly the free churches were more numerous than the state churches. The "error" of the Anabaptists—I intentionally set the word "error" in quotation marks, for it in no way involves guilt—was that they went to work too soon. The collision between the Zwinglian and the Anabaptist views of the church was the tragic conflict of two significant syntheses, one of which was premature.

After 1530, as we have seen, Anabaptism was largely destroyed in the city and canton of Zürich. But many of the persecuted had fled, and the movement lived on in Germany,

---

9 Three men from the Anabaptist movement had lost their lives earlier because of their convictions: Klaus Hottinger, expelled from Zürich before baptism had become an issue, Hippolyt Eberle Bolt (*ME* 1:384) and Johannes Krüsi, the latter both leaders of the Anabaptist movement in and around St. Gall in 1525, were put to death by Catholic cantons as Protestants.

Austria, and elsewhere, always under the terrible menace of death. The Diet of Spires in 1529 had officially proclaimed the Anabaptists to be heretics; every court was obliged to condemn them to death with no opportunity for defense. In Reformation times between four and five thousand men and women were executed as Anabaptists by fire, water, and the sword; Protestant and Catholic governments worked as one in the campaign of extermination.

In 1527 Michael Sattler, an Anabaptist from the Black Forest, drew up a confession of faith in seven points. It was adopted by a secret synod of South German and Swiss Anabaptists at Schleitheim near Schaffhausen, as a binding Rule of Faith, and has come to be known as the Schleitheim Confession.[10] The Schleitheim articles are Anabaptism's oldest confessional document. It is first of all striking that these articles say nothing about God, Jesus Christ, and justification by faith. The central truths of the Christian faith are not mentioned. Why? Because the men who adopted this confession were in agreement with Luther and Zwingli concerning all of these central truths. Zwingli himself emphasized repeatedly that nothing involving belief in God, Christ, and grace separated the Anabaptists from him.[11] The Schleitheim Confession deals only with those points in which Anabaptism and the Reformation differ. That is the reason for the absence of a treatment of the fundamental Christian truths. The seven articles deal with the church and the state, not with the center of Christian faith. In faith in Jesus Christ as sole and sufficient Redeemer they were of one mind with the Reformers. For this reason it is inadmissible to designate the Anabaptist churches as "sects." The characteristic of a sect is the recognition of another authority of equal weight with Christ, whereas the church honors Christ alone. The Anabaptists confess Jesus Christ alone and are therefore churches.

10 Cf. Beatrice Jenny, *Das Schleitheimer Täuferbekenntnis 1527* (Thayngen, 1951); John C. Wenger, "The Schleitheim Confession of Faith," *MQR* (October 1945) 19:243-53.

11 Hermann Lüdemann, professor at Bern, failed to see this as he accused the Anabaptists of "works-holiness" in his *Reformation und Täufertum* (1898).

III

From the above we draw three conclusions:

1) *Anabaptism and Protestantism.* Anabaptism sprang from the soil of the Reformation; it is a child, though an unsubmissive child, of the Reformation. The first congregations are found where the Reformation had already begun. The roots of Anabaptism do not go back to the Middle Ages. This must be said in contradiction of Ludwig Keller (1849-1915), who regarded the Anabaptists as remnants of the medieval dissident movements of the Albigenses and the Waldensians.

2) *Anabaptism and the class struggle.* Friedrich Engels (1820-95), cofounder of Marxist communism, understood Anabaptism as a form of the war of the classes. This is incorrect. Anabaptism was in its origin a religious and not a social phenomenon. The first churches were not representative of any one social group.[12] In Zürich in 1525 all the strata of the population were involved. Grebel was a patrician; he and Manz were educated humanists, Blaurock a former priest; beside them stood burghers and artisans. Repressed in the city, the movement shifted to Zollikon and found the support of farmers and workingmen.[13] Elsewhere we see the same development. Small groups were formed in the cities, and moved to the villages when repressed. The movement was borne principally by rural elements from about 1527 on.

Thus the origin of Anabaptism is not to be found in social conditions. Nor did the founders have specific social goals, such as community of goods or even rebellion against the state. Grebel's letter of September 1524 clearly rejected Thomas Müntzer's revolutionary intentions. Christian communism was practiced by only one branch of sixteenth-century Anabaptism, the Hutterian Brethren. The Melchiorites

12 Paul Peachey, *Die soziale Herkunft der Schweizer Täufer in der Reformationszeit* (Karlsruhe, 1954). See also Peachey, "The Social Background and Social Philosophy of the Swiss Anabaptists, 1525-1540," *MQR* (April 1954) 28:102-27.

13 It is furthermore certain that the Zollikon Anabaptists were irreproachable in their economic relationships.

brought about a political revolution in Münster (Westphalia) in 1534, but this bloody venture was an exception condemned by the majority of the Anabaptists. This must be expressly emphasized, because the claim that Anabaptism and the Peasants' Revolt were related is encountered again and again. It is a commonplace affirmation, to be found in every schoolbook, that the Anabaptists were responsible for the great German Peasants' War of 1525. This, however, is impossible. Anabaptism only came into existence in 1525, and was at that time an urban movement, with the sole exception of Zollikon. It reached Basel and Bern only in the course of 1525, when the Peasants' War was already over. That war was a German, not a Swiss phenomenon. When it began in Germany Anabaptism hardly existed in Switzerland. A connection between the two movements is impossible, unless it be in the reverse direction. Perhaps, so writes Paul Peachey,[14] the collapse of the Peasants' Revolt prepared the way for Anabaptism; after their failure the embittered German peasants, expecting nothing more from state or church, were ready to turn to Anabaptism.[15]

3) *Anabaptism and the state.* The attitude of the earliest Anabaptists is not anarchy or enmity toward the state. They recognize the civil order. For they were Biblicists, and in their Bible stood the words: "The magistrate bears not the sword in vain." They accepted Romans 13; every state is for them an institution willed by God. But they go further; a disciple of Christ can accept no civil office, no sword, no military service. Thereby the government is left to the non-Christians. This is not anarchy; it is apolitism, withdrawal from responsibility for the life of the state. One may object that this position is unsatisfactory; that one cannot admit that government is instituted by God and at the same time refuse

14 Peachey, *op. cit.*, 55.

15 A further remark should be added concerning the agitation in Zürich's Oberland in 1525. Here again the Anabaptists were not the agitators; they appeared only after the fermentation had passed the critical point. Hans Nabholz in *Die Bauernbewegung in der Ostschweiz* (1898), 95, wrote that when the Anabaptists arrived "the religious issue pushed the political issue more and more into the background."

to accept office. This position is indeed no solution, as occasional representatives of Anabaptism, such as Hubmaier and Marpeck, realized already four centuries ago.

Nevertheless we must seek to understand the Anabaptist attitude toward the state, even if we disapprove of it. In the century of the Reformation the governments affirmed their Christian character with great self-confidence. Political measures were described as Christian. The state itself was a Christian state. This unquestioned fraternization of Christianity and government was too much for the Anabaptists. The alliance of state and church, in which each uses the other for its own ends, was unacceptable to them. All the more impossible was the conception that the church was identical with the people. In other words, the Anabaptists rejected the *Corpus Christianum. Corpus Christianum* means that state and church form one whole, encompassing all of life, a "Christian body." This conception was born A.D. 380 when the Roman Emperor Theodosius proclaimed Christianity the state religion, and has influenced occidental history down into modern times. One expression of the *Corpus Christianum* mentality was that the Roman Catholic and the Protestant churches claimed the guardianship of all cultural and public life, a claim which could not be realized without coercion. The Anabaptists recognized that Theodosius' manner of relating state and church to each other was unwholesome for both parties. Therefore their rejection of the *Corpus Christianum*.

But with what shall we replace it? With withdrawal from political life, apolitism? The Anabaptists had no sympathy at all for the state. This was naturally also wrong. *Corpus Christianum* is no more acceptable than apolitism; but neither is it worse. We must find a solution which goes beyond both. May this much be said toward an understanding of the thought world of the Anabaptists. I shall be grateful if I have succeeded only in demonstrating that the judgment of their movement which we have taken over from the Reformers is in need of re-examination. The problem, Anabaptism and the Reformation, must be posed anew.

✠ N. VAN DER ZIJPP ✠

The Early Dutch Anabaptists

It is a well-known fact that both in Switzerland and South Germany the Täufer or Anabaptist movement early developed into a large number of congregations after the pattern of the first Anabaptists in Zürich. It was particularly after the principles and practices of the movement had been laid down, in the so-called Schleitheim Confession[1] of February 1527, that a local church life of an autonomous congregational type emerged. Although the leaders (usually the elders together with the ministers and deacons) of these autonomous congregations had a genuine influence on the course of affairs, their views and ideas were not obligatory for the congregation. In the management both of the organization and of the spiritual life of these congregations each member of the brotherhood had privileges and responsibilities equal to those of every other member. This democratic process was the consequence of their rejection of the state church and every kind of hierarchy, and of their restoration of the church of Christ after the apostolic pattern.

On the other hand, however, it was also commonly accepted that such democracy had its limits; for every member was expected to believe and to act in accordance with the Scriptures. Although as yet there was no "creed" as that term is commonly understood, the brotherhood nevertheless felt itself united within the objective bounds of the Bible. This is what Michael Sattler meant by the expression "fenced

* N. van der Zijpp is Professor of Church History in the Doopsgezind Theological Seminary, Amsterdam, and author of *Geschiedenis der Doopsgezinden in Nederland* (Arnhem, 1952).

1 The Schleitheim (Schlatten am Randen) resolutions are found in *Brüderlich Vereinigung etzlicher Kinder Gottes sieben Artikel betreffend.* I used the Dutch translation after a copy of 1560 edited by S. Cramer in *Bibliotheca Reformatoria Neerlandica*, Vol. 5 (The Hague, 1909.)

territory of the Scriptures;"[2] and it was the vision of Sattler's confessionalism and congregationalism, more than the individualistic spiritualism of Hans Denk, which characterized the Täufer movement among the Brethren of Switzerland and South Germany.

Although the nature and the character of early Dutch Anabaptism are less clear, it is certain that it took a somewhat different turn than did that of Switzerland and Germany. Notwithstanding a large number of early historical sources, however, it is difficult to get a completely true and objective picture of Anabaptism in the Netherlands during the years 1530-40. The following, for example, are a number of questions for which we have no definitive answer:

1. To what extent was early Dutch Anabaptism influenced by religious movements and reforms of the late Middle Ages? Historians agree that Waldensian influences are out of the question;[3] but what was the influence of the Biblical revival of the Brethren of the Common Life?[4]

2. To what extent did the economic situation and the social conditions of the lower classes provide a fertile soil for the astonishingly rapid growth of Dutch Anabaptism in the years 1530-34? Certainly, early Dutch Anabaptism is not to be identified with an economic,[5] and still less with a socialistic movement, as has been proposed. On the other hand, however, a social woof in Anabaptism cannot be completely

---

2 *BRN*, 5:615. This expression is found in a letter written by Sattler from prison to the congregation of Horb.

3 The Waldensian influence theory was defended in the 17th and 18th centuries by Mennonite authors such as Galenus Abrahamsz and Herman Schijn, and in the 19th century by J. H. Halbertsma and S. Blaupot ten Cate; the German historian Ludwig Keller was also of the opinion that the Waldensians had a great influence upon the Mennonites. W. J. Kühler, quoting a passage from the outstanding Dutch church historian W. Moll, refused to accept Waldensian influence on the Dutch Mennonites. See Kühler, *Geschiedenis der Nederlandsche Doopsgezinden in de zestiende eeuw* (Haarlem, 1932) 23 ff.

4 See Kühler, *op. cit.*, 24-32; and N. van der Zijpp, *Geschiedenis der Doopsgezinden in Nederland* (Arnhem, 1952) 27 ff.

5 This is the opinion of K. Vos in his papers, "Kleine Bijdragen over de Doopersche beweging in Nederland tot het optreden van Menno Simons," in *Doopsgezinde Bijdragen* (1917), and "Revolutionnaire Hervorming," in *De Gids* (December 1920). The same view is presented in the book of A. F. Mellink, *De Wederdopers in de Noordelijke Nederlanden 1531-1544* (Groningen, 1954).

denied as is clearly seen from the many confessions of Anabaptists during their court trials.[6]

3. Did the Swiss-South German movement have a direct influence on the rise of Anabaptism in the Netherlands? It seems not to have had, even though there are many striking similarities.[7]

4. The so-called sacramentists or evangelicals in the Netherlands, the number of whom in many towns must have been large, are known to have been averse to Roman Catholic doctrines and practices such as the mass and indulgences, although as a rule they had not broken from the church completely, nor practiced adult baptism upon confession of faith, nor founded special evangelical congregations. Why did the majority of these people now decide for Anabaptism?[8] No satisfactory answer has been found.

In the fall of 1530 Anabaptism rapidly spread throughout Friesland and North Holland, and also around the town of Maastricht in the southeastern part of the country. A large number of preachers, most of whose names remain unknown, were traveling all over the country, and everywhere congregations emerged. Until at least 1534 this was a spontaneous movement more than a well-organized church. Prophets are said to have been numerous and each brother and even sister was entitled to read and explain the Scriptures; at least they did so, and baptism was administered by every member of the church who was asked to baptize. The only definite office which we find in this early period is that of the deacon, who cared for the poor.[9] Gradually, however, a more formal or-

6 Striking examples are found in G. Grosheide, "Verhooren en vonnissen . . . in 1534 en 1535," published in *Bijdragen en Mededeelingen van het Historisch Genootschap* (Amsterdam, 1920) Vol. 41.

7 Dutch Mennonite historians before 1640 seemed unaware of Anabaptism in Switzerland and even until recent times no attention was given to the question whether the rise of Anabaptism in the Netherlands was connected with the *Täufertum* in Switzerland and South Germany. See also Kühler, *op. cit.*, 20 ff.

8 Note the striking facts mentioned by W. Bax in *Het Protestantisme in het Bisdom Luik en vooral te Maastricht* (The Hague, 1937) 1:76-93.

9 Jan Pauw, who died as a martyr at Amsterdam on March 6, 1535, is expressly said to have been a deacon (as early as 1533); in other towns there is mention of *buideldragers* (those who bear the purse).

ganization emerged. In the larger congregations such as Amsterdam and Leeuwarden there was a bishop (soon the word "bishop" was replaced by elder), who was the head of the congregation. The prophets disappear, and more and more elders and preachers who had been appointed by the members of the congregation became the leaders, together with the deacons. A regular church life had now begun. This did not take place everywhere at the same time, however, and often it was hindered or even made impossible by persecution. It was not always possible to act as Sattler recommends in the Schleitheim Confession: "Should it happen that through the cross the shepherd (*Hirt*) should be banished or led to the Lord (through martyrdom) another shall be ordained in the same hour so that God's little flock and people may not be destroyed."[10] Often the congregations were without elders and preachers. Many elders too, in the early years, did not have charge of special local congregations. Rather, they were traveling evangelists going from place to place like the Apostle Paul. This was true, for example, in the case of Menno Simons.

Among the early Dutch Anabaptists there were great divergences and it cannot be said that there was one universal Anabaptist vision. Nearly all agreed on the coming of the kingdom of God in the near future. This made the question of organization relatively unimportant, rather incidental, or even superfluous. The Anabaptist movement in the Netherlands, much more than that of Switzerland and South Germany, was strongly eschatological. Concerning the realization of the eschatological expectation, however, there were differences of opinion. The majority believed that "the end of this world and the realization of the world to come" would be a spiritual experience: one had to wait patiently and peacefully and to suffer faithfully until "the day of the Lord."[11]

---

10 *BRN*, 5:609.

11 This fact clearly emerges from the martyr books. The oldest of the Dutch martyr books, the *Offer des Heeren*, has only one case of a cry for revenge. Cf. Kühler, *op. cit.*, 263.

Others, always a minority although a strong one, believed that the coming kingdom would not only bring peace on earth and absolute fulfillment of the sovereignty of God in all things spiritual, but that it would bring the end of material needs as well.[12]

Economic conditions, such as unemployment, poverty, famine, and social injustices, made their contribution to the development of this point of view. After certain leaders had declared it to be God's will that unbelievers (that is, all who persecuted the Anabaptists, or who helped to perpetuate social injustice) should be uprooted, and after they had summoned the Lord's "true servants" to respond to the "call of God" to take up the sword and eradicate the "enemies of God," the tragedy of revolutionary Anabaptism occurred.[13] The culmination of the movement was Jan van Leyden's kingdom of Zion at Münster in Westphalia. It is, to be sure, historically incorrect to regard "Münster" as representative of Dutch Anabaptism, as has frequently been charged by Catholic and Reformed historians, a view which has been supported even in our own time by writers such as Vos and Mellink. Kühler's thesis, that there were peaceful, nonresistant Anabaptists prior to Münster, as well as at the time of the kingdom and afterward,[14] is much more according to the truth. It is clear, however, that the roots of this deplorable *deraillement* were present on the religious scene in the Netherlands from the earliest beginnings of Anabaptism in that region.

Another divergence within Dutch Anabaptism, also present from the beginning, had to do with the Christian's relation to the world. One group believed that the disciples of Christ must remain absolutely separated from the world; that they must be gathered as the chosen *cleyn hoopen* (little flock), keeping themselves unspotted until the day of God. Others permitted believers to associate with the world to a

12 See Mellink, *op. cit.*, 362-64 *et passim*.
13 As an illustration see the booklet *Van der Wrake (On Vengeance)*, written by Bernard Rothmann in Münster, and which had a wide circulation among the Anabaptists in the Netherlands.
14 In his paper "Het Anabaptisme in Nederland," in *De Gids* (1921) 250.

certain degree, regarding a large number of practices and even principles as adiaphora which could be engaged in without sinning. The latter found their leader in David Joris,[15] an elder who had many adherents, more than is usually admitted, even as late as 1546.

Another divergence among the Anabaptists of the Netherlands was that between those of what might be called the congregational vision and those of the spiritualistic vision. In Switzerland this difference never became a source of dispute or schism, congregationalism being largely prevalent. In the Netherlands, however, the two schools of thought continued side by side for some time, each with its body of adherents. It is true, of course, that in the early period, before it was possible for a church organization to be effected, the question did not arise.[16] As soon as there were congregations, however, with ministers, established religious practices, and disciplinary procedures, the differences between these two points of view emerged. Such questions as the competency of the ministers and the validity of baptism and of discipline then came under discussion.

Above all, however, was the question of the congregation as the visible body of Christ, as opposed to the primacy of individual faith, with the congregation regarded as of secondary importance. The question might be formulated as follows: Shall the congregation be thought of as the true and holy church, administering the Word of God and directing the faith of its members, who as obedient servants accept the authority of the congregation and submit themselves to its

---

15 Concerning David Joris see *Mennonite Encyclopedia*, 2:17. Joris was of the opinion that it was allowed "with Jacob to put on the clothes of Esau" and "to simulate with the world." That is, it was permissible not to separate from the world and occasionally even to visit the Roman Catholic church in order to deceive the government officials. Against this view of Joris, Menno stated that it should be a characteristic of true Christianity to have "sorrow and suffering because of the Word of God."

16 In the court trials of the martyrs information concerning the organization of the church is scarce; in the letters written by martyrs after about 1550 and inserted in the martyr books there are occasional references to the church as a well-organized body.

ministers as the ministers of God? Or shall the emphasis be placed upon the operation of the Holy Spirit in the heart of the believer, in this way opening the Scriptures and making known to him the will of God, and giving to the believer the direct experience of peace restored and of sins forgiven? Those holding to the former view regarded the congregation as all-important, striving for the realization of a church without spot or wrinkle (Eph. 5:27). Much attention was given to the objective holiness of the church; the ban was rigorously applied even in the case of minor sins; and the need for a uniform creed, a confession of faith, was emphasized. An ordained ministry, also, was a strict necessity under this pattern of church life. It is self-evident that much support for this type of church life can be found in the New Testament, especially in the pastoral epistles, as well as in the practices of the apostolic church.

Spiritualism, on the other hand, also goes back to the Bible, although it is usually not inclined to rely upon proof texts from the "outer word" for the support of its position.[17] Like congregationalism, spiritualism also has its pitfalls, always being exposed to the danger of disdaining the visible church. Emphasis upon inner security ("My grace is sufficient for thee," II Cor. 12:9) often includes the rejection of an objective formulation of doctrine or confession of faith. The experience of faith as a purely personal relationship between God and the individual soul can be the source of a vigorous religious and moral life. Frequently, however, it also tends toward a low view of the communion service, and even of baptism; and occasionally it runs off into an unsound mysti-

---

17 Sebastian Franck, the "father of spiritualism," who had a great influence on the left wing of Anabaptism, writes that "die Schrift und die äusseren Worte nur des wahren, wesentlichen, inneren Wortes, Bild, Scheide, Monstranz, Krippe, Schatten, Mund und Laterne seien," nay even "der finster todt buchstab der schrift on glauben und gottes geist gelesen ist nit gots wort sunder der todt und seelen gift." For the principles and views of spiritualism see particularly J. Lindeboom, *Stiefkinderen van het Christendom* (The Hague, 1929) 170-72. On congregationalism and spiritualism see also my paper, "Das Glaubenszeugnis unserer Väter von der Gemeinde," read at the fifth Mennonite World Conference, Basel 1952, and published in *Die Gemeinde Christi und ihr Auftrag* (Karlsruhe, 1953) 102-10.

cism. (The spiritualism here referred to is that Christian spiritualism which basically believes in the Holy Spirit who operates within the hearts of men, and not a philosophical spiritualism according to which men are convinced that they are able to produce eternity out of their own mind by mere self-concentration.)

The antithesis between congregationalism and spiritualism was present in early Dutch Anabaptism from the beginning, and during the first years undoubtedly spiritualism was dominant.[18] Obbe Philips, elder from 1533 to the time of his defection in 1540, was the champion and promoter of spiritualism. With his brother Dirk Philips, Menno Simons, and other leaders he energetically opposed the principle of revolutionary Anabaptism and the fantastic Biblical interpretation of David Joris, the spiritualist who had completely separated the "inner word" from the "outer word." Obbe did much for the founding of the Anabaptist congregations. In a period of great confusion he traveled widely, preaching and baptizing, and exposing his life to danger as he did so. Both Dirk Philips and Menno Simons were ordained as elders by him. In course of time, however, particularly after 1536, as local congregations were gradually being formed, as the basis for their administration had to be considered, and as questions of creed and discipline, banning and shunning came up for discussion, Obbe Philips more and more proved to be a spiritualist, averse to strict organization and binding regulations. In 1540, unable to accommodate himself to the growing congregationalism, he left the church. Somewhat spitefully, and not altogether with objectivity, Menno declared that Obbe had become a Demas, "having loved this present world" (II Tim. 4:10).[19]

Worldliness, however, was not the cause of Obbe's departure from Anabaptism. The reason was that he was

18 See H. W. Meihuizen, "Spiritualistic tendencies and movements among the Dutch Mennonites of the 16th and 17th centuries" in *MQR* (October 1953) 27:259-304.

19 Menno Simons, *Opera Omnia* (Amsterdam, 1681) 312a; *The Complete Writings of Menno Simons* (Scottdale, 1956) 761-62.

unable to accommodate himself to the growing congregationalism among the brethren. In his *Bekentenisse* Obbe formu-
lates it thus: In the beginning of Anabaptism each disciple
tried to revere and serve God as best he could. After some
time, however, in which many pious hearts had served God
in this simple way after the pattern of the patriarchs, without
preachers, elders, and a visible church (*wtwendige vergaderinghe*), some of them were not satisfied with this quiet service of pure hearts, but desired visible gods which they could
hear, touch, and feel, and they suggested that a visible church,
congregation, ministerial office, and ordination (*Ghemeente,
vergaderinghe, sendinghe, ampt ende ordeninge*) should be
established, as if one could not be saved unless he stood within such a congregation.[20]

Dirk Philips and Menno Simons opposed this spiritualistic vision, both in their preaching and in their writings.
Menno, not only to meet the views of Obbe but also to refute
the extreme teachings of David Joris, placed increasing emphasis on the significance of the visible congregation as the
church of God. In his first writings, as Kühler has pointed
out, Menno gave relatively little attention to the church on
earth. As early as 1539, however, in his *Foundation of Christian Doctrine* he deals with the organization of the church,
and gradually Menno's teachings developed into a congregational theology.[21] It is particularly Dirk Philips, however, the
greatest Dutch Anabaptist theologian, who in his *Verant-
woordinghe ende Refutation op twee Sendtbrieven Sebastiani
Franck* deals principally with spiritualism: Christ Himself
has commanded the founding of the church which is on earth
and visible; He Himself commissioned His apostles to gather
the believers in a visible church and to baptize them; and
according to His own word the apostles did organize congregations, providing them with elders, ministers, and deacons.[22]

20 *Bekentenisse Obbe Philipsz* (published after a printed copy of 1584 by
S. Cramer), *BRN* (The Hague, 1910) 5:122.
21 Kühler, *op. cit.*, 217, 237, 291; Cornelius Krahn, *Menno Simons* (Karlsruhe,
1936) 113-19.
22 *BRN*, 10:499, 503; see also 211-25, 380-414.

Both Dirk and Menno proceeded to build the church in line with their congregational vision. They did so because they saw no other way to save the Gospel in this wicked world. Their principles and arguments were based on the Scriptures, but it was not only a question of faith which impelled them to found and organize congregations. There were also practical considerations, yes of urgent necessity, which compelled them to follow this course.

The spiritualist view which considers it sufficient to believe that God's Spirit will move and act in the hearts of men without the aid of a visible church is a glorious vision; but it has small chance of realization in the actual world. This vision will survive only with the aid of an eschatology which expects the absolute reign of Christ to be realized upon the earth in the imminent future. As soon as it is believed that the kingdom of God will be realized only in His time, and that this can be in the far as well as the near future, the building of the visible church in this world becomes a necessity. Believing that without such a visible house of God His children would be homeless in this world, Dirk Philips and Menno Simons proceeded to organize the church.

The consummation of this task was fraught with great difficulties. In the first place, after 1540 neither Dirk nor Menno was able to remain in the Netherlands except for a few inconsequential brief periods. This meant the entrusting of the work into the hands of elders who were less capable and sometimes also less faithful. Secondly, after 1535 the Anabaptists suffered heavy persecution. The magistrates laid hands on the elders and ministers in particular so that the flocks without shepherds might the more easily return to the Catholic fold. This brought with it special problems of organization, the lack of ministers often being serious. Thirdly, the attempt to convert the numerous followers of David Joris and the large remnants of former Münsterites required untiring effort and exertion. In order to bring this gigantic task to a good conclusion Menno and Dirk felt it necessary to define the nature of the church with rather clear and definite circumscriptions. Menno described the character of the true Christian church under six heads: 1) unfalsified pure doctrine; 2) use of the sacramental symbols according to the Scriptures; 3) obedience to the Word of God; 4) a sincere brotherly love; 5) a frank avowal of God and Christ; 6) and sorrow and suffering because of the Word of God.[23] Dirk Philips enumerated nearly the same points, adding the washing of the saints' feet.[24]

As early as 1539 Menno pointed out in his *Foundation of Christian Doctrine* that ministers should not exercise their office of their own accord *(loopen van hemselven),* but only after having been chosen in a regular way by the brethren of the congregation.[25] This was the first point to be regulated: without true ministers no true congregation. This point was very important, hence the tendency, found as early as 1540 but especially appearing in the resolutions of the meeting of elders at Wismar in 1554, to have the elders appointed by a conference of elders, and to have the ministers appointed by the elders.[26] Dirk Philips in particular was at great pains to keep the ministerial office in safe hands, even if it meant the abridgement of the rights of the congregation.[27]

A second important point requiring regulation was faith, which is a gift of grace given by God through the Scriptures. Increasingly Menno stressed the obedient acceptance of the Bible, and particularly the New Testament, as the basis of the Christian's faith, emphasizing the "ringing letter of the New Testament" and the "simple command of Christ."[28] Conversion is defined as a renunciation of sin, a changing of one's life, and a following of Christ in humility before the law

23 Menno Simons, *Opera Omnia* (1681) 300b; *Complete Writings,* 743.

24 Dirk Philips, *Van de Gemeynte Godts,* in *BRN,* 10:393-407.

25 Menno Simons, *Dat Fundament des Christelycken leers* (1539) J V (recto); *Complete Writings,* 161.

26 The Wismar resolutions were published by S. Blaupot ten Cate in *Geschiedenis der Doopsgezinden in Groningen* (Leeuwarden-Groningen, 1842) 1:252-54.

27 See *Doopsgezinde Bijdragen* (1893) 54-72.

28 *Opera Omnia* (1681) 437a, 17a, 447a; *Complete Writings,* 292, 129, 507-8.

of Christ.[29] Menno and Dirk reproached both the Roman and the Lutheran churches in that they limited faith to an acceptance of the creed, thus neglecting the bringing forth of good fruits and proving themselves to be corrupt trees.[30]

A third matter requiring regulation, which came into the picture at a later date, was church discipline. The point of beginning is Matthew 18:15-20. At first the emphasis was placed upon the sinner's own need for discipline. He was disciplined and even banned in order that he might become repentant and be saved. From this point of view Menno called the ban "a work of love."[31] Later, however, the emphasis came to be placed upon discipline as a means of maintaining a congregation without spot or wrinkle.[32] Sinners were now to be excluded from the church in order that the church might maintain its holiness. This later view of the ban included severe shunning, which was rigorously defended by Dirk Philips,[33] and which soon after the death of Menno caused a lamentable division of the church into several branches. It should be remembered, however, that during the lifetime of Menno there were only a very few cases of banning because of heterodoxy; the ban was merely applied in cases of moral misconduct.

The church as a whole, and each member in particular, according to the vision of Menno Simons and Dirk Philips, must keep itself separate from the world.[34] For the church as

29 *Ibid.*, 124b, 125a, 419b; *Complete Writings*, 91-93, 265-66.

30 *Ibid.*, 29a, 402b, 78b, 79a; *Complete Writings*, 150, 238, 333-35. As to Dirk Philips see *BRN*, 10:324 ff. 219, *et passim*.

31 Kühler, *op. cit.*, 239; Krahn, *op. cit.*, 151.

32 This is the trend of Menno's later work *Grondelyk onderwys ofte bericht van de excommunicatie (Instruction on Excommunication)* of 1558. The same view is found in Dirk Philips' treatise *Van den Ban*, reprinted in *BRN*, 10:250-65.

33 In the spring of 1556 Menno was still averse to strict avoidance as pertaining to married couples; but in a meeting held at Harlingen in the summer of 1556 he was convinced by Dirk Philips and his coelder Leenaert Bouwens that in case of the ban even marital avoidance is necessary.

34 Krahn, *op. cit.*, 170: "Wie sich die Herauslösung aus der *Welt* vollzogen hat, so muss diese auch ferner gemieden werden. Zwei vollkommen gegensätzliche Bereiche finden sich hier vor: das Reich Christi und das Reich des Antichrists. So verschieden die Reiche sind, so verschieden sind auch ihre Lebensordnungen."

a whole this meant that it could not be a state church in which good and evil are mixed together, and which is not directed by the commandments of Christ, but by the "cares of this world and the deceitfulness of riches" (Matt. 13:22) which lead to lawsuits and wars in which a Christian should not be engaged. For the individual Christian separation from the world meant simplicity in food and dress and in every manner of life, and "the continuous crucifixion of the flesh with its affections and lusts" (Gal. 5:24).

This was the vision of Menno Simons and Dirk Philips. They had numerous followers, not only in the German territories of East Friesland, Mecklenburg, and Prussia where they labored and lived, but also in the Netherlands, particularly in the provinces of Groningen and Friesland. It is largely due to the firm and basic faith, and to the untiring leadership of these men, that Anabaptism in the Netherlands was not lost to the lax morals and the vagaries of David Joris and his followers; that Münsterism with its violent and polygamous practices was overcome; and that everywhere congregations were permanently established, well organized and well governed by capable and pious ministers able to conquer both the dangers which threatened the life of the church from within and to defy the severe persecutions which for four decades harassed the church from without.

Nevertheless, this light had its shadows. The exclusive stress laid upon the letter of Scripture sometimes led to formalism; the attention given to the simple and clear commands of Christ often became a dead legalism; the power given to the elders all too frequently deteriorated into unrestrained ambition and arbitrary rule; the high ideal of a holy church and the conviction that theirs was the only true church often led to overestimation and to an unchristian Pharisaism; and the ban, far from being a "work of love" as Menno had called it in the earliest period of his leadership, often rigorously applied at random, did not build up the church, but broke it down, and divided the church into schismatic groups, detesting and maligning one another to the derision of the outside world and their own detriment.[35]

In 1557, after Menno, Dirk, and other Dutch elders began to practice severe banning and rigorous shunning the more moderate South German Anabaptists separated themselves from them. About the same time, or even earlier, a large group of the Dutch Anabaptists, later known as the Waterlanders, also left the main body. Among the Waterlanders, though congregational in their views and practices as is shown by their church regulations (*gemeente-ordeningen*) of 1568 and 1581,[36] spiritualistic tendencies also emerged. These Waterlanders declined to accept the vision of Menno Simons and Dirk Philips. They rejected the name Mennonite, choosing to call themselves *Doopsgezinden* instead. They laid much stress upon the inner word (the inward light) and they were of the opinion that a holy church on earth is an illusion, that shunning is not according to the love of Christ, and that banning is to be used in only very grave cases. They did not hold tenaciously to an absolute separation from the world as the strict Mennonites did, and among them the more moderate advice was heard: to be "in the world, but not of the world." Eventually they even came to have no objection to the holding of government offices. In course of time, moreover, the Waterlander vision and practice came to be predominant among the Dutch Mennonites as a whole, although this was a matter of later development, of two centuries or more.[37]

35 Many Mennonites left the church because banning and shunning thus had been pushed to extremes. One of them wrote his memoirs in *Het Beginsel der Scheuringen onder de Doopsgezinden* (1615), reprinted in *BRN*, Vol. 7; see particularly pp. 526-33. Because of their many schisms and different denominations an opponent, the Reformed minister, Hermanus Faukelius, compared them with Babel in his book entitled, *Babel dat is Verwerringhe der Wederdooperen ondermal kanderen* (1621).

36 Published in *Doopsgezinde Bijdragen* (1877) 62-93.

37 For this later development see N. van der Zijpp, *op. cit.*, chapters 7-13; see also H. W. Meihuizen, *Galenus Abrahamsz* (Haarlem, 1954), and by the same author the paper "Die Gemeinde in der Welt, aber nicht von der Welt" read at the fifth Mennonite World Conference, Basel 1952, published in *Die Gemeinde Christi und ihr Auftrag* (Karlsruhe, 1953) 210-18.

The Hutterian Brethren and Community of Goods

The great movement of the evangelical Anabaptists of the sixteenth century was by no means uniform in character. Three distinct groups developed which may be distinguished as follows: 1) the Swiss Brethren, since 1525, led by Conrad Grebel, Felix Manz, and Jörg Blaurock, whose spiritual descendants in America are the Mennonites; 2) the Dutch Mennonites, since 1536, led by Menno Simons and Dirk Philips, today represented by the Doopsgezinden of the Netherlands and the Mennonites of northern Germany and Prussia, many of whom later emigrated to Russia and some descendants of whom are now settled in the western parts of the United States and Canada; and 3) the Hutterite Brethren in Austria, particularly in Moravia, since 1529, or more specifically since 1533, when Jacob Huter became their leader. The Hutterite group alone developed that remarkable system of communal living which should be called "Christian communism."

The amazing thing is that the communal type of living established by the Hutterian Brethren in the sixteenth century has persisted for 425 years, a phenomenon truly unique in social and religious history. In the mid-twentieth century there are approximately 110 Hutterite *Bruderhofs,* located in the northwestern section of the United States and in western Canada, and numbering about 10,000 souls. Were it not that they emphasize married life, the nearest comparison of their communities would be with monasteries where similar principles of organized communal living prevail. However, the

* Robert Friedmann is Professor of History and Philosophy in Western Michigan University, author of *Mennonite Piety Through the Centuries* (Goshen, 1949), and a recognized authority on the Hutterites. The present article is a reprint of a section, slightly revised, of an article, "The Christian Communism of the Hutterite Brethren," which appeared in the *Archiv für Reformationsgeschichte* (1955) 46:196-208. Reprinted by permission.

difference in spirit and motivation is too great to allow any further comparison.[1]

Social scientists have tried to study and understand these people, interpreting them sociologically, economically, and genetically. But it is obvious that they all have missed the central point, the deep Christian foundation upon which the Hutterites have built and still continue to derive their strength and courage. Only by a thorough study of the rich Hutterite manuscript literature of the sixteenth and seventeenth centuries can we discover the underlying principles which motivated these people in the first place and made possible a survival through all these centuries. This paper is an attempt to make just such an interpretation. Since all human actions have many and often contradictory motives, such an analysis is by no means a simple matter; hence the following discussion is submitted merely as an essay in interpretation, although its basic orientation at least is undoubtedly correct.

It might be useful to look briefly at earlier attempts at such interpretation. There is above all the sociological explanation according to which the Hutterites were primarily simple peasants, who as such were unsympathetic to our entire civilization as it had developed since Renaissance and Reformation, with its urban and highly individualized spirit. It is true that an antagonism of this kind actually existed, however not so much because of a sociologically determined hostility of one class against another,[2] but rather because of a radical Biblicistic outlook, emphatically dualistic, in which the kingdom of God and its righteousness was contraposed to the "world," our secular civilization. Thus the reference to sociological determinism fails to a large extent to explain this particular way of life, so hard and full of sacrifices. The same holds true for what Kautsky and other socialists claim to

---

1 Roland H. Bainton of Yale is inclined to compare the Hutterian Brethren with the Franciscan Tertiarians who also accepted a married status. I would admit that there actually exists some similarity which, however, should not be carried out too far.

2 In the sixteenth century by no means all brethren were peasants. Compare P. Dedic, "Social Background of the Austrian Anabaptists," *MQR* (January 1939) 13:5-20.

see in these communities, namely, the early beginnings of socialism. Nothing is farther from the truth. Where the Bible rules there is no room or need for social utopianism.

Likewise unsatisfactory is the reference to certain economic emergency conditions during the earliest period of Anabaptism. True, a need of taking care of the many indigent among the Brethren, reminiscent of the situation of the primitive church at Jerusalem, did actually exist and led to the pooling of goods in 1529.[3] But such an emergency motivation would never have produced survival for any protracted period of time. The primitive church in Jerusalem itself soon abandoned its experiment in communal living. Above all, it was not such a situation in 1529, but Jacob Huter's radical reorganization in 1533, which actually established the new communal pattern and point of view. It went far beyond the vague experimentation prior to this year 1533.

When we consult the Hutterite writings of the seventeenth century (by Claus Braidl, Joseph Hauser, and Andreas Ehrenpreis) or of present-day members of the Hutterite brotherhood, we almost uniformly meet but one answer: the reference to the primitive church as described in the Book of Acts, chapters 2, 4, and 5, plus some further texts interpreted in the light of these chapters. The Brethren understood themselves as obeying to the letter the Holy Scripture, following strictly the model of the first church without any further questioning.

Although this explanation comes nearer to the center of our problem because of its strong Scriptural orientation, it does not really explain how this great venture in communal living started and throughout its first century maintained such a strong attraction for many seekers. After all, the mere

3 The *Great Chronicle* of the brethren, written by Caspar Braitmichel (around 1560-70), reports this event, thoroughly in the style of the Bible, as follows: "At this time these men spread out a coat before all the people, and everyone put upon it his possession, with a willing and unconstrained mind, and they did so for the support of the needy according to the teachings of the prophets and the apostles." Rudolf Wolkan, *Geschicht-Buch der Hutterischen Brüder* (Vienna, 1923) 63; or A. J. F. Zieglschmid, *Die älteste Chronik der Hutterischen Brüder* (Philadelphia, 1943) 87.

reference to an historical antecedent lacks that spiritual vigor which alone makes such a sectarian movement possible and capable of growth and survival. Hence we must seek further to find a more satisfactory answer. Fortunately, the earliest writings of the Brethren allow us to gain deeper and more adequate spiritual insight. And it is this early period alone which matters and reveals a power and charismatic authority never again reached in later generations.

The epistles and confessions of faith and the tracts by Jacob Huter, Peter Riedemann, Ulrich Stadler, Peter Walpot, and all the less-known Brethren, the innumerable martyrs and witnesses to their faith, clearly disclose three major motives which produced the facts here discussed: 1) brotherly love in action, the strong longing of Christians for brotherly sharing and togetherness; 2) *Gelassenheit,* a term derived from the mystics and almost untranslatable. It means yielding absolutely to the will of God with a dedicated heart, forsaking all selfishness and one's own will; 3) obedience to the divine commandments, understood as the inevitable consequence of the attitude of *Gelassenheit.* As one gives up one's own will, one naturally accepts God's commandments as the basis and guidepost for all further actions.

Motive one: the idea of love—brotherly togetherness and mutual giving and sharing—was present among the Brethren at all times. It was the very center of Jacob Huter's work. He visualized the brotherhood as a great family. Since in such a family all material things are shared as a matter of fact, this should also be the case in a true *Gemeinschaft,* or community. And so we read throughout our records confessions like this: "Love is the tie of perfection. . . . Where she dwelleth she does not work partial but complete communion. It means having everything in common out of sheer love for the neighbor."[4] "Where Christian love of the neighbor does not produce community in things temporal, there the blood of Christ

---

4 This quotation is taken from the confessional document called "The Five Articles of our greatest quarrel with the world, etc." *(Die Fünf Artikel des grössten Streits zwischen uns und der Welt)* contained in the *Great Chronicle,* and inserted

does not cleanse from sin."[5] In short, "private property is the greatest enemy of Christian love." In love all men are considered equal and united in the oneness of the Spirit. The reference to the Book of Acts in these early tracts, however, serves not as a motivation but rather as an undergirding of this love-motive, as an exemplification of how it works, and as an assurance that this way is the right one. It was never to be understood as a strict commandment of God to be followed in obedience without any further questioning.

The *second motive* is *Gelassenheit*, a term of great richness, meaning self-surrender, yieldedness, the giving of one's self to God's guidance, even unto death. Among the Hutterites it also means the forsaking of all concern for personal property, thus leading almost naturally to a complete community of goods.[6] At the earliest period this idea of *Gelassenheit* almost dominates the thought of the brethren. "To have all things in common, a free, untrammeled, yielding, willing heart in Christ is needed," writes Ulrich Stadler about 1536.[7] "Whosoever is thus inwardly free and resigned (*gelassen*) in the Lord is also ready to surrender all temporal possession." To the rejoinder that such a community of goods is not a commandment of the Lord, the same brother answers as fol-

---

to the year 1547. The third article deals with *Von der wahren Gelassenheit und Christlicher Gemeinschaft der Güter*. Cf. Zieglschmid, *Aelteste Chronik*, 285-96.

5 Andreas Ehrenpreis, *Ein Sendbrief . . . Brüderliche Gemeinschaft das höchste Gebot der Liebe betreffend* (written 1650, printed for the first time 1652). *Aufs neue herausgegeben von den Hutterischen Brüdern in Amerika* (Scottdale, Pa., 1920) 49. The entire "epistle" (actually a long tract) is a defense of the principle of community of goods as the true expression of Christian love. In 1954 this epistle was reprinted by the Brethren in Canada.

6 Cf. this writer's article "Gelassenheit" in the *Mennonite Encyclopedia* (1956) 2:448-49, where the different connotations of this concept are discussed at some length. At this place it is in order to call attention to a possible confusion of the concept *Gelassenheit* (which in no sense means passivism in life) with the similar concept of "quietism" (as taught by Madame Guyon or Gerhard Teerstegen) which intentionally shirks all activities in order to become a more perfect vessel of divine influence. Anabaptism never went to this extreme as it also never was individualistically minded after the manner of quietism.

7 This and the following quotation is taken from a beautiful meditation of the brother, Ulrich Stadler, entitled *Von der Ordnung der Heiligen in ihrer Gemeinschaft und Leben* (about 1536-37), published by Lydia Müller, *Glaubenszeugnisse Oberdeutscher Taufgesinnter* (Leipzig, 1938) 225-26; now also in an excellent Engl. translation by B. H. Williams, *Spiritual and Anabaptist Writers (Library of Christian Classics*, XXV) (Philadelphia, 1957) 283 f.

lows: "To serve the saints in this way with all one's possession is true and genuine self-surrender *(Gelassenheit),* and it is also the way of brotherly love. In summa: one brother should serve the other, live and work for him, and no one should do anything for himself." Elsewhere we read: "If you want to become a disciple you must resign to such a *Gelassenheit* and must renounce all private property."[8] At this place it might be well to stress that this attitude led to the establishment of complete community of goods; while other Anabaptist groups, likewise intent on practicing love, were satisfied with a "community of charity," a caring for the needy without the demand of giving up private property altogether. Such a community of charity was typical among the Swiss and Dutch Brethren.

The Hutterites, however, in their strict Biblicism, became particularly sensitive and alert to the pitfalls of "mammon" in all its forms. "As the beetle lives in the dung, and the worm in the wood, so avarice (or greed) has its dwelling place in private property"[9] (1599). Whosoever refuses communal living, they taught, shows obvious sympathy for avarice (or greed). And then they quote the example of the rich young man in the parable who could not enter the kingdom of God because he was not willing to sell all that he had and give it to the poor. Avarice, the demon of possession, must therefore be overcome if true *Gelassenheit* is to be achieved. But once it has been overcome, there follows a complete community of goods in brotherly togetherness and sharing. The ready acceptance of such complete community, incidentally, became the very touchstone of the regenerate. In particular

8 *Das Grosse Artikelbuch* of 1577, sometimes also called *Ein schön lustig Büchlein* etc. (its author was most likely Peter Walpot, the bishop of the brotherhood, 1565-78). It is an elaboration of the "Five Articles," mentioned in note 4. This quotation, taken from the original codex, is quoted by R. Friedmann, "Eine dogmatische Hauptschrift der Hutterischen Täufergemeinschaften in Mähren," in *Archiv für Reformationsgeschichte* (1931) 210. Cf. also R. Friedmann, "A Notable Hutterite Document: Concerning True Surrender and Christian Community of Goods," *MQR* (January 1957) 31:22-62.

9 Johann Loserth, "Der Communismus der mährischen Wiedertäufer" in *Archiv für Oesterreichische Geschichte* (Wien, 1894) 81:240, quoted from a manuscript of 1599.

it was also an indication whether or not a brother was capable and worthy of becoming a leader of the group.

Taken all in all, the Hutterites represent a most original type of "theocratic society" or "theocratic communism," as it was once aptly called,[10] a venture otherwise rather foreign to the western world. The brethren were aware of this antagonism to world and culture, but affirmed time and again that no other way to salvation was possible. "It is but through *Gemeinschaft*, that is, communal living, that the blood of Christ may cleanse sinful man. Christ cannot help us unless we follow Him all the way, without any reservation."[11]

This concept of "theocratic communism" naturally implies also the *third motive*, the principle of unconditional obedience by which we "bring into captivity every thought to the obedience of Christ" (II Cor. 10:5, as quoted now and then in Hutterite tracts). It means what the brethren never tired of repeating, that what really is needed for a true disciple is this: walking the "narrow path," breaking the self-will, and subsequently submitting to the will of God, whatever He may command.

It is quite obvious that this principle of obedience involves a certain paradox: on the one hand, it is the most profound and most spiritual principle imaginable where the individual surrenders completely to divine guidance and asks nothing for himself, doing only that which he feels is required of him, even if it should lead to martyrdom. "Not my will be done, but Thine." It means genuine discipleship, and represents the spirit of the first generation of Anabaptists, in particular the Hutterites, who gave up everything in order to obey God. Suffering was accepted almost gladly as the inescapable consequence of such acts of obedience.

10 Franz Heimann in his excellent study, "The Hutterite Doctrines of Church and Common Life, a study of Peter Riedemann's Confession of Faith of 1540," in *MQR* (January 1952) 26:32 (English version of a Vienna Ph.D. thesis of 1928, translated by R. Friedmann).

11 This is a statement made to the writer by one of the elders of the present-day Hutterites in Alberta, in the autumn of 1954. It expresses a general conviction of the entire brotherhood. Cf. also the reference cited in footnote 5 above.

On the other hand, such prophetic conditions hardly persist in the long run; and among the second, third, and fourth generations of Anabaptists this principle of obedience becomes more and more formalized and external. "This is the time-honored rule and regulation," and the individual must conform to it. Occasionally such "obedience" can become a real burden and a dependence upon the leader (bishop) and his bigness or smallness in matters of the spirit. Moreover, the danger is at hand that those who now meticulously obey these rules, laid down by the forefathers, readily believe that they are the righteous ones and consider all nonconformists unrighteous. In the long history of the Brethren, this danger of legalism was not always avoided. But it should be said that the Brethren in the beginning were well aware of this pitfall. In one of the finest tracts of early Anabaptism, called *Two Kinds of Obedience,* a clear distinction is made between childlike and servile obedience, and a warning is given to beware of the latter. The tract, although not of Hutterite origin, is found in several Hutterite manuscripts.[12]

Although this new life in perfect community of goods did bring a certain external security through mutual help and service, it meant a hard, daily internal struggle with that part of man's nature which insists upon self-will and personal possession. The Brethren by no means ignored this desire. In fact, they liked to quote in this connection a jingle which in the *Great Article Book* of 1577 occurs here and there in the third article "Concerning Community of Goods":

> Die Gemeinschaft wär nit schwer
> Wenn nur der Eigennutz nit wär.

Or in a free English translation:

> Communal living would not be hard
> If there were not such self-regard.[13]

12 "Two Kinds of Obedience: an Anabaptist Tract on Christian Freedom," translated and edited by John C. Wenger, *MQR* (January 1947) 21:18-22; see also H. E. Fosdick, *Great Voices of the Reformation* (New York, 1952) 296-99.

13 John Horsch, *The Hutterian Brethren, a Story of Loyalty and Martyrdom* (Goshen, 1931) 74, also *MQR* (January 1957) 31:25 and 34.

The Theology of Anabaptism

✝ JOHN H. YODER ✝

The Prophetic Dissent of the Anabaptists

One of the most glaring injustices of modern historiography, certainly the one which has done the most harm to Protestant Christendom, by rendering self-evaluation impossible, has been the failure to see the movements of dissent within Protestantism as consistent, self-conscious, serious phenomena in their own right. For centuries historians could conceive of the existence of the spiritualists, the Anabaptists, or the anti-Trinitarians of Reformation times only as diabolical antagonists of the heroes of Wittenberg, Zürich, or Geneva. Their only significance lay in their negation of essential Protestant dogma or ecclesiastical form; they denied what the Reformers affirmed and affirmed what the Reformers denied. That any of the dissident men or movements might have been theologically mature, might have found an original and consistent solution to the problem of the reformation of the church, never entered the minds of historians; still less did the possibility that among the dissidents there might have been groups clearly distinct from one another, separated by disagreements far deeper and more far reaching than their common opposition to state church Protestantism, ever take shape in their minds.

It has been only just that historical research has come to understand the sixteenth-century dissidents, and the Biblical Anabaptists in particular, as historical realities in their own right, capable of being grasped honestly and accurately only on the basis of their own theological and historical presuppositions. Yet with this rehabilitation the task of the church historian has only begun. For if the study of church history as an ecumenical ministry is to be justified, it must deal with

* John Howard Yoder is a doctoral candidate at the University of Basel.

the fact that the manifold personal and institutional realities with which the historian deals all stood in relations of assent and dissent to one another. Ascertaining how a church or theology sprang from its own presuppositions may be an interesting exercise in logic or sociology; but the stuff of church history lies in the assent and dissent, in the communication and excommunication, the conversations and the conflicts which went on within the context of faith.

Of the numerous streams which flowed from the religious eruption of the early sixteenth century, only two brought forth men and churches capable of inter-group conversation. The spiritualists and the anti-Trinitarians, refusing by the nature of the case any norms over against their own insights, were by principle incapable of conversation. The Roman Catholics, the Münsterites, and to a great degree the Lutherans, by maintaining the strictly confessional character of the state, and equating dissidence with blasphemy, were sociologically incapable of conversation, since no interlocutor could exist except in the form of a hostile state.

True conversation was thus possible only between the Anabaptists and the Reformed churches, first of all in Switzerland and Strasbourg, later in the Palatinate, Hesse, and the Netherlands. For conversation to be more than a talking-past-one-another, there are two formal prerequisites. There must be an epistemological norm, under the authority of which both parties stand in the common search for truth; and each party must recognize the other party's right to exist. The Reformed and the Anabaptists agreed as to Scripture's being the touchstone of truth, fulfilling the first requirement. The Anabaptists stood consistently,[1] and the Reformed occasionally, usually with reluctance and for a limited time, for the principle of tolerance. Thereby the formal conditions

---

1 The best survey of the original contribution of the Anabaptists to the struggle for religious liberty is Harold S. Bender's "The Anabaptists and Religious Liberty in the 16th Century," in *Archiv für Reformationsgeschichte* (1953) 44:32-50: also *MQR* (April 1955) 29:83-100. It might be said more strongly than Bender says it, that this originally grew not only from a different conception of faith but also from a revival of the New Testament view of the state.

94

were met, and (usually with reluctance and for a limited time) a real dialogue could take place.[2] We shall seek here to analyze that encounter and to ascertain where the essential theological differences really lay.

I

The Anabaptists began, as did Huldrych Zwingli, with the intention of reforming all of church and society according to the norm of Scripture. This did not mean (at least not necessarily) a slavishly legalistic use of Scripture; it meant only that no *other* norm be set up beside the Bible. In January of 1523 Zwingli, debating against the episcopal vicar Johannes Faber, stated the "formal principle of the Reformation" in the most radical terms conceivable, with the full accord of those who came later to be called Anabaptists. To our day the picture of Zwingli drawn by popular historians makes of him a lifelong champion of the *sola scriptura*. But the fact is that soon after January 1523 Zwingli's position underwent a radical change. Already in the summer of the same year, as with the peasants' refusal to pay tithes and interest the Reformation took on for the first time the dimensions of a social crisis, Zwingli was able rapidly to calm those whom his Biblicism had inspired. He declared that although every form of interest was strictly forbidden by both Old and New Testaments, the ultimate authority in such matter belongs not to Scripture but to the magistracy, which has been established by God to administer everything "outward." In October this distinction was carried further and applied to the mass. It does not lie within the competence of government, he explained, to teach that the mass is a sacrifice; for the teaching is not "outward." Yet the state may well ordain that the mass must continue to be celebrated, and Zwingli will

2 According to our present knowledge at least some forty serious "conversations" took place in the course of the sixteenth century, either in the form of "Disputations" or as exchanges of written arguments. Especially the earliest of these, those taking place within Reformed Switzerland between 1523 and 1538, serve as source material for the dissertation from which the generalizations in the present article are drawn.

then bow to the powers that be, for the celebration of mass is an "outward" matter. This is the point, both chronologically (October 27, 1523) and theologically, where the "Anabaptist dissent" began. This issue was not the state church, nor the mass, nor baptism, nor tolerance, as such, but whether there could be beside Scripture any other norm for Christian behavior and church order. Zwingli supports this analysis with his own testimony in his book on baptism of May 1525; there he notes that the Anabaptists cite against him his own example, appealing to the strong Biblicism he had stood for in 1523. In reply he distinguishes between the "outward" realm, where the state is competent, and the "inward," where the Bible has the last word. The other Reformers used other arguments against the Anabaptists, being less able than Zwingli to take for granted such an Hellenistic view of the relationship of "inward" and "outward," but it remained generally characteristic that whoever undertook to refute the Anabaptists began by limiting the authority of Scripture.[3]

II

If the starting point of the pre-Anabaptist movement in 1523 was a view of Scriptural authority, the end point, which enabled the movement to become a force in history, was a view of the church. Negatively expressed, the product of the development from October 1523 to January 1525[4] was the

3 We shall have to omit the comparisons with Lutheranism which could be made throughout this paper. In general the forms of dissidence which Luther encountered were less articulate and consistent than the comparable phenomena in Switzerland. Yet at this point a very near parallel may be found, in Luther's argument with Andreas Carlstadt about the application of the Decalogue to the use of images in worship. Carlstadt and the simple folk of his congregation in Orlamunde thought that "Thou shalt not make unto thee any graven images" would also apply to Christians, and that therefore the statues should be taken out of the churches. Luther replied that one must distinguish between that part of the Decalogue which corresponds to the order of nature, and that part which is specifically Jewish. The prohibition of images is a particularly Jewish prescription, just as the *Sachsenspiegel* is a particularly Saxon code of law. Only that part of the Decalogue which corresponds to the order of creation is ultimately valid; thus the order of the creation, or whatever Luther thought the order of creation to be, stands as a norm over Scripture. *Works*, Weimar Ed., 18:80-82.

4 This development has been described excellently by Harold S. Bender in *Conrad Grebel* (Scottdale, 1950) 89-135, and in Fritz Blanke's *Brüder in Christo* (Zürich, 1955) 5-22.

Anabaptists' rejection of the *Corpus Christianum*.[5] Following the revolutionary changes in the relations of church and world which we associate with the names of Constantine, Theodosius, and Augustine, medieval Christendom had no room for the Biblical concept of the "world." The consequences for ethics, for the doctrine of the church, for evangelism, and for eschatology, were revolutionary and yet were hardly noticed. So unconscious and so all-pervading was the acceptance of the identity of church and society that the Reformers, each working closely with the local magistracy and seeking to reform medieval Catholicism with as little commotion as possible, were not even aware of a problem and were able to pass off as political revolutionaries anyone who raised the question. Nor did men like Carlstadt or Müntzer, or even Hubmaier, really see the point.

Only among the Zürich Anabaptists and those who learned from them was a new answer to the problem reached. Led by their simple Biblicism, abetted by the opposition of both civil and ecclesiastical authorities, they learned that the "world" was just as significant a theological quantity in the sixteenth century as it had been in the first, and that the church is not simply an administrative subdivision of a monolithic society, charged with giving that society moral sanction and psychological stability, nor an invisible mystic communion of true believers, but a new kind of disciplined fellowship, taking shape within history by the gathering of confessing believers. Already in Grebel's letter to Thomas Müntzer in September 1524 this new view of the church had led to a new view of the world. Thereby evangelism, which for the "Constantinian" reformers was by definition inconceivable, became a real possibility; alone of all the churches of the

5 Our use of this term does not imply our taking part in the learned debate about whether the term is adequate or whether it was ever used in the Middle Ages or the sixteenth century. We refer simply to the situation in which the church and human society coincide numerically. How the church and the state as institutions are related to one another within that completely baptized society is of relatively little significance for our present concerns. Cf. Paul Peachey, "Social Background and Social Philosophy of the Swiss Anabaptists, 1525-1540" *MQR* (April 1954) 116 ff.

Reformation, the Anabaptists considered evangelism as belonging to the essential being of the church.[6] Church discipline; a level of ethical requirements distinct from the average behavior of the average citizen; economic fellowship within the local congregation, whether through common ownership of goods or through the deacon's office; baptism upon confession of faith; refusal of the oath and of civil office; all the foci of disagreement with the Reformers fell into place as parts of a consistent whole once one dared, at the price of scandal and persecution, call into question the Constantinian synthesis, and to conceive of the church as being distinct from the world.

III

This by no means signifies that the Reformers were so naive or so proud as to believe that their mass churches were by virtue of the baptism of every infant, true churches of true Christians. This would in many ways have been the consistent conclusion from their views on the sacraments, for Luther and Calvin, if not for Zwingli; but they knew better than to make such a claim. The Constantinian synthesis had merged the institutional church, as an historical phenomenon, dispenser of the sacraments, with society; but the true church, formed of true believers, is another thing. Since only God knows true faith, the true church is invisible, not an historical reality at all.

Consistently applied, their doctrine of the invisibility of the true church should have led the Reformers, like the spiritualists, to reject all concretizations of faith within history.[7]

6 Cf. F. H. Littell, *The Anabaptist View of the Church* (The American Society of Church History, 1952) Ch. 5.

7 Franklin H. Littell has rightly pointed out, in the *MQR* (January 1955) 29:34 ff., that the spiritualists really must be classed, not with the Biblical Anabaptists, with whom historians have grouped them for centuries, but with the mass-church Reformers. Their arguments against the Anabaptists were practically identical; both rejected the Anabaptists' intention to give clear historical form to the Scriptural imperatives; the spiritualists because they wanted no form at all; the Reformers because they coveted the freedom to maintain non-Biblical forms. Since the spiritualists could not take on form in history, they were no serious danger for the Reformers, and were not persecuted in the same way as the Anabaptists.

Actually, the opposite happened; the Reformers chose a very clear concretization, namely, the persecuting state church; but at the same time they were protected themselves against any criticism which might have objected that their church was not what a church should be by the fact that their church, being visible, could never be the true church anyway. Since our church is not the true church, they said in effect, the state is free to organize and administer it as seems best. This concession to Hellenism, the admission that the invisible and timeless is more real than the visible and historical, has avenged itself a hundredfold in occidental piety, ethics, and social responsibility.

IV

That Christ alone is Lord and Saviour was, although it is the most precious insight of the Reformation, limited by the Reformers to one field of application. In soteriology and church order, Christ's uniqueness enabled a polemic against the mass, against hagiolatry and the hierarchy. Yet Christ's authority remained strangely circumscribed; He could not be normative for ethics. Christ's perfect obedience is, for orthodox Protestantism, no criterion for the obedience of the believer, but merely the prerequisite to an innocent and therefore vicariously valid death. The guide for ethics for the Reformers was neither Christ Himself, nor the New Testament, but the "Rule of Love." "Love" in this usage signified for them not that quality of God's Being which is seen in Christ, but rather whatever seemed to them to be required by the best interests of the social order.[8] They assumed with touching naiveté, that the precise requirements of the Rule of Love were self-evident, and could be doubted only by the willfully recalcitrant. Whether the non-Biblical norms, drawn from what was thought to be best for society, should be evaluated by the historian as a remnant from the Middle Ages

8 The term "Rule of Love" in this meaning was especially important in the conversion of Hans Pfistermeyer in 1531 and in the Zofingen debate of 1532; but it can be traced back to Oecolampad and Zwingli in 1524-25. The concept of vocation had a similar function in Lutheran ethics.

or as an early kind of theological liberalism, will be a matter of taste. But in any case the observation must be made. What the Anabaptists spoke of as "discipleship" was, in a nutshell, what twentieth-century theologians think is a new insight, when they argue that ethics is an integral part of dogmatics, and that the sole criterion in dogmatics is Christ Himself.

For the Reformers such an attitude, giving immediate *ethical* relevance to the human obedience of Christ, so that the Christian should love as He loved, be persecuted as He was persecuted,[9] was at the best pride, and at the worst blasphemy. The Reformers were so fully conditioned by their anti-Catholic polemic that they fell prey to the temptation to affirm simply the opposite of what the Roman Church had taught. Against Catholic immanence they leaned toward an almost Docetic transcendentalism;[10] against Catholic legalism they tended toward antinomianism. They were far too close to the Gospel to be frankly antinomian; but they had enormous difficulty in finding a place to attach ethics to the rest of their doctrine. Having thus thrown out the baby with the bath, they condemned Protestantism to a centuries-long pendulum movement between ethical liberalism and nonethical orthodoxy. There being no essential structural connection between Christ and ethics, except the negative one that we are saved by Christ instead of by works, Protestants have had to choose between a high Christology and a high ethic. The Anabaptist claim that Christ is authoritative in ethics in the same way as for soteriology, so that only the disciple can really *know* Him (Denk's "Niemand vermag Christum wahrlich zu erkennen, er folge ihm denn nach im Leben"), avoided such a posing of alternatives, and perceived that a high ethic and a high Christology are possible only together.

9 Cf. the expositions of discipleship as the formal principle of Christian ethics in: Harold S. Bender, "The Anabaptist Vision," *MQR* (April 1944) 18:67-88; Ethelbert Stauffer, "The Anabaptist Theology of Martyrdom," *MQR* (July 1945) 19:179-214; Bender, "The Anabaptist Theology of Discipleship," *MQR* (January 1950) 24:25-32.

10 In a strictly philosophical sense this reproach applies only to Zwingli; the incapacity or the refusal to find a bridge from doctrine to ethics is however just as clear in Luther's thought.

V

The problems of the *Corpus Christianum* and of the relationships of the visible and the invisible church, already treated above, pose the ultimate question of eschatology. The Anabaptists revived the two-aeon doctrine of the New Testament through their discovery that the "world" is not simply an amorphous conglomerate of evil impulses but a structured reality taking concrete form in the demonic dimensions of economic and political life. They could have such a realistic view of the world because the church was, in their view, an equally concrete historical reality already incarnating the coming aeon. Thus they were able to grasp the tension between the "already" and the "not yet" and between church and world in a way which maintained the priority of the coming aeon. For the Reformers, the New Testament eschatology was fulfilled and thereby dissolved in the *Corpus Christianum*. Now that there is a Christian government, there is no longer a difference between church and world (or, what means the same thing, the difference lies on the same nonhistorical level as the true and invisible church). The Reformers were no freer from the apocalyptic feelings of their time than were the Anabaptists,[11] but only with the Anabaptists did eschatology take on present historical relevance. With Augustine, the Reformers identified the millennium with the Christianization of the Roman Empire.[12] Thereby Christian society became its own norm. Instead of belonging to the upper pole of the tension between the two aeons, the Christian finds himself at the lower pole of the tension between divine and human justice, and is quite content to stay there. Sin, and not grace, has the last word in history.

11 In late 1521 Luther was quite sure that the world would end in February 1524. (*Works*, Weimar Ed., X/I² 108.) Zwingli ended his anti-Anabaptist pamphlet, *Vom Predigtamt* (summer 1525), with a reference to the imminent coming of Christ.

12 This view of history is most explicit in Martin Bucer's *De Regno Christi Libri Duo* (Paris, 1955) 36 ff. Bucer follows Eusebius in identifying the age of Constantine with the reign of peace in the end time foreseen by the Old Testament prophets. The Christian lawgivers, notably Theodosius and Justinian, possess for him a kind of infallibility.

An unsympathetic critic would say that it was consistent with their own principles, notably with their subordination of the church to the necessities of the world, that the three great Reformers of the first generation, Luther, Zwingli, and Bucer, all ended their days assailed by doubts as to whether their lives had been worth while.[13] It would be not only uncharitable but also inaccurate to evaluate these signs of disappointment on the level of personal judgment; yet they must be seriously faced, as Reformation historians have not yet faced them, as indications that the pragmatic confidence in the Christian state, which characterized the young Reformers and has entered history as *the* Protestant view of history, is not supported by the maturer judgment of the Reformers themselves.

These summary observations might be supplemented by others of a more speculative nature. It might be pointed out how many of the insights of the contemporary "Theology of the Word of God" were anticipated in the brief work of Hans Denk.[14] It could be shown how the Anabaptists preceded state church theologians in the insight that the New Testament is the norm for the interpretation of the Old. But it will already have become clear in what sense the Anabaptists dissented from the Reformers. We have found no specifically Anabaptist starting point, fundamentally in contradiction to that of the state churches. The difference lies rather in the fact that in the common search for the shape of a Scriptural reformation the Anabaptists dared, partly because they were not politically committed to the maintenance of the existing

13 Zwingli attempted to resign from his responsibilities in Zürich just a few weeks before his death. Bucer died in exile after the very spirit of moderate accommodation to political necessity and Christian unity whch he had fostered in the Strasbourg church finally drove him out; and his *De Regno Christi* (p. 40) is deeply despondent about the present state (1550) of the Reformation in Germany. The despondency and pessimism of Luther's later years is notorious.

14 The concept of evil as *Das Nichtige*, the understanding that the command of God is the *Gestalt der Freiheit*, the rejection of a deterministic view of double predestination, the identity of justification and sanctification; much in short, which modern theology owes to Karl Barth, was already expressed embryonically in the fragmentary works of Denk, the only one of the speculative spiritualists to have maintained for a time positive relations with the Biblical Anabaptists.

system, partly because their lay Biblicism was unhampered by medieval or Erasmian presuppositions, to call into question the *Corpus Christianum* mentality and all the distortions which it had brought with it in other areas of faith and life. This was the one point at which the Reformers had abandoned their formal principle and had openly affirmed that, notwithstanding the New Testament, the world can become the church. The Anabaptists, by insisting that Scripture remains valid also at this point, were nothing more than faithful children of the Zwinglian Reformation. Before the choice between living by faith and surviving by alliance with the world, the originality of the Anabaptists was simply that they stood by the decision which Luther had made in Worms, and Zwingli in January 1523, and refused to let the problem of survival interfere with their submission to Scripture. They had neither the leisure, nor the interest, nor the conceptual equipment, to frame their dissent in theological terms as we have here attempted to do. But now that those whose preoccupation with techniques of survival and with the necessary compromise between church and world have brought the "Christian Occident" to the verge of suicide, the hope may not be vain that God might grant to His church to listen afresh to the testimony of those who knew four centuries too soon that Christian Europe was an illusion and Reformation a never-finished renewal.

*　　*　　*

The reader who is a student of Reformation history may well feel that the position of the Reformers as here sketched is an unfair caricature. Such a reaction would be well-grounded, and calls for further comment.

a) Just as we have here been dealing with the Anabaptists only in so far as they dissented from the Reformers, so also have we seen the Reformers only in their reaction to the Anabaptists. In the relations of the Reformers to Rome, in which tradition sees their main activity, and in the debates between the Reformed and the Lutherans, in terms of which the peculiar personality of each Reformer is usually described, the traits which we have dwelt on here would be frequently irrelevant and sometimes clearly false.

b) The study of Reformation history has in the past taken too little account of the deep changes which took place in the Reformers' thought and work when they discovered, Luther beginning in 1522 and Zwingli in 1523-24, that the Reformation they had begun would, if put into effect consistently, lead further than they had meant to go. The historian who has not learned to distinguish the Luther of 1517 and of Worms from the Luther of 1525, and the Zwingli of 1522 from the Zwingli of 1525, will certainly consider as unjust the above treatment, which deals with the Reformers solely in their post-1525 form.

c) The Reformers themselves caricatured themselves. Defending their compromises against their own spiritual children, they used arguments which clashed visibly with their own starting points. Contemporary Catholics observed pointedly that the Reformers were defending themselves against the Anabaptists with arguments which if used consistently would drive them back into Catholicism. A man like Zwingli had sufficient confidence in his own spiritual authority to be able to ignore some of these contradictions; the "second string" Reformers like Haller in Bern, more objective, less self-confident, tending more to consistency, bring them clearly into the open.

The Doctrine of the Two Worlds

It has often been asked whether one may properly speak of an Anabaptist theology as such or whether the Anabaptists simply aimed to follow the footsteps of the Master in a simple and unsophisticated manner without theological speculation or foundation. As to the basic doctrines of Christianity, it is certain that they were orthodox, teaching nothing foreign to the Apostles' Creed. Since the center of their concern lay elsewhere, however, they have often been described as theologically naive. A deeper search, however, makes one wonder whether such a judgment is tenable. A movement of such strength is unthinkable without a definite theological foundation, without specific ideas concerning man's relationship to the divine and the meaning of earthly life. Even if these foundations were not expressed in a systematic way, one must assume that they were implied in all the doings and witnessing of the Anabaptists. The rediscovery of these presuppositions is a challenge to present-day research.

Several years ago Harold S. Bender, almost casually and without elaboration, proposed a possible answer to this question. Musing about the deeper motivations of the Anabaptists for their pacifistic stand, he made the following highly suggestive remarks:

"The answer is to be found rather in their [the Anabaptists'] doctrine of the two worlds. The new kingdom of God which is being established in their terms and through them . . . is of necessity distinct from the world order which is dominated by Satan. That the church and state join in persecuting the true church is only one more bit of evidence of the wickedness of the world order, they concluded. The old church (both Roman Catholic and Protestant) has failed particularly in its mixing of the two kingdoms, hence the true church must be, and is being, re-established separate from the world. This true church is the present kingdom of Christ which is being established in the midst of and alongside of the kingdom of this world; it is not to be deferred to some millennial future."[1]

Here then is a challenge. Is it true that this "doctrine of the two worlds" represents the deepest layer of the Anabaptist theological outlook, and if so, what constitutes its difference from the main stream of Protestant thought? Furthermore, what are the implications of this doctrine for faith and practice? These are questions which deserve more careful examination than they have hitherto received.

The main line of Protestant theology is a kind of one-sided interpretation of the Pauline teaching on justification by faith. Although including this doctrine in its foundation, sixteenth-century Anabaptism shows definitely a different orientation, emphasizing above all the commandment of discipleship. As Roland H. Bainton so appropriately put it: "The Anabaptists went back further than any of the other groups [of the age of the Reformation]. They tended even to neglect Paul and to push back to Jesus. That is why the ideal of Restoration (common to all groups of that age) tends to coincide now with the ideal of the imitation of Christ."[2] Certainly, Luther himself did not overlook Christ's teaching concerning discipleship, but unfortunately there was no organic place for it in his differently slanted system of Pauline-Augustinian theology. Thus, even though both the Reformers and Anabaptists alike claim to be strict Biblicists, a noticeable tension prevails in their way of reading the Holy Scriptures. The Anabaptists paid more attention to Christ's commandment concerning *Nachfolge*, being certain that if it was commanded it can also be carried out under proper conditions, while the Reformers focused nearly all of their atten-

1 Harold S. Bender, "The Pacifism of the Sixteenth Century Anabaptists," *Church History* (June 1955) 24:128. (A paper read before the American Society of Church History, New York, December 28, 1954.) See also *MQR* (January 1956) 30:15.

2. Roland H. Bainton in a personal letter to the writer, November 23, 1953.

tion upon man's sinful nature which makes him utterly helpless in the pursuit of the good. Consequently they came to rely almost exclusively upon the Pauline teachings regarding salvation of the individual sinner by faith, disclaiming even James's admonition to be doers of the Word as well as hearers.

In connection with Anabaptism, Harold S. Bender has introduced the term "theology of discipleship." The idea of discipleship or *Nachfolge,* however, does not yet constitute a theology in the proper sense of the word. It is rather an element of that implied theological system which enabled the Anabaptists to carry on so forcefully, and in which discipleship assumes but a constitutive character. The numerous confessions of faith and confessional tracts of the different Anabaptist groups do not give much help in the further elucidation of the question since, as stated above, they simply affirm their formal orthodoxy in the acceptance of the doctrine of the Trinity and of the Apostolic Creed, plus the call to unconditional obedience to the divine commandments: "Christ said so, . . . hence we have to do it."

It is certainly true that in the New Testament a theology in the more formal sense of the word is most explicit in the writings of Paul; but that does not mean that the teachings of Christ Himself as recorded in the Synoptic Gospels are lacking in theological foundations. It has been only in recent decades that we have come to recognize this "implied" theology of the Synoptics, so long by-passed and overlooked, as exactly the one which became so central for the Anabaptists in the sixteenth century. The teachings of Paul are essentially not different from those of Christ, but the emphasis and the categories applied are different, or at least could be so interpreted. In any case it is possible to speak of a Pauline tradition, elaborated later by Augustine, and of a Synoptic tradition, preserved in the main by those groups which Ludwig Keller once called old evangelical brotherhoods.

As we now study this Synoptic tradition or emphasis,

we find that central for it is the teaching of the two kingdoms, together with the message of what the kingdom of God actually means and implies. I think it is justified to call these doctrines a genuine theology in the proper sense of the word, even though its forms of expression are different from the above-mentioned more sophisticated Pauline-Augustinian tradition. It is proposed to call this teaching "kingdom theology." In a certain sense it is a continuation of the teachings of the Old Testament prophets, in the main of Isaiah, where this basic dualism of the two realms already appears. Most important in this connection is the idea that the "other kingdom" is not merely something transcendental, something of another aeon, or something to be experienced only after death, but a reality to be expected and experienced in this life, even though in a sort of metahistorical situation.

As a matter of fact, the kingdom theology (as we see it, the very center of Christ's message and witnessing) is to be distinguished from a theology whose primary concern is personal salvation (the Protestant interpretation of Paulinism). These two theologies are complementary to each other and of equal importance. The Reformers knew this fact very well.[3] In fact their outlook on history was decidedly kingdom-oriented, but they had their reasons for underemphasizing this two-facet content of the New Testament theology. The Pietists a century and a half later revived the kingdom idea, but being themselves the offspring of traditional Protestantism, they interpreted it in a non-Synoptic way. The real representatives of the Synoptic kingdom theology have always been the old evangelical brotherhoods, but none were more outspokenly kingdom-oriented, hence none more true to the spirit of the Master Himself, than the Anabaptists.

In the Pauline teaching the idea of original sin has a central position, making personal salvation and justification by

---

3 Compare, for instance, the most recent treatment of this subject, Franz Lau, *Luther's Lehre von den beiden Reichen* ("Luthertum," Berlin, 1952). The traditional interpretation, however, reduced the dualism of "this world" and the kingdom to the simplified dualism of Law and Gospel. This is certainly not the understanding of the Anabaptists.

faith a most urgent matter, while the kingdom comes to occupy apparently a secondary position. In the teaching of Jesus, on the other hand, the sense of urgency seems to be associated predominantly with the kingdom,[4] which, of course, includes the certainty of personal salvation. To be sure, Jesus taught by means of parables and pictures rather than by way of concepts and theories, and parables allow no easy translation into a system. And yet, the doctrine of the two worlds—the kingdom of God which is to come here and now, and the kingdom of darkness which rules over all those who do not see the light—this doctrine represents definitely a very specific outlook or theology. As will be shown below, it has its own characteristic 1) value system; 2) view of history; and 3) social ethic. In short, it implies a real theology although of a character rather different from that of the Pauline tradition as interpreted by Augustine and the Reformers.

While Paul by no means taught only a theology of justification by faith *alone* (as the Reformers, in particular Luther, have done),[5] he gave enough attention to it to make possible the development of a one-sided theology at the hands of the Reformers, running something like this: The law has come to an end; all men have inherited original sin; Christ died for us; and thus the individual can and will be saved (i.e., justified before God) if only he puts all his confidence and faith in the atoning quality of Christ's supreme sacrifice. The essential element here is faith, not works, however the latter may be interpreted. This one-sided emphasis in a fully developed Protestantism, which tended to ignore both the remainder of Paul's teaching and the Gospels as well, produced a theological system which assumed an extremely individualistic outlook. The individual, a sinner through and through who cannot do good, craves for salvation and eventually finds it by believing.[6] The neighbor, the brother, im-

4 Cf. Albert Schweitzer, *The Mystery of the Kingdom of God* (New York, 1950).
5 The term "alone" was added by Luther to the text of the epistle to the Romans in order to make the idea more understandable and emphatic. Paul would have turned it down, not up.
6 A good illustration of this type of thinking may be drawn from the follow-

portant though he is, is in no way constitutive to this outlook on salvation. Love, we learn, is the fruit of faith, but such love adds nothing essential to the drama of completely unearned and even undeserved redemption, else it would assume the quality of works. No specific social implications could be deduced, and both Lutheranism and Calvinism became exceedingly individualistic in their teachings, while civilization at large went on independently and autonomously.

Kingdom theology is essentially of a different kind. The outlook is dualistic as throughout the New Testament. Yet while Paul preferredly contraposes *spirit* and *flesh,* categories suggesting above all a conflict in the personal and private sphere, kingdom theology distinguishes two other concepts in polarity. These concepts are *the world* (being ruled by "the prince of this world," i.e., Satan), and *the other world,* the kingdom, which is God's world. Two possibilities are here to be contemplated: either that these two realms are coexistent, although on different levels, and the kingdom of God is already present in or among those who have been born again or who are united in the name of the Master ("where two or three are together in my name . . ."); or the kingdom of God is to come, in fact its coming is imminent, and one ought to prepare himself for this imminent coming by purification and a new life. The latter idea was present already in the teaching of the Essenes, of John the Baptist, and of some Ebionites. This second interpretation of the kingdom idea we may call eschatological,[7] while the first has no special systematic name, yet is more closely associated with the idea of rebirth and conversion. These two views, the kingdom present in every reborn Christian (or present where two or

ing quotation from Luther: "When God speaks and gives signs [i.e., sacraments], man must firmly and wholeheartedly believe that what God says and signifies is true. . . . Then God, in turn, will count *this* faith unto our righteousness, good and sufficient to salvation." *Martin Luther's Works* (Ed. Jacobs, Philadelphia) 3:20 f.

7 It might be well to compare at this point the eschatological outlook of the Gospels (such as Matt. 24, Mark 13, and Luke 21) with that of the Book of Revelation (Rev. 20). The latter never received much emphasis among the old evangelical brotherhoods.

three are assembled in the Master's name), and the kingdom as the new order to be expected at any moment and for which proper preparation is needed, are intermixed in Anabaptist thought just as they are in the original source of that teaching, the Gospels. But the eschatological hope was subdued and never dominated the thinking of the Anabaptists, just as in the Gospel the implied eschatology was never to outdo the positive teachings concerning the kingdom as the newly revealed other-reality which is within the reach of everyone who earnestly longs and desires to enter the same.

As suggested earlier, the kingdom theory implies first a new set of values. Certainly, the Sermon on the Mount is the best illustration: love, forgiveness, self-surrender, hating not even one's own persecutors, these values are so radically different that they seem paradoxical and unrealizable to an unregenerate mind. Certainly they go far beyond mere ethics. Rather they imply a different dimension, the world of the pure Spirit, in contrast with all secular this-worldly valuations. In fact, these new values are unobtainable except through rebirth and a radical change of mind, concepts not too much at home in orthodox Protestantism, the religion of the many. Historically, this has produced within Christendom what the sociologists of religion like to call sectarianism, meaning that the disciples, the *Nachfolger,* the citizens of the kingdom, intentionally separate themselves from the "world," in order to share as little as possible in the affairs of the natural realm and of its citizens. They are highly suspicious of the values of this world, including even that which is usually called "culture," and they sense in it the working of destructive, non-divine forces in the background. All cathartic or puritanical tendencies have their roots in this new value system.

In the second place, kingdom theology has its own specific outlook on history, a fact much forgotten today but very much alive even in the age of the Reformation. The two realms, the kingdom of God and the kingdom of darkness,

111

are engaged in a perennial struggle, a world drama, in which each person must choose and take his side. In the end the kingdom of God will triumph over the powers of darkness. This is the eschatological expectation.[8] Hence the sectarian feels a high sense of responsibility in this cosmic-historic process, and therefore accepts suffering and martyrdom without flinching. Only by witnessing to the kingdom of Light can the latter ever become full reality. That this outlook, although prominent in the New Testament, especially in the Gospels, recedes with the Reformers' interpretation of Paul hardly needs further elaboration.

Thirdly, the kingdom theology includes also a social ethic, different, to be sure, from what usually goes by that name. A lack of "social ethics," or at least of what may better be called a concern for the social order of this world, was often observed in the teaching of the New Testament. The absence of any doctrine of "natural law" was observed at an early date in church history, but it was soon supplied from Stoic philosophy to promote a more adjustable foundation of church life. Thus far, however, very little attention has been given to the genuine social ethic of the Gospel message of the kingdom of God, most likely because it does not fit too well into the ways of the world at large and into the social exigencies of civilization. We mean here the brotherhood idea, the idea of the *Gemeinde,* the *ecclesia* in its first meaning, the idea of the *koinonia,* a closely knit fellowship of believers and disciples, not in the form of conventicles as in later Pietism, but in the form of the brotherhoods as we know them in the early church, and in all old evangelical brotherhoods including the Anabaptists. All individualism and individualistic concern for personal salvation is ruled out. No one can enter the kingdom except together with his brother. The old saying that "there is no salvation out-

8 This particular outlook on history is actually much older than the New Testament. According to N. Söderblom, "Ages of the World," in Hastings' *Encyclopedia of Religion and Ethics* I (1928) it is found in Iranian (Zoroastrian) ideas which entered later postexilic Judaism. Of course, the New Testamental kingdom theology gave this outlook a new and different significance.

side the church" does not exactly express the underlying idea
of this brotherhood ideal; actually that doctrine belongs to a
different frame of reference. And yet, it simply is so that the
kingdom of God means from its very beginning a togetherness, else it is no kingdom. The mere aggregation of saved
souls, as in Pietism, does not constitute the kingdom; it remains just an aggregation, nothing else. The horizontal man-
to-man relationship belongs to the kingdom just as much as
does the vertical God-man relationship. In fact, the belief
prevails that one cannot come to God (that is, attain salvation) except as one comes to Him together with one's brother. The brethren, the body of believers, constitutes the realm;
hence brotherly love, *agape*, is more than mere ethics. It is
one of the basic qualifications of the kingdom in the here
and now.

Kingdom theology is hostile to *Kultur*, man's autonomous creation and setting of values. Actually *Kultur* or civilization is a Graeco-Roman and a Renaissance concept, not a
Christian one; hence the apparent coolness of the Anabaptists
toward human achievement and cultural advancement. Since
the latter does not belong to the system of values embodied
in the kingdom theology they meet it with suspicion, fearful
lest it contain elements of destruction, elements of despondency and nonsalvation, in short, that it miss the essentials of
Christ's message and world outlook. The Middle Ages, being
steeped in the philosophy of history of the two realms, knew
more about this tension between man-made civilization and
God's kingdom than has any time since the fifteenth century.

The kingdom theology is concerned with the concrete,
the life in the here and the now, although in a dimension
other than the material. By no means does it teach that the
kingdom is found in heaven only, and attainable only
after death. This is a post-New Testament interpretation.
Kingdom theology does not mean merely a glorious expectation of life after death to be reached by the pious and the
ascetic; it means a radical turn in life itself, the breaking in

of a new dimension into the physical existence of man. Due to its new system of values, so highly challenging to anything known to "natural" man, the group life of the disciples has always been misunderstood and disliked, in fact persecuted by the world. Hence a "theology of martyrdom" developed among the Brethren, an understanding that the citizens of the kingdom of God will necessarily meet suffering in this world. This suffering, however, is of a redemptive character and represents a necessary element in the building of God's kingdom. It was this way in the early centuries A.D., and all through history. The Anabaptists in particular accepted the idea of the suffering church in an almost matter-of-fact fashion, and every member of this group understood it without much explanation. In fact, we often discover even a kind of longing for martyrdom, a desire to be allowed to testify for the new spiritual world through suffering and supreme sacrifice.

This martyr-mindedness is usually mellowed by a restrained eschatological outlook: God will soon change the world altogether. Wait but a little while, and yours will be the triumph. Save for a few exceptions, such as that of Melchior Hofmann, the Anabaptists did not calculate the end of the world, being mindful of the words of Christ that no one knows the day, not even the Son, but the Father alone. Nevertheless, they frequently speak of "these last and dangerous times," and of the "last fury of the beast." Here they use a figure from the Book of Revelation which is otherwise little used and quoted. Beyond this, however, eschatological expectations were seldom talked about. After all, is not the kingdom realized even now through the brotherhood of the reborn? Thus, although the kingdom theology always has an eschatological slant, implying a philosophy of history, it nevertheless does not lead to unbalanced expectations such as chiliasm, adventism, millennialism, and the like.

The question may be raised whether or not the Anabaptist sources actually support this thesis of their kingdom theology.

The kingdom theology was never systematically formulated by the Anabaptists; implicitly, however, it is very much there. Even as Jesus spoke mainly in parables, thus revealing His theological ideas but indirectly, so it is also with the Anabaptists. Very clear, even radical is their dualism concerning the two realms. Their disparagement and even fear of the world goes beyond that opposition which we would find in Paul's derogation of the flesh. While the latter leads to asceticism and celibacy, the Anabaptist dualism is of a rather different kind, requiring complete separation from the world as the realm of the prince of darkness. The Anabaptists, however, were not Puritans. The mere practice of purity of morals would mean little to them even though the idea of a "church without spot and wrinkle" is quite common with the Anabaptists. The Puritans certainly had one element of the kingdom theology, the strictness of discipline; but they lacked certain other elements, due to their Calvinistic outlook.

The terms most often used by Anabaptists are *Nachfolge* (discipleship) and *Gehorsam* (obedience); that is, the acceptance of Christ's leadership and that spirit which permeates His teachings. In short, their way of thinking and of evaluation is that of the kingdom theology, even though an explicit theology of this kind might not be so easily demonstrable. They felt absolutely certain that they were citizens of that other (spiritual) world here and now, and accepted the values, the outlook on history and the social consequences which follow with this position as a matter of course.

This theology, however, needs one further analysis to exclude misunderstanding. Frequent attempts have been made to integrate kingdom theology and the typical Protestant theology of salvation, i.e., justification by faith alone. The outstanding attempt in this direction is Pietism, which likewise speaks of God's kingdom and its building up, mainly through intensive mission work. As in so many other areas, Anabaptism and Pietism have certain similarities also at this point. The Anabaptists, too, were intent on mission work and they were aware that by this work they were instrumental in the building God's kingdom here and now. Likewise the Pietist emphasis upon the new birth is quite similar to that of Anabaptists, although the accompanying methodic struggle of repentance (the *Busskampf*) of Pietism is totally foreign to Anabaptism. In spite of all these similarities the concept of the kingdom in Pietism is yet basically different from that in Anabaptism. To Pietism of all shades the kingdom means the assembling of all those who have passed through the *Busskampf* experience and know themselves now as the reborn; they represent then the citizens of that kingdom, the conventicle of the saved who now enjoy their state of salvation in quiet withdrawal and devotional uplift (edification). The world outside is not challenged, and accordingly does not react against the Pietist. In Pietism the dualism of the two realms is never dynamic, and the world is not decried as darkness, but is marginally accepted. Above all the brotherhood idea is not present, at least not in the sense of the old evangelical brotherhoods with their togetherness and sharing.

To the Pietist the kingdom is the assembly or society of the redeemed, who join in a sort of conventicle; to Anabaptism it is a closely knit, nonindividualistic brotherhood where the brother is *constitutive* to the idea of the kingdom and its realization, and where the concern with one's own salvation from original sin is but marginal, and any thought of its "enjoyment" completely foreign. Obedience stands here in opposition to enjoyment (edification). In Anabaptism the kingdom idea is the primary concern, and thus becomes dynamic, challenging, and extremely other-dimensional. With Pietism individual salvation is the primary concern, and the kingdom idea assumes a non-dynamic and only mildly dualistic character, thus leading to less tension with the kingdom of this world. In Pietism the idea of the cross becomes more emotional than existential, just as the idea of the Spirit is further reduced to a psychological uplift without the existential "I cannot do otherwise" of the Anabaptists. Finally, Pietism places undue emphasis on death and dying, as if the kingdom of God were synonymous with heaven or paradise. Nothing is farther from Anabaptism than that. Thus, although the kingdom idea and even a kind of kingdom theology occurs also within the respected circles of Protestantism, namely, the pietistic wings of Lutheranism and of Calvinism, the difference between this and the kingdom theology of Anabaptism is nevertheless very real and tangible, and forbids any confusion between Anabaptism and Pietism.

It was only in fairly recent times that a more adequate appreciation of this kingdom theology was promoted and with it a new understanding of the life and work of Christ and the meaning of discipleship. Two men were primarily instrumental in this regard: Albert Schweitzer, whose first book on this subject was published 1901,[9] and Leonhard Ragaz, the Swiss theologian, whose magazine *Neue Wege* began to appear in 1907 and whose major books were published between 1922 and 1925.[10] Unfortunately, neither of these two men were too successful in their endeavor as they challenged too strongly the traditional viewpoints of most Protestant theologians. This is particularly true of Ragaz whose work was an unceasing "prophetic" fight for the recovery of the original meaning of the kingdom theology and its consequences. In this connection he likes to speak of *Die Sache Christi,* that is, loyalty or devotion to that which Christ stands for and is most concerned with, instead of "Christian religion" with its concentration on institutional church bodies. He also urges a "going back from Paul to Jesus," very outspokenly connecting discipleship with the kingdom idea.

9 Albert Schweitzer, *The Mystery of the Kingdom of God; the Secret of Jesus' Messiahship and Passion (Das Messianitäts-und Leidensgeheimnis: Eine Skizze des Lebens Jesu)* was written in 1901 (translated into English in 1913; new edition with an introduction by Walter Lowrie, 1950).

10 Leonhard Ragaz, *Weltreich, Religion und Gottesherrschaft,* 2 Vols. (Zürich, 1922); *Der Kampf um das Reich Gottes in Blumhard, Vater und Sohn,-und Weiter* (Zürich, 1922); and the magazine *Neue Wege* (Zürich, 1907 ff.). See also his *Gedanken aus Vierzig Jahren geistigen Kampfes, Ausgewählt von Freunden,* 2d ed. (Bern, 1951), with exhaustive bibliography by Lejeune.

From a historical viewpoint we might also mention the work of Rudolf Otto, who in his *The Kingdom of God and the Son of Man*[11] offers perhaps the finest scholarly treatment of the ideas here discussed, helpful also in the reinterpretation of Anabaptism. In contradistinction to the work of Ragaz, it remains a strictly historical analysis. I myself have likewise tried to clarify the issues in my *Mennonite Piety Through the Centuries*,[12] discussing the idea of the kingdom and its difference from the doctrine of justification by faith alone. But then I was not yet prepared to carry the analysis as far as in the present paper. Very little has been said concerning the consequences of this theology of the kingdom for the outlook on history. Otto Piper's *God in History*[13] emphasizes rightly the difference between secular history and holy (sacred, redemptive) history, but the consequences as to withdrawal and opposition to secular civilization are not clearly drawn.

The meaning of the present paper is then to propose a comparatively new viewpoint and to invite further discussion and exchange of thoughts and research. I hope that our younger friends and co-workers will answer, correcting or setting aright whatever was said above. They should remember, however, that the idea of salvation by faith alone looks very different from this point of view than from that of the official Protestant interpretation. To be concerned with one's own salvation first and foremost is not the same as to feel a burning passion to serve the *Sache Christi* through *Nachfolge* and obedience, through the creation of a nucleus of the kingdom here and now. The latter is the never-ending concern of those who have a vision of that other dimension which alone is the place where Spirit may truly become flesh.

11 Rudolf Otto, *The Kingdom of God and the Son of Man* (published in German, 1930; first English edition, 1938; revised 1943).

12 Robert Friedmann, *Mennonite Piety Through the Centuries* (Goshen, 1949) 85-88.

13 Otto Piper, *God in History* (New York, 1936).

✠ FRANKLIN H. LITTELL ✠

The Anabaptist Concept of the Church

In his review of my book, Harold S. Bender concludes: "But I am still inclined to make discipleship the central controlling idea more than primitivism and restitution."[1] This conclusion is in line with his well-known presidential address, "The Anabaptist Vision,"[2] and seems at first blush to imply a basic disagreement as to the "central controlling idea" in the Anabaptist movement. Is this really the case?

The emphasis upon the view of the church as central to Anabaptism has been developed by various historians, both hostile and friendly. The study by Fritz Heyer, which unfortunately must be classed in the former category in spite of wide use of sources, expresses the opinion that, "The core of the *Schwärmertum* of the sixteenth century is found in the view of the church."[3] R. J. Smithson, author of one of the few reasonably adequate books on the movement, says: "The real issue between the Anabaptists and the other reformers was on the question of the type of Church which should take the place of the old Church." He goes on to quote the great church historian, Philip Schaff, to the effect that "The reformers aimed to reform the old Church by the Bible; the radicals attempted to build a new Church from the Bible."[4]

Among the more fair-minded of the historians of the

* Franklin H. Littell is Representative in Germany of the Franz Lieber Foundation, St. Paul, Minnesota, and author of *The Anabaptist View of the Church* (American Society of Church History, 1952).

1 Franklin H. Littell, *The Anabaptist View of the Church* (Chicago and Philadelphia, 1952), reviewed by Harold S. Bender in *MQR* (July 1953) 27:249-53.

2 See pp. 29-54.

3 Fritz Heyer, *Der Kirchenbegriff der Schwärmer* (Leipzig, 1939). LVI *Schriften des Vereins für Reformationsgesichte*, No. 166, Part 2, 3.

4 R. J. Smithson, *The Anabaptists* (London, 1935) 14-15.

Reformation there has been a general agreement on this point. According to Lindsay, writing in 1907, for instance: "The Anabaptists would have nothing to do with a state Church; and this was the main point in their separation from the Lutherans, Zwinglians, and Calvinists. It was perhaps the *one* conception on which all parties among them were in absolute accord. The real Church, which might be small or great, was for them an association of believing people; and the great ecclesiastical institutions into which unconscious infants were admitted by a ceremony called baptism long before they could have or exercise faith, represented to them an idea subversive of true Christianity."[5]

Harold Grimm, writing in 1954, states: "It was Grebel's conception of a free church, consisting of freely committed and practicing believers, as opposed to the *Volkskirche,* or inclusive state church of the Catholics and most Protestants, which formed the basic doctrine of the Anabaptists."[6]

Walther Köhler, the great Heidelberg church historian who, according to his widow, would have "preferred to die a Mennonite," attested: "The crystallization of the Reformation in territorial churches or in parishes led by city political authorities gave the impulse for the building up of Anabaptist circles. . . . The Anabaptists are the Bible Christians of the Reformation. . . . They wished to restore the Early Church at Jerusalem as a community of saints sharply separated from the world."[7]

Fritz Blanke concludes a study with the words: "The rise of the Anabaptist group in Zollikon was the birth of a brotherhood of a purely religious character. The young plant was soon violently suppressed, but that does not decrease its significance. In Zollikon a new type of Church had begun to differentiate itself, the Free Church type. Zollikon is the cradle of this idea, which from here entered upon its trium-

5 T. M. Lindsay, *A History of the Reformation* (New York, 1941) 2:443.

6 Harold Grimm, *The Reformation Era: 1500-1650* (New York, 1954) 266.

7 Walther Köhler, "Wiedertaufer," in *Die Religion in Geschichte und Gegenwart* (Tübingen, 1927-31) 5:1915-17.

phal march through four centuries and through the whole world."[8] The idea of the Anabaptists as forerunners of the free church view is thus widespread, and undoubtedly explains their fascination to a growing number of out-group historians and churchmen who consciously or unconsciously are dissatisfied with promiscuous political or social establishments.

Among Mennonites, also, the centrality of the view of the church has frequently been accepted. C. Henry Smith wrote in his *History:* "In fact the whole movement was an attempt to reproduce as literally as possible the primitive apostolic church in its original purity and simplicity; and restore Christianity once more to a basis of individual responsibility."[9] Robert Friedmann has recently stressed the importance of the church covenant and the collective responsibility of brethren which differentiated Anabaptism from other Protestantism.[10] According to Cornelius Krahn, the central theological concern of the Anabaptists was in the church, and he goes so far as to term their thinking *ecclesio-centric.*[11] Some years before he had already established the central concern in Menno Simons: "nevertheless the basic lines of his theology can be established, when you work out from the center, from which he managed, worked, and lived as a Christian and as elder in the churches. This central point was for him making actual the apostolic model in the local Christian church. Almost all other questions of Christian life and teaching are determined from here."[12]

Thinking on this, one cannot read without being deeply moved the opening sentence of a recent article by van der Zijpp: "Menno is reported to have said, while on his sickbed

---

8 Fritz Blanke, "The First Anabaptist Congregation: Zollikon, 1525," *MQR* (January 1953) 27:33.

9 C. Henry Smith, *The Story of the Mennonites.* Third edition, revised and enlarged by Cornelius Krahn (Newton, 1950) 21.

10 Robert Friedmann, "Anabaptism and Protestantism," *MQR* (January 1950) 24:18-19.

11 Cornelius Krahn, "Prolegomena to an Anabaptist Theology," *MQR* (January 1950) 24:10-11.

12 C. Krahn, *Menno Simons, 1496-1561* (Karlsruhe, 1936) 103.

—which was to become his deathbed—that nothing on earth was as precious to him as the church."[13] For the struggle in Protestantism today, again challenged by persecutors without and spiritualizers within,[14] is precisely about the church. As revealed in crisis, so it seems to me, the Protestantism of the political and social establishments has tended to dissolve the church and stifle the Holy Spirit. It is my further conviction that study of the classical Anabaptist testimony, and renewal of the church accordingly, can provide again a clear guidance as to how Christians can withstand persecution without and betrayal within the movement.

Does all this in some fashion contradict Harold S. Bender's view as to what was central in the Anabaptist movement? Are "discipleship" and "the church view" necessarily at odds with each other? It is in the last phrase of the quotation from the late C. Henry Smith that I find the worm in the apple: "and restore Christianity once more to *a basis of individual responsibility*" (italics mine). For "discipleship," in our day and age, has become a matter of individual picking and choosing. In the first place, the objective validity of Scriptural truth has been obscured by the wisdom of men. In the second place, a quite spurious doctrine of "individual conscience" has replaced collective responsibility and obedience to the Lord of the church; credibility is thereby given to the utterly pernicious notion that civic freedom and "the glorious liberty of the children of God" (Rom. 8:21) are one and the same thing.

13 N. van der Zijpp, "The Conception of Our Fathers Regarding the Church," *MQR* (April 1953) 27:91.

14 Cf. my discussion of the parallel challenges to the Anabaptists and the church today, in "Spiritualizers, Anabaptists, and the Church," *MQR* (January 1955) 24:34-43. Evidently the Dutch Mennonites are prepared to find more evidences of spiritualizing carry-over in the Anabaptist-Mennonite tradition and to view such a thought more kindly than I am. Cf. N. van der Zijpp, *loc. cit.*, pp. 95-97; also H. W. Meihuizen, "Spiritualistic Tendencies and Movements Among the Dutch Mennonites of the 16th and 17th Centuries," *MQR* (October 1953) 27:259-304. I agree wholeheartedly with Robert Friedmann's denunciation of the doctrine of "the invisible church" as alien to Anabaptism, *MQR* (April 1954) 28:148-54. This teaching, which is spiritualizing in effect and perhaps in origin, has been from the 16th century to the present day the major underground tunnel by which leaders of established Protestant churches have been able to escape from the position to which their Biblical insurgency at first has led them.

In a discussion of C. Henry Smith's *History*, Robert Friedmann has expressed approximately the same misgivings as mine. His comments are so forceful, and so illuminating for the present crisis in the Protestant churches, that the temptation is strong to quote at greater length than here feasible. Contrasting other Protestant movements, including renewal movements, with Anabaptism, he writes:

"Everybody still remains alone, seeking his personal salvation, and he only enjoys the sharing of edification with the like-minded coreligionists. Or to put it in other words: the brother is not absolutely necessary for the salvation of the individual, which rests alone in the possession of one's faith. It is but one further step from this position to the liberal concept of individualism of the last hundred years, [which] almost atomized society and destroyed church life at large. . . .

"Now then, the central idea of Anabaptism, the real dynamite in the age of Reformation, as I see it, was this, that one cannot find salvation without caring for his brother, that this 'brother' actually matters in the personal life. . . . This interdependence of men gives life and salvation a new meaning. It is not 'faith alone' which matters (for which faith no church organization would be needed) but it is brotherhood, this intimate caring for each other, as it was commanded to the disciples of Christ as the way to God's kingdom. That was the discovery which made Anabaptism so forceful and outstanding in all of church history."[15]

The bane of Protestantism has been its increasing identification with individualism in the generations since the Enlightenment and the French Revolution. "Magisterial Protestantism"[16] has always been weak on the doctrine of the church and the doctrine of the Holy Spirit. By and large, the

15 Robert Friedmann, "On Mennonite Historiography and on Individualism and Brotherhood," *MQR* (April 1944) 18:121.

16 This expression has been coined by George H. Williams to cover the various forms of legal establishment and control in the formative decades of the Reformation: magistrate=*Obrigkeit;* see his introduction to the source book in the Christian Classics Series which he edited and largely translated: *The Radical Reformation* (Westminster Press, forthcoming), Philadelphia.

Protestant establishments have either uncritically admitted into the church ideas of individual rights and privileges which properly are limited to the unbaptized areas of life, or succumbed to "high church" restorationist tendencies (usually sacramental and liturgical) which in the end betray the whole burden of the Protestant Reformation of the church. Here is precisely the juncture where the free church,[17] which is bound neither to *sola fide* nor *ex opere operato,* can bring a needed theological assistance to the whole Ecumene. In giving concrete evidence of "the brotherhood of the reborn" (i.e., the second Israel), the free church fathers (the Anabaptists) considered both the forms of doctrine (confession= *Bekenntnis*) and the patterns of witness (moral, ethical, and church organizational) to be subject to the guidance of the Holy Spirit.

This, again, was no promiscuous inspiration, but rather precisely the Spirit of Whom the Bible speaks:[18] Comforter, Spirit of Truth, the Divine Presence among His folk following Pentecost (John 14:16 ff). When a matter of confession or witness has been "talked up" among the faithful (and this may take minutes, hours, or even decades), the decision is called in human terms a *consensus.* Biblically speaking, the act of holy government is reported: "It seemed good to the Holy Spirit, and to us" (Acts 14:28). In this context Dono-

17 The Anabaptists were forerunners of the free church pattern, and thus are the classical reference for purposes of comparison with later developments—not only for Mennonites, but for many contemporary denominations who have strayed much further from the testimony of the fathers. Cf. my Menno Simons Lectures, 1954: *The Free Church* (Beacon Press, forthcoming), Boston. In this they were radically different from both Catholic and Reformation parties. "The Anabaptist-Mennonite tradition, theologically understood, is seen to represent not simply a branch of Protestantism with a particular 'talent,' but a historical incarnation of an entirely different view of the Christian life, of the work and nature of the church, and fundamentally also of the meaning of redemption." Cf. John Howard Yoder, "The Anabaptist Dissent: The Logic of the Place of the Disciple in Society," *Concern* (Scottdale, June 1954) 1:57.

18 "The primary, begetting force which gathers the church, is and remains for Riedemann the Holy Spirit." Cf. Franz Heimann, "The Hutterite Doctrines of Church and Common Life," *MQR* (January and April 1952) 26:39. "*Anabaptism rests ultimately on perpetual spiritual re-creation which derives its authority from the work of the Spirit among men thereby united, and not from ecclesiastical stucture.*" Cf. Paul Peachey, "Anabaptism and Church Organization," *MQR* (July 1956) 30:217.

CONCEPT OF THE CHURCH

van E. Smucker is certainly correct in asserting that the Anabaptists rediscovered the theology of the Bible:[19] i.e., the burden of the elect of God, a visible "vanguard" who carry the meaning of human history and who are continually subject to His governance. It was this, and not any consequent "form" (including believers' baptism),[20] which made them offensive to the well-ordered monopoly of hierarchy and canon lawyers who ran the monolithic structure of the establishments.[21] The

[19] Donovan E. Smucker, "The Theological Triumph of the Early Anabaptist-Mennonites," *MQR* (January 1945) 19:6.

[20] Harold S. Bender, "The Anabaptist Theology of Discipleship," *MQR* (January 1950) 24:27.

[21] Paul Peachey, "Social Background and Social Philosophy of the Swiss Anabaptists, 1525-40," *MQR* (April 1954) 28:120. Because of their own predilection to concern themselves primarily with Biblical issues and matters of discipleship, and because of the speed and efficiency with which their movement was buried in a bath of blood by the persecutors, it has been customary even for many latter-day friends of the movement to assume that the Anabaptists contributed nothing to social and political thought as such. I long thought that study of the contribution of the free churches to democratic development as such must be postponed until the Commonwealth Period in England. However, the implications for a constitutional and just government are also there, and some of the direct teachings as well. Michael Sattler, when he heard the barbarous sentence passed upon him, first reaffirmed his faith and then said: "You know that you with your fellow-judges have sentenced me contrary to law; therefore take care and repent." Gustav Bossert, Jr., "Michael Sattler's Trial and Martyrdom in 1527," *MQR* (July 1951) 25:215. One of the relatively unworked areas of Anabaptist thought is this: To what extent did the Anabaptists, albeit indirectly or as appendage to their prior concern with the nature of the true church, also have something to say about the nature of the just state? Although the whole intellectual framework of natural law was foreign to their commitments as it is bound to be foreign to those of any thoroughgoing evangelical, nevertheless the documents indicate a wide area of possible research in relating their views to the problems of a government which recognizes human rights and due process of law. The major conviction was that a just state does not persecute, and the political implications of this position have been beautifully summarized by the Old Catholic scholar, Professor Döllinger, in an appraisal of Cromwell: "He was the first among the mighty men of the world to set up one special religious principle, and to enforce it so far as in him lay: . . . the principle of liberty of conscience and the repudiation of religious coercion. It must be clearly understood how great the gulf, is which divides the holders of this principle from those who reject it, both in faith and morals. He who is convinced that right and duty require him to coerce other people into a life of falsehood . . . belongs to an essentially different religion from one who recognizes in the inviolability of conscience a human right guaranteed by religion itself, and has different notions of God, of man's relation to God, and of man's obligations to his fellows. . . ." Quoted in A. D. Lindsay, *The Essentials of Democracy* (London, 1951) 69. The problem of political responsibility in a democratic society (where the *Obrigkeit* is the citizenry) can be solved by accommodation politically and by spiritualizing the doctrine of the church (as in Dutch Mennonitism). Robert Kreider has given evidence that Russian Mennonitism, when tolerated, "moved in the direction and exhibited many of the characteristics of the *Volkskirche* or what the English call the 'parish pattern of the church.'" Cf. "The Anabaptist Conception of the Church in the Russian

125

Anabaptist rediscovery of peoplehood and rejection of the institutionalized mass establishments, their reassertion of the Biblical role of the laity and the local congregation, were related to a view of history which I have elsewhere termed "primitivism."[22] What this means can be determined by reference to the two contrasting views of "apostolicity."

The Catholic tradition has been portrayed by John Henry Cardinal Newman in the following words: "It is sometimes said that the stream is clearest near the spring. Whatever use may fairly be made of this image, it does not apply to the history of a philosophy or a belief which, on the contrary, is more equable, and purer, and stronger when its bed has become deeper, and broad, and full. . . ."[23] In the Catholic teaching the apostolic tradition is maintained through a swelling sacramental system, guaranteed by an unbroken line of commissioned and staff officers from the beginning to the present day. Although the Protestant Reformers, especially Zwingli, had some inkling that the flow had been corrupted and that one or more "fall of the church" had occurred, Lutheran and Calvinist establishments have generally attempted to establish a continuity of pure teaching (reine Lehre).

For the Anabaptists "apostolicity" meant something else: "true to the apostolic church." To be sure, the general opinion prevailed that God had never left Himself without a community of witness; the Hutterites, indeed, listed those church-

Mennonite Environment, 1789-1870," MQR (January 1951) 25:18. This is not, although many large American Protestant demominations are in the process of becoming Volkskirchen, what disturbed "out-groupers" in America and throughout the Ecumene need from American Mennonitism. But how is a healthy tension between church and civic commitment to be retained in America? "It is at least questionable whether a definition of the separation of church and state worked out under an autocratic system of government can be made normative for a democratic system in which, theoretically, at least, the government is the people and thus inevitably includes every Christian citizen." Erland Waltner, "The Anabaptist Conception of the Church," MQR (January 1951) 25:15. Our fathers knew only two types of government: 1) that which persecuted; 2) that which tolerated, perhaps only temporarily. Has not a third type emerged, in good part as consequence of the Anabaptist-Free Church testimony? But what are the limits?

22 The Anabaptist View of the Church, chapters III and IV.

23 Quoted in Oliver Chase Quick, Liberalism, Modernism, and Tradition (London, 1922) 27-28. One is tempted to comment that Newman didn't know the great rivers (including "the Big Muddy"!) of the American geographical and ecclesiastical landscape!

es who had wandered in the wilderness during the generations of the great apostasy, thereby bridging the gulf between the early church and the restitution. This was all more or less interesting, but only later and only on rare occasions (as with John Smyth) did it become an obsession. In the interpretation of history which was common to all branches of the movement—Swiss, South Germans, Hutterites, and Dutch—the early church was the heroic age and its life and style were normative for true believers. Then a fall of the church occurred, in which imperial arrogance, hierarchical ambition, and baptized heathenism were blended together in politico-religious union. They saw the task before them as a restitution of the true church, and this radical program included vastly more than the elimination of the most heathenish cults which had accumulated or the abandonment of false or unnecessary teachings. This restored true church was to recapitulate apostolic life and virtue and, as a matter of fact, did so to a remarkable degree. The apostolicity which scholars of the Catholic and Protestant establishments have been unable to fix in their research, i.e., apostolicity as the assertion of an unbroken line of laying on of hands, the Anabaptists proved with their blood; viz., apostolicity as loyalty to the church of the disciples, martyrs, and missioners.

The church as a community of discipleship is the needed word and witness today. This can be seen in the encounter with alternative ideologies. Some time ago, as national socialism and communism were in full flood, the general secretary of the World Council of Churches expressed the problem in these words: "The main task of the Christian community, and the greatest service which it can render to the world, is . . . to be the Christian community. For the real tragedy of our time is that we have on the one hand an incoherent mass of individual Christians and on the other hand powerful impulses towards new forms of community, but no Christian community. Christians today do not form a true community; and the communities which shape the new world are not

Christian. The present-day task of the Christian community is, therefore, not to enter more deeply into the world but to rediscover itself. It must learn to understand again what Christian community means before it can go out and change the world around it."[24]

The persecutors were one of the two main enemies of Anabaptism in the sixteenth century, and in the twentieth century they have also played their role.[25] The other enemy, the spiritualizers, has likewise been prominent in the twentieth century. Thus certain parallels can be drawn between the situation of the Anabaptists and sincere Christians today. Events of the last two decades in middle Europe will show how this is true.

In the church struggle with Nazism, the German faith, and/or Germanized Christianity,[26] the Confessing Church (*Bekennende Kirche*) took her stand squarely for the community of discipline and discipleship. At Barmen (May 29-31, 1934) it was declared:

"*We reject the false doctrine* that the Church can and must acknowledge as a source of its proclamation, beside and in addition to this one Word of God, other events, powers, forms, and truth as the revelation of God.

"*We reject the false doctrine* that there are spheres of our life in which we belong not to Jesus Christ, but to other masters, realms where we do not need to be justified and sanctified by Him.

"*We reject the false doctrine* that the Church is permitted to form its message or its order according to its own desire

24 W. A. Visser't Hooft, "*None Other Gods*" (New York, 1937) 70, 76-77.

25 Cf. my "The Protestant Churches and Totalitarianism (Germany, 1933-45)," in Carl J. Friedrich (Ed.) *Totalitarianism* (Cambridge, 1954), chapter VI. Also, "Die Freien Kirchen, die Sekten und das Widerstandsrecht," in Bernhard Pfister and Gerhard Hildmann (Ed.), *Widerstandsrecht und Grenzen der Staatsgewalt* (Berlin, 1956) 56-57. The encounter of the open society with totalitarianism has been widely studied; the Christian encounter with totalitarianism, with the necessary conclusions as to the nature and life of the church, awaits further research and writing. The Nazis were not irreligious; Article 24 of the party platform espoused "positive Christianity" (approximately what our secularists praise as "non-sectarian religion"!).

26 On the three forms of anti-Christian ideology which developed in the Third Reich, see Hans Buchheim, *Glaubenskrise im Dritten Reich* (Stuttgart, 1953).

128

or according to prevailing philosophical or political convictions.

"*We reject the false doctrine* that the Church is able or at liberty apart from this ministry to take to itself or to accept special 'leaders' equipped with power to rule.

"*We reject the false doctrine* that the Church should or can beyond its special task assume characteristics, functions, and dignity of the State, thus itself becoming an organ of the State.

"*We reject the false doctrine* that the Church can, in human glorification of itself, put the Word and the work of the Lord to the service of any desires, purposes, and plans, chosen on her own authority."[27]

Just as the Anabaptist forefathers rejected the claims of the persecutors and warded off the false leadings of the spiritualizers and revolutionaries (who were—and are—in the precise sense, *Schwärmer*), so did the men of Barmen in loyalty to the Master of the church reject Nazi pressure and spiritualizing accommodation. It has been reported that "in the dialectical theology, there had emerged a new, post-liberal, restatement of the theology of the Reformation."[28] It might further be said that the issues with which they were confronted had led them to a pre-Anabaptist position on the nature and work of the church.

The tragedy is that in the years following the end of the war the true logic of such convictions has not been maintained, and no radical reformation has been carried out. To be sure, Karl Barth for a time continued to appeal for a thoroughgoing reform. The church does not exist in councils and presbyteries, and certainly not in bishops, but ". . . is present and only present, 'where two or three are gathered together in my name' (Matt. 18:20) and thereby in the visible—visible to itself and to others—community." He proposed that the true way had been tried in England in the six-

27 *The Significance of the Barmen Declaration for the Oecumenical Church* (London, 1943). Cited, pp. 13-14.
28 *Ibid.*, 35.

teenth and seventeenth centuries, in the pilgrim church, and quoted finally Friedrich Loofs to the effect: "Who knows if not perhaps, when once the territorial churches of the old world have fallen apart, the Congregational church form will also have a future among us?"[29] Barth was unfortunately not aware that the real pioneers were not the English free churchmen, but precisely the evangelical *Täufer* of a century before in South Germany and Switzerland. Doubly tragic was it that the so-called free churches on the continent were not able to bear a clear and winsome testimony along Anabaptist lines. Thus Hermann Ehlers, at the time of his early death the president of the German parliament, asserted at the Third Synod of the Confessing Church (Augsburg: June 4-6, 1935): *"We will not go out of this our church into the free churches; rather we are the Church."*[30]

There were two chief reasons for the failure of the German free churches. First, they were rather more pietist conventicles than free churches in the classical sense, with an individualistic doctrine of personal salvation and—to a considerable degree—a double membership in the territorial church. Their style of free religious association actually paralleled the position of those in the sixteenth century who "stood still" and did not accept the social opprobrium and testimony of suffering involved in a forthright free church position. Secondly, they were through the group habit of accommodation and the individual habit of stressing the authority of the solitary "conscience" early led to adjust to the claims of the Third Reich. Hermann Ehlers, like the resisting churchmen generally, did not understand the free church testimony, and it must be said that the fault lies in good part with the style of so-called free churches which had grown up in nineteenth-century Germany.

In the postwar period the occupation authorities did not

29 "Die Kirche . . . die lebendige Gemeinde des lebendigen Herrn Jesus Christus," *World Council of Churches, Commission I: Die Kirche in Gottes Heilsplan.* Printed from MSS (April 1947) 17, 23.
30 Erie Wolf (Ed.), *Im Reich dieses Königs hat man das Recht lieb* (*Psalm 99:4*) (*Zeugnisse der Bekennende Kirche*, II, Tübingen-Stuttgart, 1946) 23.

feel free to order disestablishment. Two former Religious Affairs officers in the American staff have explained this reserve:

"Although many American officers felt that established churches were undemocratic, on balance it seemed best for Military Government not to attempt to disturb the traditional adjustment of Church-State relations in Germany. The experience of England and Sweden showed that established churches were not necessarily incompatible with democracy."[31]

"Although Military Government officials felt that German churches might benefit in the long run from a complete separation of church and state, it was believed even more firmly that any such decision must be made by the German people themselves, as part of their training in democratic procedures."[32] The decision thus rested squarely with the Germans from the beginning. Those whose strongly Biblical conviction led them to resistance to Nazism did not after the war understand the free church way as a clear alternative, and one which in its classical (i.e., Anabaptist) form actually represented that churchmanship of integrity for which they were striving.

In more recent times, having failed to press forward to a genuine thoroughgoing reformation (or *restitution* of a true church), the individuals who have striven to remain true to Barmen have split into two groups. The first group consists of those who have attempted through laymen's work in Kirchentag and Evangelical Academies to make a positive contribution to postwar reconstruction, and still are asking some of the important unsolved questions. The second group contains those who in the name of a *Situationsethik* have tended more and more toward *Schwärmertum*. The territorial churches as a whole have succumbed more and more to restorative (*Restauration*) tendencies, with a reassertion of tra-

31 Marshall Knappen, *And Call It Peace* (Chicago, 1947) 48.
32 Otto G. Hoiberg, "Religious Affairs," *Weekly Information Bulletin of OMGUS*, No. 73 (December 23, 1946) 4.

ditional patterns of hierarchical control, institutional blindness, and scholastic theology interpreted by experts.

Since the second group mentioned contains most of the neutralists and pacifists of postwar vintage, some special attention to Situationsethik is worth while. In the church struggle, the primacy of the church and her claims had been restated; today the appeal is made to the individual conscience. Certainly an ethic based on given and revealed factors in a moment of confrontation and challenge has the merit of moving beyond any simple synoptical legalism, and it also denies the whole structure of an earlier ethic derived from political authority and class structure. On the other hand, it leaves completely indeterminable whether a given action at a given moment derives from hate or love, enthusiasm or divine guidance. When Martin Niemöller addressed the meeting of the Bruderrat in May 1954, he defined conscience as that which is "unconditioned." When Karl Barth addressed the Hesse state legislature on the *Volkstrauertag*, 1955, his appeal was made to the individual conscience.[33] A radical Situationsethik leads to denial of the mutual admonition and exhortation of the Christian fellowship, and in the final analysis undermines the authority of the Bible as well; it begins as a useful challenge to false legalisms and ends in spiritual anarchy.

The first group mentioned above is the most creative and most potential from an Anabaptist point of view. Reinold von Thadden-Trieglaff, founder and president of the Deutscher Evangelischer Kirchentag, and Eberhard Müller, founder and chairman of the Association of Evangelical Academies, were both prominent figures in the earlier resistance to Nazism. Both have, however, had the faith to leave the besieged fortress of the church of those years and set forth to lay conquest the land in Christ's name. To give two summary examples of issues confronted: 1) At the Frankfurt

---

33 Cf. Wolfgang Boehme, "Politik im Namen Gottes?" *Zeitwende: Die Neue Furche* (1955) 26:73-81. Also my "Freiheit als Verantwortung," in *Verteidigungswerte Werte* (Evangelische Akademie, Loccum über Wunstorf, 1956) 54-60.

Kirchentag (August 8-12, 1956) the question constantly before the steering committee was: "To whom are we addressing our findings?" Ostensibly, the whole company assembled (500,000) was composed of baptized Christians, but this was recognized to be without meaning. Was it the church or the body politic which was being addressed? (Is *Gemeinde* in German usage a political or religious concept?) A provisional solution has been found in increasing use of the term, *Kirchentagsgemeinde*. In a movement dedicated to strengthening lay initiative and conscious Christian witnessing on Biblical terms, this is but one symbol of "pre-Anabaptist" developments. 2) The work in the Evangelical Academies[34] which demands the most thoroughgoing clarity in witness and makes the greatest demands is that developed through vocational-professional conferences and groups. Lawyers, engineers, teachers, doctors are gathered in working conferences to work over problems of daily conscience and decision under the twin spotlights of the Christian imperatives and the claims of professional ethics and morals. An "ethic of relationship" is here emerging, in a process where brotherly counsel is basic to the scheme. The key words are *Begegnung* (encounter) and *Gespräch* (brotherly counsel). In the meantime the authority of the Bible is taken seriously, and questions about the nature of the church and Christian discipleship are leading not infrequently to "pre-Anabaptist" points of view.

It might be said that the present question in the Evangelical Church of Germany is this: *Whether the real encounter is that between Luther and the Schwärmer at Wittenberg, 1521-22, or that between Zwingli and the Täufer at Zürich, 1524-25.* At Wittenberg the issue was between the authority of the church in process of partial reformation and individual inspiration. At Zürich the issue lay between an imperfectly reformed territorial church and a church gathered and disciplined on New Testament principles (i.e., a free church).

---

34 Two new handbooks on the Academies and Lay Institutes have recently appeared: *A New Road in Germany: Evangelical Academy* (Hamburg, 1956); *Signs of Renewal* (Department on the Laity, World Council of Churches, Geneva, 1956).

There is grave danger that those who now espouse a doctrine of "conscience" (within the framework of a Situationsethik), which is remarkably like that principle of authority proclaimed by Storch, Zwilling, and Stübner, will—in challenging a reactionary restoration in the establishments—simply succeed in casting the whole encounter falsely; i.e., between a corrupted church and no church at all. What is needed is a clear-cut apologetic and witness along the lines of the Anabaptists rather than the *Schwärmer;* i.e., the people of God, bound by covenant and nought else, ruled by the Holy Spirit and no other.

This witness is a testimony both to the nature of the true church and to the vision of Christian discipleship. It is a brotherly enterprise, and not individualistic. It grows out of the life "under the Lordship of Christ in a covenant of discipleship"; out of "a brotherhood of love in which the fullness of the Christian life ideal is to be expressed."[35] This is the Christian life which Harold S. Bender has done so much to cast in its proper setting through historical research; viz., Christian administration and statesmanship, the ministry of the Word, love of the brethren and their Risen Lord.

35 Harold S. Bender, "The Anabaptist Vision," *MQR* (April 1944) 18:79, 87.

134

The Anabaptist Vision of Discipleship

From time to time the Christian church asks the question: What is the essence of Christianity? By essence is meant the central and all-important reality under which all other realities of faith and life are subsumed. This basic question arises especially during times of religious and social revolution.

Historically Christianity has considered its message around one aspect of the apostolic witness and then another. For example, the Greek Orthodox church has regarded Christianity in its encounter with Hellenism primarily as the ontological bridge between time and eternity. The Incarnation of the Word has been considered the most significant fact of faith. The Roman church, on the other hand, has been concerned primarily with the problem of sin for which a sacramental solution has been sought. The mass has assumed so central a position that the essence of Christianity according to Catholicism is sacramentalism. When it comes to Lutheranism, the preponderant emphasis has been placed upon man's alienation from God through his violation of the divine law. In this context Christianity has been regarded essentially as the experience of forgiveness. Around these pivotal points great Christian cultures have been built.

In some such way of reasoning, Harold S. Bender declared in the *Anabaptist Vision* in 1943 that for the Anabaptists the essence of Christianity is *discipleship*. Discipleship is said to be "first and fundamental in the Anabaptist vision."[1] Of all the elements that make up Christianity, discipleship is so important that all else is subordinated to it and,

* J. Lawrence Burkholder is Associate Professor of Bible and Philosophy in Goshen College.
1 See p. 42.

in fact, integrated by it. Therefore when we are considering the meaning of discipleship in Anabaptism we are probing at the very heart of the movement. The question which the Anabaptists asked was: What does it mean to follow Christ? Or, what does it mean to submit life in its totality to the claims of the kingdom of God? Their answer to these questions involves a statement of the Anabaptist concept of discipleship.

The fact is, however, that discipleship is one of the most ambiguous words of the Christian vocabulary. Historically almost any kind of life from that of martyrdom to inquisition has passed as discipleship. Kierkegaard observed in his day that everyone regards himself a disciple. The popes, St. Francis, James I, and Menno Simons have been upheld as outstanding examples even though their lives took radically different forms. It seems that every Christian tradition defines discipleship simply in terms of itself. Ultimately this can lead to a kind of relativism which would make the claim that discipleship is the essence of Christianity an empty tautology, a mere begging of the question.

Bender assumes, however, that discipleship implies something very definite. For its logical frame of reference is the life and teachings of Christ and this is precisely the basis for the Anabaptist concept of discipleship. The disciple is one who follows Christ. The term which the Anabaptists used repeatedly was *Nachfolge Christi*. This refers not simply to a life which is connected with the church or spiritually motivated, important as these may be, but one which is externally patterned after the New Testament. The Anabaptist conception of discipleship involves a return to what is considered the earliest and therefore the normative form of Christianity. It is the form implied by Christ's own person and work. It is assumed that the life and teachings of Christ are to be duplicated in principle and in many cases the principle determines the form. Furthermore Christ's message becomes the message of the disciple. The Lord's ministry of preaching and service, His sweeping rejection of social and political structures, His mobility and freedom from cultural attachments, His eschatological outlook, and His love and nonresistance are accepted as normative for all believers. The uniqueness of Anabaptism lies in its conviction that Christianity is much more than reflection upon Christ as the divine Being who has invaded time, and it is more than the appropriation of the benefits of the divine drama of the cross. Christianity is the concrete and realistic "imitation" of Christ's life and work in the context of the kingdom of God.

Negatively, the Anabaptist conception of discipleship stands for the rejection of all historical relativities. Anabaptism tried to cast aside all historical adaptations to the institutions of society which were regarded as a compromise of the pure Gospel. Historically this radical criticism placed them against the very structure of the society of the day and consequently they were frequently mistaken for anarchists. If Anabaptist nonconformity had touched only peripheral matters, the conflict with the Reformers would have been a passing phase. The truth is, however, that Anabaptist theology and the Anabaptist way of life contradicted the fundamental convictions of more than a thousand years of European history. For example, they challenged the very idea of Christendom as an all-embracing cultural synthesis. They sought to replace the *Corpus Christianum* as a socio-political unity with a voluntary nonpolitical reality called the *Corpus Christi*. Their conception of the church as a gathered body of the redeemed, their way of love and nonresistance, their rejection of responsibility for the social and political order, their separatistic depreciation of the forces of cultural synthesis, their pure Biblicism, and their general disregard for the claims of historical continuity made the clash with the culturally entrenched traditions of the Reformation inevitable. In fact, the tension between Anabaptist absolutism and historical realism, including modern democracy, is a permanent implication of this radical type of Christianity.

137

What are some of the outstanding features of discipleship according to the Anabaptist interpretation? Only a few can be mentioned here.

First is obedience to the Great Commission. Franklin H. Littell has given us a most illuminating account of the missionary enterprise of the Anabaptists in his volume entitled *The Anabaptist View of the Church.* He says that "no words of the Master were given more serious attention by His Anabaptist followers than His final command: 'Go ye therefore, and teach all nations, baptizing them in the name of the Father, and of the Son, and of the Holy Ghost: teaching them to observe all things whatsoever I have commanded you . . . .' "[2] The evangelical Täufer became effective evangelists who went into the highways and along the "hedges," preaching. Most significant were their assumptions that a great "Christian" culture, after a thousand years of Christian teaching, needed to hear the Gospel and that the responsibility of witnessing was not the professional task of a particular class of Christians. According to the Anabaptists, the Great Commission followed baptism and therefore it became the task of every believer. This was a revolutionary idea which if practiced generally would soon change the face of Christendom.

One significant implication of the Great Commission is the conception of the Christian calling or "vocation" according to which all cultural aims are subordinated to the missionary task. All concerns of life such as family, occupation, guild, education, political responsibility, all the elements of civilization to which men give themselves, are either subordinated or eliminated. Theologically this represents a judgment as to how far the natural order may lay claim on the Christian. A general characteristic of Anabaptism is its preoccupation with the purely redemptive processes. The orders of creation (*Schöpfungsordnungen*) are acknowledged but they are left to Providence while the Christian devotes his energies to the preaching of the Word. No necessary moral

2 Franklin H. Littell, *The Anabaptist View of the Church* (American Society of Church History, 1952) 94.

dualism between redemption and creation is implied, and certainly the Anabaptists were not ascetics. Marriage was considered sacred, and honest work was sometimes exalted. Nevertheless, as between the socially unsettling mobility of itineracy and the stability of the "station," the Anabaptists instinctively chose the former. They saw themselves in the line of Abraham, who "went out not knowing whither he went." They accepted as normative the "insecurity" of faith with Jesus who had no place to lay His head and with the disciples who were called upon to "take no thought for the morrow." Their first command was to "go." The natural demands of home and occupation were frequently regarded as "worldly concerns." Seldom in history has the issue of security been so heroically faced. Many references in Anabaptist literature speak of long periods of separation between husband and wife and, of course, severe persecution added to the anxiety of family responsibility.

The significance of the Great Commission for the Christian's vocation stands out most clearly when compared with the Reformation view. Luther reinterpreted the medieval idea of the Christian "calling" so as to give the work of the world high religious significance. He overthrew monasticism by shifting the locus of discipleship roughly from the order of redemption to the order of creation. He moved discipleship into the secular world. He divided the secular realm into "callings," "offices," and "ranks." The three main groups of orders within the secular realm were the family, the government, and the empirical church. After the pattern of the three persons of the Trinity, the family (*Hausstand*) was first, the political and secular authority was second, and the Christian ministry third.[3] It is notable that Luther made the family first, for he regarded this as the basic institution of society. In fact, it may be said that Luther's entire social philosophy was designed to reinforce the family. The stability of the family was the temporal goal of the divine order of creation.

---

3 Cf. George W. Forell, *Faith Active in Love* (New York, 1954) 122-23.

Governments were intended to maintain law and order so that the family could live in peace. Thus Christian discipleship was conceived largely in terms of what makes for a stable social order rather than, as in the case of the Anabaptists, that which advances a new and different order called the kingdom of God. As between staying at home and being a good Christian father or mother within a settled religio-social system and going from village to village to preach the Gospel of repentance, Luther's conservative and socially responsible attitude emphasized the former. The latter was interpreted to mean social revolution, whereas Luther's real interests lay in reinforcing traditional patterns by the broadest conceivable diffusion of Christian graces.

To Luther the divine calling was the "station" in which one finds himself. He considered no occupation wrong if it is integral to civil life. This included even the magistracy and the military. Although Luther was far more realistic about the incongruities of retributive justice and love than Calvin, both accepted political and military offices as appropriate callings for the disciple. In fact, Calvin held that "civil magistracy is a calling not only holy and legitimate, but by far the most sacred and honorable in human life."[4]

The differences between the Reformers and the Anabaptists become utterly irreconcilable at this point. Calvin elevated the magistracy to the highest position in society while the authors of the Schleitheim Confession placed this office "outside the perfection of Christ." What Calvin held to be the most sacred profession, the Anabaptists held appropriate only for the heathen. The basis for Calvin's appreciation of the magistracy is its necessity. "The exercise of civil polity . . . is equally as necessary to mankind as bread and water, light and air and far more excellent."[5] Thus he derived his conception of discipleship in this and other instances from an analysis of civil society and the needs of public life, which he put on a

4 John Calvin, *Institutes of the Christian Religion*, IV, xx, 4 (Seventh American Edition, Philadelphia, 1936) 2:775.

5 *Ibid.*, IV, xx, 3; 2:774.

par with natural necessities of bread and light. Behind his conception of discipleship lay a vision of the kingdom which includes public life in its totality. The Anabaptists, on the contrary, oriented their conception of discipleship in a kingdom which while historical is not of this world. Discipleship was confined to life within the committed community of believers which could theoretically exist without serious political involvement.

It may be added parenthetically that the tension between missionary mobility and biological and cultural needs such as family, security, and community inevitably tempered many an original Anabaptist enthusisam. The problems of Christianity and culture seem to appear even among those who renounce responsibility for the total order. As the Anabaptists settled in more permanent forms of existence some of the conflicts which confronted the Reformers appeared to the Anabaptists also, even though on a smaller scale and in a nonpolitical context. Possibly the Hutterites were among the most successful in doing justice to both nature and grace by regarding the colony as a base of operation for the support of bands of missionaries who preached and organized new communities. The community of Jacob Hutter was in many respects a training school for Christian witnesses. Historically, however, the Mennonite church has tended to emphasize the virtues of social stability more than the merits of evangelistic mobility. In fact, the Mennonites have tended to interpret the calling more and more in Lutheran terms along with cultural entrenchment. The radical sayings of Jesus which, for example, would have the disciple "hate" his father, mother, sisters, and brethren for the sake of the kingdom, were gradually exchanged for the commandments which supported the established community, not the least of which was Paul's statement: "But if any provide not for his own, and especially for those of his own house, he hath denied the faith, and is worse than an infidel." In defense of the Mennonites, however, it may be said that they have tried to do something even more difficult than that which was attempted by the medieval monks. They have tried to embody the rigorous ethic of Christ amid the relativities of history while taking the family along. It is one thing to transcend selfish demands apart from filial responsibilities. It is another thing to "take no thought for the morrow" with mouths besides one's own to feed.

Secondly, the Anabaptist vision of discipleship emphasizes love and nonresistance. Anabaptism renounces the sword in all its forms. This applies most dramatically to the institution of war. It was utterly impossible for the Anabaptists to reconcile the love of God as demonstrated in His redemptive work in the cross of Christ with the hatred and pride of mortal combat. It is well known, however, that Anabaptists were not political pacifists. It was a pacifism limited in scope to the personal life of the Christian and the corporate life of the church. The Anabaptists had no vision of a warless world. This was not their goal. Their dark picture of history and their acquaintance with the Biblical realism of Romans 13 enabled them to escape some of the pitfalls of a later liberal pacifist movement. They knew that so far as the world is concerned social sin requires political restraints and punishments. The sword in some of its forms is, in fact, integral to fallen humanity. In this respect the Anabaptists were far from utopian. But it is important to remember that Anabaptists would have no part in the processes of the restraint of evil. This responsibility was left to those "outside the perfection of Christ." The responsibility of the Christian according to Anabaptism is exclusively that of the construction of the new society in which strife has no part.

Obviously the implications of the principle of nonresistance went much further than the rejection of war. It implied a general attitude of social and political indifference and eventually a practical program of withdrawal from certain comprehensive structures of society which were grounded in force. Most notable is the attitude of the Anabaptists toward the office of the magistracy and the rejection of the entire dimension of political life. The problem of the relation of nonresistance to the world order was considered at Schleitheim. Here the absolute ethic of love was held over against all the relativities of society in the sharpest dualistic categories of the two kingdoms:

"Now it will be asked by many . . . whether a Christian may or should employ the sword against the wicked for the defense and protection of the good, or for the sake of love.

"Secondly, it will be asked concerning the sword, whether a Christian shall pass sentence in worldly disputes and strife as unbelievers have with one another.

"Thirdly, it will be asked concerning the sword, shall one be a magistrate if one be chosen as such?"

Schleitheim responds to the questions listed above as follows:

"Christ teaches and commands us to learn of Him, for He is meek and lowly of heart and so shall we find rest to our souls.

"Christ did not wish to decide or pass judgment between brother and sister in the case of the inheritance, but refused to do so. Therefore, we shall do likewise.

"They wished to make Christ King, but He fled and did not view it as the arrangement of His Father. Thus shall we do as He did, and follow Him, and so shall we not walk in darkness. For He Himself says: He who wishes to come after me, let him deny himself and take up his cross and follow me."[6]

There can be no doubt that the extreme position of Schleitheim, in so far as it was representative of the Anabaptist position regarding strife, was bound to make any responsible leadership in political affairs a permanent impossibility. If Christ's refusal to arbitrate a dispute over an inheritance is accepted as a principle defining the relationship of the Christian to all the power struggles of the political, social, and economic realm, it is clear that the only consistent position

---

6 Cf. John C. Wenger, "The Schleitheim Confession of Faith," *MQR* (October 1945) 19:250-51.

for the Anabaptist is a radical withdrawal. It means that the disciple cannot address himself responsibly to the problems of social ethics since these problems presuppose the stuff of human egoism. The continuous task of arriving at just divisions of goods and privileges, the balancing of personal and corporate egoism, the punishment of the criminal offense, and the continuous application of law belong to a world for which the Anabaptist's high ethic is not immediately applicable. Mennonite withdrawal, which is sometimes attributed to historical accident or severe persecution, is really the logical inference of absolute nonresistance. The conflicts between this pure ethic of love and the realities of social involvement constitute a real problem to any person or group which accepts this ethic.

It should be pointed out, however, that although the Anabaptists refused to enter into the problems of justice and the enforcement of law together with the vast areas of culture tied up with them, they co-operated with the legal structure in many ways and were grateful for the benefits of law. They accepted the legal provisions for property and contractual obligations. As Biblicists with little knowledge or interest in the tradition of civil law in Europe and the incorporation of political thought with theological thought, they realized that the Christian community which is not of this world nevertheless builds its house within the passing order and to a certain extent out of the materials of the world. Hence Anabaptists assumed their rights and privileges as citizens and entered into the normal exchange of commodities. Generally speaking they did not see any necessary conflict between the ordinary activities of day to day living in a settled social situation and their profession of love. The ordinary ethical presuppositions of civil life were not adequate, however, for the Anabaptist when he encountered what he called evil. When the "peace" was disturbed by some kind of unjust demands or the violation of life and property, the Anabaptist applied an ethic virtually unknown in its purity in social and political affairs, namely, the cross. The principle of absolute nonresistance was always kept close at hand and was made to apply to all situations no matter what the cost. In his response to evil, the Anabaptist ethic comes into its own. It is an ethic of suffering love.

We must remember, however, that the ethic of love and nonresistance was not simply an occasional response to evil. It was a positive force for good which pointed toward a new community of love. Love did not simply demand withdrawal from some of the major functions of society. It called for the creation of a new society where peace and brotherhood would reign. Love was not a mere turning of the cheek from time to time but the creation of a continuous network of relationships in which love was intrinsic. Certainly Anabaptism never arrived at a settled and generally agreed position as to just what kind of society love implied. The forms of social life within Anabaptist communities varied greatly. But all the communities were imperfect realizations of what it means to live together in Christ. The main impulse was to share and to accept each other as brethren—hence such a pre-Hutterite article of faith as the following: "Every brother or sister shall yield himself in God to the brotherhood completely with body and life, and hold in common all gifts received from God."[7] With such a powerful impulse to share, it is no wonder that Anabaptism included within its ranks an experiment in complete community, namely, Hutterianism. Possibly no more ideal concept of corporate life exists. It represents the cleanest break with the system of this world known to Anabaptism. The writer is not unmindful of the fact that the history of Hutterianism is not without its dark pages. The most ideal system does not guarantee the ideal in reality. Nevertheless, if discipleship includes nonresistance and if nonresistance implies an order of love which somehow transcends the social systems of the world, one cannot pass by the Hutterian order of brotherhood lightly.

7 Cf. Robert Friedmann, "The Oldest Church Discipline of the Anabaptists," *MQR* (April 1955) 29:164-66.

In the third place, the Anabaptist vision of discipleship emphasizes suffering in the spirit of cross bearing. The disciple is a heroic sufferer, a member of a race of heroes of the cross who follow Christ to the bitter end. The Anabaptists accepted suffering not as incidental but as essential to discipleship. Baptism is a baptism unto death. Conrad Grebel said: "Wer den Tauf hat, der ist im Tode Christi gepflanzt worden." The words of Jesus, "I have a baptism to be baptized with" (Luke 12:50), were constantly on the lips of the Anabaptist martyrs. Anneken of Rotterdam begins her familiar last words to her son on the day of her martyrdom in typical fashion as follows:

"My son, hear the instruction of your mother; open your ears to the words of my mouth. Behold I go today the way of the prophets, apostles, and martyrs, and drink the cup they have drunk. I go, I say, the way which Jesus Christ . . . Himself went . . . and who had to drink of this cup even as He said, 'I have a cup to drink of and a baptism to be baptized with. And how am I straitened until it be accomplished.' Having passed through He calls His sheep, and His sheep hear His voice and follow Him whithersoever He goes. This way was trodden by the dead under the altar. . . . In this way walked also those who were marked by the Lord."[8]

In his outstanding interpretation of the suffering of the Anabaptists, Ethelbert Stauffer shows that they had a Theology of Martyrdom. Their understanding of history as reflected in numerous writings, particularly the *Ausbund* and the *Martyrs' Mirror,* involves a struggle between the two realms in which the death of Christ is the central event. The people of God must suffer from the very beginning of history to the apocalyptic events of the latter days. In this struggle truth is vindicated. It will be finally victorious. When the church is true to its calling it is a suffering church. With the conversion of Constantine, however, it exchanged its status as a suffering church for that of a persecuting church and therefore

8 Tieleman J. van Braght, *Martyrs' Mirror* (Scottdale, 1951) 453.

lost its status as the true church. The Anabaptists encouraged one another to drink the cup because they were convinced that a deluge of suffering would paradoxically break the power of death.

Possibly the leading motive of discipleship as *imitatio Christi* is no more clearly evident than in their attitude toward the cross. "It is always the sign of the cross under which they understood their fate."[9] Christ was pictured as the one who lived under the cross before He hung on the cross. Christ's passion was an event which was to be repeated because this is the nature of Christianity.

> Gar viele in Unschuld starben
> Wie Christus auch getan.[10]

It is instructive to compare the Anabaptist conception of suffering in the Christian life with that of Luther. At the beginning of the Reformation Luther was seized by the typology of martyrdom, particularly since his own circumstance was not unlike that of a long line of sufferers. However, as time went on and as the state church under his leadership adopted a Constantinian outlook, suffering became increasingly an internal conflict within his own soul rather than a struggle with external foes. Luther follows in the pre-Reformation tradition of *theologia crucis,* but the suffering of the cross is not an external struggle against the enemies of the body who slay with the sword and the fire. It is a suffering of the spirit in the struggle against guilt. The cross for Luther is the cross of submission to the Gospel. It is the inner conflict in which all claims to righteousness are renounced and one throws himself entirely into the hands of the Spirit who can only groan for Christ (Rom. 8:26). "Inner conflict may be said to be the battleground where the decisive final struggle between the law and the Gospel, death and life, Satan and the Holy Spirit is fought. Therefore the place where we may

9 Ethelbert Stauffer, "The Anabaptist Theology of Martyrdom," *MQR* (July 1945) 19:195.
10 *Ausbund,* 382. Quoted in Stauffer, *loc. cit.,* 196.

learn to know the Holy Spirit is in the school of inner conflict."[11]

The struggles of the Anabaptists, on the other hand, were struggles against outer foes. The "warfare of the cross" was the warfare between the company of a good conscience and the company of the Antichrist, whose diabolical weapons were made of steel. The issue with Luther was guilt. Subject to attacks (*Anfechtungen*) of conscience, he struggled to surrender his guilt to God's mercy. The issue with the Anabaptists, on the other hand, was physical torture and death. They were conscious of their election as God's sheep.

Finally, the Anabaptist vision of discipleship included the separated life of holiness. If Luther rediscovered the Biblical doctrine of faith, the Anabaptists rediscovered the Biblical call to holiness. They assumed that to follow Christ meant putting away all the works of darkness including lewd conversation, pride, drunkenness, and fornication. That they actually attained a high quality of life is evident from many testimonies. Their moral standards were really a prime source of appeal. The rapid spread of Anabaptism may be attributed considerably to the desire of a goodly number of people, as in the time of the early church, for a thorough reformation of morals. Anabaptism spoke to the need for a new life full of the fruits of repentance.

For the Anabaptists rebirth implied a life of separation from the world. Separation took many forms and operated on many levels. The moral and spiritual condition of the Anabaptists was supported by the discipline of the brotherhood. The importance of discipline for the Anabaptist conception of discipleship can hardly be exaggerated. Although it turned out to be a disastrous source of division in the history of the church, it was conceived originally in the highest interests of mutual encouragement in the serious struggle against the powers of darkness.

11 Regin Prenter, *Spiritus Creator*, Tr. by John M. Jensen (Philadelphia, 1953) 208.

One could go on to describe other important aspects of the Anabaptist vision of discipleship but space does not permit. However, a few words must be devoted to an evaluation of this view. Certainly anyone acquainted with the most obvious elements of Biblical Christianity cannot help recognizing authentic Christian elements in Anabaptism regardless of his point of view. If the kingdom of God is the theme of the Bible and if such realities as repentance, righteousness, love, peace, brotherhood, sacrifice, eschatological hope, and triumphant faith lie at the center of the Christian faith, Anabaptism may be recognized as a most serious attempt to recapture the center. Few have placed greater emphasis on the primary demands of obedience and few have taken more seriously the absolute authority of Christ. Anabaptism has stood for heroic Christianity in the tradition of the early church.

It is a well-known fact, however, that the Christian church as a whole has rejected this conception of Christian discipleship. It has been rejected not only by careless men but by men who have earnestly sought God's will. In fact, the general conception of Christianity espoused by the Anabaptists has been held only by fringe groups and monastic orders since around the third century. Why is it that the most simple and obvious implications of following Christ have not been upheld regularly and uncompromisingly by the church for all of its members? Why does the church even encourage its members in certain instances to fight?

The answer seems to lie mainly in the realm of social responsibility. The church has not known how to correlate the demands of the kingdom with the demands of world order. It has not known what to do about the historical order since Christ did not return to earth in the first century as some expected. The church has not known how to face the problems of culture, the complexities of economic life, and the prevention of social chaos with the Gospel ethic alone. It has never known how to correlate the social responsibilities of a Christian majority with the ethic of complete love. It has

149

not been able to translate the personal ethics of discipleship into a social ethic embracing the structures of human society. And so the church has asked the question whether the pattern of discipleship described in the New Testament is the only one which corresponds to God's will. It has asked whether love may not take "strange" forms for the sake of the social good. It has asked whether love does not demand the restraint of evil and whether it would not be better to have Christian rulers than pagan ones even though recognizing the ambiguity of the political office. It has asked whether the church should not embrace a relative ethic such as the *Lex Naturae* of the Stoics by grafting it upon the Ten Commandments. It has asked whether the universal elements of the Gospel do not warrant the penetration of all social structures with the Christian spirit even though love must take legal forms of justice. Ironically, if the church had failed in its outreach during the first few centuries the problem of its involvement and responsibility for the social and political structures, with the consequent shift in theological and practical emphasis, would not have appeared. It was the success of the pre-Constantinian church which led to the "fall of the church" during subsequent periods.

The answer of Anabaptism to the Constantinian church was theoretically clear. Discipleship demands a return to a disciplined and socially separated church of true believers. It demands complete withdrawal from the relativities of the passing order. It means a new social order living eschatologically in accordance with the "new age." This answer has been clearer in theory, however, than in practice. It has been clearer theologically than sociologically. It has seemed more likely for small minorities than for majorities. It has been clearer to the first generation of Anabaptists than to their descendants. It has seemed more reasonable in a political order conducted by a nobility than in a democracy in which everyone is theoretically responsible for the political order. It has rung clear in conditions of poverty; but in prosperity it has been mixed with other considerations.

150

The Anabaptist concept of discipleship involves the fundamental dilemma of Christianity in a sinful world. How can Christianity penetrate history without being choked by social, economic, and political forces which do not move on the level of the Gospel? The disciple is theologically and existentially committed to Christ and His way of unqualified love, but any realistic understanding of culture with its power polarities raises the difficult problem of how Christ's ethical absolutism can be positively related to the world as we know it to be. The question assumes critical importance today as certain traditional methods of withdrawal are commonly considered no longer possible or desirable. This is particularly disturbing to those who try to be open to the full force of Christ's demands and yet who are at the same time sensitive to involvement in the ambiguities of society.

✠ J. D. GRABER ✠

Anabaptism Expressed in Missions and Social Service

In sixteenth-century Anabaptism there was no organized mission or service program. This does not mean that there was no sense of mission, nor that this sense of mission did not find effective expression. In this twentieth century we are so accustomed to thinking in terms of organization and program that we are apt to confuse the spiritual reality with the external expression of it. For example, the Russian Baptist delegation which visited America in 1956 informed us that the Baptist Church in Russia is not permitted to have her own schools, engage in social service programs, or hold public evangelistic meetings outside the church building itself. Does this mean that the church in Russia is therefore not a true church, not evangelistic, and without means of expressing Christian love and brotherhood? No, the exact opposite is the case. There is every indication that the Baptist Church in Russia is a strong, vital, and growing church. She is short on external program but long on inner vitality.

In 1956 an Anglican bishop from China, reporting to a committee in London, expressed similar convictions regarding the church in China. The following is a summary of his statement as given in religious news releases:

"The relation of the Church with God. He quoted the saying of Pascal, 'The blessed state of the Church is to be dependent on God alone.' Christians in China had not been prepared for the events of 1949, and as all supporting agencies were withdrawn they were forced back on God alone. The whole environment of the Church had certain existential

* J. D. Graber is Assistant Professor of Missions in Goshen College Biblical Seminary and Executive Secretary of the Mennonite Board of Missions and Charities.

152

qualities—vague Christianity was no help. In this new situation Chinese Christians have come to know Christ as the center of history and their hope is in His Kingship. To believe in this Kingship does not mean that the Church quests power. On the contrary the Church has surrendered its crutches one after the other. Judged by human standards the Church without its supporting medical and educational institutions looks weaker, but in reality is stronger."

The early church was in an exactly similar situation. An unfriendly government designated the church as a subversive organization and made all Christian activity illegal. There were innumerable seemingly crippling handicaps and restrictions and yet the church showed great vitality and rapid growth. There was very little by way of evangelistic or service programs but a great deal of evangelism and mutual burden bearing. In circumstances such as that in which the church of the first three centuries, as well as the Anabaptist church of the sixteenth century found herself, and in the circumstances in which the church in Russia and China finds herself today, all that is superficial is shorn off leaving only that which is of the true essence. Faith, worship, fellowship, witness, service—these are the irreducible elements of the church of Jesus Christ which become obvious in times of stress and severe repression. These may be called the elements of the true church, and these are the very characteristics that were most prominent in the Anabaptist church of the sixteenth century.

But we are not discussing the nature of the church as such. We are to examine here mainly the mission and service emphasis and expression of this Reformation period church. Yet the mission of the church can only be understood in terms of the concept of the church. The meaning of the church and the mission of the church are in a real sense interdependent if not identical. The Reformers did not see eye to eye on the meaning of the church which they brought into being in revolt against the Catholic state church. There was, moreover, a considerable confusion among the Anabaptists themselves during the first decade or two until the more revolutionary and radical fringe elements were separated out and the central core of main line Anabaptism more clearly emerged. The Reformers (Luther, Zwingli, Calvin, etc.) still conceived of the church in the pattern of the Middle Ages. "Religion was a certain phase of a civilization, controlled and bordered by the agreement of princes. The Reformers generally held that the Great Commission was binding only upon the New Testament Apostles, while the Anabaptists (*Täufer*) made it fundamental to their whole attack."[1]

Charles W. Ranson, Secretary of the International Missionary Council, evaluates the situation thus: "The churches of the Reformation, despite their firm adherence to the apostolic faith, failed to disengage themselves from the divisive nationalism of the time. They became entangled in the complexities and conflicts of the rising nation states in which they were set, and the vision of the church universal—one, holy, and apostolic—was dimmed. And as the vision of the church's oneness faded, the sense of world mission receded. Contemporary Protestantism still bears the marks of an incomplete Reformation."[2]

The fundamental concepts of evangelical Anabaptism made the movement universal, i.e., unhampered by national or territorial limitations. Franklin H. Littell writes: "The gathering of small congregations by believers' baptism went on apace, and Anabaptism spread in many areas closed to the state churches by their acceptance of the principle of territorialism. The Anabaptists represent thereby an early Protestant vision of a world mission unrestricted by territorial limitations, and in a unique fashion foreshadow the later concept of the Church as a community of missionary people."[3]

Quite apart from the binding nature of the Great Commission itself (which will be discussed later), because of the

---

1 Franklin H. Littell, *The Anabaptist View of the Church* (American Society of Church History, 1952) 32.
2 Charles W. Ranson, *That the World May Know* (Friendship Press, 1953) 67.
3 Littell, 32.

acceptance of the authority and centrality of the Bible in the life of the church, the evangelistic (missionary) motivation of the Anabaptists lay in their concept of the nature of the church. They considered the state church as the "fallen church" and understood their mission to be that of the restitution of the true apostolic church. The eschatological element could not be kept out of this concept, particularly as persecution grew and death sentences multiplied. The movement assumed something of an apocalyptic quality, and the church of now became but the prototype of the church universal which was to be consummated at the return of Christ to the earth. The church thus became not merely universal geographically but also temporally in that the present church was understood to be in direct continuity with the true church to be revealed and established at His coming, i.e., that the end was begun in their movement. The Apostle Paul gave expression to this perspective of eternity when he prayed (Eph. 3:15) ". . . of whom the whole family in heaven and earth is named."

"The Restitution of the True Church was full of meaning on the world map. The Anabaptists believed that they were forerunners of a time to come, in which the Lord would establish His people and His Law throughout the earth. Both revolutionaries and *Stille* had this vision of approaching fulfillment, although their understanding of the details differed greatly."[4]

Without a doubt this eschatological element in the concept of the church was a strongly motivating force in witness and evangelism during these early and dangerous years. The nerve of missionary endeavor is cut when we cease to believe in a new world to come, when we lose our sense of destiny, our sense of being directly in God's stream of history pressing forward to fulfillment in the coming of His kingdom. We may be pessimistic about the present social and political order; so were the Anabaptist founders. Our hope is

4 *Ibid.*, 94.

not in the reforming or refining of the present order. We live in ecstatic anticipation of God's new order which He will establish in His own time and by His own method. A mere blind obedience to the Great Commission or a mere sense of duty to snatch some "brands from the burning," based on an individualistic concept of the Christian faith, is like wood on the altar that has not yet caught fire. To be conscious of standing within a stream that moves forward to a glorious consummation by the mighty power of God alone, of such faith and conviction are ever born the flaming evangels and the singing martyrs.

This is a world view which we as the modern exponents of Anabaptism have largely lost. I cannot refrain from quoting Littell's criticism of our present-day church life:

"When we survey both historically and dogmatically the ways of 'nestling back into the world,' we are forced to the conclusion that cultural enclaves which have lost their missionary passion and sense of a new world to come are hardly more true to original Anabaptism than those who have acclimated themselves to commerce and warring. For the 'evangelical *Täufer*' linked their suffering nonresistance to the evangel of Him who commanded, 'Go ye into all the world . . .' (Matt. 28:19), and they had great expectations concerning a time to come. They were certain that after the long centuries of the Dispersion they were gathering together again the faithful people of the Lord, to be His blessed community and to live the life for which He gave precept and example. And in that restored community there dwelt the promise of great things to come on earth."[5]

THE GREAT COMMISSION

One of the cardinal principles of evangelical Anabaptism was the acceptance of the Bible as the authoritative word of God. The Great Commission was given to be obeyed; naturally, so clear-cut a command of Christ, five times repeated in

5 *Ibid.*, 93.

the Gospels and in the Acts, must be taken seriously. It is strange how the Reformers explained away its significance by declaring that it applied only to the apostles and was no longer binding after the apostolic age. Ranson, in discussing this aspect of the missionary problem, writes:

"The paradox of the Protestantism of the Reformation era is that while it called the Church back to its apostolic faith it was largely content to leave the fulfillment of the apostolic mission to the church of Rome. The leaders of the Protestant Reformation were too busy with their domestic concerns to give thought to a world mission. This strange silence of the Reformers may be explained but can hardly be excused. They were engaged in a titanic struggle for the soul of the church. They were seeking a recovery of apostolic Christianity. But this very fact only renders more puzzling their blindness to a universal missionary obligation. The Reformation, seen as a return to apostolic Christianity, was at this point seriously incomplete.

"The prevailing view with regard to foreign missions at the beginning of the Protestant era was that the command to preach the Gospel to all nations was given only to the original apostles and expired with them. This view was to persist within Protestantism for three centuries and more."[6]

This author has correctly assessed the views of the great Reformers, for the sources make frequent reference to this method of explaining away the Great Commission of our Lord. Ranson, however, has typically ignored the Anabaptist acceptance of the Lord's last command to evangelize the whole world because the standard references to the Anabaptist movement over the centuries have been disparaging and unfriendly; and it is only in comparatively recent years that church historians are trying to set forth the Anabaptist movement in a more understanding and sympathetic light.

It is clear from the record that although the Reformers sidestepped the Great Commission the radical reformers did

6 Ranson, 65.

not do so. There had been from time to time organized groups in the state church which strove to fulfill Christ's command for world evangelism, notably the Franciscans; but the Anabaptists were among the first to make the Great Commission binding not merely on the leaders but upon all church members.[7] It appears that a promise to heed the command of the Lord to make disciples of all people generally was made a part of the baptismal vow when members were admitted into the "true church." Citing as authority the historian C. A. Cornelius, John Horsch writes:

"In Catholic countries, where Protestantism was persecuted, the field was left entirely to the Anabaptists who did not shrink from dangers of torture and death. Pilgram Marpeck in 1532 said of the preachers of the state church, that they preached only in places to which the protection by the Protestant government extended 'and not freely under the cross of Christ.' . . . Menno Simons in his writings says repeatedly that he was constrained in conscience, through love to God and the unsaved, to risk his life in the endeavor to spread the evangelical truth."[8]

It is to be regretted that this early Anabaptist acceptance of the binding nature of the Great Commission was lost, especially by the Swiss and German Brethren, the ancestors of our earliest Amish and Mennonite communities. It is beyond the scope of this paper to discover just when and for what reason this came about; but it is a fact that until near the end of the nineteenth century, and much later in many quarters, the Great Commission of our Lord was almost totally ignored. It is strange that the standard rationalization for this "blind spot in orthodoxy," regularly put forth as an excuse by the great Reformers, in time became the usual stock in trade of our Mennonite and Amish forebears; viz., that Christ gave the command to make disciples of all people to the apostles only.

7 Littell, 96.
8 John Horsch, *Mennonites in Europe* (Scottdale, Pa., 1942) 315.

It is interesting to note that William Carey, the first leading light in what may be called the modern Protestant missionary movement, was constrained to meet this age-worn excuse. He published in England, in 1792, *An Enquiry into the Obligations of Christians to Use Means for the Conversion of the Heathen.* He began his historic survey with a section entitled "An enquiry whether the commission given by our Lord to His disciples be not still binding on us."

Ranson, in commenting on his matter, says: "The first point in Carey's crisp and devastating argument was that if the command of Christ to teach and baptize all nations was given only to the apostles, then the reasons for the administration of baptism as well as for the world-wide mission have expired with them. This ringing challenge marked the beginning of a new era in the post-Reformation history of the church."[9]

The church has far too often made of baptism a piece of dead ritual if not an actual supernatural influence bordering on magic. The Anabaptists did not emphasize baptism as such. The name was given them persistently by their enemies because it "afforded the authorities an issue for suppressing the radicals by force. . . . The radicals wanted to be known only as '*Brüder*' (brethren) or by some other nonsectarian name, and were far indeed from the later insistence on formal precision in ritual. . . . The movement . . . cannot properly be classified in terms of the baptismal rite."[10]

To the Anabaptists the teaching and practice of baptism lay couched within the Great Commission and they did not try to separate the two. A candidate had to be of mature mind before he could believe; and this belief was the only Scriptural ground for baptism they could find. Teaching was to follow baptism in the order laid down in the Great Commission. It appeared at times that the entire controversy with the Reformers turned on this divine order as laid down in the Lord's last command—faith has to precede baptism which is

9 Ranson, 65-66.
10 Littell, x, 29.

to be followed by teaching. With so much weight given to this portion of the command, and so much attention focused on its literal observance, it is natural that the context of the universal authority of Christ and His world-wide purposes as expressed in the definite command to His followers to make disciples of all people should also be unreservedly and enthusiastically accepted. It is difficult for us, with the fuller knowledge of several intervening centuries when our church ignored the Great Commission, to appreciate or to understand with what zeal and sacrifice our earliest forefathers carried out the Lord's last command. Let us examine briefly how this worked itself out in the life of the early Anabaptist church.

EARLY ANABAPTIST MISSIONARIES

We can do no better than first of all look at a quotation from the writings of Menno Simons himself: "In the second place, we desire with ardent hearts even at the cost of life and blood that the holy Gospel of Jesus Christ and His apostles, which only is the true doctrine and will remain so until Jesus Christ comes again upon the clouds, may be taught and preached through all the world as the Lord Jesus Christ commanded His disciples as a last word to them while He was on earth.[11]

"This is my only joy and heart's desire: to extend the kingdom of God, reveal the truth, reprove sin, teach righteousness, feed hungry souls with the Word of the Lord, lead the straying sheep into the right path, and gain many souls to the Lord through His Spirit, power, and grace. . . .[12]

"Therefore, we preach, as much as is possible, both by day and by night, in houses and in fields, in forests and wastes, hither and yon, at home or abroad, in prisons and in dungeons, in water and in fire, on the scaffold and on the wheel, before lords and princes, through mouth and pen, with possessions and blood, with life and death. We have

11 *The Complete Writings of Menno Simons* (Scottdale, 1956) 303.
12 *Ibid.,* 189.

done this these many years, and we are not ashamed of the Gospel of the glory of Christ."[13]

Nor were missionaries conceived of as being the intellectually elite among the brotherhood. Many of the early leaders of the movement were indeed educated men; but it is clear that the command to evangelize was considered binding on all believers. They accepted the view that a personal commitment to the demands of the Lord Christ was the best equipment for a missionary. They said "the craftsman might make a better missioner than the cultured man." They believed that the common man could best witness to common men. "For the Brethren that was honorable and sufficient, and better equipped him to go forth into all lands 'in order to gather the sheep to the Lord' and 'to fish for men' than the wranglings of the philosophers."[14]

The Reformers resisted this "wandering" of the Anabaptists, and condemned the irresponsibility of those who left their families and jobs to become wandering missionaries, content to live on such support as the brethren gave them. From the vantage point of our own denominational "order" it is difficult for us also to appreciate or approve of this quite general tendency of that day to become wandering preachers. But our own instinctive aversion to this type of mission work may have the same root as that of the Reformers: it disturbs the *status quo* and is so terribly unpredictable. Is it possible that our penchant for organizing and regularizing this work of the Spirit is the very thing that cuts the nerve of its effectiveness?

At least the effectiveness of the early Anabaptist "wandering missionaries" is well known. John Horsch writes on this point: "Leonard Bouwens, who had the oversight of the congregations in a large part of Holland and North Germany, kept a list of persons baptized by him. This list is still preserved. It shows that from 1551 to 1582 Leonard Bouwens baptized 10,252 persons. Obviously the greater number of

13 *Ibid.*, 633.
14 Littell, 96.

these were not of Mennonite parentage but were won through special effort put forth by local congregations."[15]

It would be difficult to overemphasize the missionary zeal that characterized these early Anabaptist founders. Persecution was a factor that drove them out into exile and, as with the believers of the first century, they went everywhere preaching the Word. A whole people thus became pilgrims, exiles for Christ, who evangelized and taught "where driven by the hounds of the established order." Persecution drove many of them to Moravia where the great settlements of the Hutterian Brethren were formed, and where the Moravian Brethren became known in later history for continuing their missionary zeal and world-wide outreach when the evangelical Anabaptists were losing their vision.

"The Hutterian Brethren developed one of the most perfect missionary organizations of the time, and strongly underwrote the work in the Tyrol, South Germany, and even in the Netherlands, with personnel and place of refuge. The original Anabaptist impulse survived most vigorously in those congregations which were most missionary."[16]

On August 20, 1527, there was convened what has come to be known as the Martyr Synod. As Littell says, this meeting "could as well be called a Missionary Synod" because here for the first time the land was divided and apportioned "on a grand map of evangelical enterprise." Brethren were sent out to various countries and centers with the express purpose of declaring the Gospel and making disciples. Those attending the Synod represented the outstanding leaders and missioners in the movement and within a few years most of them had died as martyrs. "The fate of an Anabaptist missioner ('agitator' in Christendom) was usually sealed without trial or hearing."[17] His lot when apprehended was summary execution, often accomplished by excruciating and horrible tortures. Thus these early missionaries demonstrated through

15 Horsch, 315, 316.
16 Littell, 106.
17 *Ibid.*, 101-2.

their life and by their death that they believed the church to be a "voluntary association of committed pilgrims," without racial or territorial boundaries, pilgrims on their way to join that great company which no man can number, of every tongue and nation, gathered around the throne of God.

MUTUAL AID

History records that executioners who carried out sentences of death against Christians during the early Christian centuries used to remark, "How they love one another." And this testimony of mutual love led many of them to lay down their swords and join the "despised community." Jesus said: "By this shall all men know that ye are my disciples if ye love one another" (John 13:35). It was likewise proved over and over that concern for the needs of the brethren was a cardinal virtue of the Anabaptist fathers.

In the first place they believed and practiced a vigorous stewardship of possessions. John Horsch reports: "In 1557 a member of the established Protestant church of Strasburg in Alsace visited a meeting of the Swiss Brethren near that city. A number of persons were being received into the Church by baptism on that occasion. Among the questions addressed to the applicants before the ordinance was administered was this, Whether they, if necessity required it, would devote all their possessions to the service of the brotherhood, and would not fail any member that is in need, if they were able to render aid."[18]

Hans Leopold, who suffered martyrdom in 1528 at Augsburg, said of the Brethren that "if they know of anyone that is in need, whether or not he is a member of their church, they believe it their duty, out of love to God, to render him help and aid." Horsch also reports that "Heinrich Bullinger in his work against the Swiss Brethren made the charge that they were of the opinion that to be rich is inconsistent with Christian principles (*rych syn sye böss*)."[19]

18 Horsch, 317-18.
19 *Ibid.*, 319.

The dominating "pilgrim and stranger" setting of the Anabaptist church naturally developed this spirit of mutual brotherhood aid. It is a strange psychology that makes us more willing to share out of our penury and extremity in a time of persecution and danger than to share out of our abundance in times of peace and security. A man with only two coats is somehow more willing to give one away than would be a man with many coats. If I have nothing more than a crust of bread I gladly break it in two to share it with someone else in need; but to forego one meal in a day when we are all overfed is more difficult. This explains in part the readiness of the sixteenth-century Brethren to share gladly all that they had. But it does not explain away the tact that they were motivated in their mutual aid by the command and spirit of the Gospel. The extremity of their situation only made it easier for them than the prosperity and security of our own times do for us.

A pamphlet entitled *Mennonite Relief Service,* published by the Mennonite Central Committee in 1945, lists many instances of Mennonite relief and mutual aid from the very beginning of the Anabaptist movement. Here reference is made to one group of Anabaptists in Moravia who separated themselves from others because the latter did not measure up to the standard with respect to nonresistance and mutual aid:

"This group departed from Nikolsburg in 1528 because they felt unable to worship with the Anabaptists there who did not practice nonresistance and because 'they do not open their homes to the pilgrims and refugees from other countries.' In the village of Bogenitz they chose 'ministers of temporal needs,' who 'spread a cloak before the people, and every one laid down on it his earthly possessions unconstrained and with a willing mind according to the teaching of the prophets and apostles.' This action was in conformity with their doctrine as Swiss Brethren that Christians were stewards of all their possessions."[20]

20 M. C. Lehman, *Mennonite Relief Service: the History and Principles of Mennonite Relief Work, An Introduction* (Akron, Pa., 1945) 9-10.

There are other instances of aid given by the Dutch Mennonites: to a shipload of stranded Reformed refugees from England in 1553; relief to the victims of the Huguenot persecutions in 1685; aid to the victims of persecution that swept over the Mennonites of the Palatinate in 1690; and many other similar instances. Help was given to the Schwenkfelders as they passed through Holland on their way to America, after being driven from their home in Germany. The passage money to America was advanced to them in full. After some years when the Schwenkfelders in America returned the advanced funds to the Mennonites in Holland they refused to accept them and sent them back. The amount was then placed in a relief fund which is in operation to the present day among the Schwenkfelders of Eastern Pennsylvania.

CONCLUSION

From the foregoing glimpses of the Anabaptist concept of world mission and mutual aid we can draw the following conclusions:

1) The meaning and the mission of the church are interrelated and interdependent concepts.

2) The strength of a church and the effectiveness of its witness are not dependent upon its institutional programs.

3) The true church is in direct continuity with the consummation of the kingdom of God, and the true church here is the beginning of the end.

4) This eschatological hope, the coming and fulfillment of the kingdom, in God's own time and manner, is a powerful motivation to world-wide missionary effort.

5) The church is universal, not hemmed in by national or territorial limitations.

6) The Bible is authoritative in the life of the believer and of the church and for this reason the Great Commission, even as the Sermon on the Mount, is binding on all believers and on every congregation.

7) Baptism has its chief significance, not as ritual, but in the context of God's purpose of universal discipleship.

8) The believer is but a steward of all he possesses and is willing to dedicate everything which he has to meet human need both within and outside the church.

9) The true church is a voluntary association of committed pilgrims. This concept brings under judgment our present-day denominational life in so far as it is a mere cultural enclave that has lost its missionary passion and sense of a new world to come.

✛ JOHN C. WENGER ✛

The Biblicism of the Anabaptists

I

The Anabaptists were distinguished by a diligent study of the Scriptures from the moment of their conversion. Harold S. Bender says: "From the court records of the Anabaptists who were seized at the beginning of the Reformation era it is at once evident that they possessed an amazing knowledge of the Bible."[1] Amazing is not too strong a word, for the fact is that untrained lay brethren often proved more than a match for the Roman Catholic doctors of theology who interrogated them. So overwhelming was this proficiency in the Scriptures that it was sometimes explained as being due to demon possession.[2]

This knowledge of the Scriptures was not confined to any particular Biblical book, and not even to the New Testament. Indeed the earliest Anabaptist sermon which has been preserved (1527) is that of Eitelhans Langenmantel on Jeremiah 7:3, 4 and 9:8, a sermon which sounded a call for repentance and reformation of life. Langenmantel was beheaded the next year without trial, although he was a patrician of Augsburg. It is of course true that the Anabaptists did devote more intense study to the New Testament than to the Old. "I hope to be able to learn one hundred chapters of the Testament by heart," declared an Anabaptist in a sixteenth-century personal letter.[3] In his *Vermanung* of 1542 the South German Anabaptist elder, Pilgram Marpeck, wrote:

* John C. Wenger is Professor of Theology in Goshen College Biblical Seminary and author of *History of the Mennonites of the Franconia Conference* (Scottdale, 1938), *Glimpses of Mennonite History and Doctrine* (Scottdale, 1947), *Separated unto God* (Scottdale, 1951) and *Introduction to Theology* (Scottdale, 1954).

1 *ME (Mennonite Encyclopedia*, Scottdale, Pa., 1955) 1:322.

2 John Horsch, "An Inquiry . . . ," *MQR* (January and April 1934) 8:18-31; 73-89.

3 *ME*, 1:325.

167

"We would sincerely admonish every Christian to be on the alert and personally to study the Scriptures, and have a care lest he permit himself to be easily moved and led away from Scripture and apostolic doctrine by strange teaching and understanding. But let every one, according to Scripture and apostolic teaching, strive with great diligence to do God's will, seeing that the Word of Truth could not fail us nor mislead us."[4]

As Thomas von Imbroich stood before the court in Cologne about the year 1556 he declared: "The Scripture cannot be broken, nor shall anything be added to or subtracted from the Word. It is God's Word which remains in eternity."[5] Dirk Philips (*c.* 1504-68), the most outstanding colleague of Menno Simons, wrote in his *Vindication:* "From these words it is evident that whatever God has not commanded and has not instituted with express words of Scripture, He does not want observed, nor does He want to be served therewith, nor will He have His Word set aside nor made to suit the pleasure of men. . . ."[6] One of the most accurate descriptions of the Anabaptists is that of Walther Köhler: "The Anabaptists wanted to be Bible Christians, and they were precisely that for the most part."[7]

The earliest confessions of faith of the Anabaptists took the matter of Biblical inspiration and authority for granted, as an investigation will disclose. But the Swiss Brethren confession drawn up in Hesse in 1578 includes the following explicit statement in its very first article:

"We believe, recognize, and confess that the Holy Scriptures both of the Old and New Testaments are to be described as commanded of God and written through holy persons who were driven thereto by the Spirit of God. For this reason the believing born-again Christians are to employ them for teaching and admonishing, for reproof and reforma-

---

4 *MQR* (January 1931) 5:18.
5 *ME*, 1:325.
6 D. Philips, *Enchiridion* (Elkhart, 1910) 151.
7 *ME*, 1:325.

tion, to exhibit the foundation of their faith that it is in conformity with Holy Scripture."[8]

The Swiss Brethren engaged in major theological debates with the Swiss Reformed clergy at Zofingen in 1532 and at Bern in 1538. In these debates the Brethren stated succinctly: "We hold that all things should be proven to ascertain what is founded on the Holy Word of God, for this will stand when heaven and earth pass away, as Christ Himself said."[9]

Harold S. Bender writes of the Anabaptists: "That all members should read the Bible was to them a self-evident duty, and it was often the only book in the home that was steadily used."[10] Indeed, Mennonites throughout their history have fundamentally remained "a people of the Bible."[11] In no writer is this truth more evident than in Menno Simons (*c.* 1496-1561). "All Scripture," declared Menno, "both of the Old and New Testament, rightly explained according to the intent of Christ Jesus and His holy apostles, is profitable for doctrine, for reproof . . . . But whatever is taught contrary to the Spirit and doctrine of Jesus is accursed of God."[12] "Therefore we counsel and admonish all . . . to take good heed to the Word of the Lord. . . ."[13] For Menno the Scriptures are "the true witness of the Holy Ghost and the criterion of your consciences."[14] "Do not depend upon men," cried Menno; "put your trust in Christ alone and in His Word. . . ."[15] For Menno, "the whole Scriptures, both of the Old and New Testament, were written for our instruction, admonition, and correction, . . . they are the true scepter and rule by which the Lord's kingdom . . . and congregation must be ruled and governed."[16] All doctrine and practice must be "measured by this infallible rule."[17]

8 *MOR* (January 1949) 23:27.

9 *ME*, 1:232, 324.

10 *ME*, 1:322.

11 *ME*, 1:324.

12 *Complete Writings* (Scottdale, 1956) 312.

13 *Ibid.*, 62.

14 *Ibid.*, 89.

15 *Ibid.*, 138.

16 *Ibid.*, 159, 160.

17 *Ibid.*, 160.

Since the Anabaptists were so earnestly devoted to the Scriptures it is little wonder that some of them attempted translations of parts of the Bible, this in spite of the fact that they were usually only a few steps ahead of the catchpolls and arresting officers. Perhaps the most important contribution in this area was the translation of The Prophets (1527), a work of which Luther spoke respectfully and of which he made some use in his own translation of the Old Testament. The translators were, to be sure, both fringe figures in the Anabaptist movement, Ludwig Haetzer and Hans Denk, but they did a creditable performance in their book, *Alle Propheten nach Hebräischer sprach verteutscht.* Two examples will indicate how they and Luther sometimes chose different words: In Luther's translation, Isaiah 47:13 speaks of *Sternkucker,* while the Denk-Haetzer version reads *Sternseher;* in Ezekiel 9:7 the Luther translation says *todter Leichnam,* whereas Denk-Haetzer says *Erschlagenen.*[18]

The Froschauer Bible of Zürich (1524-29) followed the Luther translation as a whole, though with slight deviation, except in the Prophets where the Denk-Haetzer version was used. This Froschauer Bible has been much used in Mennonite history. Quite famous in Dutch Mennonite circles was the Bible (many editions were of the New Testament only) printed by the Dutch Mennonite printer Nicholaes Biestkens, a work which enjoyed about one hundred editions, though it was not a Mennonite version. In common with many Christians of the sixteenth century the Anabaptists made more use of the Old Testament Apocryphal books than would be considered proper in Mennonite circles today. Both Pilgram Marpeck and Menno Simons quote from these writings. It is clear that Menno even considered the book of *Wisdom* to be inspired of the Holy Spirit.[19]

II

Not only did the Anabaptists spend much time in studying the Scriptures; they also followed rigorously the principle

18 Christan Hege, *Die Täufer in der Kurpfalz* (Frankfurt a. M., 1908) 22-31.
19 *Complete Writings,* 850.

of *sola scriptura:* only the Bible is to be followed. "It alone," says Bender, "was authoritative for doctrine and life, for all worship and activity, for all church regulations and discipline."[20] The same writer continues:

"The principle of the sole authority of the Bible for faith and life was not an exclusive Anabaptist possession, but rather a foundation principle of all Protestantism beginning with Luther himself, and was established against the Roman Catholic principle that the Bible and the tradition of the church together constitute the authoritative norm. The reformers, however, although emphatically proclaiming the principle, were not uniformly consistent in applying it, being led at times by theological and practical considerations to depart from the strict teaching of Scripture. The Anabaptists, being Biblicists and usually unsophisticated readers of the Bible, not trained theologians or scholars, and having made a more complete break with tradition than the reformers, were more radical and consistent in their application of the principle of sole Scriptural authority."[21]

It was because of this principle of *sola scriptura* that Luther defied the pope, abolished the mass, taught the principle of justification by faith, did away with clerical celibacy, restored the office of preaching to a central place, discarded compulsory fasts and other human regulations, and taught salvation by grace through faith. But he was, in the eyes of the Anabaptists, not consistent with his own principles when he wrote: "It is true that there is not sufficient evidence from Scripture that you might be justified to begin infant baptism at the time of the early Christians after the apostolic period. But so much is evident that in our time no one may venture with a good conscience to reject or abandon infant baptism which has so long been practiced."[22]

In contrast to this statement by Luther, Conrad Grebel

20 *ME*, 1:322.
21 *ME*, 1:323.
22 Weimar Ed., Vol. 26, p. 167. Cited in Horsch, *Infant Baptism* (Scottdale, 1917) 42.

says,[23] "We would ask you to discard the old ordinances of Antichrist, and to hold to the Word of God alone and be guided by it."[24] And as early as 1525 the Brethren wrote to the Zürich city council: "We desire nothing upon earth but to have these things decided according to the Word of God."[25] When Michael Sattler was on trial for heresy (and he was adjudged worthy of death, tortured, and executed), he stated earnestly: "Ye ministers of God, if you have neither heard nor read the Word of God, we would suggest that you send for the most learned men and for the book of the divine Scriptures, and that they with us weigh these things in the light of the Word of God."[26]

The most eloquent defender of the sole authority of the Scriptures, however, was Menno Simons. Space permits only a few sample quotations on the subject. "Nothing may be preached in Christ's kingdom, house, and church except her King and Husband's own commands and words. . . . Christ . . . does not say, preach the doctrines and commands of men, preach councils and customs, preach glosses and opinions of the learned. He says, preach the Gospel. . . ."[27] Against the charge that he taught contrary to the greater part of the doctors and learned men in the history of the church, Menno appealed "to the oldest, most pious, most upright, truest, and most able doctors . . . such as Moses, Isaiah, Jeremiah, David, etc., Christ Jesus, Matthew, Mark, Luke, John, Paul, Peter, James, Jude, etc."[28] "The true evangelical faith sees and considers only the doctrine, ceremonies, commands, prohibitions, and the perfect example of Christ, and strives to conform thereto with all its power."[29] After pleading for a testing of one of his books by the Scripture, Menno adds: "I dare not go higher nor lower, be more stringent or lenient, than the Scriptures and the Holy Spirit teach me; and that out of great fear and anxiety of my conscience lest I once more burden the

23 Chief founder of the Anabaptists. H. S. Bender, *Conrad Grebel* (Goshen, 1950).
24 *ME*, 1:323.
25 *ME*, 1:323.
26 *ME*, 1:323.
27 *Complete Writings*, 165.
28 *Ibid.*, 233.
29 *Ibid.*, 343.

God-fearing hearts, who now have renounced the commandments of men, with more such commandments. Willfulness
and human opinions I roundly hate, and do not want
them."[30]

With evident irritation Oecolampad addressed the Swiss
Brethren: "I know full well that you cry, Scripture, Scripture,
asking us for clear words to prove our teaching. . . . But if
Scripture would teach us all points there would be no need
for the anointing to teach us concerning all things."[31]

III

One of the shopworn charges against the evangelical
Anabaptists is that they depreciated the "outer" (written)
Word in favor of the inner Word. While this charge is true
of such fringe leaders as Hans Denk, the rank and file of the
Swiss Brethren, the Austrian Hutterian Brethren, and the
Dutch "Menists" identified the text of Scripture with the
Word of God.[32] One of the most thorough investigations of
the subject has been made by Wilhelm Wiswedel. After quoting Luther, Melanchthon, Justus Menius, etc., all of whom
bemoan the low estimate of the external Word supposedly
held by the Anabaptists, Wiswedel declares flatly, "But these
charges made against the Anabaptists by no means correspond
to the facts of history."[33] "Do you have Zwingli's word?" cried
the Swiss Brethren of Zürich, "We want God's Word!"[34] It
was on this very point that Marpeck wrote extensively. In his
Verantwortung (*c.*1543-46), addressed to Caspar Schwenkfeld,
he stated pointedly: "We say again that there are not two but
only one Word of God; and the Word of divine, evangelical
preaching (which Schwenkfeld calls the word of the letter)
is truly the Word of the Holy Spirit and of God. For the
Holy Spirit, who is God, has spoken through and out of the

---

30 *Ibid.,* 484.
31 Oecolampad, *Antwort,* sig. J3. Cited by Horsch, *MQR* (January 1931) 5:12,
13.
32 Cf. Horsch, *MQR* (January 1931) 5:17.
33 *ME,* 1:325.
34 *ME,* 1:325.

heart and mouth of the Apostles."[35] Wiswedel says that the Anabaptists "did not separate the inner Word from the outer Word."[36] And John Horsch declares, "The view held by many writers that the Swiss Brethren defended Denk's doctrine of 'the inner word' is an assumption that cannot be substantiated."[37]

For Menno Simons the Scriptures themselves are "the true witness of the Holy Ghost."[38] The text of Scripture is identical with the Word of God. Menno everywhere takes this for granted. He is fond of appealing to the Scriptures at every point as he discusses any question. The "plain, ineffable Word"[39] is his final court of appeal. He admonishes "all true Christians to cling to the Word of the Lord with all the heart, and to hold firmly to His promise."[40] In one of his books, issued in 1558, Menno declaims against the arrogance of human reason: "It has become so perverse, haughty, ignorant, and blind that it dares to alter, bend, break, gainsay, judge, and lord it over the Word of the Lord God."[41]

IV

Just as the evangelical Anabaptists insisted upon the text of Scripture as over against any doctrine of an inner Word, so they also held to *sola scriptura* in contrast with those who would appeal to dreams and visions or other supposed special revelations. In all ages of the church, of course, there have been individuals who claimed to experience miracles of divine providence, special revelations of one kind or another, and the like. The sixteenth century was not particularly critical of divine "voices" and revelations. For example, the story was told of the Lutheran reformer Johannes Brenz, that as the Spanish army approached Stuttgart he was told by an inner voice to take a huge loaf of bread, go to the upper city, enter an open door which he would find, and hide under the

---

35 J. Loserth, *Quellen u. Forschungen. . . . P. Marbecks Antwort. . . .* (Wien u. Leipzig, 1929) 528. Cited by Horsch, *MQR* (January 1931) 5:18.

36 *ME*, 1:327.
37 *MQR* (January 1931) 5:17.
38 *Complete Writings*, 89.
39 *Ibid.*, 81.
40 *Ibid.*, 348.
41 *Ibid.*, 961.

rafters in the attic. This he did, and behold, a hen came and laid two eggs daily until the danger was past and he was free to emerge from his hiding place.[42] Similar stories were told about a few Anabaptists. But the fact is that the Anabaptists as a whole were remarkably free of such claims, holding rather to the written Word of God as their only source of doctrine and religious practice.

R. J. Smithson writes to the point: "One principle which all Anabaptists held was the supremacy of the Scriptures as a rule of faith and practice. To them the Bible was the final authority."[43] As early as 1530 Sebastian Franck wrote: "There arose from the letter of Scripture, independently of the state churches, a new sect which was called Anabaptists. . . . By the good appearance of their sect and their appeal to the letter of Scripture to which they strictly adhered, they drew to themselves many thousand God-fearing hearts who had a zeal for God."[44] Michael Sattler wrote to his congregation of fellow believers at Horb: "And let no man remove you from the foundation which is laid through the letter of the Holy Scriptures, and is sealed with the blood of Christ and of many witnesses of Jesus."[45]

Once again we must turn to Menno Simons, to a writing of 1539: "You see, dearest brethren, I speak frankly with a certain and sure conviction, not by some revelation or heavenly inspiration, but by the express, definite Word of the Lord. From my inmost heart I am convinced that this doctrine is not our doctrine, but the doctrine of Him who sent us, that is, Christ Jesus. All those who are desirous to do His will, will acknowledge that this doctrine is of God and that we do not declare our own invention, dreams, or visions.[46]

"Brethren, I tell you the truth and lie not. I am no Enoch, I am no Elias, I am not one who sees visions. I am no prophet who can teach and prophesy otherwise than what is

42 *MQR* (January 1931) 5:15, 16.
43 R. J. Smithson, *The Anabaptists* (London, 1935) 122.
44 Horsch, *Mennonites in Europe* (Scottdale, 1950) 350.
45 Van Braght, *Martyrs' Mirror* (Scottdale, 1950) 419.
46 *Complete Writings*, 308.

written in the Word of God and understood in the Spirit. (Whosoever tries to teach something else will soon leave the track and be deceived.) I do not doubt that the merciful Father will keep me in His Word so that I shall write or speak nothing but what I can prove by Moses, the prophets, the evangelists and other apostolic Scriptures and doctrines, explained in the true sense, spirit and intent of Christ. . . .

"Once more, I have no visions nor angelic inspirations. Neither do I desire such lest I be deceived. The Word of Christ alone is sufficient for me."[47]

This Anabaptist Biblicism is of course not to be understood as teaching that Christians should take all of the Bible with a kind of bald literalism. Grebel, Menno, and Dirk Philips all speak, for example, of the two sacraments or ordinances which Christ instituted for the church. These Anabaptist writers did not comb the New Testament for statements which could be pulled out of context and made into a code of laws for believers—such as not to carry any money when on a journey (Matt. 10:9, 10). Indeed, one of the finest treatises on Christian liberty is the Anabaptist tract of about 1528, *Von zweyerley gehorsam,* which sets forth beautifully the difference between the Pharisaical bondage of legalism and the freedom of one who sees himself as a child of the heavenly Father.[48]

V

The Anabaptists regarded all the Scripture as the inspired and authoritative Word of God. But they placed a strong emphasis on the preparatory role of the Old Testament. They felt that God's final word was in the New Testament, not in the preparatory dispensation of the Old. They therefore insisted that all doctrine and practice must have New Testament support. Bender interprets the Anabaptist view of the supremacy of the New Testament thus: "For them the Old Testament was not binding in the same sense, and

47 *Ibid.,* 310.
48 *MQR* (January 1947) 21:18-22.

in so far as it disagrees with the New it was superseded and abrogated."[49]

John Horsch puts it this way: "They recognized the fact that the relation of the Old to the New Testament Scripture is that of promise to fulfillment, of type and shadow to reality, of the groundwork of a building to the building itself. . . . The Old Testament Scriptures were the rule of life for pre-Messianic times. The New Testament obligations . . . are more far-reaching and perfect than the Mosaic Law, and whatever of the Old Law is obligatory for the Christian is also taught in the New Testament Scriptures."[50]

Pilgram Marpeck compiled an entire book of over 800 pages, the *Testamentserläuterung* (c.1544), on the theme of the contrast of the two Testaments on a multitude of topics: forgiveness, rest, faith, sword, offerings, etc. The period of the old covenant is called "yesterday," while the era of the new is called "today." It is Marpeck's thesis that the old covenant was one of shadows with no real forgiveness and no real spiritual blessings; it was rather a time of waiting for the redemption that was to come. It was in the contrast between the Testaments that the Anabaptists grounded their two most distinctive ethical emphases; viz., no participation in warfare and bloodshed, and no swearing of oaths, although both warfare and swearing were permitted in the Old Testament. The stressing of the contrast between the two Testaments also weakened for the Anabaptists the Protestant comparison of infant baptism with Jewish circumcision.

And yet the relation of the Old Testament to the New must be seen at least partially as one of fulfillment. Hence Dirk Philips could write: "So then the Gospel and the Law are divided so far as the figures, shadows, and letter of the Law are concerned, which are all done away by the Gospel. But it is essential that we take heed to the spirit of the Law (for the Law is spiritual, as Paul says, Rom. 7:14). We will then find that the signification, purport and real meaning of

49 *ME*, 1:323.
50 *MQR* (January 1931) 5:20, 21.

the Law accords and agrees in every way with the Gospel, yea, that it is one and the same truth."[51] Dirk then relates the physical circumcision of the old covenant to the heart "circumcision" of the new, etc.[52] He laments, however, the confusion which obtains when theologians fail to make the proper distinction between the Testaments:

"The false prophets cover and disguise their deceptive doctrines by appealing to the letter of the Old Testament consisting of shadows and types. For whatever they cannot defend by the New Testament Scriptures, they try to establish by the Old Testament, on the letter of the books of the prophets. And this has given rise to many sects and to many false religious forms. Yea, from this fountain have flowed the sacrilegious ceremonies and pomp of the church of Antichrist [Roman Catholicism] and the deplorable errors of the seditious sects [Münsterites and Batenburgers] which in our day, under a semblance of the holy Gospel of the faith and the Christian religion, have done great injury and cause much offense."[53]

The Hutterian confession of faith of 1545, written by Peter Rideman, states: "Since the old covenant cometh to an end on account of its darkness and imperfection, God hath established, revealed, and brought to light a covenant that is perfect, that abideth unchanged throughout eternity. . . .

"This is the covenant of childlike freedom; of which we also are the children if we let ourselves be sealed by this covenant and submit and surrender ourselves to its working. . . . Those who have not the Spirit are not the children of this covenant."[54]

In opposition to this Anabaptist contrast between the covenants stood the state church theologians with more or less emphasis on the unity of the two covenants, a point of view which furnished logical grounds for the defense of war-

---

51 *Enchiridion*, 260.

52 *Ibid.*, 261.

53 *Ibid.*, 323 (Horsch translation, *Mennonites in Europe*, 356).

54 Rideman, *Account of Our Religion, Doctrine and Faith* (Suffolk, 1950) 67, 68.

fare, the swearing of oaths, the suppression of dissenters by armed force, and even in a case of dire necessity for the justification of the bigamy of Philip of Hesse! In still greater contrast with the evangelical Anabaptists stood the insurrectionists of Münster in Westphalia. This group envisioned an Old Testament theocracy with polygyny, an earthly king, religious wars with hostile earthly governments, and a communism of consumption. The only thing this group had in common with the Swiss Brethren and the Menists was the unfortunate label Anabaptist.

VI

The Anabaptist vision involved a free church of converted people, committed to an earnest discipleship of the Lord Jesus, following the law of love and nonresistant suffering, seeking to be salt and light in a corrupt society which gropes for the light which will bring peace and happiness. The Anabaptists sought to build Christ's kingdom here and now in the fellowship of the church, a fellowship which would exhibit the love, peace, and good will which God desires for the human race. This vision derives from the entire New Testament, not merely from the Sermon on the Mount, although that sermon does set forth beautifully the ideal society of love. For this vision the sixteenth century was not prepared. It saw it, and in some measure understood it, but ultimately destroyed with fire and sword those who held it. Perhaps the twentieth century will also reject this vision, although one would hope that the world would finally learn the futility and sin of human bloodshed and war. In any case God will, we trust, continue to raise up faithful followers of the Prince of Peace to continue this Biblicist tradition.

179

✠ ROBERT KREIDER ✠

The Anabaptists and the State

The Anabaptist view of the state must be studied from two vantage points: from the perspective of the Anabaptists and from the perspective of the civil authorities of the sixteenth century. Historians of the movement have too often failed to search out the minds of those in authority—the official opposition to Anabaptism—who were alternately perplexed and enraged by these dissenters. Our purpose here will be to study the Anabaptist view of the state by attempting, first, to project ourselves into the minds of the opposition and, second, to explore the thinking of the Anabaptists themselves.

The theater of inquiry for this study is German-speaking Switzerland in the first half of the sixteenth century.[1] Genetic aspects of this subject are slighted here because of limitations of space. One must remember, however, that the Anabaptist view of the state was wrought out step by step as this brotherhood of sixteenth-century disciple-apostles sought to bring their lives into conformity with the will of God, fashioning their convictions in the context of prayer, Biblical study, and fellowship, encompassed about by mounting hostility.

THE STATE'S VIEW OF ANABAPTISM

On first appearance it seems most strange that the Anabaptists, who Sebastian Franck declared were "drawing to themselves many sincere souls who had a zeal for God,"[2] were

* Robert Kreider is Dean and Professor of History in Bluffton College.

1 For fuller development of the issues discussed in this paper consult my doctoral dissertation, "The Relation of the Anabaptists to the Civil Authorities in Switzerland, 1525-1555" (unpublished Ph.D. dissertation, University of Chicago, 1953).

2 Sebastian Franck, "Chronica der Römischen Kätzer," Part 3 of *Chronica, Zeytbüch und Geschychtbibel* (Strassburg, 1531) ccccxliiiib.

singled out by the civil authorities of the sixteenth century for the fate of imprisonment, torture, banishment, hanging, drowning. Why were these brethren persecuted? Why did even mild-mannered churchmen like Haller, Capito, and Oecolampadius finally yield, though reluctantly, to the compelling logic of persecution?

A host of reasons were advanced by men in public office to justify the suppression. One must distinguish between the publicly avowed reasons for persecution and the probable real reasons. The essential reasons were few in number. First, the authorities believed that the Anabaptists were dismembering the church, the very body of Christ, and thus shattering the ideal of a unified civil and religious community.[3] The Swiss civil authorities were unprepared to countenance a pluralistic society. Although they had broken with Rome, they were still devoted to the vision—now more narrowly limited to the territorial community—of a *Corpus Christianum*. This concern for complete civic and religious solidarity was heightened by an acute anxiety for the safety of Reformation strongholds in a hostile world of Roman Catholicism. Furthermore, the authorities feared that the Anabaptists were undermining the authority and prestige of the magistracy. These dissenters refused to bear arms. They challenged the accepted belief that a Christian should hold public office. They declined to swear the oath, the sacred symbol of community loyalty. Moreover, the Anabaptists refused so frequently to conform to the commands of the government that the magistrates feared that this civil disobedience would produce an epidemic of contempt for governmental authority.

3 Cf. the Concordat of the cities of Zürich, Bern, and St. Gall against the Anabaptists, August 14, 1527, *Die Eidgenössischen Abschiede aus dem Zeitraume von 1521 bis 1528*, Vol. IV, Part 1a of *Amtliche Sammlung der älteren Eidgenössischen Abschiede*, ed. by Johannes Strickler (Brugg, 1873) No. 470, pp. 1140-43; Ulrich Zwingli, "Wer Ursach gebe zu Aufruhr," *Huldreich Zwinglis sämtliche Werke*, ed. E. Egli *et al.*, III (Vol. XCVIII of *Corpus Reformatorum* [Leipzig, 1936]) 374-469 (hereafter cited as ZW with the volume number of the *Werke* rather than of the *Corpus Reformatorum*); Ulrich Zwingli, *Selected Works of Huldreich Zwingli*, ed. S. M. Jackson (Philadelphia, 1901) 134 (hereafter cited as the *Selected Works of Zwingli*).

The authorities feared, moreover, the missionary expansionism of the movement. They feared what might happen if a large segment of the community became Anabaptist. They were afraid of the effects upon the military establishment, the staffing of the magistracy, the perpetuation of tradition-honored civic customs. Above all they harbored forebodings that a large body of dissent would play havoc with the carefully laid plans for a new reformed state church order.

The authorities could not erase from their minds a gnawing anxiety that this peaceful-appearing movement harbored revolutionary potentialities which might break forth with savage violence at some future time.[4] Such dread was later fanned by reports concerning the Münster revolution. This evil of persecution, it was argued, was the only way to prevent a greater future evil, a revolutionary catastrophe. In addition, the authorities were deeply annoyed by the boldness and forthrightness with which the Anabaptists challenged their political superiors. Officials viewed Anabaptist behavior as insolent, disrespectful of the hierarchical qualities of sixteenth-century society.

Despite these fears and antipathies, many of the civil authorities were prepared to work out a *modus vivendi* with the Anabaptists. They offered immunity from arrest if the Anabaptists would only remain quiet, attend church, baptize their children, and cease to evangelize overtly.[5]

The polemical literature of the time and the mandates of persecution were filled with a variety of other accusations against the Anabaptists. This propaganda offensive became wildly indiscriminate and exaggerated as the struggle against the dissenters was prolonged. The Anabaptists, it was declared, despised orthodox evangelical doctrine. They were accused of being in secret alliance with the Roman Catholics. They were charged with every conceivable kind of immorality: hypocrisy, lewdness, theft, adultery, sexual orgies, mur-

---

4 *Ibid.*, 128, 186, 187, 197, 198 206.
5 Theodore de Quervain, *Kirchliche und soziale Zustände in Bern unmittelbar nach der Einfuhrung der Reformation, 1528-1536* (Bern, 1906) 244.

der.[6] Their enemies called them communists. They were accused of preaching nonpayment of interest, taxes, and other dues imposed by the government. Above all they were "dangerous seditionaries, plotters of rebellion." The annals of the movement in Switzerland provide no evidence supporting these multifarious accusations.

The towns and territories of Switzerland were under no overriding legal compulsion to suppress the Anabaptists. The resolutions of the Swiss diet were legally binding upon member states only when they specifically concurred with particular confederation covenants, as for example, when St. Gall, Bern, and Zürich agreed to the Concordat of 1527. The imperial mandates and recesses of 1528 and 1529, echoing ancient Roman sanctions against heresy and rebaptism, constituted for the Swiss governments a more remote authority for persecution. These imperial and confederate laws confirmed the civil authorities in their prior determination to rid their lands of this nonconformist movement. The primary impetus for persecution, however, came not from the dictates of venerated legal authority so much as from the exigencies of local circumstances.

The Swiss governments resourcefully employed a wide range of methods in their efforts to suppress the Anabaptists. First, they tried the techniques of persuasion: kindly pastoral counseling, learned arguments in public disputations, polemical tracts, vigorous efforts to produce a disciplined state church. These techniques, however, were insufficient to halt the advance of Anabaptism.

Second, they tried the techniques of legal restriction. Almost from the very first appearance of the Anabaptist movement the civil authorities sought to curb the movement by prohibitory restrictions.[7] One of the first measures was simply to ban all unauthorized meetings and all unauthorized preaching. Coupled with this was legislation compelling reg-

6 *Selected Works of Zwingli*, 187.
7 *Zürich*, Vol. I of *Quellen zur Geschichte der Täufer in der Schweiz*, eds. Leonhard von Muralt and Walter Schmid (Zürich, 1952) Nos. 24, 25, 26 (hereafter cited as *Zürich*).

ular church attendance and observance of certain ordinances such as infant baptism. Censorship hampered and more often prevented the publication of Anabaptist writings. Special civic oaths were introduced in which the citizen was required to pledge himself to avoid all forms of dissent and to keep the public peace.[8] Those who recanted of their Anabaptist errors were often compelled to atone for their sins by making public confession in the city minster or village chapel. It was soon discovered by the several governments that simple legal restrictions and prohibitions could not stem the tide of an aggressive Anabaptist movement.

Third, there was the technique of physical and economic coercion. All civil authorities appear to have come to the conclusion that this was the only effective way of containing and turning back the movement. Heavy fines were levied. The citizenry was required under threat of punishment to refuse hospitality—board, room, and assistance—to Anabaptists and especially their leaders. Anabaptists were cast into prison where the treatment received varied from kindness to extreme cruelty. Apparently the jailers in the villages were more benevolent and lax, because one observes that the central authorities often demanded that Anabaptist prisoners should be brought to the territorial prison where they would be subject to more rigorous surveillance.[9] All Swiss governments appear on occasion to have used the black arts of torture. They employed it to extract information, to compel recantations, and to give warning of severer punishments yet to come. In later stages of the fight against Anabaptism the authorities confiscated the property of dissenters. Ordinances were posted, threatening to destroy Anabaptist property by fire. An effective socio-economic weapon was to declare the children of Anabaptist couples illegitimate and not legal heirs. Every government used freely the device of banishing its Anabaptists. They singled out particularly those of for-

8 Emil Dürr and Paul Roth (eds.), *Aktensammlung zur Geschichte der Basler Reformation in den Jahren 1519 bis Anfang 1534* (Basel, 1921-50) Vol. IV, No. 293.
9 De Quervain, *op. cit.*, 129.

eign residence. Most distressing to the authorities were those Anabaptists who returned in violation of their banishment. The governments often imposed on the exiles a pledge or an oath never to return. These coerced pledges or oaths were often violated, laying the Anabaptists open to charges of perjury.

The ultimate in punishment were the acts of execution— beheading and drowning. Only in Catholic lands do the Anabaptists appear to have been burned at the stake. Those who were ferreted out for execution were, of course, the leaders— the missionaries, preachers, and elders. Executions were frequently staged in a prominent central location where the populace might observe the fearful punishment. The authorities hoped that these acts of terror would compel faint hearts to return to the bosom of the established church. Concurrently with these harsh punishments, the Swiss governments held forth to the Anabaptists the olive branch of full pardon to any who would renounce their faith.

These techniques of persecution were effectively implemented by a variety of administrative techniques. The more vigilant town councils dispatched a continuous stream of instructions and orders to local officials on how to handle the problem.[10] Most governments recognized that the Anabaptist problem could not be solved on a local, cantonal basis, but required a co-operative, interterritory approach. The several governments kept one another informed, therefore, of the movements of Anabaptists considered particularly dangerous. Several Swiss governments joined forces, as in the Concordat of 1527, to correlate their legal offensive. The more effective programs against Anabaptism were centralized in the capital towns. Trials, imprisonments, and executions were usually conducted in a central location where rigorous administration of justice could be assured and where a maximum publicity value might be derived. Some governments found it useful to employ the services of special espionage agents to spy out Anabaptist meetings and activities. In sev-

10 *Ibid.*, 128.

eral territories all citizens were bound by oath to serve as informers. A very effective technique was to equip and deputize forces of vigilantes to capture Anabaptists.[11] As "Anabaptist hunters" they combed the countryside in search of dissenters and were paid by the head for their captives.

The Anabaptist issue was often inextricably bound up with local issues.[12] One observes many local rural areas seeking desperately to preserve their ancient legal prerogatives against the centralizing tendencies of the town councils. These dissident political forces gave aid and encouragement to the Anabaptists, who for essentially religious reasons were also resisting the centralizing controls of the town councils. The Anabaptists, also, often received unexpected support from certain influential elements high in the counsels of government: those who on principle favored moderation, those who opposed the power aggrandizement and centralizing efforts of the dominant faction, and those who were of the secret Catholic minority.[13]

One may inquire in conclusion what methods were most effective in attaining the objective of suppressing the Anabaptist movement. The techniques of persuasion appear not to have been very convincing to most Anabaptists. The task of suppressing Anabaptism required the services of strong, driving, single-minded leadership. Zwingli gave this kind of leadership in Zürich. Moreover, it was essential that the magistracy should not underestimate the virility of the movement. For several years Basel saw no threat in Anabaptism and the movement spread rapidly. From the outset Zürich viewed Anabaptism as a dangerous threat and quickly curbed the movement. The suppression of the movement required more than prohibitory restrictions on the statute books. The governments which were most effective in containing and eliminating Anabaptism were those which applied physical

11 Emil Egli, *Die St. Galler Täufer* (Zürich, 1887) 5; *Zürich*, No. 110.
12 Examples of this situation are to be found in the districts of Grüningen, Canton Zürich, and the Emmental, Canton Bern.
13 Note as examples Jacob Grebel, Zürich; Hans von Waldkirch, Schaffhausen; Hans Frans Nageli, Bern.

and economic coercion in a sustained, unwavering manner. There could be no respite. It was essential that the efforts be directed particularly against the leaders, the patrons, and the centers of strength of the movement. The only moderation which could be permitted in this pattern of coercion was clemency to those who would recant.

THE ANABAPTIST VIEW OF THE STATE

The views of the civil authorities toward the Anabaptists have been surveyed. We move now to an examination of the response of the Anabaptists to the authorities. One observes that in the earliest days of the movement the Anabaptists entertained hopes that leaders of church and state could be won to the brotherhood.[14] Hence, Conrad Grebel, Balthasar Hubmaier, and their colleagues sought out those in authority to gain them as converts. One sees the Anabaptists begging the governments not to suppress the movement. Repeatedly they requested official permission to publish their writings. They urged that proper public hearings be granted their cause. They petitioned councils for safe-conduct papers to enter the capital towns to plead their case. As the hand of suppression descended, the Anabaptists felt compelled to disobey the prohibitory laws. They continued to assemble and to preach despite the law. They refused under questioning to divulge the names of their brethren. The leaders roamed the land, ignoring the laws prohibiting itinerant evangelism. The Anabaptists eluded their persecutors by hiding out in forest and mountain. Hearing that they would not receive fair trial, they refused in some instances to surrender themselves to the court. Non-Anabaptists granted their harried Anabaptist neighbors hospitality and aid despite threats of dire punishment. Amidst persecution and suffering they encouraged one another in their faith. They accepted suffering patiently, convinced that persecution was the earthly lot of all true chil-

14 *ZW, IV,* 169, 171, 591; *Zürich,* No. 120; *Selected Works of Zwingli,* 132; **cf.** Harold S. Bender, *Conrad Grebel, c. 1489-1526: the Founder of the Swiss Brethren Sometimes Called Anabaptists* (Goshen, 1950) 103.

dren of God. The magistrates complained that the Anabaptists "remained intractable" in the presence of governmental authority; others conceded in moments of charity that the Anabaptists were of "unsurpassed courage" under persecution. This steadfastness, courage, and tranquillity throughout imprisonment and in the hour of execution moved many citizens to a feeling of compassion for the Anabaptists. Finally, however, some Anabaptists yielded to the persistent demands of the authorities and recanted their faith. Whereas in certain areas—notably in St. Gall—many recanted, in most regions the number who recanted appears to have been few. Persecution did not decimate the ranks of the committed brethren so much as it discouraged those interested, sympathetic folk who might have identified themselves with the movement had not the commitment appeared so dangerously costly.

Persecution eventually remolded the movement. Anabaptism was driven from the cities. It persisted in remote rural regions. Prolonged persecution dulled the missionary edge of the movement. The Anabaptists appear to have become gradually more quietistic in their attitudes toward government. They, of course, continued vigorously to defend their nonconformist ways. All that they asked of governments was to be left alone to be "the quiet in the land."

As the Anabaptists diligently searched their Scriptures and as they confronted governments in a continuous series of encounters, a theory of the Christian's relationship to the civil authorities took form in their minds.[15] In the intensely

15 For the Anabaptist views of the Christian's relationship to the state the following sources are of particular significance: "A Brotherly Union of a Number of Children of God Concerning Seven Articles," an edited English translation available in John C. Wenger, "The Schleitheim Confession of Faith," *Mennonite Quarterly Review* (October 1945) 19:243-53; the letter of Conrad Grebel to Thomas Müntzer, September 5, 1524, which is to be found in an abridged English translation in Bender, *op. cit.*, Appendix IV, 282-87; the record of the interrogation of a group of Anabaptist prisoners in Bern on May 24, 1529, in *Aktensammlung zur Geschichte der Berner-Reformation, 1521-1532*, edited by R. Steck and G. Tobler (Bern, 1923) No. 249, pp. 1040-43; the disputation at Bern, April 19, 1531, *Ein Christenlich Gespräch gehallten zuo Bern Zwüschen den Predicanten und Hansen Pfyster Mayer von Arouw/den Widertouff/Eyd/Oberkeyt/vnd andere Widertoufferische Artickel betreffende* (Bern, 1531); the disputation at Zofingen, July 1 to 9, 1532, *Handlung oder Acta*

confident early days of the movement some may have hopefully anticipated a new apostolic order where the secular magistracy would not be required.[16] From the beginning they appear to have generally accepted the view that God had destined them to be a small minority in a hostile, secular world. Consequently they were prepared to affirm that in a sinful world, government was a necessity for the maintenance of peace and order.

First, the Anabaptists acknowledged the primacy of the claims of God over the claims of government. They often quoted the words of Peter: "We ought to obey God rather than men." They rooted their theory concerning the Christian's obligation to the state in their conception of discipleship. The Christian is essentially a citizen of the kingdom of Christ and not of this world. The kingdom of Christ is alienated and sharply separated from the kingdoms of this world. The Christian knows that those who are obedient to the commandments of God will be persecuted. The Christian is prepared to suffer meekly the pain and persecution of this world because his citizenship is in heaven. From this view stemmed the conviction that a Christian is obedient to the government only in so far as the claims of the magistracy do no injury to the Christian's pursuit of the will of God.

Second, the Anabaptists affirmed the doctrine that the magistracy was ordained of God to punish the evil and protect the good. Romans 13 was the foundation and starting point for all Anabaptist discussion of the civil authority. They differed from their contemporaries in declaring that a magistrate could be a Roman Catholic, a Protestant, or even a non-Christian and still satisfactorily fulfill the divinely ordained role of the civil ruler.

der Disputation gehalten zu Zoffingen in Aargau, von den Predigern zu Bern mit den Widertauffern (Zürich, 1532); the disputation at Bern, March 11 to 17, 1538, "Acta Des Gesprächs zwüschenn Predicanntenn vund Touffbruderenn Ergangen, Inn der Statt Bernn von xja Mertzeuns, bisz of den XVIja Desselben Monats Inn MDXXXVIIIten Jar" (unpublished typewritten transcript by Heinrich Türler from Vol. LXXX of the "Unnützen Papiere" in the Staatsarchiv Bern, 1912, Goshen College Library).

16 Selected Works of Zwingli, 132, ZW, VI, 33; cf. Bender, op. cit., 255, n. 31.

Third, the record is not clear whether the Anabaptists felt the magistracy had functional value for earnest Christians. All were agreed that the magistracy was essential for non-Christians. They did not, however, state that all non-Anabaptists were *ipso facto* non-Christians. The few fragments of Anabaptist expression on this issue indicate that some asserted that everyone, even Christians, required a magistracy, while others declared that among Christians the magistracy had no essential function to perform.[17]

Fourth, the Anabaptists agreed unanimously that the Christian owes obedience to the civil authorities in so far as the prior claims of God are not violated in those duties. The Christian gives this obedience freely and not grudgingly. He pays taxes, tithes, interest, and customs as required by the magistracy. No evidence can be found to substantiate the frequently made accusation that the Anabaptists refused to pay these obligations. The Anabaptists consistently taught that a Christian should suffer nonresistantly the rule of all princes—even tyrants. The Christian might be compelled by dictates of his conscience to disobey the magistrate in particulars, but the Christian disavowed completely any recourse to general rebellion. The Swiss Anabaptists were eager for change, but only peaceful change. No evidence supports the accusation that they were proponents of violent revolution.

Fifth, the Anabaptists were generally of the conviction, that a Christian could not occupy the office of the magistrate. Some who became Anabaptists appear to have continued, at least for a while, as local officials of government. Some Anabaptists declared categorically that no Christian could be a magistrate. Others granted that a Christian might under certain circumstances be a magistrate, but they added that it would be extremely difficult for a magistrate who became a Christian to remain long in office without compromising his faith. The principal reason given why a Christian could not hold office was that the magistrate ruled by force while the

17 Cf. Ernst Müller, *Geschichte der bernischen Taufer* (Frauenfeld, 1895) 42-43.

Christian was nonresistant. Moreover, a Christian was a servant, not a ruler. If a Christian were a magistrate it would undermine the equality of the brotherhood. The Christian could not be a judge in civil and criminal cases without violating Scriptural precepts. Finally, the Christian had another vocation in the world than that of heading secular government. The Anabaptists were quite unimpressed by arguments that Christian occupancy of the magistracy was essential to good government. Whereas the issue was often discussed whether a new convert could remain in the magistracy, the Anabaptists never raised the question whether the Christian, out of a sense of civic-Christian duty, ought to enter the magistracy. In the context of that day it would have seemed utterly unrealistic to discuss whether a separatist, nonresistant, Anabaptist kind of Christian could or even should have a place in the magistracy.

Sixth, the Anabaptists were convinced that a government-established church violated the precepts of Scripture. They advocated disestablishment. They insisted that the state had absolutely no rights or responsibilities of supervision, interference, and coercion in the affairs of the church. The Anabaptists reserved their most caustic words for the state clergy and the established church. To them the state clergy were "hirelings of the rulers." They charged that the clergy preached under the protection of their state paymasters and not freely under the cross of Christ. They condemned particularly the benefice system based on income from interest, rents, and tithes—to them an iniquitous form of usury. They saw the established church as a broad, inclusive, lax institution filled with many unrepentant and undisciplined sinners. They saw it as an institution under the domination of the government. They urged that the true church should be a gathered, exclusive, heroic, disciplined church of believers completely severed from all control by the state. As advocates of the disestablishment of the state church, the Anabaptists were essentially calling for a government of limited powers.

191

Seventh, the Anabaptists were devoted believers in nonresistance. As such they renounced all warfare and all use of the sword. Their simple, all-sufficient reason for nonresistance was that Christ had forbidden His followers to use the sword. They added that a Christian "suffers rather than resists evil." Apparently military service did not then have the universal compulsory character which would make it an acute problem for the Anabaptists. No evidence can be found that they engaged in military service. A suggestion of an exception was that of two Anabaptists from Waldshut who refused combatant duty but offered noncombatant service to their beleaguered town. Balthasar Hubmaier was a lone voice raised in defense of the Christian's use of the sword. The Anabaptists viewed as more immediate and crucial the issue of the magistrate's use of the sword to punish dissenters and evildoers. All Anabaptists appear to have agreed that in matters of faith no one should be physically coerced. It is not clear, however, whether all Anabaptists would have insisted that the government should renounce all use of capital punishment. The Schleitheim Confession, for example, states: "In the law the sword was ordained for the punishment of the wicked and for their death, and the same sword is now ordained to be used by the worldly magistrates."[18] Hans Marquardt found the sword of government "good and necessary."[19] Other Anabaptists, however, specifically condemned any use of capital punishment. One brother stated that even a non-Christian magistrate ought not to execute thieves or murderers. It appears that the prevailing conviction among Anabaptists was that magistrates should abandon the use of the sword in the punishment not only of religious dissenters but also of common criminals.

Eighth, the Anabaptists refused to swear the civil oath on the grounds of Christ's admonition: "Let your communication be Yea, yea; Nay, nay." Since the ancient loyalties and

---

18 Wenger, *loc. cit.*, 243.

19 Joachim von Watt (Vadian), *Deutsche Historische Schriften*, edited by Ernst Götzinger (St. Gall, 1879) 3:455-502.

traditions of the community found their symbolic center in the civic oath, this rejection of the oath was deeply disturbing and puzzling to the authorities. The Anabaptists were prepared as an alternative to make a simple affirmation where an oath would otherwise be required.

Ninth, the Anabaptists believed that the New Testament dictated that no Christian should bring suit in a court of law. The Christian should suffer patiently the loss of possessions or status rather than demand redress in the secular courts. Although the Anabaptists refused to sue in court in behalf of their rights, they did not hesitate to appeal to the authorities for the rights of fair hearing and trial customarily accorded the defendant.

Tenth, the Anabaptists refused in many ways to conform to civic mores. They declined to carry the traditional ceremonial side weapon. They failed to participate in the civic assemblies. Much of the ceremonial ritual of civic life was to them a worldly abomination from which true Christians were to separate themselves. This nonconformity of the Anabaptists was scarcely intelligible to the good burghers who loved their town's venerable traditions.

The prolonged encounter between the Anabaptists and the civil authorities in the sixteenth century exposed issues which continue to this day to be fundamental in the problem of church and state relationships. The Anabaptists made an impressive contribution in their day. Committed to a Biblical faith, and earnest in their search for the leading of God, they sought in fresh, new, courageous ways to face the competing claims of Christ and Caesar.

Brotherhood and the Economic Ethic
of the Anabaptists

In all Anabaptist literature there is frequent reference to the concept of brotherhood. Anabaptists were known for their predominantly lay character as over against the more clerical and hierarchical structure of the Reformed and the Catholic churches. A prominent feature was the mutuality which existed among members of the Anabaptist-Mennonite groups. The brotherhood concept had in it the central idea of discipleship and this meant a close following of Jesus Christ in matters pertaining to this life. Obviously, the whole matter of the way people lived was important, and this affected the way in which they earned their living.

The God-consciousness of the Anabaptists definitely affected their economic relationships. Fritz Blanke reveals this in discussing the congregation at Zollikon, a suburb of Zürich, where the first organized Anabaptist congregation was established. The court records show that a group of Anabaptists held a communion service in the house of Jakob Hottinger where the members agreed "that they would now henceforth lead and live a Christian life." Another Anabaptist, Jörg Schad, testified that they broke and ate the bread with the intention that "they would always have God in their hearts and think of Him." The Lord's Supper was thus "an obligation of love to God" and devotion to each other as fellow believers. The Lord's Supper is described as "a bread of love and Christian spirit," also "a sign of brotherly love in peace, as an occasion to show brotherly love to everyone." "Thus," as Blanke says, "the communal eating of the bread and drinking of the wine symbolizes mutual fraternal union;

* J. Winfield Fretz is Professor of Sociology in Bethel College and author of *Christian Mutual Aid* (Akron, 1947) and *Pilgrims in Paraguay* (Scottdale, 1953).

communion is the meal of community and love, with obvious reference to I Corinthians 10:17."[1]

The Anabaptist attempt to build a genuine believers' church, based on an apostolic pattern with the New Testament as its guide, sought to emphasize the concerns of their members in all matters of this life so that they would be consistent with the teachings of Jesus and thus acceptable to God, their Father. They were conscious of trying to establish an earthly kingdom, as Menno Simons described it, "without spot or wrinkle."

One of the best evidences that the early Anabaptists achieved a measure of brotherhood is the seeming absence of class distinction among its members. A careful study of the occupations from which the early Anabaptists came indicates a rather wide range in the occupational strata of the time.[2] There were peasants, craftsmen, merchants, engineers, and learned professors among them. All of them seem to have been bound together by their common faith and an intense devotion to their new concept of discipleship under Christ's love. The religious life of the group seems not to have been affected significantly by occupational and economic differences.

An examination of sixteenth-century Anabaptist writings leads one to feel that there was little concern about an economic system as such; but rather their major concern was the quality of their spiritual devotion to Christ, and their expression of helpfulness and good will to all men.

THREE SOCIOLOGICAL TYPES

Looking at the Anabaptists from a sociological point of view, there appear to be three rather clearly defined types. The first is that of the revolutionary, apocalyptical, chiliastic type. This group was led by such men as Jan Matthys and Jan of Leyden. This element of Anabaptism wished to bring

1 Fritz Blanke, "The First Anabaptist Congregation: Zollikon, 1925," *MQR* (January 1953) 27:19-20. The passage in I Cor. 10:17 says: "Because there is one loaf, we who are many are one body, for we all partake of the same loaf."

2 Robert Kreider, "Vocations of Swiss and South German Anabaptists," *Mennonite Life* (January 1953) 8:38-42.

about a change in the social order by means of violence and force. There is some resemblance in this group to the radical wing of the Taborites of a previous century. They were millenarians who interpreted the New Testament in the light of its Messianic hopes rather than of its ethics. Through divine revelation and mystical experiences they claimed direct commands from God to establish a kingdom of God on earth.[3] This was attempted by trying to kill all the people they considered a hindrance to their goal. This radical wing of Anabaptism was short-lived in comparison to the other two Anabaptist groups.

The Münsterites practiced an enforced communism. The duty of the Brethren, they said, was to "possess as though they possessed nothing." The democratic idea of the equality of all Christians was constantly stressed. This presents an interesting paradox, however, because while the Münsterites held to a program of compulsory communism in matters of property they advocated a thoroughgoing theory of the right of private judgment in matters of religion. Each man was taught to believe that God communicates with every man directly in mysterious ways. Thus we have on the one hand, in matters of economic goods, a complete communism; and on the other hand, in the realm of ideas, a thoroughgoing individualism. The Münsterites were undoubtedly affected in their social behavior by their strong belief that the end of the world was rapidly approaching.

A second type of Anabaptism, clearly distinguishable from other forms, is that of Christian communism, best illustrated in the life of the Hutterian Brethren. This communism, unlike that of the Münster type, was purely voluntary. The leaders of this group held to a peaceful, nonresistant way of life. It originated in the Tyrol region and may have been influenced by the descendants of the Moravian Brethren of an earlier day.

3 John Horsch, "The Rise and Fall of the Anabaptists of Münster," *MQR* (April and July 1935) 9:92-103; 129-43; see also Horsch, "Menno Simons' Attitude Toward the Anabaptists of Münster," *MQR* (January 1936) 10:55-72.

The third sociological type of Anabaptism is that which might best be characterized as the brotherhood type. Like the two previous types, it held to a principle of separation from the world, but the term "separation" was not as literally interpreted as in the case of the Münsterites and the Hutterites. This group found its following chiefly among the Swiss Brethren around Zürich, and the followers of Menno Simons in Holland and North Germany. These Anabaptists tended to draw close together and to live in compact communities. Although certain communal tendencies appeared among them, complete ownership of goods and living together in single households was never the practice. Anabaptists of the Swiss Brethren type, like the Hutterites, adhered strictly to the principle of nonresistance and strongly renounced the chiliastic character of the Münsterites. The Hutterites of the present day are directly descended from the communal Hutterian Brethren, and the Mennonites from the sixteenth-century brotherhood type of Anabaptists.

We see evidence of the extent to which mutual aid operated as a factor in the life of the Anabaptists as we look at their teachings and practice. Hans Leopold, a minister of the Swiss Brethren in Augsburg, who suffered martyrdom in 1528, said that "if they know of anyone who is in need, whether or not he is a member of their church, they believe it their duty, out of love to God, to render him help and aid."[4] Heinrich Seiler, who in 1535 was executed by drowning at Bern in Switzerland, said in regard to the ownership of property: "I do not believe it is wrong that a Christian has property of his own, provided he will do right and share his goods with the needy, for he is nothing more than a steward."[5] One of the early sources says that it was the practice among the Swiss Brethren to administer baptism only to those who vowed "to consecrate themselves with all their temporal possessions to

4 J. Kühn, *Toleranz und Offenbarung*, 231, quoted in John Horsch, "The Faith of the Swiss Brethren," *MQR* (April 1931) 5:139.

5 Ernst Müller *Geschichte der Bernischen Täufer* (Frauenfeld, 1895) 44, quoted in Horsch, *loc. cit.*, 5:139.

the service of God and His people."[6] In the Swiss Brethren congregation at Strasbourg in 1557, applicants for membership were asked whether they were willing to devote "all their possessions to the church and its needs, if necessity requires, and not to fail any member that is in need, if they are able to render aid."[7]

Heinrich Bullinger, an enemy of the Swiss Brethren, says that according to their teaching "every good Christian is under duty before God to use from motives of love all his possessions [if need be] to supply the necessaries of life to any of his Brethren."[8] It must be remembered that this testimony comes from an enemy of the Anabaptists who would therefore not be prejudiced in their favor. A contemporary writer says concerning the Brethren at Augsburg that "in their brotherhood there was in evidence the purpose to render each other the greatest possible help from motives of brotherly love."[9] All of these statements are so clear that they need no explanation. Not only does the evidence come from their own pen but from the mouths of opponents and critics as well. The Swiss Brethren had great concern for the economic and social welfare of all their own members and, at least on several known occasions, for those outside the brotherhood as well.

In a disputation at Frankenthal, in 1571, in which the Brethren were evidently being accused of holding to community of goods, one of their spokesmen had the following statement to make: "We confess that Christians may have private property without violating Christian love, always with the provision that they do not misuse it but at all times let their abundance serve the needs of the poor, as Paul teaches in II Cor. 8 and 9."[10] In the frequent references to the poor there is no way of telling whether this means those needy in the

6 Horsch, *loc. cit.*, 5:139.
7 *Ibid.*, 5:139-40.
8 *Ibid.*, 5:140.
9 Meyer, "Wiedertäufer in Schwaben," *Zeitschrift für Kirchengeschichte* (1897) 18:252, quoted in Horsch.
10 *Protocoll Franckenthal*, 553, quoted in Horsch, *loc. cit.*, 5:140.

brotherhood alone or whether it refers to the poor wherever they may be found. Apparently it refers to their own needy first, but is not confined to their own poor. Balthasar Hubmaier, one of the outstanding leaders of the Brethren, says in answer to accusations brought against him that he never held to a view of community of goods in spite of the accusation. He declared himself in favor of the kind of community of goods that he believed the early Christians in the Jerusalem community practiced. This, he thought, was to the effect that Christian believers should hold property subject to the needs of the brotherhood.[11]

What has been said about the Swiss Brethren is also characteristic of the Dutch Anabaptists. For instance, Van Benthem, a non-Mennonite Dutch author, wrote in 1698: "We may learn much that is good from these people, namely, humility, contentment, moderation, and especially mercy toward the needy. For although the people of the Reformed Church of Holland deserve to be commended for their benevolence toward the poor, yet this virtue is particularly true of these people. Also they are very careful to dress unassumingly."[12] In a public debate with Martin Bucer at Marburg in 1538, George Schnabel speaking for the Anabaptist Brethren stated his reason for leaving the Lutheran state church. He said that he had been in charge of the treasury for the poor in the Lutheran Church. He noticed that the management of the funds was not carried out in the Biblical spirit, and the pastor gave no attention to his complaint in regard to the matter. He felt conscience-stricken about the custom of lending out money of the church on interest, while many of the poor people in the community were in great need. For this reason he told the pastor, the mayor, and the council of Marburg, he was separating himself from the state church and becoming an Anabaptist.[13] It appears that the Anabaptist

11 H. C. Vedder, *Balthasar Hübmaier* (N.Y., 1905) 164 ff.

12 Horsch, "The Character of the Evangelical Anabaptists as Reported by Contemporary Reformation Writers," *MQR* (July 1934) 8:133.

13 Christian Hege, "The Early Anabaptists in Hesse," *MQR* (July 1931) 5:167.

practice of social responsibility and the habit of generous sharing attracted this man to them.

Another aspect of Anabaptist life which throws light on the extent to which mutual aid was practiced is reflected in their attitude toward the accepting of interest on money loaned. The New Testament, they said, knew nothing about interest and usury. They quoted Scripture in support of their contention (although it was the Old Testament rather than the New that they quoted). "You must not exact interest on loans to a fellow countryman of yours, interest on money, food or anything else that might be exacted as interest."[14] Again in the Psalms they found justification for their opposition to usury: "He does not put out his money on interest, nor takes a bribe against the innocent."[15]

Being opposed to the principle of lending money at interest they consistently refused to accept interest themselves and paid it unwillingly to others. They held to the common-sense notion that money should be lent for the benefit of the borrower rather than of the lender.[16] They looked upon the charging of interest as a form of exploitation and felt it improper to exploit anyone. As far as we may judge from all evidence the Anabaptists treated nonmembers of the brotherhood in the same way as they treated their own. That is to say, they had no dual ethic, one for themselves and another for those outside the group. This opposition to the accepting of interest is another evidence of the law of love and brotherhood found earnestly being practiced among the Anabaptists everywhere.

An examination of Anabaptist literature does not reveal a preference for any one type of economic system except for the Hutterian emphasis on Christian community of goods.

14 Deut. 23:19.

15 Ps. 15:5.

16 In contrast to this attitude of the Anabaptists toward money and property stands Calvin's position. Georgia Harkness, *John Calvin, the Man and His Ethics* (New York, 1931) 218, says, "Calvin stood firmly for the right of every man to possess his own. His fierce attack upon the Anabaptist tendencies toward religious communism reveals clearly his sanctity of private property."

Otherwise the literature reveals almost a total unconsciousness of economics *per se*. No specific occupations seem to be preferred above others, although it was emphasized that only such trades and professions must be engaged in which are consistent with the way of Christian discipleship. On these grounds Peter Rideman ruled out the making and selling of implements of warfare, of fashionable clothing, and of alcoholic beverages. That which could legitimately be produced could also be sold for a price, but merchandising, that is, the purchase of goods which one did not produce and its resale at a higher price, was looked upon as endangering the law of love. Menno Simons recognized that some merchants were God-fearing, but was nevertheless fearful lest they lose this quality since the business in which they are engaged is a dangerous one.[17] The one central point of emphasis which runs through Anabaptist literature like a symphonic theme is the duty of all disciples to live by the one law of love, the love of God as demonstrated by Christ. The assumption seems to have been that the genuine disciple was purely motivated and thus his relations with his fellow men would be worthy no matter what the occupation nor the system of property holding.

The goal of the Anabaptists was to be good disciples first; occupation was secondary. They placed spiritual virtue and moral attainments above everything else and hence philosophical speculation and business acumen were goals not sought after nor activities engaged in. The Anabaptist economic ethic can best be characterized by its strong emphasis on brotherhood sharing.

17 See Peter Rideman, *Account of Our Religion, Doctrine and Faith* (Suffolk, 1950) 3, 112, 126; Menno Simons, *Complete Writings* (Scottdale, 1956) 368-69.

✠ JOHN S. OYER ✠

The Reformers
Oppose the Anabaptist Theology

The early Reformers, without exception, were violently opposed to the Anabaptists. They differed in their analyses and evaluations of those intrepid missioners, as one might expect. But they were unanimous in the opinion that the sternest possible sanctions must be employed against the sect to prevent its further increase and even to eradicate it. This paper is an attempt to discover the reasons for this opposition to the Anabaptists. It will not catalogue the entire range of sometimes wild and always angry charges. Rather it will suggest those reasons, not always explicit, which form the basis for the Reformers' fears.

An examination will be made of the writings of two leaders from each of two centers of the Reformation. Zürich is selected because it was the fountainhead of Anabaptism, and because its leaders formulated the basic Reformed pattern of opposition to Anabaptism, a pattern repeated in Strasbourg and Geneva. Here Zwingli and Bullinger are the obvious choices because of their close acquaintance with the movement and the extent of their polemical activities. Wittenberg is selected as the second Reformation center because of its influence on Protestant historiography of Anabaptism. Melanchthon is the most comprehensive of its writers on the topic. Luther is selected, not because of any eminence in the battle with the Anabaptists, whom he rarely if ever encountered even in their writings, but because his total view of left wing elements in the Reformation has helped to shape a vast literature which has inaccurately included Anabaptism.

* John S. Oyer is Assistant Professor of History in Goshen College.

I

Both Zwingli and Bullinger condemned the Anabaptists on two major counts: they disrupted the religious order and they threatened the peace and even the existence of the civil order. Both men considered the actual issues on which there was open conflict to be incidental, and even trivial.[1] The entire conflict should be seen in the light of an attempt by both parties to discover and put into practice a new Christian order founded upon New Testament principles. They disagreed sharply on the nature of that order, and on the manner and speed at which it should be instituted.

The earliest attacks against the Anabaptists came from the pen of Zwingli. Characteristically his attacks centered on the point of Anabaptist public departure from the Reformers' church, the issue of baptism. Zwingli devoted far more space to the refutation of Anabaptist errors on this point than on any other.[2] There was no insurmountable barrier between the Anabaptists and Zwingli on the nature of the sacrament; both believed it to be essentially a symbol, and not in any sense a conveyor of grace. The disagreement arose as to what specifically the act symbolized. The Anabaptists administered it as a symbol of an experience of regeneration of the individual through faith, and of his promise to obey Christ, a pledge of ethical behavior. Obviously infants could not receive baptism because they were incapable both of faith and of voluntary commitment to any program of ethics.[3] Zwingli viewed baptism as a symbol of membership in the religious body, as a New Testament parallel to the Old Testa-

1 See John Horsch, "The Struggle Between Zwingli and the Swiss Brethren in Zurich," *MQR* (July 1933) 7:158, for Zwingli's view. Heinrich Bullinger, *Von dem unverschampten fräfel, ergerlichem verwyrren unnd vnwarhafftem leeren der selbsgesandten Widertöuffern* . . . (Zürich, 1531) XXIIIa. (Hereafter referred to as: Bullinger, 1531.)

2 See his polemics: *Von der Taufe, von der Widertaufe und von der Kindertaufe* (1525), *Zwingli Werke*, 4:188-337; *Antwort über Balthasar Hubmaiers Taufbüchlein* (1525), *ZW*, 4:577-647; *In Catabaptistarum Strophas Elenchus* (1527), *ZW*, 6:1-196. English translation printed as *Refutation of the Tricks of the Catabaptists* in Samuel Jackson, *Selected Works of Huldreich Zwingli* (Philadelphia, 1901) 123-258. (Hereafter referred to as: *Refutation.*)

3 Harold S. Bender, *Conrad Grebel* (Goshen, 1950) 207.

ment practice of circumcision. As such, infants must be baptized. Indeed, not to baptize them was both impious and inhuman, since it relegated them to a position—"among baggage and goods rather than among believers."[4]

Zwingli believed he could prove the necessity for infant baptism by the application of synecdoche to Scriptural exegesis. Whenever a group activity was described in Scripture, all aspects of that activity applied equally to each segment and individual of the group. Thus infants were included among "our fathers" when they crossed the Red Sea (I Cor. 10:1). Likewise they were included among those baptized in the household of Stephanas.[5] The Anabaptists were arch-literalists. As Zwingli quoted them in the *Elenchus*, they countered his synecdoche with a refusal to recognize any addition, no matter how trivial or how compellingly logical, to the literal Word.[6] Armed with his beloved synecdoche, Zwingli contemptuously decried the Anabaptist debaters as boors.[7]

In his final, definitive work against the Anabaptists, Zwingli had interpreted their rejection of infant baptism primarily as an attack on the existent church with its inclusion of infants within the religious body.[8] Heinrich Bullinger, Zwingli's successor as leader of the Zürich Reformation, added nothing new to his predecessor's arguments on baptism except a clearer elaboration of this particular point.

The baptism issue to Bullinger was pre-eminently the issue of the church. "From the very beginning it was principally a matter of separation for the purpose of creating a divided church. Therefore . . . because they wished to abandon the Papists and the Evangelicals . . . and live in the new Baptist order, which they called the true, blessed, Christian Church, their leaders received rebaptism . . . as a sign of separation."[9]

---

4 *Refutation*, 173.   5 *Ibid.*, 131, 154-57.
6 *Ibid.*, 131, 163-65. See also Bender, *op. cit.*, 176.
7 *Refutation*, 157-58.   8 *Ibid.*, 134, 137.
9 Heinrich Bullinger, *Der Widertöufferen vrsprung, fürgang, Secten, wäsen,*

Both men considered the Anabaptists guilty of a deliberate attempt to overemphasize the baptism issue as a screen for the division of the church.[10] In point of fact, the Zürich Reformers and the Anabaptists disagreed fundamentally on the nature of the church.

Zwingli believed that the church of Jesus Christ was an invisible community of true believers. Its members exist in all places at all times.[11] But although God alone ultimately knows who is a member of the church, nevertheless it is possible for men to assemble believers into a community which would become in fact a segment of the church. The bridge between the invisible church of Christ and the visible congregation is the Word. Wherever the Word is truly proclaimed, at that place the number of believers will increase. Thus the two criteria for determining a given congregation's adherence to the true church were the existence of believers and the proclamation of the true faith. Historians have disagreed as to the relative importance of these conditions in Zwingli's thought, because Zwingli underwent a change of mind. Whereas he once entertained the hope that men can recognize assembled Christians as believers and therefore as the church, and fortified this hope with a strong faith in the compelling power of the Spirit to transform the hearts of unregenerate men until they became faithful believers, he later came to doubt completely man's ability to detect the true believers. He therefore began to emphasize the proclamation of the pure Gospel as the sign whereby a congregation might be recognized as the church.[12]

fürnemen vnd gemeine jrer leer Artickel, ouch jre gründ. . . . (Zürich, 1561), 15b. (Hereafter referred to as: Bullinger, 1561.)

10 For Bullinger see *Ibid.*, 68b. For Zwingli see Horsch, *loc cit.*, 158.

11 Alfred Farner, *Die Lehre von Kirche und Staat bei Zwingli* (Tübingen, 1930) 3-6. By 1530 Zwingli tended to designate the church of Christ as the church of the elect, rather than the church of true believers. The change in terminology reflected an increasing emphasis on the doctrine of election in Zwingli's later years, and his growing conviction that a church of true believers was impossible of fulfillment. See Farner, 7-9.

12 Bender, *op. cit.*, 92 c.; Farner, *op. cit.*, 3-9; Walther Köhler, *Zwingli Werke*, 4:234-35.

Zwingli intended to establish a reformed church in the commonwealth of Zürich, a church patterned after the New Testament. Many of his followers, including Grebel, Manz, and Stumpf, accepted the idea with enthusiasm. They disagreed violently with him, however, and abandoned his camp for an uncertain future at that point in the second disputation (October 1523) when he agreed to postpone the abolition of Romish practices in accordance with the wishes of the city council. For if Zwingli advocated the establishment of a believers' church, he also was convinced that its realization lay in a process of gradual change—change that did not antagonize the more conservative elements in Zürich society by its radical character. And if Zwingli conceived of the New Testament church as a pattern for the commonwealth of Zürich, he also believed that the civil authorities were to help establish it.[13] The Anabaptist line of dissent was devoted to the view that the New Testament church should be instituted only after a decisive separation from the established Roman church had been made, with the removal of all vestiges of popery.[14] The Anabaptists regarded a program of church reform geared to the approval of civic authorities as contrary to the nature of the true church. It had already lost the essential autonomy of a genuine church of believers and had become a territorial church. The precipitate action of the "Anabaptists" in October 1523 was probably instrumental in diminishing Zwingli's hope in the possibility of attaining a believers' church.[15]

Bullinger's view of the church did not differ substantially from that of Zwingli, except that he was more concerned, or at least more articulate, about the necessity for unity. He considered separation from the church the worst of all possible heresies. Indeed, the very meaning of the word *Ketzer* is "divider."[16] He had in mind Zwingli's true church of the

13 Bender, *op. cit.*, 92, points out that any change in ecclesiastical affairs had to be approved by the council, since it had assumed full control of the church after the nullification of the authority of the Bishop of Constance in 1522.
14 *Refutation*, 132; Farner quoting Zwingli, *op. cit.*, 6.
15 Farner, *op. cit.*, 6.
16 Bullinger, 1531, XXIIIa.

elect, in both its invisible form in various places at various times, and its visible manifestation where the pure Gospel is proclaimed.[17]

The Anabaptists had deep convictions on the necessity for ethical living as a measure of true Christianity. Bullinger interpreted their insistence on "newness of life" in the reborn Christian, as exemplified in holy living, as the real foundation of their believers' church.[18] He of course did not deny the desirability of ethical behavior on the part of Christians. Nor did he deny the reality of moral improvement in the lives of the Anabaptists, a fact that surprises us in view of his predecessor's charges of licentiousness among the radicals.[19] He believed, however, that it was wrong to regard post-conversion ethical behavior as a corroboration of the authenticity of the convert's claim to be a Christian. It was heresy to found a separate church on such a principle; it was precisely the heresy of the Cathari.[20] He believed that the Anabaptists' pious behavior was hypocritically designed as a lure to draw the simple people from the church of the Reformers.[21]

The second level of opposition to Anabaptism developed around the Zürichers' belief that the Anabaptist program of church reform and Christian ethics constituted a threat to the civil order. Zwingli was repelled early by the radical character of some of the Anabaptists. They swarmed through the streets and squares of Zürich preaching repentance, threatening the city with woe, and denouncing Zwingli himself as "the old dragon."[22] Zwingli sensed in Anabaptism a subjective character which manifested itself in excesses of public behavior.

A fundamental antagonism between the Zürich Reform-

---

17 Heinrich Bullinger, *Questions of religion cast abroad in Helvetia* . . . (London, 1572) 2a. (English translation by John Coxe.)

18 Bullinger, 1561, 224b.

19 See *Refutation*, 167-72. Bullinger reiterated the charges briefly with little comment.

20 Bullinger, 1531, LIIa.

21 Bullinger, 1561, 16a-17a; Bullinger, 1531, LIIa.

22 *Refutation*, 134-35.

ers and the Anabaptists stemmed from their differences in emphasis on the Sermon on the Mount. Zwingli found in the Bible primarily the majestic power of God, and the manifestations of His irresistible will throughout the world, past and present.[23] To this view the Sermon on the Mount was incidental. The Anabaptists, on the contrary, made it central in their emphasis. Zwingli interpreted their emphasis as an attempt to replace civil authority with the authority of the love ethic in a Christian community. Any attempt to erect a new community of love, based on the hope that Christians would not require the restraints of secular power, Zwingli considered impossible of attainment. Men are inherently sinful; wherever Christians dwell together, even there infractions of the civil law will take place. Moreover, to replace the state with a community of love is nothing else but an attempt to erect a new legalism based upon the Gospel. This represents a misuse of the Gospel; for the Gospel is the power to change an individual, not a blueprint for a political-social order.[24]

Zwingli had emphasized the Anabaptist belief that civil authority was unnecessary for Christians. Bullinger repeated the charge, and refuted it in the same manner as Zwingli had done.[25] He then enumerated additional errors of the Anabaptists in regard to the civil order. In the first place, they taught outright disobedience to government. Their belief in nonresistance constituted a refusal to obey at precisely that moment when complete obedience was a prime necessity, in time of war. Bullinger defended Christian participation in the just war, which meant principally the defensive war.[26] Secondly, he perceived in their refusal to swear the formal oath the collapse of the social and political order. The Zürich city council, the Swiss confederacy, the relation of citizen to magistrate, and peace itself—all were in some way based upon the oath.[27] Finally, he rebuked them severely for denying that

23 J. L. Neve, *A History of Christian Thought* (Philadelphia, 1946) 1:244-46.
24 Farner, *op. cit.*, 52-53.
25 Bullinger, 1531, CIIb-CIIIb.
26 Bullinger, 1561, 176a-177a.
27 Bullinger, 1531, CXVb-CXXIb.

a Christian could be a magistrate, or occupy any office that required the use of the sword. Bullinger believed that government as it then existed was not only ordained of God; it was also in fact Christian in character and members. There could be no excuse for opposition to a Christian civil authority.[28]

Both of these Reformers tended to exaggerate Anabaptist ethical concerns to that point where they had virtually created for the radicals a program of social and political action which had as its ultimate goal the overthrow of the state. Münster did indeed have such a program. The Swiss Brethren did not. It might be suggested that this exaggeration had two causes: fear of Anabaptism's effectiveness in gaining adherents among the common people and a desire to dissociate themselves completely from the Anabaptists in the eyes of all observers. For the Anabaptist views on the church, and even on baptism, were derived in large part from those of Zwingli in particular. Hence he advertised to the entire world that "they have gone out from us, for they were not of us."[29]

II

The Reformers at Zürich had abundant personal contacts with the Anabaptists. They knew intimately the Swiss Brethren, a moderate manifestation of Anabaptism. The Wittenberg Reformers, on the other hand, had no such opportunity to know the Anabaptists, for which Luther at least gave dutiful thanks to God.[30] Anabaptism did not penetrate central Germany until the latter part of the 1520's. And it never did become a problem at Wittenberg itself. A few of its devotees entered the Electorate of Saxony on the southern fringes. But for the most part they confined their activities to Hesse because of the relatively tolerant attitude of the ruler of that principality. Hence the sources of information

28 *Ibid.*, Ca, CIIIa-CVa.
29 *Refutation*, 137.
30 Martin Luther, *Von der wiedertauffe an zwen Pfarherrn, ein Brief* (Nürnberg, 1528), A *verso*.

about Anabaptism for the Wittenberg theologians were generally secondhand, or worse. Melanchthon, it is true, had seen and talked with a few Anabaptists. Some of his earliest information seems to have come from, if not personal contacts with the radicals, at least discussions with persons who had encountered them.[31] On one occasion, in 1535 at Jena, he presided at a theological examination of four captive Anabaptists, during which a wide range of topics was discussed.[32] Supplementing this information with certain details which he obtained from friends, or from writings of the Anabaptists,[33] he was able to present a systematic outline and refutation of Anabaptist dogma, something which Luther for lack of time and adequate information never accomplished. Melanchthon possessed a fuller, more exact knowledge of Anabaptism than did Luther. The latter's record bears no hint of personal encounters with them. He obtained some information about them from Melanchthon, much more from friends such as Menius and Rhegius, and possibly some from the students who came to Wittenberg.

The historian dealing with the Zürich Reformers' relations with Anabaptism has a relatively clear picture of the type of Anabaptism being described. With the Wittenbergers, especially with Luther, the situation is vastly different. Bombastic, voluble, imaginative, Luther invented words to fit his descriptive needs, and used them in baffling profusion. *Rottengeister, Schwärmer, Sacramentirer,* or the more conventional *Wiedertäufer* were terms he applied with almost no precision to a motley array of left wingers. It is very difficult to know whom Luther is talking about, and therefore to ascertain the nature of Anabaptism as he perceives it. It is probably correct to say that he never did see Anabaptism with any degree of clarity, but rather confused it constantly with all non-Catholic opposition to himself, including that of

31 Letter to Camerarius, August 11 (?), 1527, *Corpus Reformatorum*, 1:881.
32 *Corpus Reformatorum*, 2:997-1003.
33 For his works on the Münsterites he had access to their publications, at least to Rothmann's *Restitution*. See his *Etliche propositiones wider die lehr der Widerteuffer* (n.p., 1535), A *verso*.

Zwingli.[34] Melanchthon, on the other hand, if he distinguished types of Anabaptism, refused to consider them other than as degrees of Anabaptism. The species was the same; only the degree of revolutionary character differed. Thus he mixed thoroughly the doctrines of the Münsterites, the Davidians, and the Menists.

Anabaptism for the Wittenbergers began with the Zwickau Prophets and Thomas Müntzer. In the Prophets Luther met for the first time the serious denial of the validity of infant baptism. They did not propose adult or believers' baptism; but they thoroughly challenged infant baptism in a manner characteristic of some of the later Anabaptists: baptism is contingent on the faith of the individual and hence should not be administered to infants who are incapable of faith. Luther's reply to this argument was fundamentally his answer for the remainder of his life. These Prophets have not properly understood the nature of the sacrament. The sacrament is in no way contingent upon the faith of the individual recipient, which faith is at best a weak, vacillating thing. Rather the sacrament is based upon the command of God. As such it is true; and accompanied by the Word it becomes the certain conveyor of God's grace.[35]

Luther discerned and condemned the subjective character of the religion of the Zwickau Prophets. He was suspicious of their revelations. He laid it down that the true test for the validity of extrascriptural revelations must be the God-given ability to perform miracles. The Prophets produced no miracles, though they hinted that wonderful things might occur. But Luther had learned as much as he wanted: the "spirit" of the Prophets was much more akin to that of Satan than to the Holy Spirit.[36] Luther met subjectivism in Müntzer's mysticism, and scorned it with equal fervor. Müntzer rejected

---

34 Luther's *Vorrede* to Menius' *Von dem Geist der Widertäufer* (Wittenberg, 1544), Aij *verso*.

35 Letter to Melanchthon, January 13, 1522, in J. G. Walch, *D. Martin Luthers . . . Sämtliche Schriften* (Halle, 1739-53) 15:221-27 (Appendix No. 103).

36 *Ibid.* Also excerpt from Tabletalk in Preserved Smith, *The Life and Letters of Martin Luther* (Boston, 1911) 143-44.

what he considered Luther's dead literalistic interpretation of the Scripture. The ultimate authority for Müntzer was experience, by which the written Word was to be interpreted. This experience was an internal suffering, borne in the spirit of Christ's suffering on the cross (the true *Nachfolge Christi* to Müntzer), through which all sensual pleasure and lust was killed and an earnest desire for truth was kindled. God's spirit then moved the heart to understanding. Luther considered such subjectivity utter folly, if not the work of Satan.[37]

A third basic element in the programs of the Prophets and Müntzer which Luther later associated with Anabaptism was the threat to the established civil order. The Prophets were more than mildly iconoclastic. The confusion and disorder which they helped to foster in Wittenberg forced Luther to leave his Wartburg refuge at considerable personal risk, to return to quiet the tumult. Luther was of the opinion that innovations in religious practice were to be made only with much careful planning and instruction.[38] More fundamentally, he opposed any attempt to usher in a church reform by physical force, such as clearing a church of all physical vestiges of popery by mob action. He relied instead, with the utmost confidence, on the power of the Word to perform unaided the task of reform. To supplement the Word with a program of force was unnecessary and wrong; such was not the manner of God's work among men.[39]

Müntzer was even more violent; he determined to destroy not only images, but also persons who blocked the progress of his kingdom of God, all done in the name of God. Even before the Peasants' Revolt Luther was convinced that the iconoclast of Allstedt would sooner or later become a shedder of blood.[40] At that point where the iconoclast grasped

37 Carl Hinrichs, *Luther und Müntzer* (Berlin, 1952) Chap. I *passim.* Letter to the Princes of Saxony, July 1524, in Preserved Smith and Charles Jacobs, *Luther's Correspondence and Other Contemporary Letters* (Philadelphia, 1918) 2:243.

38 Letter to Nicholas Hausmann, March 17, 1522. Translated and printed in P. Smith, *Life and Letters of M. Luther,* 149.

39 *Ibid.,* 148.

40 Hinrichs, *op. cit.,* 156.

the sword it was necessary to call upon the magistrate; the matter was no longer one of religious differences, but rather of civil disobedience.[41]

Here are Luther's *Schwärmer*, the religious enthusiasts who swarm over the entire country usurping to themselves the right to preach and teach the Word, showing no respect for the lawful holders of religious office. It was in this context that Luther regarded Anabaptism. In those letters, sermons, and tracts in which he considered the Anabaptists, he repeated the identical charges, only with greater elaboration: they did not understand the sacrament of baptism; their ultimate authority in religious matters was subjective in character; they trafficked in sedition and fomented revolution in the name of Christianity.[42] He seemed to have recognized the existence of a type of Anabaptism not organically related to the Prophets or Müntzer. Through a Wittenberg student he learned of Conrad Grebel early in 1525, and sent greetings to him, though he disliked some of Grebel's ideas.[43] In his major work against the Anabaptists, written in 1528, he declared that Electoral Saxony had not been visited by the Anabaptists, and that he therefore did not know their doctrines.[44] Indeed, he hoped his brochure would provoke them to answer with a clear delineation of their doctrines.[45] Since the Prophets and Müntzer had certainly troubled Electoral Saxony, Luther must have known that there were other "Anabaptists." He persisted nevertheless in viewing them as of the same mind and spirit as the Prophets and Müntzer.[46] He tended to regard the Anabaptists as a monstrous obstacle to the progress of the Word, the devil's angels incarnate.

41 Letter to the Princes of Saxony, July 1524, Smith and Jacobs, *Luther's Correspondence*, 2:246.

42 His principal works touching Anabaptism are: *Von der wiedertauffe an zwen Pfarherrn, ein Brief* (1528); *Vorrede* to J. Menius' *Der Widder-tauffer lere vnd geheimnis* . . . (1530); Sermon on Matt. 5, 6, 7 (1532); *Vorrede* to Menius' *Von dem Geist der Wiedertäufer* (1544).

43 Letter of Erhard Hegenwalt to Conrad Grebel, January 1, 1525. Discussed in Bender, *op. cit.*, 119 ff.

44 Luther, *Von der wiedertauffe, A verso*-Aij *recto*.

45 Letter to Spalatin, February 5, 1528, in *D. Martin Luther's Werke* (Weimar, 1883-1914) 4:376 (Brief Nr. 1218).

46 Luther's *Vorrede* to *Von dem Geist der Wiedertäufer*, Aij *verso*.

Melanchthon had been utterly unable to refute the arguments of the Prophets against infant baptism. Despite his erudition, he felt himself helpless against the spiritual authority which the Prophets professed. Luther gently reprimanded him for this hesitation,[47] which was probably due not so much to indecision on the question of infant baptism as to an irenic temperament which sought constantly to temporize and placate in religious disputes. He displayed this same quality of spirit in the Lutheran-Zwinglian controversy concerning the Lord's Supper.[48] When he later turned to a defense of the practice of infant baptism, he did so with a vigor which perhaps was a compensation for his earlier uncertainty and devoted a major portion of his Anabaptist polemics to this topic. In this connection it is well to remember that he wrote to instruct pastors on the Lutheran frontiers on how to refute the Anabaptists, and the issue of baptism was the point at which the Anabaptist was normally detected, i.e., when he refused to have his children baptized. Melanchthon's view on the topic did not differ substantially from Luther's. Baptism was a sacrament which, accompanied by the Word, fortified one's faith. Administered to infants, it removed the guilt of original sin.[49]

But baptism aside, by far the major concern to Melanchthon when he came to deal with "Anabaptists" from the Prophets through Münster was their tendency toward a disruption of the civil order. He charged them repeatedly with propagating ideas which undermined authority in society and which tended toward revolution. The specific Anabaptist teachings which provoked him to the charge were these: no Christian should be a magistrate, or hold any office which required the use of the sword; Christians should admit no authority except that of the religious office; no Christian should swear an oath; Christians should possess no private property;

---

47 Letter of Luther to Melanchthon, January 13, 1522, in Walch, *op. cit.,* 15:221-27.

48 See Neve, *op. cit.,* 1:260-61.

49 Philip Melanchthon, *Underricht Philip Melanchthon wider die Lere der Wiederteuffer* (Wittenberg, 1528), Aij *verso*-Aiij *verso;* Biij *verso*-Ciiij *verso.*

a true Christian should leave his non-Christian spouse.[50] Melanchthon was convinced that the civil authority as it then existed was ordained by God; its highest function was that of promoting the honor of God. As such it was truly Christian government. To deny that a Christian might be a magistrate stood therefore as a condemnation of Christian government as it then existed, which, if dissolved under the pressure of Anabaptist arguments, would leave utter anarchy. Melanchthon, horrified, pictured for his readers the uncontrollable outbreak of theft and murder if everyone would adhere to Anabaptist dogma.[51] It is clear that Melanchthon perceived civil disorder (at least potentially) in the teachings of the peaceful Anabaptists. He buttressed his case with a concrete example: the kingdom of Münster. Even if by false humility and hypocrisy the Anabaptists appeared to be pious Christians, they would eventually, if given a chance, develop as the Münsterites had. For all Anabaptists rejected some concern of the citizenry. They would proceed quickly then to insurrection, if means were at their disposal. The events at Münster stood as a testimony to this fact.[52]

Melanchthon compiled a formidable list of Anabaptist errors during his thirty-odd years as principal polemicist among the Wittenbergers. The Lord's Supper, the nature of Christ, original sin, extrascriptural revelations, works-righteousness were the most important of these. Unlike the Zürichers he charged the Anabaptists only implicitly with the heresy of dividing the church, except on one occasion. In 1536, in response to a request for counsel from Philip of Hesse, he wrote a treatise on how Anabaptists ought to be punished in which he accused them of dividing the church, as the Donatists had done. But it appears that he did so pri-

50 Philip Melanchthon, *Das Weltliche Oberkeitt den Widertauferen mit leiblicher straff zu weren schuldig sey* (Wittenberg, 1536), Aij *verso*. Philip Melanchthon, *Prozess wie es soll gehalten werden mit den Wiedertäufern*, in Gustav Bossert, *Quellen zur Geschichte der Wiedertäufer* (Leipzig, 1930) 1:162, 163.

51 Melanchthon, *Das Weltliche Oberkeitt*, Aiij *recto*.

52 Philip Melanchthon, *Verlegung etlicher unchristlicher Artickel welche die Wiedertäufer vorgeben* (Wittenberg, n.d.), Aiiij *verso*.

marily to enable him to claim the same punishment for the Anabaptists that Roman law accorded the Donatists—the death penalty.[53] It is surprising that he did not elaborate and repeat the charge.

Melanchthon's experience with the Zwickau Prophets undoubtedly prepared him for the view that all Anabaptists, even those whom he recognized as teaching nothing against the magistracy or the social order, were to be condemned as destroyers of public authority. For he viewed all Anabaptism as coming from the Prophets.[54] Thus, just as some of the followers of the Prophets (i.e., Münsterites) fomented revolution, so all Anabaptists would act if not restrained. Melanchthon was bitter about his own docility in the face of the Prophets when they had come to Wittenberg in 1521.[55] He became in turn, though by nature mild in temperament, more dedicated than Luther to the application of the sternest punishment, the death penalty, to Anabaptists of all types.

53 Melanchthon, *Das Weltliche Oberkeitt*, B *verso*-Bij *recto*.

54 Letter to Myconius, February 1530, quoted in Paul Wappler, *Die Stellung Kursachsens und des Landgrafen Philipp von Hessen zur Täuferbewegung* (Münster, 1910) 13.

55 *Ibid.*, 13.

Anabaptism in History

✠ CORNELIUS KRAHN ✠

Anabaptism and the Culture of the Netherlands

The Netherlands provide an unusual opportunity for he study of the relationship of Anabaptism and culture: the nfluence of Anabaptism upon culture, and how Anabaptism tself was influenced and modified by culture. Dutch Ana-baptism differed somewhat from the Swiss stream of the novement. Although Melchior Hofmann transplanted some eatures of Swiss Anabaptism to the North, certain basic ele-nents of the Anabaptist movement of the Netherlands were native.[1] They grew out of the Sacramentarian movement of he Low Countries, created in part by native religious forces, and in part by Luther's Reformation. It was in this soil that Hofmann planted his seed. To the Sacramentarian concepts, Hofmann's message added the practice of believers' baptism as a seal of the New Testament covenant, his symbolic inter-pretation of the Scriptures, and his peculiar emphasis on the second coming of Christ. The latter were a deviation from Anabaptism, causing disaster among the Dutch Anabaptists. In the case of the peaceful Anabaptist wing, however, it must be said that the native Dutch Sacramentarian ideas and the genuinely Swiss Anabaptist beliefs survived.

At first the Sacramentarian movement was predominant among the Reformation forces at work in the Low Countries. After 1530 this movement became for some decades almost entirely identical with Anabaptism. Later on, militant Cal-vinism assumed the lead and overthrew the Spanish Catholic occupational authorities. Nonresistant Anabaptism, severely

---

* Cornelius Krahn of Bethel College is Professor of Church History, editor of *Mennonite Life,* and author of *Menno Simons* (Karlsruhe, 1936).

1 For literature see Cornelius Krahn, "The Historiography of the Mennonites in the Netherlands," *Church History* (September 1944) 13:19.

persecuted by the foreign oppressor, now became a tolerated minority. Thus the Dutch Anabaptists were not aggressive or even active participants in creating and shaping Dutch culture and national life after the Spanish occupants had been forced out. The new government and the Reformed Church of the Netherlands were co-operating in this task.

On the other hand, the Anabaptists gradually joined in with the pioneer culture bearers of the Golden Age which the Netherlands entered soon after having obtained national and religious independence. The early Swiss leaders of Anabaptism belonged to the educated or middle class. In the Low Countries the participation of the lower, uneducated class in the Anabaptist movement was more conspicuous. The laboring class and the peasants were predominant at times and often held the leadership. Thus the followers of Anabaptism in the Netherlands did not belong to the "cultured" population. This does not mean, however, that there were no educated, cultured, and well-to-do people among them. It is merely to state that the predominant constituency was of the lower class.

Numerous studies have been made of the economic and social background of the Dutch Anabaptists.[2] Although the conclusions arrived at differ greatly, one thing is clear. Swiss Anabaptism emerged in cities with an educated leadership and survived in remote places as peasants only. In the Netherlands Anabaptism began primarily within the lower level urban population and survived there, gradually participating in a wider range of occupations, and benefiting fully by the prosperity of the Golden Age of the Netherlands. Many became prosperous. This observation caused the Mennonite historian P. M. Friesen to state that piety results in prosperity. We could add that prosperity opens the door to greater participation in social and cultural activity.

---

2 Greta Grosheide, *Bijdrage tot de geschiedenis der Anabaptisten in Amsterdam* (Hilversum, 1938); A. F. Mellink, *De Wederdopers in de noordelijke Nederlanden 1531-1544* (Groningen, 1954); W. L. C. Coenen, *Bijdrage tot de kennis van de maatschappelijke verhoudingen van de zestiende-eeuwsche Doopers* (Amsterdam, 1920). See also Krahn, "The Historiography . . . ," 15.

INDIVIDUAL FREEDOM, BROTHERHOOD, AND DISCIPLESHIP

The Dutch Anabaptists adhered to a specific church concept which implied a rigid separation from the world, which they practiced even more consistently and tenaciously than did the Swiss Brethren. They considered themselves citizens of the heavenly kingdom to which their dwelling upon the earth was merely a preface. The brutal persecution during the early sixteenth century only strengthened their conviction that the true children of God are and will always be persecuted. The pages of the *Martyrs' Mirror* illustrate the fact that their otherworldly views were emphasized and strengthened through this experience. For this reason the early Dutch Anabaptists had only a limited contact with their contemporary culture. Their attitude toward many phases of culture was negative. They practiced nonconformity and nonresistance.

The Anabaptist concept of sin and salvation, of the church and the world, of the sinful life of the world and the fruitful life of the Christian, and of the relationship of state and church implied great contrasts. The church exists on an entirely different level from that of the world. Salvation places a person who is doomed in the Pauline sense of the word, from one level of being into an entirely new one. His being, although to some extent in anticipation and hope, is different from that of the unregenerate person. One is of divine origin; the other is carnal and of the earth. One is within the church, and the other outside of it. The church, the Ark of Noah within which redemption is experienced, takes its members and passengers securely from one shore to the other surrounded by the lurking dangers of the sea of life. From within, threats are also present and sin is in evidence. The members of the body of Christ are not immune to the temptations of the world around them. Therefore disciplinary measures are necessary to keep the demarcation line clear, or to prevent the water from entering the ark. The ark is in the sea, but the waters of the sea must be kept out. The goal of the ark which the pilot aims to reach must be a fixed and unmovable goal.

With Paul the Anabaptists believed in Christ as the head of the church whose members receive all directions from Him. Each member must be in close contact with the head, the central office. Any local disturbance is noticeable throughout the body and can easily paralyze it.[3] This brings us to the question which has been raised at times as to what was most basic for the early Anabaptists in their beliefs and practices. Were they pioneers of an individualistic piety in which responsibility in religious matters rests with the individual only? Was each individual his own priest in this fellowship of believers with the concept of the priesthood of all believers?[4] Was discipleship the central idea, based on the challenge of Christ: "Follow me"?[5] Or was their view of the church the unique Anabaptist idea? All of these and other views have been expressed as typically Anabaptist. We would like to present here a synthesis in the following manner.

It is true that the early Anabaptists were extreme individualists, defying the institutionalized religion of their day, pioneering along the lines of freedom of conscience, separation of state and church, and other areas. With possibly few exceptions, however, this was only one aspect of their concern. Their strength, courage, hope, and faith were not motivated by a revolutionary and negative attitude. Basically, their revolutionary and individualistic personal attitude and program were closely connected with their desire to restore the true church of Christ Jesus founded on the rock against which the gates of hell cannot prevail. Or as expressed in Menno's motto: "For other foundation can no man lay than that which has been laid which is Jesus Christ" (I Cor. 3:11).

3 Cornelius Krahn, "The Anabaptist-Mennonites and the Biblical Church," *Proceedings of the Study Conference on the Believers' Church* (Newton, 1955); Franklin H. Littell, *The Anabaptist View of the Church* (1952).

4 H. W. Meihuizen, "Basic Beliefs of the Dutch Mennonites," *Mennonite Life* (October 1956).

5 Harold S. Bender, "The Anabaptist Theology of Discipleship," *MQR* (January 1950) 24:25-32.

With Paul they accepted the idea that the true church is the body of Christ which "should be holy and without blemish, . . . for we are members of his body, of his flesh, and of his bones" (Eph. 5:27, 30). Or again Paul speaks of this when he says: "Now ye are the body of Christ" (I Cor. 12:27). With Martin Luther they believed that a Christian is free and at the same time a servant of all. They believed in a freedom which is guided and directed toward a goal. Indifference and unrestricted liberty were unknown to them. They believed in the freedom to which Christ had called them, namely, to become members of His body, and to follow Him.

This at the same time was their idea of discipleship. Discipleship does not take place in a vacuum; it is possible only in relationship to Christ and the other members of the brotherhood, fellowship, or church. The mystic, quietist, and pietist can dream on an island of bliss about "My God and I"; but his Christianity is tested only in the frame of the larger fellowship, in a community or brotherhood. Anabaptism at its best was a component of individual freedom obtained through Christ within the fellowship of disciplined members which received their direction through Christ, the head of the church. Discipleship is not equal to mysticism or pietism. Discipleship implies directed and disciplined living and action . This takes place within the fellowship, the brotherhood, or the church. It is true that on the periphery of Anabaptism there were some who were not willing or able to identify themselves fully with the movement. Among these were Sebastian Franck, Obbe Philips, and possibly Hans Denk. The fault was no doubt not entirely on their side. Certain developments within the Anabaptist main stream were also causes for this attitude.

Most of the martyrs were severe critics of existing conditions, primarily within the Catholic Church. There was no complete uniformity of thinking. Many died giving their witness at the time when Anabaptism was emerging out of the Sacramentarian movement of the Netherlands. Yet there were some basic thoughts and ideas prevalent in their testimonies. Their severe criticism was inspired and based on positive convictions which they found in Jesus Christ as a personal Saviour: the conviction of a fellowship of the redeemed, and of a challenge to live a dedicated, consecrated, and disciplined Christian life within the brotherhood. Their concepts were not final and fixed; they were still flexible depending upon the conditions in which they lived.

Thus we must say that there need be no conflict or contrast between the idea of an individual Christian life rejoicing in its freedom, sincerely seeking to follow Christ all the way, and the idea of a disciplined body of Christ, the church. This church is composed of individuals who voluntarily choose to withdraw from the commonplace life and join the fellowship. Personal freedom, brotherhood, and discipline have found a synthesis. A slavish incorporation into the body of Christ would be a deadening weight to the body. Undisciplined exploitation of the members of the body by one member would represent a cancerous growth which must be removed in order to keep the body without "spot or wrinkle" (Eph. 5:27).

FROM MARTYRDOM TO THE GOLDEN AGE

Realizing that the ideal church without spot or wrinkle could not be fully established on earth, some Dutch Anabaptists began to lose hope. They visualized themselves as having attempted to build the tower of Babel, and felt that the Lord Himself had confused their tongues. The main lines of their original concern had become obscured by the details of controversies about them. In the second generation of Anabaptism the vision and zeal of the early fathers were not always matched by love for the brother. In disillusionment some gave up the original ideals and substituted others for them. Those who felt that their individual initiative and freedom had been curbed now placed emphasis on the freedom of the individual conscience, the fruits of faith and the free will. This was also done in contrast to the predestinarian Calvinist majority of the Reformed Church which emphasized a rigid orthodoxy in matters of faith. Thus Calvinism and the Reformed Church of the Netherlands must be taken into consideration in reviewing the development of Dutch Anabaptism. Without this background we cannot fully understand nor appreciate the development and contributions made by the Dutch Mennonites. No religious group or movement remains alive when it is isolated for any length of time. Either it dies in isolation or it is challenged by its environment. If this challenge is accepted the group will adapt itself in some areas and in others it will develop characteristics of its own. It will fill a gap and it will fulfill a mission.

The process of growing into the culture of the country and the acceptance of it was a gradual one that was brought about through a number of factors. When persecution was relaxed, and the piety, frugality, and industry of the Mennonites brought about prosperity, the foundation was laid for a greater participation in cultural activities. The Golden Age of the Netherlands and its prosperity and progress in culture and the fine arts speeded up this process. After the Anabaptists had tried to define the demarcation line between the church of Christ and the world around them, in their relationship to state and society, disagreements arose. They became divided into many groups, some very rigid in their nonconformist views, while others gradually accepted a more positive attitude toward participation in matters pertaining to culture.

After having gradually given up some of their original tenets, the Dutch Mennonites found a new mission in their day. In an age of cold Calvinistic orthodoxy they were attracted by a personal creedless type of piety which also found expression in Arminianism, the Remonstrants, and the Collegiants. In a country of rigid Calvinism, and the land of Erasmus and Rembrandt, they joined the pioneers of a Christian humanism. Roots of this development can be traced back to original Dutch Anabaptism and early Sacramentarian views. The outcome, however, was conditioned by the developments of the latter part of the sixteenth and the early part of the seventeenth centuries. But throughout this time, an individualistic and quietistic piety which is primarily concerned with its own salvation, nourishing its spiritual life in an ivory tower unrelated to the questions and the life of the day as was at times the case in German Pietism and in English Methodism, remained foreign to Dutch Mennonitism, although there are some traces of it in the theology of J. Ph. Schabaelje, Pieter Petersz, Johannes Deknatel, and others, which influenced European and American Mennonites. A greater danger for the Dutch Mennonites was a shallow moralism lacking a deep religious and theological foundation. These dangers already noticeable in early Anabaptism became more pronounced at this time. The ethical emphasis was still strong; but the Pauline emphasis on the sinful state of man and the power of grace were lacking at times. The writings of the early leaders in which this emphasis is strong were no longer read. "Think well, speak well, do well," became a widely accepted motto.

By now the otherworldly nature of the church concept had undergone a considerable transformation. The sea in which the Ark of Noah was floating seemed no longer to be inhabited by furious beasts which were a constant threat to the believers in the ship. In a century during which the Dutch had a merchant marine in all the seven seas bringing in the riches of the world, the elements of the sea were no longer considered to be a danger. The adventure of the sea had become challenging. Life on earth was not merely a preface to life in heaven; it had a value in itself and the utmost care had to be taken in order to bring it to fruition. The values of this life became ever more precious and desirable. Contact with the cultural environment was not kept to a minimum, but accepted and enjoyed. This was a gradual process, with a step by step development, in which all groups sooner or later followed. Out of the church of martyrs, who had been willing to give their life for a heavenly cause, seeking a kingdom not made by hands, came a fellowship well established on earth, industrious, sincere, honest, simple, and enjoying prosperity and helpfulness. An anonymous versifier said in 1682 (free prose translation):

> "Formerly the Mennonites
> (What I say is true)
> Were in the world, but now
> The world is in the midst of them."[6]

What kind of world was it that was in the midst of them at this time? Of course, the environment had changed to some extent. The martyrs had died at the hand of a foreign occupational power guided by medieval concepts which used the inquisition machinery to suppress every deviating thought or movement in the religious, political, and social life. The Dutch government and public opinion of the Golden Age, on the other hand, were enlightened and tolerant to some degree. In this time of tolerance and prosperity the values of the earthly life rose in the eyes of the public, including the descendants of the martyrs. It was so much easier to appreciate the culture and to be at peace with the world which, although not perfect, was no longer persecuting its subjects for religious reasons.

AGRICULTURE AND BUSINESS

The German historian H. L. B. Bentheim called the Mennonites of Europe "the honeybees of the state."[7] Their pioneer spirit, industry, frugality, and contributions in general were appreciated by friend and foe. That they became agricultural pioneers in many areas was due in part to the fact that their industry and perseverance were rooted in their religious convictions, and in part to their willingness to withdraw into uncultivated areas, making a livelihood where no one else could. Since not all places and occupations were

---

6 N. van der Zijpp, *Geschiedenis der Doopsgezinden in Nederland* (Arnhem, 1952) 152.
7 *Holländischer Kirchen- und Schulenstaat* (Frankfurt, 1698) 1:823.

open to them, they often became experts in whatever area they were tolerated. Outside of the Low Countries the Mennonites for a long time were restricted to agricultural activities. In later generations at times there was a conflict between their singing *Von der Erde reiss mich los* on Sunday, and their actual clinging to the soil during the week. The Lord's command "to till the soil" they fully accepted and observed. In this development they became *Die Stillen im Lande,* observing the motto "to live and let live" or "to believe and let believe." The burning zeal and witness of the martyrs had been channeled into other areas. Often they became quite tolerant and understanding of an environment that differed from theirs. Their witness had lost the sharp edge which it formerly possessed.

In the Netherlands prosperity, integrity, honesty, frugality, and reliability opened to them channels of service formerly closed to them. New contacts with the ladder of society were established and used. The radical views of the early days about nonparticipation in matters of the world and nonconformity, and even nonresistance and the holding of public office, were reviewed and at times modified. According to N. van der Zijpp, however, the Mennonites of Holland likely held no significant public offices before 1795.[8] This was due in part to the fact that such offices were not yet open to them. In many instances the adjustment was a gradual process in which the full weight and impact of the outcome was not foreseen nor felt immediately. When called upon to participate in military drills or actions, they would make financial contributions instead, which were used for the same purpose.

The situation in the realm of the economic and cultural life was different. Around 1650 the Mennonites constituted 20 per cent of the population in some places, as for example in Amsterdam, and in the provinces of Friesland and Groningen.[9] Some industries such as whaling and the herring fisheries were almost entirely in the hands of the Mennonites. They

8 N. van der Zijpp, *op. cit.,* 149.
9 *Ibid.,* 149.

did not participate, however, in the East Indies Company because this would have obligated them to break the principle of nonresistance by fighting the pirates. On the other hand, their trade with Russia and the Baltic States was extensive. The lumberyards of Zaandam, Amsterdam, and Harlingen were in many cases in the hands of Mennonites. Well known are the contacts of Peter the Great with the Mennonites. The Mennonite, Nicolaas Bidloo, sponsored by Peter the Great, established the first medical school in Moscow. The cities of Deventer and Middelburg were also centers of Mennonite business enterprises. In the province of Twente and in Gronau, Westphalia, and in Crefeld on the Lower Rhine, Mennonite weavers laid the foundation for the present-day big scale weaving industry.[10]

EDUCATION AND FINE ARTS

In the realm of education Mennonites had no objections. However, education was for them not an end in itself. It was only a means toward an end. The primary objective of education for the early Anabaptists was otherworldly. It was a means toward a better understanding of the Bible and of God's plan for mankind. When the Friar Cornelis heard Jacob de Roore expound the Scriptures he exclaimed: "You Anabaptists are certainly fine fellows and understand the Holy Scripture; for before you are rebaptized you can't tell A from B, but as soon as you are baptized you can read and write. If the devil and his mother have not a hand in this, I do not understand anything about you people."[11]

The Anabaptist motivation in aiming to obtain an education was primarily religious. Gradually, however, with a greater appreciation for cultural values, education of itself

10 Heinz Münte, *Das Altonaer Handlungshaus van der Smissen 1682-1824* (Altona, 1932); B. K. Roosen, *Geschichte unseres Hauses* (Hamburg, 1905); Abram Fast, *Die Kulturleistungen der Mennoniten in Ostfriesland und Münsterland* (Emden, 1947); Gerhard van Beckerath, *Die wirtschaftliche Bedeutung der Krefelder Mennoniten im 17. und 18. Jahrhundert* (Crefeld, 1952; unpublished dissertation at Bonn University); *Mennonite Encyclopedia* (Scottdale, 1955) 1:483.

11 *Martyrs' Mirror* (1950) 275.

became more desirable. The value and significance of higher education among the seventeenth-century Mennonites of the Netherlands is illustrated from the fact that they not only had a great number of physicians in their midst, but that they also began to select their ministers of the Gospel from the ranks of the physicians. They were not quite ready to give their ministers a full theological training; but neither were they satisfied to continue with the ministry of lay preachers who had no higher education.[12]

In another field the Anabaptists of the Netherlands early demonstrated an appreciation of culture. This was in the field of the fine arts. Carel van Mander (1548-1606) was one of the first among the writers and artists. His hymnal entitled *De Gulden Harpe* was used not only among the Mennonites of the Netherlands, but also of Prussia. A considerable body of literature exists dealing with the works of art and literature produced by him, and a considerable number of his paintings are extant.[13] Joost van den Vondel (1587-1679), the "Shakespeare of the Netherlands," for a time was a deacon of the Mennonite Church in Amsterdam. In 1640, however, he joined the Catholic Church.[14] Peter Langedult[15] (born about 1648), Claas Bruin[16] (1670-1732), and Peter Langedijk[17] (1683-1756) were outstanding Mennonite writers who achieved national fame. One of the best-known writers and artists was Jan Luyken[18] (1649-1712), who wrote many devotional books. His etchings adorn the *Martyrs' Mirror* and many other books. Among the artists, we should name also the minister Lambert Jacobsz[19] (1598-1636); Michiel

---

12 W. J. Kühler, *Geschiedenis van de Doopsgezinden in Nederland* (Haarlem, 1950) 3:2 ff.; "Amsterdam Mennonite Seminary," *ME*, 1:108-10.

13 *Het schilder-boek van Carel van Mander* (Amsterdam, 1946); R. Jacobsen, *Carel van Mander (1548-1616) dichter en prozaschrijver* (Rotterdam, 1906); "Mander, Carel van," *ME*, Vol. 3.

14 W. J. Kühler, *Geschiedenis van de Doopsgezinden in Nederland* (Haarlem, 1940) 2:159; P. Leendertz Jr., *Het leven van Vondel* (Amsterdam, 1910).

15 "Langedult, Peter," *ME*, Vol. 3.

16 "Bruin, Claas," *ibid.*, 1:450.

17 "Langedijk, Peter," *ibid.*, Vol. 3.

18 P. van Eeghen, *Het werk van Jan en Casper Luyken* (Amsterdam, 1905) 2 vols.; "Luyken, Jan," *ME*, Vol. 3.

19 *Herdenkings-Tentoonstelling Lambert Jacobsz* (Leeuwarden, 1936).

Jansz van Mierevelt[20] (1576-1641); Dirk van Hoogstraten (1596-1640); his son Samuel van Hoogstraten[21] (1627-78); Jacob Adriansz Backer[22] (1608-74); Salomon van Ruysdael[23] (1602-70); Jacob van Ruisdael[24] (1628-82), who later joined the Reformed Church; Govert Flinck[25] (1615-60), a pupil of Lambert Jacobsz and Rembrandt, who later joined the Remonstrants; Abraham van den Tempel[26] (1622-72), a son of Lambert Jacobsz; and Jan van der Heyden[27] (1637-1712). Rembrandt, it has been claimed, was also a Mennonite. However, recent investigations indicate that he never joined the Mennonite Church, although he was closely related to the Mennonites by spiritual and friendship ties.[28] Our observations on the active Mennonite participation in the fine arts are limited to the period of the Golden Age. During the later period, naturally, their interest and participation increased. Works of art of all those mentioned above can be found in many European museums, particularly in the Netherlands, but also in America.

As in the case of education, the voluminous literature of the early Anabaptists was not merely a form of self-expression; it was created for a definite goal. From the earliest edition of *Het Offer des Heeren* to the last edition of Menno's writings and in all the confessions of faith and devotional books, the primary objective was to instruct, inspire, and challenge the new generations to live a Christian life and to appreciate their own heritage. Not only did this literary output serve the needs of the Dutch Mennonites for generations to come; some of the books were also translated into German and English to be used among the Mennonites of the Vistula

20 "Mierevelt, M. J. v.," *ME*, Vol. 3.
21 "Hoogstraaten, Dirk and Samuel van," *ibid.*, 2:806.
22 "Backer, Jacob Adriaensz," *ibid.*, 1:204.
23 W. von Bode, *Die Meister der holländischen und flämischen Malerschulen* (Leipzig, 1951) 215; "Art," *ME*, 1:165-72.
24 W. von Bode, *op. cit.*, 233 ff.
25 "Flinck, Govert," *ME*, 2:340.
26 "Art," *ibid.*, 1:170.
27 W. von Bode, *op. cit.*, 365; "Heyden, Jan van der," *ME*, 2:736.
28 Irvin B. Horst, "Rembrandt Knew Mennonites," *Mennonite Life* (October 1956); see also January 1952 issue of *Mennonite Life*.

region, and of Russia, South Germany, Switzerland, and America.[29] Had it not been for the literary and devotional books of the Dutch Mennonites, Anabaptism and Mennonitism would have become a spiritual desert. Among the early writers, we name only a few: Hans de Ries, Cornelis Ris, P. J. Twisk, Jan Cents, and Jan Philipsz Schabaelje.[30] Of course, not all of the writings were purely devotional and theological in character. Much of the literature was devoted to the defense of the "true" teachings and practices against opponents outside the church, as well as against those within the brotherhood who deviated from the true path.

SCIENCE, TECHNOLOGY, AND PHILANTHROPY

In the realm of scientific and technical invention the Mennonites were just as active as in the fine arts. The above-mentioned Jan van der Heyden invented a fire engine; Jan Adriaensz Leeghwater[31] was an expert in draining swamps; and Jan Kops[32] was noted for the agricultural program which he introduced in Holland. In the draining of swamps and in agriculture the Dutch Mennonite refugees made outstanding contributions in East Friesland, in Schleswig-Holstein, and in the Vistula Delta. This contribution was continued by their descendants on the plains of Russia and North America, and in vast undeveloped territories of Latin America.

In welfare work, the Dutch Mennonites made outstanding contributions in helping the Swiss Mennonite refugees establish new homes in the Netherlands and in North America. They pioneered in raising the educational level of their country, and in rehabilitating the poor in their own church as well as on a national scale. In philanthropic and social work the Mennonites of Holland became pioneers on a large scale through men like Jan Nieuwenhuizen (1724-1806) who founded during the eighteenth century the welfare organization *Maatschappij tot nut van t'algemeen* which is playing

---

29 Robert Friedmann, *Mennonite Piety Through the Centuries* (Goshen, 1949).
30 *Ibid.*
31 "Leeghwater," *ME*, Vol. 3.   32 "Kops, Jan," *ibid.*, Vol. 3.

an outstanding role in the Dutch commonwealth even in the twentieth century.[33] At the same time Pieter Teyler founded the Teyler Institute at Haarlem to promote scientific and philosophical research. The Teyler Institute is still exerting a considerable amount of influence. Among the social reformers of Holland Peter Cornelisz Plockhoy was an outstanding pioneer of social progress. He implored the Dutch and English governments for an opportunity to establish an ideal society where there would be no class distinction, no racial discrimination, no exploitation of any kind, and he established such a colony in the present state of Delaware in 1663.[34]

LAMENTING A LOSS

During the middle of the seventeenth century, the Dutch Mennonites consisted of two major groups, although they were subdivided into many smaller groups as a result of the numerous schisms which had occurred. The two major groups were classified as conservatives and progressives. The conservatives, such as the Groningen Old Flemish, were usually grouped together as *Fijne Mennisten* (fine Mennonites) who endeavored to enforce regulations and standards, and to prevent their members from mixing too freely with the world, in order to keep the church pure. They forbade such innovations as shoes with high heels, shaving of the beard, silverware, ornaments, etc. They enforced simplicity and nonconformity to the world by making use, among other things, of regulations along these lines. These congregations gradually gave up some of their rigid practices; those who consistently adhered to them died out.[35]

The progressive groups, such as the Waterlanders, were known as the "coarse Mennonites." They were more willing to adjust themselves to the environment and to give up some of the concepts of the early Anabaptists, including their view

33 Winkler Prins, *Algemeene Encyclopedie*, fifth ed. (1936) 11:569; "Nieuwenhuizen, Jan," *ME*, Vol. 3.
34 Leland and Marvin Harder, *Plockhoy from Zurik-zee* (Newton, 1952).
35 N. van der Zijpp, *op. cit.*, 153.

of the church and its relationship to the world. At times they were in danger of giving up their Anabaptist heritage and accepting the surrounding culture uncritically. Even Galenus Abrahamsz de Haan of the Lamist group, in many ways a progressive leader, had this criticism to offer for those who accepted uncritically that with which they came in contact. During the Reformation, he says, the council of devils succeeded in dimming the flame of the Gospel everywhere except among the Anabaptists. The persecution which the devils used as a means to crush their faith only strengthened it. Their new tactics, in trying to break the Anabaptist witness by dividing them into many groups, also failed to accomplish the task. The third attempt to put out the flame of the Gospel was to give the Anabaptists freedom and prosperity. Galenus concludes that this effort was successful, and that "the love of the world" destroyed the witness of the Anabaptists.[36]

Another critic, P. Langendijk, wrote the poem in 1713 in which he describes the impressions which the newly arrived plain Swiss Mennonite refugees received when they met their highly cultured and prosperous Dutch brethren who had made peace with the world. The translated title is "Swiss Simplicity Lamenting the Corrupted Manners of Many Dutch Mennonites or Nonresistant Christians." He states (literal translation, disregarding the verse):

> She (simplicity) had no coach with trotting horses
> When hither coming down the Rhine in boats,
> And saw with alarm the brethren at Amsterdam
> In unrestrained pomp which brought tears to her eyes
> And moved her to lament with two complaints:
> Is this the selfsame land for which I longed,
> When I was bound in chains and shackles?
> Do my eyes deceive me: Are these the selfsame brethren,
> Who helped me in my need, with God, preservers of my
>   people?

*　　*　　*

36 *Ibid.*, 153.

You preached nonresistance, while bearing the banners
Of the Flemish armies and the Waterlander hosts,
Armed with contention, armored with the ban;
Each with a sharp tongue, which hearts can wound,
Direct a war, not to destroy nations,
Or precious human blood, no, but what is worse—souls.

*   *   *

How many a "doll" we see in gay attire,
When walking with our people on the street!
See, here comes one now, strutting like a peacock.
For shame, half clothed, with naked shoulders!
Shut, children, shut your eyes. But say, where is she
    going?
Oh, to the church! Not for worship I surmise,
But rather to display her fine attire.[37]

*   *   *

In 1701 Lambert Bidloo wrote a treatise declaring that
unlimited tolerance (indifference) would cause the downfall
of Mennonitism. Herman Schijn (1662-1727), a physician
and minister of Amsterdam, wrote in a similar vein. Many
of those who had given up their Anabaptist heritage attempted a complete adjustment to their environment and culture.
Many joined the Reformed Church during the eighteenth
century. "The salt had lost its savor." Fortunately, however,
some did not completely relinquish their heritage. They carried the torch from generation to generation, from century
to century, and were letting their light shine in a dark world
in need of this light.

CHRIST AND CULTURE

The question could be raised: Is it possible to retain the
pure Gospel and pure concepts within the same group from
generation to generation? Did not Christ say that He could
raise up children out of stones if Israel were unfaithful? Does
not the Spirit of God move wherever He pleases? He is not
under any obligation to restrict His attention to people who
have broken His covenant.

37 *Mennonite Life* (July 1955) 129, translated by Irvin and Ava Horst.

The question about the relationship of Christ to culture is never answered for all time. Each generation of Christians and each Christian from day to day confronts this question. Neither rules and regulations, hedges and fences around the vineyard of the Lord, nor the removal of the landmarks solves the disturbing question: "What are we doing with Christ?" Christ confronts the Christian in every walk of life and in every phase of his religious, economic, and cultural experience. Guideposts can be helpful as an aid in finding the general direction, and they can be harmful when they become ends in themselves. Christ condemns and judges all unredeemed aspects of culture and has come to restore and redeem all of them. He is judge and Saviour of all aspects of our life. All culture is in need of His cleansing judgment and redemptive work.

The early Anabaptists were fully aware of this fact. At times they probably oversimplified the possibility of extrication from all aspects of culture which seem to be in conflict with those who seek to live as children of God through Jesus Christ. Their awareness, however, of the gap between Christ and culture, the church and the world, was sound and Biblical. This insight and awareness has been lost to a large extent within modern Mennonitism, which has become so thoroughly a part of western culture, be that in western Europe or in North America. A thorough examination along these lines, and a clarification of issues, is essential if Mennonitism of today and tomorrow is to fulfill the mission which is received during the days of the Reformation and which it continues to receive in the challenge of the day in which each generation lives.

Anabaptism, Pietism, Rationalism and German Mennonites

EARLY ANABAPTISM

Although the main line of sixteenth-century Anabaptists renounced the use of the sword, their adherence to the principle of nonresistance did not mean that their religious life was passive in character. Indeed, Anabaptism was noted for its active, even aggressive character, especially with respect to its missionary outreach. Blaurock and others did not hesitate to disturb services in established churches in order to preach the Anabaptist doctrine to the assembled meeting. In Lower Bavaria in 1528 an artisan evangelized a fellow artisan in the very churchyard with such effective zeal that he prevailed on the brother not to attend mass in the church, but to attend instead the meeting led by the Anabaptist preacher Würzlburger in a nearby barn.[1]

We read of mass baptisms. In 1525 Conrad Grebel baptized a whole procession of men and women at St. Gall. In the same year nearly the entire community of Hallau (canton Schaffhausen) was baptized at the hands of Johannes Brötli and Wilhelm Reublin, while Reublin and Balthasar Hubmaier baptized 360 at Waldshut (Baden). In 1530 Melchior Hofmann baptized 300 at Emden, and in 1534 in Münster 1,400 baptisms occurred in one week. In 1527 the Martyrs' Synod of Augsburg sent out delegations of missionaries as did the Münsterites in 1534. The Hutterites continued for decades to commission itinerant preachers and missionaries. In a few cases the Anabaptists even controlled local governments

* Ernst Crous is director of the Mennonite Research Center, Göttingen, and assistant editor for Germany of the *Mennonite Encyclopedia*.
1 Karl Schornbaum (Ed.), *Quellen zur Geschichte der Täufer V: Bayern, II. Abteilung* (Gütersloh, 1951) 23.

for brief periods of time, as at Hallau, Waldshut, and Nikolsburg, not to speak of Münster. This early aggressive evangelization was followed by terrible persecution, long lists of martyrs extending from Switzerland in 1525 and the Netherlands in 1531 to the Bregenz Forest (Austria) in 1618. More tolerant governments committed Anabaptists to prison for life, as at Strasbourg and in the territory of Philip of Hesse.

RESTRICTED MENNONITISM

As a result of the persecutions Anabaptism became extinct in many localities during the sixteenth and seventeenth centuries. That which survived became Mennonitism in the modern sense. The Anabaptists had been a part of the general population, though distinctive in their faith, and seeking to win others for their faith. The later Mennonites, on the other hand, came to be cultural enclaves, linked together by family ties and tolerated on account of their economic proficiency, but not permitted to carry on any missionary propaganda. The once offensively aggressive *second baptism* had been reduced to a harmless *adult baptism*. The legal settlement and residence permits now granted by the authorities frequently required precisely that. The Friedrichstadt (Schleswig-Holstein) permit of 1623 specified that the Anabaptists must cause no religious annoyances in private or in public. That of East Friesland in 1626 forbade the enticement of converts with sweet words. Permits granted at Altona (near Hamburg) in 1641 and in the Palatinate in 1664 had similar restrictions. The alternative to such restricted residential privileges, more often than not, was expulsion without mercy, as in the case of München-Gladbach (1654) and Rheydt (1694) in the Duchy of Jülich. In Elbing (West Prussia) the Mennonites were denied full citizenship until 1585; in Crefeld until 1678; in Königsberg and Marienburg until about 1750; and in Danzig and the Palatinate until about 1800.

When we remember that for decades and even centuries

in most parts of Germany the Mennonites lived under conditions similar to those of the Jews in their ghetto, we can understand why the character of their faith came to be changed. Typical is the attitude of Gerhard Roosen, the great leader of the Hamburg-Altona congregation in the second half of the seventeenth century. Robert Friedmann says of his books: "In them he tried to prove to the non-Mennonite world the full 'harmlessness' of Mennonitism; and to his own brethren he tried to make that precious heritage warm and digestible. Thus, without changing any essential point, he filled Mennonitism with a very different spirit. . . . The *Christliches Gemütsgespräch* is the catechism of a well-settled religious body, a denomination rather than a brotherhood, and this determines the tone of the whole. . . . The allocation of space to the parts of the whole subject is worth-while noting: while much space is devoted to doctrinal items, those fundamental points of Mennonitism such as nonresistance, aggressive faith, and suffering, are confined to but three questions. Nonresistance is treated on less than one page, and even then in a strikingly mild and inconspicuous way (questions 136 to 138). . . . One could describe it [the *Christliches Gemütsgespräch*] best as 'Mennonitism in minor key' . . . in transition . . . in assimilation. . . . Roosen wanted to cover up anything that might have been shocking to his non-Mennonite fellow citizens of Hamburg-Altona, and to make his faith as like as possible to that of general Protestantism. Mennonites have become the *Stillen im Lande*."[2]

In the nineteenth century nonresistance became the crucial issue. After 1801 whoever adhered to this principle was

2 Robert Friedmann, *Mennonite Piety Through the Centuries* (Goshen, 1949) 143-46. The *Christliches Gemütsgespräch* referred to was one of the most popular catechisms among the Mennonites of Europe and America. It was drawn up by Gerhard Roosen in 148 questions and answers in 24 sections, and first published in 1702. The full title in English translation is: *Christian Spiritual Conversation on Saving Faith and the Acknowledging of the Truth which is after Godliness in Hope of Eternal Life (Tit. 1:1, 2), in Questions and Answers for the Rising Youth, by which they may be Incited and Encouraged to a Wholesome Practice of Life.* At least 22 editions are known to have been published, six in Europe between 1702 and 1838, and 16 in America since 1769, five of these being in English since 1857.

239

disqualified to purchase land or to make converts in West Prussia. After 1830 the same was true in the Rhineland. In southern Germany the principle of nonresistance disappeared early in the nineteenth century. The emigration of large numbers of Mennonites (some of them in search of a home where their nonresistant principles would be recognized) served to weaken still further those remaining in Germany. The membership declined both numerically and in proportion to the total population. In West Prussia in 1834 the Mennonites, fearing for their privilege of 1780, given for eternity (*auf ewig*), even suppressed a new edition of the writings of Menno Simons, the author and leader who himself had first published them at the risk of his own life. It is clear that in the nineteenth century the petrifaction or the dissolution of the Mennonite congregations in Germany was imminent. It was only the coming of new forces, Pietism and Rationalism, together with the process of assimilation, which saved the denomination, and even so only by changing its character to something different from that of the early brotherhood.

ANABAPTISM AND PIETISM

Robert Friedmann was the first to devote thorough research to contacts between Anabaptism and Pietism and to the contrast between the two types of faith. Taking as his starting point the saying of Max Goebel that Pietism may be regarded as the grandchild of Anabaptism,[3] Friedmann himself undertook a much more specialized comparison.

"Both groups desire the new birth, the inner transformation of the entire man, and therefore unite in two fundamental rejections: (1) The general state church (the *allgemeine Volkskirche*), and (2) Confessional dogmatism (as a system of thought remote from life) . . . . Both groups truly sought to comprehend the whole of life in their systems. That is, both believed in the possibility of a sanctification of

---

3 Max Goebel, *Geschichte des christlichen Lebens in der rheinisch-westfälischen evangelischen Kirche* (Koblenz, 1849-60) 1:137 and 2:697.

life, in contrast to the theology of the ineradicable depravity of human nature. . . . We recognize a faith in a positive content of life, and therewith also a faith in a new way of life. However, it also becomes evident at once that this new way is unfortunately not the same way for both groups. . . ."[4]

The emphasis of Anabaptism is distinctly different from that of Pietism. Anabaptism stresses the fear of God (*Gottesfurcht*), Christian discipleship, following Christ (*Nachfolge Christi*) in love and the cross, and the fellowship of the unity of the Spirit (*Gemeinschaft der Geisteseinheit*). Pietism, on the other hand, stresses *Gottseligkeit,* a blissful devotional experience which enjoys the assurance of individual salvation; *praxis pietatis* in daily life, blissful form of devotion, together with a mild friendliness and morality, as well as the fellowship of the regenerated. In Anabaptism the new birth is sealed in baptism, sending the pilgrim forth on the strenuous way of discipleship and love in action with the kingdom of God as its final goal. Pietism begins with the struggle for personal repentance from sin (*Busskampf*), followed by assurance of salvation and freedom to enjoy the new possession with relatively little concern for the strenuous responsibilities which confront the Anabaptist disciple. "Two external phenomena may seem to be very similar, and yet be fundamentally different."[5] Thus even the writings which the Pietists took over from the Anabaptists now assumed a different meaning without changing the words.

MENNONITISM UNDER THE IMPACT OF QUAKERS AND DOMPELAARS

The Quakers and the Dompelaars were the precursors of Pietism proper among the German Mennonites. The former, giving pre-eminence to the "inner word," reached Kriegsheim in the Palatinate in 1657, Hamburg in 1659, and Crefeld in 1667, in each case gaining adherents from among the

4 Friedmann, *op. cit.,* 72-73; *MQR* (July 1940) 14:155-56.
5 *Ibid.,* 72; 155.

Mennonites. Within a year, however, the Quakers and Mennonite-Quakers were expelled from Hamburg. In 1683 they departed from Crefeld and in 1687 from Kriegsheim, turning to the newly established province of Pennsylvania in North America.

The *Dompelaars* or *Tunkers,* who seem to have originated under Dutch Collegiant or English Baptist influence, or both, were strongly pietistic in character and were known for their emotional preaching and the practice of baptism by immersion. In the Hamburg-Altona congregation a schism occurred in 1648 when a group of Dompelaars withdrew from the main body of Mennonites. The outstanding Dompelaar-Mennonite leader was Jacob Denner (1659-1746), who preached to all denominations. Although the Dompelaar congregation in Hamburg-Altona became extinct following Denner's death his writings continued to have great influence within Mennonite circles and beyond for some time to come. In 1792, for example, 500 copies of a newly published edition of his sermons, a book of 1,718 pages, was brought to Pennsylvania and quickly sold among the Mennonites of the Franconia Conference. The Crefeld congregation also experienced a Dompelaar episode from 1709 to 1730, although this movement was more local in origin than that of Hamburg-Altona. Also an actual schism was avoided in Crefeld in that one of the ministers, Gossen Goyen, administered baptism by immersion, while the other, Jan Crous, baptized by aspersion.

MENNONITISM UNDER THE IMPACT OF PIETISM PROPER

If Pietism with its emotional emphasis fitted into the general trend of eighteenth-century thought it also found a ready response from the Mennonites in their restricted conditions of life. The Pietism of the Crefeld Mennonites was more or less a continuation of the Dompelaar movement, although omitting baptism by immersion. If Gossen Goyen was associated with the Dompelaars, his brother Arnold was equally close to the Pietists. From 1738 to 1761 he was in correspondence with Gerhard Tersteegen, the Pietist leader of the Lower Rhine region. Besides this, August Gottlieb Spangenberg, the Moravian bishop, introduced Pietism among the Mennonites of Hamburg through his contact with Gisbert van der Smissen III (1717-93), and in Holland through the conversion of the Dutch Mennonite minister Joannes Deknatel (1698-1759). Deknatel also was in communication with Count Zinzendorf and John Wesley, and through his influence on the Mennonite lay minister Peter Weber (1731-81) was instrumental in kindling a pietistic flame among the Mennonites of the Palatinate.

In 1766-67 Jacob Gisbert van der Smissen, a son of Gisbert III, in company with his cousin engaged in their *Kavalierstour* (a journey for the completion of their education) in England and on the continent. In England they visited with Quakers, Baptists, and Methodists, including George Whitefield. In Germany they saw Gerhard Tersteegen in the Rhineland, the Mennonite Pietist minister Lorenz Friedenreich at Neuwied, and even Goethe's *Schöne Seele,* Fräulein von Klettenberg. The itinerary was climaxed by a visit with Spangenberg at Herrnhut, the Moravian center, and with the Pietists of Minden-Ravensberg (Pastor Weihe). The first Mennonite Pietist in West Prussia was Isaac van Dühren (1725-1800), whose conversion to a large extent was due to the influence of a book by August Hermann Francke, the Pietist of Halle.

It is characteristic of the time that, beginning in 1731 in the Netherlands, and after 1743 including other countries as well, directories of Mennonite ministers were compiled to facilitate contact among ministers in different regions. From 1768 to 1773 an extensive correspondence was carried on between ministers of the Rhineland and the Vistula region. In the Palatinate a new interest in the martyrs is seen in the publication in 1780 of the only German edition of the *Martyrs' Mirror,* and in West Prussia in the publication in 1787-88 of an extract from this work by Isaac van Dühren. The boundaries between the denominations were losing their significance. In 1751 Tersteegen preached in the Mennonite church in Crefeld to Christians of all faiths, while Heinrich Jung-Stilling, the famous Pietist, spiritual adviser, physician, and economist, was a friend of the van der Smissens in Hamburg and of the Möllingers, Rissers, and Webers in the Palatinate. The Mennonites were gradually emerging from their seclusion and entering a wider circle.

MENNONITES UNDER THE IMPACT OF THE AWAKENING

Following the French Revolution and the Napoleonic era (1789-1815) the Mennonites found themselves and their congregations in a changed situation. Those who remained loyal to the principle of nonresistance continued to suffer some restrictions, but most of them eventually emigrated to the new world. The life of the European Mennonites, however, underwent a gradual change. Their long ghetto-like existence had converted the renunciation of missionary propaganda into something like a dogma; and the influence of Pietism had weakened those Anabaptist principles which were in conflict with the world. Thus when the second wave of Pietism, the Awakening following 1815, reached the German Mennonites it found a ready acceptance among them.

Crefeld again went its own way, Isaac Molenaar (1776-1834), its minister, being in close touch with the Dutch revival. In South Germany, France, and Switzerland the new pietistic schools began to influence the life of the Mennonite congregations. This was especially true of St. Chrischona, near Basel, founded in 1840, whose influence went out to the Mennonites of Baden, Alsace, and the Palatinate, as well as to the congregations of Switzerland. The Mennonite elementary school, beginning in 1826 at Rodlofferhuben, and after 1836 at Bröske in West Prussia, was a pietist institution. The secondary school on the Weierhof in the Palatinate was founded in 1867 by Michael Löwenberg, a product of the pietist school of Beuggen near Basel. In 1814 Jacob Gisbert van der Smissen became the cofounder and secretary of the

Hamburg Bible Society; in his home Johannes Evangelista Gossner, the missionary, for a time had a refuge. Jacob Mannhardt, pastor of the Danzig congregation, was a member of the board of directors of the Danzig Missionary Society.

In 1823 and 1824 William Henry Angas, the English Baptist preacher and missionary, stimulated interest in mission work among the Mennonites of the Palatinate and of West Prussia where, beginning in 1830, missionary conferences were held annually for more than a century. Year after year Montau-Gruppe, a rural congregation on the Vistula, took up collections for the support of foreign missions and Bible distribution work. Even Johann Heinrich Wichern, the "father of home missions" in Germany, visited this congregation in 1852 and praised it highly. The Mennonites of Baden also came under pietistic influence through the Hahnish movement, as the following of Johann Michael Hahn (1758-1819) was known, and which in 1920 had about 15,000 members. Three of Hahn's (approximately 2,000) hymns came to be included in the hymnal of the South German Mennonites. In 1858 the two congregations most influenced by the movement, Dühren-Ursenbacherhof and Heimbronnerhof, separated from the *Badisch-Württembergisch-Bayerischer Gemeindeverband* (one of the two South German Mennonite conferences), and were known as the Hahnish Mennonites. In 1857, when the Evangelical Alliance (founded in London in 1846) assembled in Berlin with more than a thousand delegates, there were eight Mennonites present: five from West Prussia, two from the Palatinate, and one from Hamburg. Half a century later, in 1903, Hinrich van der Smissen, the Mennonite pastor of Hamburg, was a member of the German board of the then reorganized Evangelical Alliance.

MENNONITISM UNDER THE IMPACT OF
THE GEMEINSCHAFTSBEWEGUNG

A few years after the establishment of the German empire in 1871 a third wave of Pietism reached the German

Mennonites, who now included those of Alsace. Strangely, though coming from America, the movement is known only by its German name, *Gemeinschaftsbewegung.* In 1875 Robert Pearsall Smith, a layman, introduced to Germany a new type of evangelism with its emphasis on sanctification. In 1892 about one third of the *Reichslieder,* the representative hymnbook of the movement with a circulation of millions of copies, consisted of American and English Gospel songs in translation, although in later editions the percentage of non-German hymns gradually declined. The new spirit entered older institutions, such as St. Chrischona. Then new schools followed: the Missionsanstalt in Neukirchen (Kreis Mörs) in 1882; the Johanneum (in Bonn in 1886, Wuppertal-Barmen since 1893); the Allianz-Bibelschule (in Berlin in 1905, in Wiedenest near Gummersbach since 1918). These schools trained and influenced the Mennonites, as did also the Evangelische Predigerschule in Basel beginning in 1876, as well as the Baptist seminary in Hamburg-Horn, beginning in 1881.

Pastors of the state churches who belonged to the *Gemeinschaftsbewegung* often received their best support from the Mennonites in their parish. Missionaries of the Basel Mission regarded the Lamprechtshof (Karlsruhe-Durlach) as an "asylum of godliness." In West Prussia the congregation of Thiensdorf-Preussisch Rosengart in particular embraced the new movement. Here Mother Eva (von Tiele-Winckler) obtained homes and means for the erection of further homes for the homeless. The difference between born-again Lutherans and born-again Mennonites had come to be insignificant. Prominent in the Blankenburg Alliance in Thuringia, the center of a renewed Darbyism (Plymouth Brethren), was Jacob Kroeker, a Russian-born Mennonite, most of whose life was given to work in Germany, "Christian being his name, Mennonite only his surname."[6] As Robert Friedmann says, this movement had become a second nature to the Men-

6 Friedrich Heitmüller, in *Evangelische Allianz* (Witten/Ruhr, 1949) 2:4.

nonite Pietists to such an extent that they more or less identified it with their own, really so different, Anabaptism of the sixteenth century.[7]

RATIONALISTIC MENNONITISM

But this is not the complete story. There are the congregations of artisans, manufacturers, and merchants in the cities of North Germany. Pietism, as far as I am able to see, never reached the congregations of East Friesland. Here trained ministers from Amsterdam brought with them the theology of the Dutch Mennonites, which had been strongly influenced by Socinianism and rationalism. The old families were open to the influence of the surrounding world in cultural life and in politics, and at the same time remained loyal to their little church. In Crefeld, which since 1770 had had trained ministers from Holland, Pietism—as often occurs—was succeeded by the Enlightenment. Isaac Molenaar, though his awakening was only an episode for the Crefeld congregation, was the first minister to preach in the German language and to be in contact with the German cultural life; and so, beginning with him the face of the Crefeld congregation turned also in religion and theology to the state in which they lived and worked. The liberalism which was the result both in East Friesland and in Crefeld found its way also into the eastern settlements. In West and East Prussia were the progressive urban congregations of Danzig, Elbing, and Königsberg. Even among the Amish in the rural areas in South Germany for some time the influence of the Enlightenment was to be seen in their hymnbooks, as at Wiesbaden in 1843 and Regensburg in 1859, and also for instance in the Memel congregation of East Prussia which in 1905 added a printed supplement to the Lutheran hymnbook. It wished to continue the use of the rationalistic hymns which had been dropped by the 1884-86 edition of the Lutheran hymnal!

7 Friedmann, *op. cit.*, 67.

THE CURRENT OUTLOOK

However, when the urban congregations attempted to form a Union of German Mennonite Churches (*Vereinigung der Deutschen Mennonitengemeinden*), with a teaching center like the Dutch Mennonite General Conference (*Algemeene Doopsgezinde Societeit*) and its theological seminary at Amsterdam, the pietistic rural congregations were very slow in joining, and the proposed teaching center never did come into being. The *Badisch-Württembergisch-Bayerischer Gemeindeverband* remained independent even in the time of the Third Reich as it does to the present day. In maintaining this independence great emphasis was placed upon the experience of the new birth, a doctrine which in the mind of the southern congregations was not sufficiently recognized by those of the *Vereinigung*.

Thus there are two groups of German Mennonites, those modified by Pietism and those modified by Rationalism. This schism is not the fault of the present generation. It is a twofold legacy backed by two centuries of history. It is in North Germany especially, where the presence of thousands of refugees from the East makes the contrast between the two schools of thought particularly sharp, that the need for more contact is most keenly felt. The *Gemeindenausschuss in Norddeutschland,* something like a conference, formed in 1951, is at least the beginning of an effort to enable the various congregations to understand and to help one another. The common name and the common heritage constitute an obligation for the different groups, as throughout world Mennonitism so especially in North Germany, Berlin being the outpost of them all.[8]

8 See also *Mennonitisches Lexikon,* articles "Pietismus" and "Reveil oder Erweckungsbewegung" (the latter to be published in installment 41); *Mennonite Encyclopedia,* articles "Berlin" and "Germany"; Ernst Crous, "Mennonitentum und Pietismus," *Theologische Zeitschrift* (Basel, July-August 1952) 8:279-96; Ernst Crous, "Vom Pietismus bei den altpreussischen Mennoniten in Rahmen ihrer Gesamtgeschichte 1772-1945," *Mennonitische Geschichtsblätter* (Karlsruhe, 1954) 11:7-29.

✠ E. K. FRANCIS ✠

Anabaptism and Colonization

Like every religion, Anabaptism has shaped the destinies of men and has found its expression in human action far beyond that sphere of life which is defined as sacred or religious. Those who have professed it have been able to achieve things in this world which others would and could not do. In the present essay we shall consider Anabaptism as an active social force which has set a peculiar pattern for one of those worldly activities by which man has subdued the earth: colonization. On the other hand, the different aspects of human existence—religious, economic, political, and so on—are so interlocking that no institution, not even religion, can impose its characteristic form upon all the others; but every one influences the others as much as it is influenced by them. Thus we must also ask to what extent a religious system like Anabaptism has been changed by other social factors.

When we trace the history of the Russian Mennonites, which shall serve us as an example and which in this context may be presumed to be known,[1] we are struck by the fact that the problem which had to be solved in the beginning was quite different from the problems which emerged in the course of their migrations from the Netherlands to Prussia, thence to Russia, and again to Canada or Paraguay. At first the Mennonites were faced with the problem of how to maintain their social existence in a world hostile to their religion. Later when their compact colonies were well established the

* E. K. Francis is Professor of Sociology in the University of Notre Dame and author of *In Search of Utopia* (Altona and Glencoe, 1955), the story of the Mennonites in Manitoba.

1 Cf. E. K. Francis, *In Search of Utopia: The Mennonites in Manitoba* (Altona, Manitoba: D. W. Friesen and Sons Ltd., and Chicago: The Free Press of Glencoe, Illinois, 1955); an extensive bibliography by the same author will be found in *Mennonite Quarterly Review* (July 1953) 27:238-48.

question arose how to preserve the purity of the Anabaptist idea in the face of forces from within the community. Finally the preservation of the Mennonite ethnic community took precedence over that of the faith, which had become an almost peripheral concern. Before we proceed to consider these typical situations, some concepts with which we intend to operate should be clarified.

When we speak of religion we are inclined to think primarily of ideas and beliefs. Yet faith finds its expression in symbolic behavior, in ritual and in social action. Believers profess and teach their creed, gather for acts of common worship, and are organized in groups for specifically religious purposes. Sometimes there is but one religion, the religion of a total society; its members and all the faithful are the same; one religion permeates its whole way of life. Nevertheless even here the sacred is set apart from the profane; not all activities are religious and the village or tribe gather only on certain occasions to act as a religious community or "church." The church may or may not be a central concern of a society, provide guidance for most other activities of its members, unify all of them for a common goal which lies beyond life in society: salvation. In any event it is a partial social system in that it does not include in itself all the activities of the members of a society however strongly it may influence them. The state on the other hand is the political order of a society. It, too, is but one aspect of the totality of a society. Although the regulation of religious convictions and activities may be included in its functions, this is often explicitly excluded. Sometimes religious and political authority reside in the same persons; more often the two spheres are kept apart, although the question as to whose authority takes precedence, or to which activities of the members of the society each authority should have the first claim, remains a source of conflict.

In the early days the evangelical Anabaptists were confronted with a situation where the claim of the Roman

church to being the only legitimate religious organization of
the total society was being challenged, and the relationship
between the authority of the state and the church was con-
roversial. Their answer is too well known to require elaboration beyond recalling that they considered neither the visible
organization of the Catholic church as the true and only
church of Christ, nor all baptized Christians as real members
of the true church; and that they denied to secular government authority over the religious convictions and practices of
those within its jurisdiction, or even the right to command
anything which, though not sacred in itself, was yet clearly
forbidden by religious prescription, as for example, the bearing of arms. We are here only concerned with the social consequences of their doctrine.

Those who adhered to it were yet members of several
communities and states, and lived by necessity intermingled
with others who held different views on religion and considered themselves members of different religious organizations. The Anabaptist vision precluded the course of action
taken by other Protestants, namely, to substitute, wherever
they could within individual communities and states, their
own kind of Christian church for the Roman church, making
it the religious organization of all the members of that particular society to be safeguarded by the state. The Anabaptists' answer was rather withdrawal from the world in an attempt to arrange their life as much in accordance with their
faith, and with as little interference from the outside, as possible. Alas, this possibility was always limited and depended
on the good will and the power of those who did not share
their beliefs. For by its very essence a religious brotherhood
is even a more segmental social group than is an established
church, since it excludes the majority of the total society who
neither join it voluntarily nor give proof of personal consecration.

As long as the Anabaptists continued to live intermingled with others in the same communities their withdrawal

was necessarily imperfect. Moreover, their very survival remained in jeopardy unless the large society and its state were willing to grant religious freedom; although outside pressure and martyrdom tended to multiply and strengthen the inner bonds between the members of the brotherhood beyond the strictly religious sphere. The migrations of the Mennonites reflect their search for countries offering tolerance: Holland, Poland, Russia, the New World. They always involved sacrifice. Withdrawal from the world, or what is really the same, from a total society, was both a means to avoid friction with it and to keep the Anabaptist way of life unadulterated. The more complete the withdrawal, the more secure the brotherhood became on both counts. This is one reason why colonization appeared to many as such a welcome opportunity, even to those who were not prepared for the toil of a pioneer. When the Mennonites went from Holland to Poland they were not only guaranteed a livelihood and religious tolerance, but in many instances they were able to form compact settlements. The self-sufficiency of village life in those days, as well as ethnic-cultural and linguistic segregation from most of their neighbors, permitted a high degree of isolation. Still isolation and withdrawal were never as complete in Prussia as later in Russia and the New World; and this decreased with the progress of assimilation, economic interdependence, and cultural exchange.

The particular conditions under which the Mennonites settled in Russia seemingly brought fulfillment of all their hopes. Not only were their colonies homogeneous, largely self-governing and self-sufficient, but they were kept by law separate from the rest of society. The right to live and to make a living in the colonies was reserved to those who were recognized members of the brotherhood and to their descendants. In turn they were charged with the concerns of life in the world, including local government, enforcement of laws, social welfare, and in certain emergencies as in some instances during the Russian Revolution even self-defense. Yet a brotherhood, as we have said, is not meant to include all the members of a total society, baptized adults and unbaptized children, saints and sinners. Membership is on principle voluntary and selective, and is forfeited upon perseverance in grave sin. Moreover the Anabaptist brotherhood had explicitly rejected responsibility for government, which by its very nature implies the use of force, and had insisted upon the separation of church and state. Accordingly the Mennonite brotherhood could not as such undertake the administration of the Russian colonies; but their members had to organize themselves into secular communities with special officers to manage their affairs, and had to arrange their life in this world as the world is wont to do. Nevertheless, the very fact that now the members of the secular and the religious community were by and large the same, and membership in the secular community required good standing in the brotherhood, changed the character of the latter. The brotherhood was transformed into what we have earlier called a church, the "parish church" of a Mennonite colony, which took its name from that colony (Altkolonie, Bergthal, etc.), and which coincided with the population of a colony assembled and acting as a religious community.

By the very nature of things these changes in the structure of the Mennonite community affected its religious foundation, the Anabaptist Vision. It has been summed up with incomparable insight and clarity by Dean Bender[2] in these terms: For the Anabaptist the church was not an institution, but a brotherhood of love in which the fullness of the Christian life was to be expressed. He denied the possibility of Christianizing the entire social order, at the same time rejecting the idea of compromising with a world order that remains sinful. Nor did he anticipate that all people would enter the brotherhood with its high ideals, but believed that the church would always be a suffering church.

If we translate this vision so that it applies to the small

2 Harold S. Bender, "The Anabaptist Vision," *MQR* (April 1944) 18:67-88.

yet almost closed and complete world of the Mennonite commonwealth in Russia, we find that it was above all a secular social order, and that imperceptibly and unconsciously the church became one of its several institutions.[3] While it had hoped to transfer the rule of brotherly love to the Mennonite community also in its secular aspects, and to permeate it wholly with the Christian spirit, it soon had to compromise with the evils inherent in every secular order which also includes sinners. When exclusion meant loss of all civil rights in the colony, the parish church could not rid itself of wrongdoers as easily as in the case of the brotherhood. In many respects the secular community and its powerful men now relied on the authority of the church in the pursuit of purely secular goals, while means of social control had to be condoned which were not quite in line with Anabaptist ideals. On occasion the established church, particularly in the New Colony, went so far as to violate the principles of voluntary membership and religious freedom, and to invoke the assistance of the secular power in order to enforce conformity when new Mennonite brotherhoods (Kleine Gemeinde, Mennonite Brethren, and others) made their appearance in an attempt to revive the lagging religious spirit.[4]

The dilemma of the Mennonite church in Russia, its partial secularization and its division into several quarreling denominations, however, must not obscure the inner strength of the common Anabaptist heritage as a factor in the organization of prospering colonies. Without their religious sense of mission and election the Mennonites could hardly have undertaken so difficult a task and have brought it to such a highly successful conclusion. It is true that most, if not all, of their peculiar institutions which so decisively supported community building were not their own creations; nor had they originally any religious implications, like village habitat,

3 Cf. E. K. Francis, "The Mennonite Commonwealth in Russia, 1789-1914: A Sociological Interpretation," *MQR* (July 1951) 25:173-82, 200.

4 P. M. Friesen's *Die alt-evangelische Mennonitische Brüderschaft in Russland* (Halbstadt, 1911) is in this sense to be regarded as an indictment of the established Mennonite churches in Russia, however partisan he may be in many respects.

communal organization, practices of inheritance, or fire insurance.[5] Yet each one of their cultural traditions was sanctioned by the church and received a religious meaning, guaranteeing their strict observance and preservation in a manner which would not have occurred had they been considered merely an expression of secular ideals and of understandings between men. There also existed a kind of transferal of the loyalty which is the prerogative of religion to the total social system of Mennonites, so that any violation of the secular social order was responded to as if it were a direct threat to their most sacred values.

Perhaps such strengthening of the social order is not confined to a particular religion. But Anabaptism stressed moral values and instilled virtues which in a special way aided the Mennonites in their enterprise. Among these the cultivation of brotherly love above all comes to mind. Not only did it command the respect of outsiders; it also greatly facilitated the maintenance of a solidaristic social organization and the avoidance of serious rifts which often have brought the downfall of similar experiments. An unusual amount of mutual help has always been extended by the Mennonites to their brethren, and has greatly mitigated the consequences of misfortune and personal failure, thereby relieving the community of many responsibilities for the care of the poor or infirm, and for public welfare in general. At the same time differences in wealth and consumption were minimized, and class cleavages were prevented, once more strengthening the cohesion of the group as a whole. Other Mennonite virtues fostered by their religious convictions and training included their frugality and industry, which have decisively enhanced their social and economic successes, and their almost proverbial honesty which has kept their colonies free from the scourge of crime, and which in criticial moments has secured for them financial support and loans literally saving their lives. The moral fiber of a people is said to be the best safe-

5 Cf. E. K. Francis, "Mennonite Institutions in Early Manitoba: A study of Their Origins," *Agricultural History* (1948) 22:144-55.

guard for their survival. The careful student of the ways of men cannot help being impressed by the characteristics of peacefulness, quiet moderation, uprightness, and Christian kindness which he finds in the personality of so many of the Russian and other Mennonites.

Let us look into history for a more concrete example of the role played by religion and church in colonization and community organization. The migrations of the Russian Mennonites to Canada, and hence to Latin America, are sufficiently documented to serve the purpose. The movement in the 1870's was sparked by the threat of the Russian government to revoke vital rights granted corporatively to the Mennonite colonists. Although economic and cultural factors were involved which affected the preservation of the ethnic community more than that of the religious brotherhood, it is significant that the question of military exemption was consistently kept in the foreground. In reality the migration went under way while promising negotiations were in progress which after their departure resulted in an agreement favorable to those who remained in Russia. A social movement of such magnitude and consequence as the relinquishing of homeland and homestead for an uncertain future on the part of almost one third of Russia's Mennonite population could hardly have crystallized, and could not have been sustained, unless it was justified on religious grounds. It was part and parcel of their Anabaptist tradition to respond to the encroachment of the world and of a secular government upon their sacred values in a typical manner through withdrawal, flight, emigration, and, if possible, retreat to remote places of the globe which seemed to offer still greater isolation and to hold out the promise that it would not easily be violated in the future.

The means by which this more complete withdrawal from the world could be achieved was once more the colonization of virgin land where no pre-existing society would challenge them. In some instances whole communities transferred from the Old to the New World, so that it was possible to leave their institutional fabric more or less intact. But there also were groups like the Kleine Gemeinde which had lived intermingled with other Mennonites, and were united only through membership in a particularistic religious organization. In any event, emigration meant a disruption of the normal functioning of the secular community and, by cutting it off from its moorings in the larger society, left civil authority in a vacuum. In this situation it was only the church which could provide leadership and a rallying point for all activities, secular as well as religious. Even after the Mennonites had succeeded in reorganizing their communities in Manitoba as faithful facsimiles of their colonies in Russia, the church retained this central position.

In Russia Mennonite institutions had been sanctioned by law and backed by the state, while in Canada they could be restored and maintained only on a voluntary basis, and in part against the social order of the larger society. Besides tradition and custom there remained but one authority on which the secular community and its officers could lean, namely, the assembly of the faithful under the leadership of elders and preachers. Appeal to Canadian courts and governmental agencies was made a religious offense, and deviants were ultimately kept in line through religious sanctions. Even the economy was largely controlled through the *Waisenamt*, a church institution whose functions extended far beyond the protection of orphans. Already during the migration it had been instrumental in financial assistance to indigent members of the community. Other funds obtained from loans by the Ontario brethren and the Canadian government, which helped the Manitoba Mennonites to weather the emergencies of the first few years, were administered by the *Brotkasse*, an institution without direct church connection. Still, it was the elders and preachers who had to guarantee the repayment of any sum drawn out by individuals. In their attempt to keep their economy independent and to prevent land within their colonies from falling into the hands of outsiders, the Mennonites utilized the *Waisenamt* not only as a trust company and guardian over the transfer of property from one generation to the next, but also as a central savings bank and finance institution through which individual economic behavior in the whole colony could be influenced and directed.

Finally, the role of the church in social welfare and school has to be mentioned. Poor relief was blended with the charities organized by the church. This was at first in addition to the poor tax levied by the organs of the secular community; but after the breakdown of Mennonite local autonomy the moral obligation to contribute a set portion of the harvest to stores kept in the fortified attics of church buildings became all the more important. The school, too, was for some time the responsibility of the church, which laid down general rules, appointed teachers, and exercised a strict supervision. Eventually the school became the stumbling block which not only caused fatal conflicts among different branches of the Mennonite church in Manitoba, but paved the way for schisms and the multiplication of Mennonite denominations. On the other hand, the cleavages within the church, combined with increasing outside pressures in favor of a secular, tax-supported, and state-controlled school, led to the withdrawal of various Mennonite groups from each other, and finally to the exodus of some to Latin America.

These renewed migrations were once more under the auspices of individual churches, and followed the familiar pattern. Especially in Mexico the Old Colony church has been able to retain a measure of control otherwise unknown among Mennonites, and to preserve as a sacred trust traditional institutions which elsewhere have been largely forgotten.[6] But also for Paraguay J. Winfield Fretz has been able to report recently that "the church, next to the family, is the most pervasive single institution. In many ways the Mennonite colony organization suggests something of a theoc-

---

6 Cf. J. W. Fretz, *Mennonite Colonization in Mexico* (Akron, Pa., 1945).

racy."[7] This is particularly true of the Mennonites who came from Canada. Once more the Mennonite colony has become a state within a state, where political decisions are largely influenced by a powerful church. Still more important is the fact that crime is partly controlled by religious sanctions. According to Fretz criminal offenses are effectively dealt with by either the church elders or the secular officers of the colony. The Bible is considered the only law, and offenders are treated "in the light of Scriptural teaching and Christian common sense." Ecclesiastical punishment consists in excommunication, punishment by the civil authorities with money fines, forced labor, corporal punishment, and banishment from the colony.[8] It seems that the earlier history of the Mennonites in Russia and Manitoba is repeating itself in the Gran Chaco.

Another observation by Fretz indicates that the early stages of colonization which are accompanied by extreme isolation and heightened group cohesion are more favorable to religious unity and church authority than later stages when the secular community has become established and more susceptible to outside influences. He noticed an earlier tendency toward close co-operation between the different branches of the Mennonite church in Paraguay and even toward union in a single religious organization. More recently, however, he says, a growing emphasis is put on denominationalism due to promptings by North American Mennonites. Earlier in this paper a distinction was made between the brotherhood and the institutionalized church. The denomination represents a third type[9] which is characterized neither by the identification of church and secular community nor by a withdrawal of the brotherhood from the world. The denomination considers itself as one of many congregations which may gather for religious purposes, and which must tolerate each other,

7 Cf. J. W. Fretz, *Pilgrims in Paraguay: The Story of Mennonite Colonization in South America* (Scottdale, 1953) 83.

8 *Ibid.*, 110.

9 Cf. J. Wach, *Types of Religious Experience: Christian and Non-Christian* (Chicago, 1951) 187-208, who cites the relevant literature. See also Robert Friedmann, *Mennonite Piety Through the Centuries* (Goshen, 1949).

and must be tolerated by the secular community. It insists on the separation of the religious from the secular aspects of life but defines the religious sphere more narrowly than either the church or the brotherhood. Any member of the secular society is free to join a denomination of his own choice or to help form new congregations.

Denominationalism is of course a condition which generally prevails in North America. It has increasingly colored the religious attitudes of the Russian Mennonites in Canada as they have submitted to the cultural influences of the large society. By the end of World War II there were no less than twenty-four religious bodies of Mennonites in Manitoba listed by separate names, more than half of which, however, were closely associated in the General Conference Mennonite Church. Some of them approached the church type of religious organization; a few resembled the brotherhood type, while perhaps a majority had taken on many of the aspects which characterize other Protestant denominations, and had assimilated some of their teachings and practices which are not entirely appropriate to strictly Anabaptist traditions. There even were individuals who considered themselves, and were considered, members of the Mennonite community although they belonged to no church whatever or had joined various non-Mennonite denominations. Thus Mennonite religious life displayed the same kaleidoscopic variety as did religious life in the Protestant society at large.

It is true that a core of common religious principles and memories of a common church history still differentiated all branches of the Mennonite church from non-Mennonite religious bodies, and drew them together in emergencies like the military draft during the war. Yet the fractionizing of the church and denominational particularism had shifted the center of gravity from an overriding concern for the preservation of the Anabaptist-Mennonite faith and way of life to a more strongly felt sense of the cultural-ethnic unity of the Russian Mennonites, and a struggle for survival as a distinct ethnic group as well as for the preservation of its distinctive cultural values. Even those Mennonites to whom religion had become but a thin veneer had however retained value orientations which were in the Anabaptist religious tradition and which were felt to be intimately related to its institutional expression in the various branches of the Mennonite church.

The problem of denominationalism and secularization is common to all Mennonite communities in modern society, and its authoritative discussion has to be left to more competent pens. Nevertheless, the problem has to be faced in all its severity now that opportunities for further retreat to isolated colonies have almost disappeared, and withdrawal from the world has become more difficult than ever when conformity with the ways of the world is demanded so pervasively by the large society.

Discipleship Expressed in Alternative Service

Alternative service, meaning work rendered to the state or society in lieu of compulsory military service, is a comparatively new term in Anabaptist-Mennonite history, but the spirit and the theology of the concept can be traced back to the days of Menno Simons and, for that matter, can be discovered in all those periods of Christian history in which the church had not made its peace with the world. In its broader sense, the concept covers the work of a Christian whose primary loyalty is to the kingdom of God rather than to the kingdom of this world. Recognizing the existence as well as the opposite characteristics of the two kingdoms, he chooses not to serve the forces of evil (the kingdom of this world) in any area of culture, whether that be in the political, economic, social, intellectual, aesthetic, or spiritual realms. Since he is a conscientious objector to every influence or program in any or all of those fields of culture that is opposed to the kingdom of God, the plan of service that he chooses to follow is an alternative to that which the forces of secularism and materialism offer him. He chooses alternative service rather than the enticing propositions which tempt him to a life of temporal power.

Although in all areas of culture the Christian is subjected in varying degrees to the pressure of "worldly" public opinion and practice, the one area in our western culture in which the Christian has faced the compulsions of the kingdoms of this world most dramatically has been in the realm of church-state conflicts. Even before the days of state conscription for military service, the citizens of western countries

* Melvin Gingerich is Director of Research of the Mennonite Research Foundation and author of *The Mennonites in Iowa* (Iowa City, 1939) and *Service for Peace: A History of Mennonite Civilian Public Service* (Akron, 1949).

through the power of public opinion sometimes brought great pressure to bear upon their young men to persuade them to volunteer for military service even if the men may have had conscientious scruples against warfare. Thus during the American Revolutionary War, when the Pennsylvania assembly warned the public against mob violence which had broken out against Mennonites and others who had failed to join the activities of the volunteer military associations of the province, the Continental Congress assured the objectors that their religious beliefs would be respected, but recommended that they "contribute liberally in this time of universal calamity, to the relief of their distressed brethren in the several colonies, and do all other services to their oppressed country which they can, consistently with their religious principles." This may be the first instance in history of a national government recommending that its citizens whose consciences forbid participation in war perform alternative service in lieu of military service.

Mennonites and Dunkers (Church of the Brethren) in a joint petition read in the Pennsylvania assembly on November 7, 1775, after thanking the assembly for granting freedom of conscience, made it clear that they recognized a responsibility to society, declaring that they were ready at all times to help those in need, "It being our principle to feed the hungry and give the thirsty drink." They added that they had dedicated themselves "to serve all men in everything that can be helpful to the preservation of men's lives; but we find no freedom in giving, or doing, or assisting in anything by which men's lives are destroyed or hurt." As an illustration of how conscientious objectors to war applied this principle during the American Revolution, there is the story of the Mennonite preacher, John Baer, and his wife who helped to nurse wounded men at Ephrata, Pennsylvania, and as a result received infections from which they died in 1778.[1]

During the American Civil War (1861-65) conscientious

---

1 For a more complete account of Mennonite experiences with war see Guy F. Hershberger's *War, Peace, and Nonresistance* (Scottdale, 1953).

objectors were permitted to hire substitutes or to pay a commutation fee of from $300 to $500 in lieu of personal military service. Although Mennonites recognized this as unsatisfactory, in the absence of a better solution they made use of it. It is worth noting, however, that the military service act passed by Union government in 1864 authorized hospital duty and service to freed slaves as additional alternatives, although these proposals were never carried out. The Southern Confederacy's proposal of labor in salt mines as a further alternative was not put in effect either. Although they struggled with the question it is evident that during the American Civil War neither the Mennonites nor the governments involved had arrived at a clear or consistent policy with respect to conscientious objectors and the military draft.

It was the Mennonites in Russia who had the first organized program of civilian service as an alternative to military service.[2] After 1880 they for the first time were subjected to conscription. At that time as conscientious objectors they were granted the privilege of serving in the Russian state forests instead of being compelled to serve in the army. The resultant program of alternative service was under the direction of the government's technical service, which provided the tools and paid the young men a small wage during their four-year term. The Mennonite Forestry Service Commission fed, housed, and clothed the men, and also provided a spiritual ministry for them. In the first years the average number of men serving in the program was approximately 400, but this number increased to about 1,000 in the year before the beginning of World War I. To maintain this increased number of men, the Mennonites of Russia annually contributed a total of approximately 350,000 rubles. During the first World War approximately 12,000 Mennonite CO's (conscientious objectors) were engaged in alternative government service, about one half in forestry work and the other 6,000 in the Mennonite hospital and medical corps. Under the latter form

2 See Guy F. Hershberger, "Conscientious Objector," in *The Mennonite Encyclopedia* (Scottdale, 1955) 1:692-99.

of service, the Mennonites organized and financed complete hospital units, which gathered soldiers from the battlefields and took them back to hospitals on hospital trains operated by their drafted men. The expense of this service was met by the Mennonites themselves. During 1917 alone the Mennonites contributed over 3,000,000 rubles for the support of their men in these two forms of service. For a time following the Revolution the Soviets continued the recognition of CO's in principle, but as time went on application of the principle became increasingly difficult.

For the first time after the Civil War, the American Mennonites faced conscription in 1917. The World War I conscription law provided for the exemption of conscientious objectors from combatant military service but it did not excuse them from noncombatant service in the army, a type of service which most Mennonites could not conscientiously accept. The government then agreed to segregation in the army camps of those CO's who rejected noncombatant military service, until a final solution could be found. In June 1918 a newly enacted law designed to meet an acute labor shortage and authorizing furloughs to men in the army "to engage in civil occupations and pursuits" was applied to CO's. At the same time a civilian Board of Inquiry was established to visit the military camps for the purpose of interviewing the CO's. Those adjudged sincere were to be granted furloughs either for farm work or for relief work in Europe under the American Friends Service Committee. When the war ended, the Board of Inquiry had not completed its work, but it had selected 1,300 sincere objectors from many religious groups for farm work or service in European relief.

World War I convinced the Mennonites that service within the army even if classified as noncombatant service was a compromise with the conscientious objectors' position. During the war the Mennonites made at least two official proposals to the government for the assignment of CO's to agricultural projects not connected with the military, one of them suggesting that they engage in agricultural development and education on an Indian reservation. There is evidence that these proposals received consideration by the government, although no action was taken upon them before the war ended.[3]

The witness of several thousand CO's who consistently took their stand against all military service, including 360 religious objectors (138 of them Mennonites) who received court-martial sentences, convinced the government as well as the "peace churches" that in the event of a future war a better way of dealing with objectors must be discovered. The "Plan of Unified Action in case the United States is Involved in War," adopted by the Historic Peace Churches (Brethren, Friends, and Mennonites) in 1935, was only one of the more significant of numerous actions which contributed to the formulation of the liberal provisions of the Selective Training and Service Act of September 16, 1940, providing for the assignment of CO's to work of national importance under civilian direction.

During the six and one-half years that men were drafted under this law, approximately 12,000 young men were assigned to Civilian Public Service (CPS) camps, there to perform "work of national importance." More than 4,600 of these men, or 38 per cent, were Mennonites. The three denominations with the next highest number of men in CPS were the Brethren, the Friends, and the Methodists. A total of 87 denominations were represented in the camps by three or more men each.[4]

In May 1941 the first Mennonite CPS camp was opened near Grottoes, Virginia, for work under the Soil Conservation Service. By December 1945 more than sixty camps and other CPS units had been established by Selective Service to be operated under Mennonite direction. A total of ten groups, including the Mennonite Central Committee (MCC), operated the 151 camps and units approved by Selective Service.

3 Guy F. Hershberger, *War, Peace, and Nonresistance*, 125-32.
4 Melvin Gingerich, *Service for Peace* (Akron, 1949); "Civilian Public Service," *ME*, 1:604-11.

Twenty-six of the MCC camps and units were engaged in soil conservation, dairy testing, and other agricultural services; 10 were engaged in forestry and national park service; and 34 in mental health, public health, and other health services, including a unit operating under the Puerto Rico Reconstruction Administration and another under the Office of Scientific Research and Development where the men submitted themselves as "guinea pigs" in experiments designed to gain information having to do with nutrition and disease. By August 1945 Mennonite units had more than 550 men engaged in dairy work, among whom were a considerable number engaged in dairy herd testing. By December 1945 more than 1,500 men had served in mental hospitals under MCC administration.

During the 1941-47 period of CPS, the men assigned to Mennonite camps performed 120 different types of work as classified by the reports of the Selective Service records, and gave 2,296,175 man-days of service, exclusive of the work in four camps which were operated jointly by two or more agencies. Since the draftees were not paid for the work performed in the base camps, and were given only a maintenance wage of $15 per month in the special projects, using the basic army pay of $50 per month for estimation, men in Mennonite CPS contributed approximately $4,000,000 worth of labor to the federal and state governments. The federal government spent approximately $1,333,000 on CPS. If this entire cost is charged against the Mennonite camps, the United States benefited to the figure of $2,666,000 from the contribution of men drafted to Mennonite CPS camps.

To operate the camps under Mennonite direction, the churches contributed a total of over $3,000,000 in money and goods to the MCC. This amount was raised by a quota plan which for a time asked a contribution of fifty cents per month per member and which by the end of CPS had produced a total contribution of about $21.45 per member. In addition to the monies and gifts collected for Mennonite CPS, congregations and individuals often gave individual gifts to men in the camps. Special efforts were made to help those men who had dependents, and certain conferences and congregations gave their men money payments at the time of demobilization to partially offset the economic handicaps resulting from several years of service without wages.

In the Canadian alternative service program the camps were operated by the government, the churches appointing religious advisers for the camps. The work was principally forestry service and highway construction, the men receiving maintenance, traveling expenses to and from camp, and fifty cents a day allowance. In 1943 the system was removed from military control and placed under the Ministry of Labor, a civilian agency, which now assigned many CO's to work on farms and in factories. The wages of these men were regulated so that they received maintenance plus $25 per month for themselves, all earnings beyond this amount being given to the Canadian Red Cross. By August 1946, when the program closed, more than 10,000 men had served in some phase of the Alternative Service Work program. Statistics as of 1944 showed that 63 per cent of Canadian CO's in World War II were Mennonites, and 20 per cent Dukhobors. At that time the Red Cross had received $300,000 in contributions from the earnings of the CO's.[5] During the decade following 1946 Canada had no conscription.

In the United States wartime conscription came to an end in 1947, only to be followed by a peacetime conscription law enacted in 1948, although CO's were not drafted until after the law was amended in 1951 to provide for their conscription for two-year terms to perform "such civilian work contributing to the maintenance of the national health, safety, or interest as the local board may deem appropriate." Under this law a new program of alternative service, considerably different from Civilian Public Service during World War II, was begun in 1952. Under the new plan the drafted

5 Melvin Gingerich, "Alternative Service Work Camps," *ME*, 1:76-78; *Service for Peace*, 412-24.

men were to be paid prevailing wages and instead of being sent to camps they were to be assigned to work under either government or private agencies. Among the 1,700 agencies approved by Selective Service for the employment of CO's were many hospitals and welfare institutions. The nonprofit private agencies included the Mennonite Central Committee, the Brethren Service Committee, and the Near East Foundation. By April 1, 1956, a total of nearly 6,500 men had been assigned to alternative service, nearly 4,000 of whom had already completed their two-year terms. It was estimated that approximately 2,400 men were actually in service as of this date, 1,600 of whom were Mennonites. Next in number were the Church of the Brethren with 200 and third the Friends with 95.

Of the 2,400 CO's in service as of April 1, 1956, 60 per cent were serving in public institutions and agencies, 20 per cent in church-related services such as foreign builders' units in Europe, 19 per cent in other Protestant agencies such as children's homes, and 6 per cent in Catholic agencies such as hospitals. Among those working in institutions, 40 per cent were serving in mental hospitals, 30 per cent in general hospitals, and 30 per cent in such institutions as Veterans Administration hospitals, tuberculosis hospitals, boys' training schools, and homes for children. Forty-five per cent of the 2,400 men were hospital attendants, 14 per cent were engaged in maintenance work, 12 per cent were doing housekeeping, 5 per cent were farming, and 24 per cent were performing other types of services, including research, teaching, community services, relief, reconstruction, medical, and "guinea pig" experiments. Most of these men were serving within the United States and its territories; but 122 had served or were serving at that time in twenty other countries around the world.[6] Because of the decrease in the number of men called by Selective Service, by October 1, 1956, the number of Men-

---

6 These statistics were taken from "Our Peace Witness in Relation to Government," a paper read by J. Harold Sherk at a Peace Conference in the Eden Mennonite Church, Moundridge, Kansas, June 17, 1956.

nonite and Brethren in Christ[7] CO's in alternative service had dropped to 1,458, with 102 serving in overseas projects.

In their witness to the state the Mennonites of the United States and Canada have consistently testified against conscription and its contribution to the spirit of militarism and its attendant evils. Since they recognize coercion as a function of the state, however, without which it cannot operate in a sub-Christian society, they have not refused to serve the state under conscription when the nature of the service itself was not considered to be in conflict with Christian teaching. They have therefore acquiesced to alternative service under conscription, whereas many Friends, for example, reject this as conscription of conscience. During World War II the Friends co-operated officially with CPS in the beginning, but withdrew before the program was ended, and they did not co-operate at all in the new draft program begun in 1951. Some drafted Friends to be sure were serving in the alternative service program, but Friends administered no projects or institutions to which drafted men were assigned for alternative service, as in the case of the Mennonites and the Church of the Brethren.

During World War II the Mennonites accepted CPS as a workable plan of alternative service under conscription, and in general they were fairly well satisfied with the results, although the new alternative service program inaugurated in 1951 is generally regarded as more acceptable than CPS. The work was generally considered to be more significant than that under CPS. The fact that 85 per cent of the men who entered alternative service "volunteered" before their induction date rather than to wait to be drafted indicates that they did not dread their term of service. Many were attracted by the foreign service which the program permitted and since the men employed by the state were paid prevailing wages

7 The Brethren in Christ Church although not Mennonite is affiliated with the Mennonite Central Committee, and the MCC statistics for Mennonites generally include the Brethren in Christ, a small denomination who share most of the doctrinal views held by the Mennonites.

hardship cases did not arise as in CPS. The government also was pleased with the service which the men were giving. In June 1956 J. Harold Sherk, the director of the MCC Peace Section, said: "Because of the service record which they established very quickly, the requests for their services increased, with the result that the demand today is considerably greater than the supply of men available."[8]

The general satisfaction of Selective Service with the plan is reflected by a statement of Victor A. Olsen, an administrator in its manpower division, who in addressing a group of alternative service men about to leave for Europe, said: "Your service is just as honorable as those of the armed forces, although it is not as spectacular. You are going into a man's service and you have a joint responsibility with military men in making good international relations as you represent your nation and church. You are going into an area where your forefathers were driven out. You have an opportunity to show them the love of Jesus and that the way you have been brought up is better than communism."[9]

The western world is slowly accepting the principle of alternative service as a legitimate expression of religious conviction. In contrast with the intolerance of World War I, public opinion toward CO's in World War II was surprisingly tolerant, and even friendly. In 1950 the official report of the Selective Service System of the United States declared that although "the average American citizen was somewhat skeptical of an objector program on work of national importance under civilian direction, . . . by the end of the 6½ years' experience which the System had with the program . . . there was a marked difference in attitude throughout the country. . . . Therefore the work-of-national-importance idea for conscientious objectors resulted in a distinct and valuable contribution to the emergency effort of 1940-47."[10]

8 See J. Harold Sherk's paper, "Our Peace Witness in Relation to Government," 3.

9 *The I-W Mirror* (Akron, Pennsylvania) Vol. IV, No. 14, 2.

10 *Conscientious Objection* (Special Monograph No. 11) by Selective Service System (Washington, 1950) 179-80.

The British policy is even more liberal than that of the United States and Canada; here CO's with religious objection to all service under conscription are exempted altogether. All of the Scandinavian countries have alternative service provisions for CO's, Denmark having inaugurated a system of government camps for civilian service as early as 1917. Following World War II, Holland inaugurated a similar program, with government camps similar to the Canadian camps of World War II and also with service in mental hospitals. In 1952 several hundred Dutch CO's, including about 30 Mennonites, were engaged in alternative service. In 1956 West Germany was in process of setting up a system of alternative service for CO's. Countries like France and Switzerland where a considerable number of Mennonites reside have no adequate provision for CO's, although in 1951 the French Mennonite Conference took official action petitioning its government to provide a plan for alternative civilian service. It is hoped that such a policy may be adopted not only in France but in other countries where it does not exist at present.

It needs to be remembered that Christian nonresistance rests on a much broader foundation than a revulsion to war. It is based on Christ's command to love all men and from this point of view Christian service is more than alternative service. It is a positive ministry of sacrificial service to men who are in need at all times and under all circumstances. The idea of voluntary service among the Mennonites was not born with CPS, although this experience did greatly stimulate the idea and led to its development into a well-rounded program of service for men and women not subject to the draft within all the Historic Peace Churches.

During World War II, service units of conscientious objector young women worked in mental hospitals and other needy areas where CPS men were serving. At the close of the war hundreds of Mennonites, young and middle-aged, many of whom had already given society from two to five years of free service in CPS, served in the war-torn and other needy countries around the globe, on a voluntary basis for two- or three-year terms, working usually on a simple cost-of-living income plus a monthly ten-dollar allowance for clothing and incidentals. An alphabetical list of all MCC summer service personnel for 1956 contains more than 340 names of persons from no less than thirteen countries, a small minority of whom were from non-Mennonite church groups. These persons worked in twenty-nine projects, seven of which were in Europe. The list of the longer term MCC personnel as of September 14, 1956, contained over 450 names of individuals serving in twenty-two countries, most of whom were working on a voluntary service basis in a variety of institutions, where they were performing many types of social services. In addition to the MCC voluntary service program, there were programs sponsored directly by several Mennonite groups, including the Mennonite Church, the General Conference Mennonite Church, and others, in which more than 240 persons were engaged in voluntary service.

Another significant result of the growing awareness of opportunities for offering voluntary social service can be seen in the development of men's service organizations, variously known as Mennonite Disaster Service and Mennonite Service Organization. The first of these organizations was formed in Kansas after World War II, and since that time the movement has spread throughout the Mennonite churches so that by the end of 1956 organizations were in existence in at least 18 states and provinces. Mennonite laymen during recent years have given greatly appreciated aid to the victims of tornadoes, fires, and floods. Their efficient service has won the praise of Red Cross and state officials and has resulted in considerable favorable publicity in the American press. Mennonites have always practiced mutual aid and have gone to the relief of their unfortunate neighbors, but their enlarged vision of the world's needs and of the possibility of increasing the effectiveness of their work by means of organization which came to them through their World War II experiences has been a major stimulus for this new movement, the most significant spontaneous movement among American Mennonite laymen in this century. It is of course true that they have also been aware of their responsibility to set examples of sacrificial service for their sons who are conscripted for social service. Nor have they been unaware of the fact that there must be an acceptable type of alternative action for those whose consciences will not permit them to become a part of Civilian Defense, which often seems to them to have primarily a military philosophy and orientation.

As stated in the opening paragraphs, in a broad definition of alternative service one can include many forms of work and expressions of protest in addition to civilian service rendered in lieu of military service. In the broader area one would include the choosing of a vocation as far removed as possible from the munitions and war industries. Although in a war economy such as that of the United States it is difficult to avoid involvement completely, Mennonites have constantly witnessed against the inconsistency of conscientious objectors entering jobs directly connected with war effort or military preparation. In a similar way they have preferred to buy civilian bonds rather than war bonds even when they were aware of the fact that their money would release other funds for military purpose. During World War II Mennonites purchased almost $5,000,000 worth of civilian bonds. This was a gesture, a symbol, and a protest in the face of great public and government pressure to bring about the wide scale purchase of war bonds.[11] Their conscience against participating in strife and violence has also made Mennonites uneasy concerning membership in labor unions, which might call upon them to participate in strikes operated contrary to the principles of love and nonresistance. Consequently when employed in situations governed by unions they have sought to discover ways and means of maintaining alternative relationships consistent with the way of love and nonresistance.[12]

11 Melvin Gingerich, *Service for Peace*, 355-59.
12 Hershberger, *War, Peace, and Nonresistance*, Ch. 10.

✠ MARY ELEANOR BENDER ✠

The Sixteenth Century Anabaptists in Literature

It is general knowledge that because the radical Anabaptist elements were more spectacular than the quiet, main line Anabaptists, they became more commonly known. In fact for many people they came to represent Anabaptism per se, an idea which has only slowly been dissipated as modern research has brought to light the essence of genuine Anabaptism.[1] Since the surface interest of spectacular movements also lends itself more easily to fictional treatment than does the quieter and subtler contribution of stable groups, it is not surprising that most literature on "Anabaptist" themes concerns not genuine Anabaptism, but its aberrant and violent forms, particularly the Münsterites. More frequently than not, sensational elements associated with Anabaptism are exploited, sometimes with intentional dishonesty, sometimes as a result of naiveté on the part of the author. It is the rare but significant exception which grasps the essence of the Anabaptist effort to face without compromise the claims of Christ and the paradoxes which that attitude presents, and transforms them into tragic literature of high quality. Slightly more often a simple admiration for some of the elements of Anabaptism's contribution to the society from which it differed is expressed in fiction which grasps a part of the spirit of Anabaptism. In general, however, there is little resemblance between the fictional treatments of even the main line Anabaptists and the Anabaptists themselves.

---

* Mary Eleanor Bender is Assistant Professor of English in Goshen College.

1 See Robert Friedmann, "Conception of the Anabaptists," *Church History* (December 1940) 9:341-65, and Roland Bainton, "The Left Wing of the Reformation," *Journal of Religion* (April 1941) 21:124-34.

THE SIXTEENTH CENTURY

The only literary treatments of the sixteenth-century Anabaptists by their contemporaries on the continent of which we are now aware are a few German poems treating Münster satirically and didactically,[2] and some Dutch verse. Although the German poems are of no significance from either a literary or an historical standpoint, the Dutch verse was written by leading poets who do treat genuine Anabaptism with some degree of penetration. One poem, for instance, was written by Dirk Vzn. Coornhert (1522-90), a Catholic poet, philosopher, and theologian, whom W. J. Kühler calls a "friend as well as an enemy of the Anabaptists," and who is so significant for religious tolerance in Holland that he is sometimes called the Dutch Sebastian Franck. It is a satire, *Aertzney der Sielen* (1570), in which Coornhert treats Menno Simons as well as the pope, Luther, and Calvin.[3] Another poem, *Olijf Bergh* (1590), was written by Carel van Mander (1548-1606), a Mennonite aesthetician, one of the leading poets of the Dutch Golden Age, and according to tradition the teacher of Frans Hals.[4] In the *Olijf Bergh* he "portrays with deep sympathy the industry, the strict and quiet manner of life, the peacefulness and piety of the Anabaptists."[5]

One reason for the difference in character between the German and the Dutch treatments is that as early as the second half of the sixteenth century the persecution of the Dutch Anabaptists had subsided, and in the resulting assimilation with Dutch society they lost many of their original distinctive Anabaptist tenets and became accepted and often important citizens. This departure is evidenced by the very fact that there was an Anabaptist aesthetician. The degree of departure from original Anabaptism which van Mander represents

2 Hugo Hermsen, *Die Wiedertäufer zu Münster in der deutschen Dichtung*, *Breslauer Beiträge zur Literaturgeschichte* No. 33 (Stuttgart, 1913) 30-34.
3 H. F. W. Jeltes, "Mennonites in Dutch Literature," *MQR* (April 1937) 11:150, translated from the article "Literatur," *Mennonitisches Lexikon* (Weierhof, 1937) 2:669-72.
4 *Ibid.*, 143-44.
5 *Ibid.*, 151.

is evidenced by the fact that he wanted to establish in Holland the aesthetics of the Italian Renaissance! One questions whether the literature on the Dutch Mennonites written even in the late sixteenth century can rightly be termed Anabaptist.

The best Anabaptist literature of the sixteenth century is undoubtedly found in the letters and devotional writings of the Dutch Anabaptists themselves, written during the time of persecution. Jeltes says: "In these stirring, at times deeply moving, and always very personal testimonies—of human suffering, of devotion to husband and wife and children, of the torturing concern of the future of loved ones, of the unshakable devotion of faith and readiness to suffer which rises high above all suffering and thinking, we often come suddenly upon an innocent, ingenuous beauty which the writer did not consciously strive for and which he very likely was wholly unconscious of."[6]

These songs and hymns were collected in two sources: 1) *Het Offer des Heeren* (1562), to which a *Liedtboecxken* was added in 1563 and which was published in 1904 by Samuel Cramer in *Bibliotheca Reformatoria Neerlandica;*[7] 2) Van Braght's *Martyrs' Mirror* (1660).

In England, where there probably were no established Mennonite congregations but only scattered groups of Anabaptist refugees from the continent, Anabaptism never occurs as a major theme. Incidental mention of it, and especially of the Münsterites, does occur fairly frequently, however. "Writers and churchmen," says Irvin B. Horst,[8] "joined public officials in making capital of 'the Münster-business' in campaigns against both separatism and nonconformity." Horst singles out several of the more important allusions to Anabaptism for discussion: John Bale's historical play, *King John,* which alludes to Münster, the coming of the Anabap-

---

6 *Ibid.,* 142.
7 *Ibid.,* 142-43.
8 Irvin B. Horst, "The Anabaptists in English Literature: A Research Note," *MQR* (July 1955) 29:232-39.

tists to England, and Queen Elizabeth's suppression of them; two pamphlets, one by Sir Thomas More, *The second parte of the confutacion of Tyndals answere* (1533), and one by William Barlow, *A dyaloge descrybyng the orygynall ground of these Lutheran faccyons* (1531); Thomas Nashe's story, *The Unfortunate Traveller* (1594), in which the hero becomes involved with the fanatical Anabaptists in Germany; and a probable allusion to the Anabaptists by Spenser in his *Faiery Queene* (Artegall's victory over the "mighty gyant" is considered by such scholars as Frederick Padelford to represent the overthrow of the Münsterites).

THE SEVENTEENTH CENTURY

The single seventeenth-century Dutch literary allusion to the Anabaptists confuses seventeenth-century Dutch Mennonitism with early Anabaptism. It is found in Gerbrandt A. Bredero's farcical drama, *Het Moortje* (1616), which refers to the Anabaptist revolt in Amsterdam in 1535. In treating his "Anabaptists," Bredero satirizes such Mennonite (but certainly not Anabaptist) characteristics as a propensity for rich food and drink.[9]

Seventeenth-century English belletristic reference to the Anabaptists (according to Horst) is largely incidental to the frequent satirical allusion to the Puritans, the term "Anabaptist" being applied in a pejorative sense to all nonconformists. Horst mentions several Anabaptist "characters," especially those by Samuel Butler; an anonymous ballad, "The Lecherous Anabaptist" (1681); and Ben Johnson's *The Alchemist* (1612), in which two Anabaptists appear. One of the Anabaptists is a deacon whom Johnson ridicules for "blind obedience to Scripture texts"; the other is a pastor who is ridiculed for "worldly-wise compromise of principle."[10]

The only German treatment of the theme is also the most significant of all seventeenth-century literary treatments

9 Jeltes, *loc. cit.*, 151.
10 Horst, *loc. cit.*, 233-34.

of Anabaptism. This is Johann Christoph Grimmelshausen's *Der abenteuerliche Simplizissimus* (1669), the leading German baroque novel and one of Germany's most important novels of development. Grimmelshausen's hero is influenced to return to religion by his contact with the Moravian Hutterites, in whom he finds those principles which he had come to admire through previous study of religion, and whom Grimmelshausen praises strongly for their ethical integrity and strength of character. The fact that Grimmelshausen calls the Hutterites *Ketzer,* and has his hero finally turn away from them because they are heretics, is clearly a concession to the spirit of the times and is not meant to represent Grimmelshausen's own attitude. As Elizabeth Bender emphasizes, the fact that Grimmelshausen was able to see strength in the Hutterites at a time when they were almost universally rejected is a tribute to him.[11]

THE EIGHTEENTH CENTURY

In the eighteenth century, which took pride in its objectivity, there are scattered attempts to distinguish genuine Anabaptism at least vaguely from its violent cousins. For instance, a German poem about Menno Simons in *Der Alten und Neuen Schwärmer Widdertäufferischer Geist* says:

Menno ist auch nennenswerth
Der sich mühte bey den Leuten
Seiner Widdertauffer Lehr, alles Fleisches auszubreiten;
wiewol mit gelindern Mitteln, als der man sogleich gedacht:
Er hat Gleichsam, was verdorben,
Wiederum ins reine bracht.[12]

Of more significance is Voltaire's Anabaptist in *Candide,* characterized by selflessness and an absolute position against

11 Elizabeth H. Bender, "The Mennonites in German Literature" (unpublished M.A. thesis, University of Minnesota, 1944) 39-46.
12 Otto Schowalter, "Die Mennoniten in der deutschen Literatur," *Mennonitisches Lexikon,* 2:663.

violence, the only personality to escape Voltaire's satire. *Candide* contains the only literary reference to the Anabaptists of any importance in France, where Anabaptism has remained relatively unknown.[13] After *Candide,* no literary treatment of the Anabaptist theme occurs outside Germany until the twentieth century.

Understandably, the period of storm and stress found the Münster theme attractive. In the last 25 years of the eighteenth century three dramas on the Münster rebellion, all of poor quality, appear in Germany. In 1777 Christoph Bernhard Schücking, an uncle of the noted Levin Schücking and himself a citizen of Münster, wrote a drama on Elizabeth Wandscherer, Bockelson's wife, entitled *Elisabeth.* Although the drama is freighted with excesses, which are explained not only by the period in which it was written but also by the youth of the author, and although it lacks any finished artistry, it foreshadows the tragic presentation of personality conflict in Jan of Leyden as tragedy which is more fully developed in later works. In his *Jan von Laiden oder die Belagerung von Münster* (1786) von Nesselrode senses the dramatic possibilities in the Münster episode, although his characters behave with too much flattering dramatic nobility to be in good taste. Christian August Vulpius's *Johann von Leiden* (1793) portrays Jan of Leyden as a titan.[14]

THE NINETEENTH CENTURY

In nineteenth-century Germany the Münsterites appear as a literary theme with relative frequency, and their treatment is adapted to the century's changing moods. The only work of literary value to mention them, however, is Achim von Arnim's romantic novel *Die Kronenwächter* (Vol. I, the only completed volume, *Bertholds erstes und zweites Leben,* 1817). Arnim places the imperial crown in Münster, and considers the Münster episode a positive step in the develop-

13 *Ibid.,* 2:663.
14 Hermsen, *op. cit.,* 35-53.

ment of the German concept of empire. Despite his fantastic main theme, Arnim strives for historical accuracy of detail and may well have set the trend, growing especially in the second half of the century, toward greater historical objectivity regarding the Anabaptists.[15]

As a result of the nineteenth-century interest in historical fiction, five historical novels on the Münsterites, all distinctly inferior from a literary point of view, followed *Die Kronenwächter*. Van der Velde's *Die Wiedertäufer* (1821) is a superficial bit of entertainment literature. Under the influence of Scott Karl Spindler, in *Der König von Zion* (1834), the novel which more than any other awakened the interest of the Germans in the Münster episode, attempts to view the characters of his story in the light of their historical situation. He does not really succeed, however, since he considers all Münsterites to be either evil or insane and has no insight into the tensions of the Reformation reflected in Münster.[16] Adolf Görling, in *Die Wiedertäufer* (1859), attempts to give a picture of the entire Reformation. The fifth work is J. D. Mallmann's *Johann von Leyden, eine Geschichte fürs Volk* (1844).[17] The Münster theme is also used in Meyerbeer's opera, *Le Prophete* (1845), in which Jan of Leyden, the hero, is praised and his failures blamed on "the times." The German translation of the opera in 1846 strongly affected the German attitude toward the Münsterites.

Six works on Münster appear in the third quarter of the nineteenth century. In 1854 Adolf Mützelburg published a novel of 1,100 pages, entitled *Der Prophet* and based to a large extent on Spindler's work. *Johann von Leyden* by Heinrich Brinckmann (1855) is a meaningless drama in blank verse. In his drama *Der König von Zion* (1865), Robert Hamerling, an active promoter of German liberalism, makes Leyden a representative of modern social problems, a cham-

15 *ML*, 2:663.
16 Hermsen, 53-72.
17 Wilhelm Rauch, *Johann von Leyden, der König von Sion in der Dichtung* (Leipzig, 1912) 47-53.

pion of freedom. The influence of Hebbel is shown in Ernst Mevert's drama, *Der König von Münster* (1869), in that Leyden's downfall is attributed to the fact that he is not in line with the "general laws of events in the world." Mevert is the first to exploit to any real extent the tragic potential in Münster, and Hugo Hermsen considers his to be the best of the nineteenth-century dramas on the Anabaptists. Ludwig Schneegans, in *Jan Bockhold* (1877), sees Leyden as an emotionally sick man. Also in 1877 Rudolf Weber published an exceedingly poor historical novel, *Die Wiedertäufer von Münster*, obviously borrowed for the most part from that of Mützelburg.

During the last quarter of the century, the Münsterites receive only programmatic treatment. Hermann Tiemann's novel, *Die Wiedertäufer in Münster* (1892) is a Victorian warning to the German people not to abandon traditional virtues. Tiemann tries to interpret Jan of Leyden psychologically, but he cannot comprehend the spirit of the Reformation and succeeds only in comparing him with enthusiasts of his own time. The politically fraught atmosphere of the era in which he wrote is evident in his attempt to make the naive Münsterites represent sophisticated political ideas, an attempt which of course fails. Victor Hardung's drama, *Die Wiedertäufer in Münster* (1895), is a partly naturalistic picture of what Hardung calls "the baseness of the great human rabble" ("der Niederträchtigkeit des grossen menschlichen Gesindels") which is completely unsuccessful. Hardung calls his characters cattle (*Viecher*). Two equally unsuccessful works were written by A. J. Cüppers: a drama, *Der König von Sion* (1900), so weak from both dramatic and psychological standpoints that it was never performed, and a historical novel, *Im Banne der Wiedertäufer* (1897).[18]

Fiction treating the main line Anabaptists does not appear until the second half of the century, but it is on the whole of good literary quality. It comes to us in the form of

18 Hermsen, *op. cit.*, 72-142.

three Novellen: Stern's *Die Wiedertäufer* (1866); Wilhelm Heinrich Riehl's *Mein Recht* (1875); and Gottfried Keller's *Ursula* (1870). *Die Wiedertäufer* treats refugees from Münster in the marshes of the lower Ems who, forty years after the Münster episode, have re-established themselves and have returned to the original Anabaptist tenets. Stern is the first of the nineteenth-century authors to make a valid distinction between the genuine Anabaptists and the Münsterites. *Mein Recht,* which takes place in 1577, is the story of a man in search of justice for himself against a fellow citizen, and whose contact with the Anabaptists causes him to realize that the New Testament principle of love precludes that justice to which he has dedicated his life. He loses his mind in the resulting conflict. Riehl presents with depth of insight both the Anabaptist position and the hero's conflict. On the contrary, Keller's *Ursula,* which takes place among the Zürich Anabaptists, is a complete misrepresentation of Anabaptism, historically and ideologically. Written under the influence of Feuerbach, it is actually meant to discredit conservative Christianity and at the same time to avenge the blot of Anabaptism on the Zürich record. Keller's Anabaptists are by his own description "beschränkte und unsaubere Gesellen," and their behavior consists of a series of lunatic excesses.[19]

THE TWENTIETH CENTURY

Fiction based on Anabaptist themes appears in great volume in the twentieth century. The works vary greatly in their attitude toward the Anabaptists. Three early novels portray the same theme, the conflict of main line Anabaptism with the state: Pastor Wilhelm Staehle's (alias Philipp Spiess) *Der Reichsprofos* (1904); Peter Cürlis' *Die drei Brüder vom Brockhof* (1908); and Ernst Marti's *Zwei Häuser, Zwei Welten* (1911). Spiess's novel is a story of kind treatment which Aichelin, hated provost of the Swabian League, receives from an Anabaptist whom he has persecuted. In

19 Bender, *op. cit.,* 57-96.

Cürlis' book, three brothers are divided by the varying views of the Reformation; Menno Simons, sympathetically portrayed, represents the Anabaptist point of view. Although both stories are sympathetic toward the Anabaptist, they contain much historical error, and both consider the Anabaptists to have been simply absorbed by the state church. Marti, on the contrary, understands the basic distinction between the Anabaptist and state church concepts, and portrays the two views as irreconcilable, an idea which he symbolizes by a permanent cleft created by the Anabaptist controversy within a family.

The second major theme among the novelists is the mysticism of the Anabaptist Hans Denk (1500-27). In her completely fantastic novel, *Das Marienbild der Nonne Zeitlose* (1911), Lotte Gubalke views Denk as a propounder of supernatural libertinism which results from his mysticism. Hermann Kosel in his biography *Albrecht Dürer, ein deutscher Heiland* (1923-24) treats Denk as a scoundrel. Although neither Denk nor the main line Anabaptists had political interests, Ludwig Huna, in *Ein Kampf um Gott* (1931), a novel which presents the Anabaptists correctly as advocates of religious tolerance, bases Denk's tolerance not on Biblicism, the basis of all Anabaptist ideas, but on modern political theories.[20]

As usual, the Münsterites are again a favorite theme in the twentieth century. In 1915 Wilhelm Schmidtbonn, depressed because of the war, wrote his rather raw drama on Münster, entitled *Die Stadt der Besessenen*. Hans Freimark's novel, *Johann von Leiden* (1919), deserves only passing mention. In 1935 Bernhard Kellerman wrote a drama on Münster, *Die Wiedertäufer*, which is fairly similar to Schmidtbonn's, although it is impressionistic.

In 1926 two Zwingli biographies appeared, one by Emanuel Stickelberger and one by Wilhelm Schaefer sub-

---

20 *ML*, 2:665-67.

titled, significantly, *Ein deutsches Volksbuch,* both of which treat the Anabaptist controversy. Both are written from the Reformed standpoint and both portray the Anabaptists as ridiculous fanatics; especially in Schaefer's book they are foils to Zwingli's strength. Beginning with Schaefer's biography, and until World War II, literary reference to Anabaptism is largely a product of German interest in national local color, sociology, and history. In 1936 Maria Veronika Rubatscher, an ultra-patriotic pan-German, wrote a novel entitled *Das lutherische Joggele,* in which, without any insight into its religious nature, she praises Anabaptism as a folk movement that originated in resistance to too much French influence in the church. She maintains that the Anabaptists were absorbed into the state church when the latter finally became capable of absorbing the various Germanic folk elements.[21] In 1939 Lulu von Strauss und Torney, whose work springs to a large extent from a love for her native Westphalia and its history, wrote a novel entitled *Der Jüngste Tag.* In it a mentally ill Westphalian weaver, inspired as a prophet by the Münsterites, is accused of setting fire to a village when the millennium does not come on the date he has predicted, and is stoned to death. *Der Jüngste Tag* is generally considered Strauss und Torney's best novel. In 1936 Ricarda Huch, a gifted and versatile author, included an unusually understanding treatment of the Anabaptists in her belletristic history, *Das Zeitalter der Glaubensspaltung.* In the same year, E. G. Kolbenheyer, an author frequently criticized for ultra-patriotic attitudes, published a three-volume biography of Paracelsus in which he also discussed the Anabaptists.

The large volume of Anabaptist fiction and drama appearing after 1945 forms part of a prolixity of historical fiction both on the continent and in the United States, which may be partially explained as a result of despair among intellectuals and a consequent desire either to escape into the

21 *Ibid.,* 2:667-68.

past or to save the situation, one means of salvation being the portrayal of historical parallels with their appropriate lessons.[22] In this literary climate Anabaptism seems to have a strong appeal. Both the radical and the quiet types symbolize to some postwar authors the dedication and faith lost in their own age of relativism and doubt. To others the violent left wing of the Reformation mirrors the turmoil of their times; it provides a setting in which to discuss the contemporary experiences of dictatorship, violence, and mass hysteria at arm's length, without becoming too painfully involved in them.

Since World War II, three noted contemporary authors, Friedrich Dürrenmatt, Franz Theodor Csokor, and Helmut Paulus, have written fiction on the Münsterites. Dürrenmatt, a young Zürich dramatist, has won much acclaim especially among students for his experimental dramatic techniques. At its premier in Zürich *Es steht geschrieben* (1948), his drama on Münster, was greeted with excitement mingled with catcalls. It combines admiration for the firm faith of the Münsterites and their obedience to it under stress with the realization that this faith was also infinitely dangerous to its followers. Dürrenmatt's drama is original in idea as well as in technique. The Austrian Franz Theodor Csokor has gained recognition both as a novelist and as a dramatist. His novel on the Münsterites, *Der Schlüssel zum Abgrund* (1955), is a serious effort to understand the Münster episode as an expression

22 "Es wimmelt von verschwommenen Weltverbesserern, persönlich Verzweifelten unter den Verfassern, die statt Menschen und echte Gegenspieler zu bilden, bestenfalls Zeitsymptome in der schwarz-weiss Technik darstellen oder mit kabarettischen Mitteln karikieren. Die Kehrseite solcher verrutschten Aktualitätensucht markiert sich immer wieder in Ueberangebot der historischen Stücke, jenen umweltfremden, substanzlosen Epigonendramen, in die sich bekanntlich so viel Gefühl, so viel falsche Mystik hineintreiben lässt. Historische Tragödien sind aber gedichtet worden, weil es die Dichter reizt, durch die Vergangenheit hindurch und in ihrer Spiegel, Bild und Schicksal, Gesetz und Notwendigkeit der eigenen Zeit besser erkennen zu lassen. Gerade an diesem Aktualisierungsprozess, der beileibe nicht äusserlich zu verstehen ist, scheitern so viele unserer Autoren, wenn sie Gedankentiefe, eigene Gesinnung und persönliche Emotionen mit lebensechter Kunst verwechseln, . . . Darum schwelgen die Personae dramatis so oft in gepflegter Konventionalität, darum stelzen sie . . . so tief in überkommenen Moralbegriffen herum . . . . Es ist Angst und krampfhaftes Zurückstreben zum Alten, das ehedem gross war und Halt gewähren möchte." Axel Kaum, "Wie steht es mit der deutschen Dichtung?" *Welt und Wort* (Tübingen, 1955) 7:151.

of the turmoil of the Reformation and thus to understand the Reformation itself more fully. However, in spite of moments of insight and artistic power, it is disturbing in its unconvincing exploitation of some of the more sensational traditions which have grown up around Münster. Helmut Paulus (1900-), though not strikingly original in technique or idea, is a master storyteller and a popular author. The motif of his works is didactic, and his principal theme is that only a life for others is fruitful. This is also the message of *Die tönernen Füsse* (1954), his novel on the tragic disillusionment caused by the selfishness of Jan of Leyden.

In 1937 Friedrich Reck-Malleczewen, a physician who was a member of the East Prussian aristocracy and who suffered spiritually under the Nazi regime, wrote a biography of Jan of Leyden which he entitled *Bockelson-Geschichte eines Massenwahns,* and which was intended as a warning to the Germans against their mass hysteria under Hitler. During the war his book was passed from hand to hand in the underground. Reck-Malleczewen himself was executed at Dachau in 1945. His book was published a year later. In 1948, Erich Müller-Gangloff, a friend of Reck-Malleczewen and at present director of one of the evangelical academies in Germany, published a series of sketches of tyrants under the title, *Vorläufer des Anti-Christ,* which he dedicated to his martyred friend. He includes members of the violent wing of the Anabaptists, especially Bockelson, whose portrait he bases on that of Malleczewen, and he calls the Anabaptists the *Rattenfänger der Reformation.* His attempt to find a recurring pattern among tyrants which might aid in an understanding of Hitler is interesting, but his treatment of the Anabaptists is seriously in error. Following is a typical sentence from his book: "Die Täuferbewegung war ja von vornherein eine weit über die Stadt Münster hinaus verbreitete Erscheinung, die in vielen Landschaften des damaligen Reiches unter der Oberfläche gärte, und explosionsartige Ausbrüche ähnlich dem des Bauernkrieges erwarten liess" (96).

287

David Joris is the subject of one novel, written by Rudolph Stickelberger, editor of the Lucerne newspaper *Neue Nachrichten*. Stickelberger entitled his story "Schwarmgeister" and published it with a biography of Bernhardin von Ochino in a volume called *Narren Gottes*. The only purpose of the book appears to be entertainment, and Stickelberger distorts the facts of Joris' life in order to increase its entertainment value. He has obviously no understanding of Anabaptism, for he considers the followers of Joris to be Anabaptists *per se,* and all Anabaptists to be unbalanced *Schwarmgeister.*

One novel and one *Novelle* having as their theme the Dutch-North German Anabaptists have appeared since World War II. Neither has much literary value. The novel, Heinrich Specht's *Heil'ge Feuer* (n.d.), was written during the war. Based on the Reformation legend of Anna Holmer, which Arnold Fokke put into writing in Dutch in 1876, it treats Münster, the North German Anabaptists, and political conflict on the Frisian-German border. The Novelle, "Die Geburt der Liebe," a romanticized story of Menno Simons by the popular, prolific Swiss author and Hollywood director, Hans Müller-Einigen, was published in a collection of historical Novellen entitled *Die Menschen sind alle gleich* (1946).

The Swiss-South German Anabaptists appear in fiction more frequently than does the Dutch-North German group. In his biography of Sebastian Franck, Hans Franck treats Hans Denk and the Nürnberg Anabaptists associated with the so-called "ungodly painters" (*gottlosen Maler*). His work is based on inaccurate sources, such as Will-Erich Peuckert, and although he is sympathetic with the Anabaptists and portrays them as redeeming some weaknesses of the state church, he dismisses them ultimately as *Schwärmer.* He gives no indication of understanding that there is an Anabaptism different from the mystic fanaticism which he pictures in Nürnberg.

A large proportion of the writers interested in Anabaptism at the present time are Swiss. In 1945 Erich Diebold, a Swiss journalist, wrote a novel on the Anabaptists of Canton Zürich entitled *Folge dem Licht*. It is a poorly written book, lacking as much in historical understanding as in depth of character portrayal and convincing development of plot. The author's thesis seems to be that the Anabaptists had excellent ideas, of which he mentions "Die Bekehrung zur Gerechtigkeit und brüderlichen Liebe, die Selbstentäusserung und die Nachfolge Christi" (Foreword, 8), but that they were wrong in trying to overthrow the existing government (as he incorrectly maintains they did) in order to introduce those ideas by force into a society not yet ready for them. Conrad Grebel becomes Diebold's mouthpiece when at his death he admits his error in attempting to establish the kingdom of God on earth by transforming the state! He now realizes, he says, that the kingdom of God is within the church and that he should have restricted his attention to the church rather than working for political reform!

Two Swiss dramas of unequal value, Heinrich Künzi's *Barbara* (1948) and Caesar von Arx's *Brüder in Christo* (1947), were published almost simultaneously. *Barbara*, a Bernese dialect drama produced by the Berner Heimatschutz Theater, portrays an Anabaptist girl who clings firmly to her faith in the face of persecution by church and state, her love and strength putting her accusers to shame. The play has dramatic weaknesses and errors in historical interpretation, especially in the final act, in which the Anabaptists escape *en masse* to the Jura mountains. The drama by von Arx, on the contrary, is a tragedy strong from the standpoint of both idea and execution. Its hero, city councillor Falk, is a friend of Zwingli who becomes convinced of the correctness of the Anabaptist position, but because of a chain of tragic circumstances considers himself unworthy of becoming an Anabaptist and thus remains in the state church, his sensitive spirit broken because he does so. Von Arx treats this genuinely

289

tragic motif not only with penetrating understanding of the human problem involved, but also with astounding insight into the nature of Anabaptism as well as of the Reformed tradition; and he portrays the essential conflict between the two with magnificent clarity. His knowledge of the historical setting is also exceptionally good. Von Arx, whose works are primarily historical tragedies of the nature of *Brüder in Christo,* is generally considered to be Switzerland's leading modern dramatist, and *Brüder in Christo* is probably his best.

There have been two attempts by Americans, both Mennonites, to interpret Anabaptism in novel form; neither can be considered on a serious adult basis. The first, *The Clemen Family* (1922) by John Horsch, the story of a Waldensian family, was published only in installments in *The Christian Monitor* (June 1922-September 1924). The second is Christmas Carol Kauffman's *Not Regina* (1954), the story of a Bernese housemaid in the home of a persecutor of the Anabaptists whose sympathy for the Anabaptists leads her to adopt their position and to become an Anabaptist herself. The novel is intended primarily for adolescents.

It is only in German literature that one finds a penetrating treatment of the ethical issues in Anabaptism. In Holland, England, and America, all fictional treatments of Anabaptism are either relatively superficial criticism or primarily entertainment. An English or Dutch novel coming to grips honestly, authentically, and artistically with the Anabaptist idea remains to be written and could make an important contribution to contemporary ethical and religious thought.

✠ DON E. SMUCKER ✠

Walter Rauschenbusch and Anabaptist Historiography

Studies in left wing Reformation history have reached an all-time peak in both quantity and quality. The continent has been studied by German, Swiss, and English scholars along with the special studies at Yale, Harvard, Chicago, and Goshen. In America, because of linguistic and cultural ties to Great Britain, the Anglo-Saxon left wing has had even wider attention than has that of the continent.

Walter Rauschenbusch's closest relationship was to the continent but the evidence also shows that he related himself to the English nonconformists as well. Actually, his spiritual and scholarly understanding of the continental left wing is a legacy from his father. The information in *Leben und Wirken von August Rauschenbusch*[1] reveals that his father had a deep interest and sound knowledge of the Anabaptists as the radicals of the sixteenth-century Reformation. The most revealing aspect of this concern was a trip to Germany, 1868-69, in order to gather material for a history of the Anabaptist movement. He visited Waldshut, a town in Lower Austria, where Balthasar Hubmaier had preached and where the Peasants' Revolt had broken out. At this time he went to key universities such as Freiburg, Zürich, and Basel, seeking the remains of Waldensian and Anabaptist literature. With true scholarly concern for primary sources, he made copies of

* Don E. Smucker is Professor of Biblical Theology and Christian Ethics in Mennonite Biblical Seminary and author of *The Theological Basis of Christian Pacifism* (Akron, 1955).

1 Walter Rauschenbusch, *Leben und Wirken von August Rauschenbusch* (Kassel, 1901) 221. See also a similarly revealing article on August Rauschenbusch by Ernst Crous in the *Mennonitisches Lexikon* (Karlsruhe, 1953) 3:430-32. The English edition of the *Lexikon*, revised and enlarged, is being published as the *Mennonite Encyclopedia* (Scottdale). Volumes 1 and 2 of the *ME* appeared in 1955 and 1956 respectively. The remaining volumes are scheduled to follow in the near future.

many original documents and other rare publications. August Rauschenbusch also sought out scholars who could help him in understanding the left wing of the Reformation. Among them were a Catholic priest in Waldshut, three Catholic professors at Ulm, Dr. Schreiber of Freiburg, and Professor C. A. Cornelius of Munich, the leading Anabaptist scholar of his day. Professor Cornelius had published a source book on the Anabaptists under the title, *Geschichte des Münsterischen Aufruhrs* (Leipzig, 1855-60). This work was read by both August and Walter Rauschenbusch and no one could have started with a sounder tutor than the Old Catholic professor from Munich, C. A. Cornelius, whose books are still listed in basic bibliographies in this area of interest.[2]

Unfortunately, this splendid orientation in left wing research and materials never culminated in the book which August Rauschenbusch had hoped to write and which was badly needed on the American scene.[3] He did write three articles for the German encyclopedia edited by Professor Schem in New York. These articles dealt with Baptists, Mennonites, and Tunkers, now known as the Church of the Brethren. In 1851 he made a trip to Canada where he met the Mennonites of Ontario. Their stress on moral conduct, as well as their church life, made a deep impression on him. But their nonmissionary outlook and their failure to demand con-

2 A thorough investigation at Freiburg, Zürich, and Basel, along with Professor Cornelius, and at other key libraries of Switzerland and Germany very likely would have disclosed the additional works available in 1869: Sebastian Franck, *Chronica, Zeytbuch und Geschychtbibel* (Strasburg, 1531); H. Bullinger, *Von dem unverschampten fräfel . . . der selbstgesandten Widertöuffern* (Zurich, 1561); and *Der Widertäufferen Ursprung* (Zurich, 1561); J. H. Ottius, *Annales Anabaptistica* (Basel, 1672); Gottfried Arnold, *Unparteyische Kirchen- u. Ketzer-Historie* (Frankfurt, 1699, Schaffhausen, 1740-42); Max Göbel, *Geschichte des christlichen Lebens in der Rh.-W.-Ev. Kirche*, 3 v. (Coblenz, 1849-60); Menno Simons, *Fundamentboek* (Amsterdam, 1539); Tieleman J. van Braght, *Het Bloedig Tooneel of Martelaers-Spiegel* (1660, 1685).

3 The materials in English concerning the left wing groups on the continent were very small when August Rauschenbusch went abroad in 1869 to collect materials for his book. Guido de Bray's *The Rise, Spring and Foundation of the Anabaptists* (Cambridge, 1668) and J. Newton Brown's *The Life and Times of Menno* (Philadelphia, 1853) were about the only books available. Walter Rauschenbusch's English Baptist friend, Richard Heath, published his *Anabaptism from the Rise at Zwickau to Its Fall at Münster 1521-1536* in 1895; it was the first modern work after the translation of de Bray! Of course, the Anglo-Saxon left wing is another matter.

version sent him on to other groups, eventually leading him to the Baptists. His contacts with the Mennonites later became the occasion for a long scholarly article about him in the *Mennonitisches Lexikon.*

In general, the basic conception of August Rauschenbusch stressed the continuity of the sectarian-pietist motif from modern times back to the apostolic era *via* the Anabaptists. He believed that true Christian congregations always existed even when in secret. In writing his father's biography, Walter Rauschenbusch suggests that the Baptists overstressed external continuity. He made a counter proposal that *ubi Spiritus Sanctus, ibi ecclesia* (where the Holy Spirit is, there is the church) would convey the true norm.

Harold S. Bender believes that August Rauschenbusch knew the best scholars and soundest materials on continental left wing groups available at the time of his career at Rochester Baptist Seminary, 1858-90.[4] During those years the left wing was generally either ignored or caricatured. August Rauschenbusch neither ignored nor caricatured the Anabaptists. Out of this background was to come one of the most formative influences in the development of Walter Rauschenbusch's social gospel.

The foregoing analysis is not to make August Rauschenbusch a sectarian of the sectarians. In the presidential address of Carl E. Schneider to the American Society of Church History, December 30, 1954, August Rauschenbusch is described as having four phases: Rationalist, Pietist, Pietist-Puritan, and Baptist.[5] Of these the influence of Pietism, broadly conceived in the German context, is the major one. Professor Schneider's analysis is underdeveloped in relation to the Ana-

4 Personal conversation with the writer, July 7, 1954.

5 Carl E. Schneider, "Americanization of Karl August Rauschenbusch, 1816-1899," *Church History* (March 1955) 24:3-14. Professor Schneider is one of the leading authorities on the religio-cultural aspects of the German migration to the United States. See his *The German Church on the American Frontier* (St. Louis, 1939); and David Georg Gelzer, "Mission to America: Being a History of the Work of the Basel Foreign Missions Society in America" (unpublished dissertation, Yale University, 1952). See pages 290 and 296 for references to Walter Rausenbusch.

baptist materials but, on the whole, provides a profound setting for the background of Walter Rauschenbusch.

As for Walter Rauschenbusch himself, the evidence is also clear that he was explicitly related to the main stream of Anabaptist scholarship. A vivid example of this is his translation and commentary on Conrad Grebel's letter to Thomas Müntzer.[6] Note the following aspects of Walter Rauschenbusch's labors in translating this letter.

1. It is a translation of a letter published originally in Professor Cornelius' *Geschichte des Münsterischen Aufruhrs*, the book discovered by his father in 1868. Here is proof of the way in which the father's scholarly concerns were utilized by the son. The opening paragraph is an interesting commentary on the bilingual, left-wing-minded Rauschenbusch:

"The letter of Conrad Grebel and his friends at Zürich to Thomas Münzer, of which a translation is here presented, was published by Professor C. A. Cornelius in his *Geschichte des Münsterischen Aufruhrs*, Book II, P. 240 (Appendix I), 1860. It is information about the Swiss Anabaptists in their earlier stage, but, so far as I have seen, no really adequate use has been made of it. For English and American students of Anabaptist history its use is hedged about with several difficulties. The book of Cornelius is becoming rare. The German text not only presents the usual difficulties of literal reprints from the first quarter of the sixteenth century, but it is filled with Swiss idioms, so that even those who read German fluently might find it hard to get more than the general thought."[7] Thus, in order to make this rare document available for English and American students of Anabaptist life, Rauschenbusch undertook the translation and commentary.

2. It is significant that fifty years after its publication this material appeared in most standard bibliographies on the Reformation radicals. It is the first quotation in Littell's chapter on "The Quest for the Essence of Anabaptism," in

6 Walter Rauschenbusch, "The Zürich Anabaptists and Thomas Münzer," *The American Journal of Theology* (January 1905) 9:91.
7 *Ibid.*, 91.

his *The Anabaptist View of the Church*.[8] It is used at Yale, Harvard, and Chicago where concern for the left wing is prominent. Thus, Walter Rauschenbusch not only pioneered with Anabaptist materials but displayed sound scholarship which has survived a half century.

3. Finally, it is interesting that this paper appeared in *The American Journal of Theology* in 1905, a journal published by the University of Chicago from 1897 to 1920 for historical and theological materials. It suggests his close relationship with another essentially Baptist faculty.

Walter Rauschenbusch did not limit his Anabaptist investigations to this one article. At his funeral in Rochester, July 27, 1918, Professor Henry B. Robins, a colleague of Rauschenbusch, referred to his basic approach to church history:

"Professor Rauschenbusch did not attempt to cover the whole broad chronological stretch of Church History, but, especially in those early years, focused upon two great creative epochs—the period down to and including Nicea and the *period of the Reformation. . . .*

"As one listened, he could see *men* emerging from that past—*real people,* both individuals and groups; he could realize somewhat the world which conditioned these folks, the ideal which controlled them, the passions which made them great or covered them with· shame; and somehow that dead past came alive, human, full of intensest interest."[9]

Then in a passage which deals specifically with both the early church and the Anabaptists, Professor Robins notes: "How could one follow his account of the new and greater manifestation of love in the Christian Agapai, or in those fraternal Christian groups among the first European churches, which did so much more for the spirits of men than ever the great sodalities could have done—how could one follow

8 Franklin H. Littell, *The Anabaptist View of the Church* (American Society of Church History, 1952) 19.

9 *Rochester Theological Seminary Bulletin* (69th Year, No. 3) 33.

him here and not be impressed also with the deeply Christian spirit that enabled him to discern all this behind the conventional narratives and in spite of fragmentariness of the records? *Nor could one work with him through Anabaptist history without feeling that the actual course of the social movement which conditioned the religious upheaval known as the Reformation has never been adequately traced and probably never can be because the peasant and commoner were held of so little account; without feeling much more, the passionate interest in the lives of plain people which gave our beloved scholar so great a measure of interpretive insight.*"[10]

In another significant passage Professor Robins observes: "It was borne in upon us that life is all of a piece, and we saw how close together lie the interests of the state, the church, and the common man, and how impossible is the rebirth of religion in a wholly conventionalized world, or the entrance of an individual or class into their full Christian birthright apart from a complete realignment of life."[11] This, then, is a survey of Rauschenbusch as a teacher of church history by a former student and a colleague on the faculty. He affirmed the normative character and then the fall of the early church along with the Anabaptists as the key to the Reformation. Both the early church and the Anabaptists were seen against the background of church history as a dynamic aspect of a total situation where state, church, and society interact on one another, demanding a total change or else a futile irrelevance.

Let us hear from Rauschenbusch himself on the basic role of the Reformation sectarians. This was his sermon, "The Freedom of Spiritual Religion," preached before the Northern Baptist Convention in Chicago, May 8, 1910. It is very revealing of his total view of the Reformation:

"The organization of our denomination began in the last grand transitional age, in the Protestant Reformation. In that transition we were far to the front, on the skirmish line. We were the radicals of radicals. Of the three great reform-

10 *Ibid.*, 33-34. (Italics mine.)
11 *Ibid.*, 34.

ers—Luther, Calvin, and Zwingli—Zwingli was the most radical, so that Luther and Melanchthon were anxious to disavow the Anabaptists. The first great creed of the Lutheran Church, 'The Augsburg Confession,' point by point makes it clear that the Lutheran party would have nothing to do with the Anabaptists. The epoch-making theology of Calvinism, Calvin's 'Institutes of the Christian Religion' was first written to prove to the King of France that the Protestants were good people and had nothing to do with such extremists as the Anabaptists. When the Baptist movement was in its cradle, nobody expected that baby to sit on the brakes of the chariot of progress."[12]

If there was any doubt about the radical perspective from which Rauschenbusch viewed church history, it was clarified in the following passage from the same address:

"We were for a 'reformation without tarrying,' even if we had to leave the old church and break it in pieces. We were against clericalism and against all hierarchies. We were for the religious emancipation of the laity. We went as far as the most radical Calvinist in purging religion of superstition, and when he stopped we went on. The others reformed the Lord's Supper, and cleared it of the abuses which had grown up about it, but they feared to attempt the reformation of baptism, for they knew that would shake the foundation of church life. The abolition of infant baptism meant not simply the modification of one church rite, but a revolutionary reconstruction of the very conception of the church.

"That is the kind of movement which our fathers initiated. They paid for their understanding with their blood, but the God of history has vindicated their daring. *In the long, slow sweep of four centuries, often by devious and pathetic ways, the course of religious development for the Protestant world has been in the direction marked out by the swift rush of radical parties of the Reformation.* That course has been

12 Walter Rauschenbusch, *The Freedom of Spiritual Religion* (Philadelphia, 1910) 12.

fastest and most decided where Christianity has been allowed to follow its own genius with least hindrances from the conservatism of the past. Its triumph has been most complete in our own country. . . ."[13]

Surely there could be no more consistent and thoroughgoing reading of modern ecclesiastical and cultural history than this Anabaptist-centered conception of Rauschenbusch. His conclusion that the Reformation radicals were determinative in shaping American life is similar to the conclusion of Ernst Troeltsch that democratic institutions as a whole stem from this free church background.

Up to this point, the stress has been on the continental radicals, and properly so, since Rauschenbusch's roots and studies are concentrated there.[14] On the other hand, he identified himself with the English left wing as well. For example, his address at Boston, November 30, 1908, shows his grasp of the Anglo-Saxon background. The quotation is from a newspaper report in the Springfield *Daily Republican*:

"Professor Rauschenbusch spoke on 'The Revolutionary Ancestry of the Congregationalists and Baptists.' He undertook to show that they originated together in a revolutionary age. They were the exponents of that revolution and its prime movers, both in religion and politics. Apparently, they were defeated at the time, but in fact they were successful and their great aims have helped to create the modern world. The revolutionary spirit is embodied in their constitution and traditions. This constitutes both a call and a qualification to do their full duty in the social revolution which is now upon us.

"The speaker made it plain that he meant by 'revolution' not a transitory violent outbreak, but a large historical change in fundamental convictions and institutions of a nation or an age. It might last a century or two. He then

---

13 *Ibid.*, p. 13. (Italics mine.)

14 For references to the Anabaptists in his books see: *Christianity and the Social Crisis*, 331, 401, 402; *Christianizing the Social Order*, 83; *A Theology for the Social Gospel*, 195, 205.

sketched the progress of the Puritan movement in England at the beginning of the 17th century and the rise of the independents. They proposed to create churches of believers who united freely on a basis of equality in little church democracies, repudiating both the help and the interference of the state. This ideal of the church was revolutionary at that time, and ran far beyond the ideas realized by the Reformation on the Continent. These early Congregationalists and Baptists at first lived in exile in Holland. Some of them came to America, e.g., the Pilgrims of the Mayflower. The Puritans who followed them did not at first hold this ideal but in the free life of the virgin continent they tended that way by a sort of spiritual gravitation, and Congregationalism found its first large development in America. The men and ideas bred by it here went across the sea and were a powerful influence in promoting radical thought in England."[15]

Once again one detects a Troeltschian sense of the creativity of radical Protestantism and free institutions, in this case *via* the Puritans. Rauschenbusch is actually less aware of this stream of thought because it was English rather than continental. Nevertheless, it is obvious that he *was* aware of it as his lecture in Boston clearly indicates. Indeed, he was aware that in Germany the Anabaptists were crushed out with tragic effects.[16] On the other hand, English Puritanism was vital and dynamic in its effect on society. His words are these: "Religious life in so far as it affects political life in England is the humanitarian democracy begotten by Puritanism. German religion has been taught to confine itself to the inner life, the family, and the personal calling. When religion effects political action in Germany it is by ecclesiastical considerations rather than by ethical spirit."[17]

15 Walter Rauschenbusch, "The Revolutionary Ancestry of the Congregationalists and Baptists," the Springfield *Daily Republican,* Dec. 1, 1908. A photostatic copy of this report was supplied through the courtesy of the City Library Association, Springfield, Mass.

16 Walter Rauschenbusch, "The Influence of Historical Studies on Theology," *American Journal of Theology* (January 1907) 11:65.

17 *The Watchman* (1899), quoted by Conrad H. Moehlman. *A Rauschenbusch Sourcebook with Commentary* (privately printed) 41.

DON E. SMUCKER

As far as the Baptist Church in America and England is concerned, the roots are clearly in English Puritanism. As Moehlman points out, the Philadelphia Confession of 1742 is closely related to the Westminster Confession of 1646. The London Confession of 1677 is largely a reproduction of Westminster, suggesting to Moehlman that the Baptists look more to Calvin's Geneva than to Hubmaier's Zürich. Winthrop Hudson of Colgate-Rochester feels very strongly about this latter point and has written an essay totally repudiating any Anabaptist background for the Baptists, blaming Thomas Crosby's *The History of the English Baptists* (1738-40) for launching the Anabaptist-Baptist connection which Rauschenbusch accepted and which most Baptists still accept.[18]

Hudson's view is rejected by a number of impressive scholars. Ernst Troeltsch in his *Die Bedeutung des Protestantismus für die Entstehung der modernen Welt* (published in English as *Protestantism and Progress*) argues that the Cromwellian Independency generated the ideas of the separation of church and state, the toleration of various churches alongside each other, the principle of voluntarism in the establishment of denominations, freedom in both religion and culture. All this, Troeltsch continues, is the end of the old medieval culture concept and the beginning of modern individual, nonecclesiastical culture. The fact that the continental expressions of this were secular and rationalistic must not obscure the fact that in England its religious roots were in the Puritan revolution.

The crucial point then is made that: "This is not properly speaking the work of Protestantism but of the revived (Ana) Baptist and Spiritualist movements in combination with Calvinism of a radical tendency.[19] It was now at last the turn of the stepchildren of the Reformation to have their great hour in the history of the world."[20]

18 Winthrop Hudson, "Baptists Are Not Anabaptists," *The Chronicle: Journal of the American Baptist Historical Society* (October 1953) 16:171-78.

19 Ernst Troeltsch, *Protestantism and Progress* (New York, 1912) 126.

20 *Ibid.*, 124.

Ernest A. Payne, leading English Baptist historian who is vice-chairman of the World Council of Churches Central Committee, believes that the English Puritan left wing drew a great deal of its inspiration from the Swiss, German, and Dutch Anabaptists.[21] Likewise Rufus Jones in his *Studies in Mystical Religion* wrote that the continental Anabaptists provide "the soil out of which all nonconformist sects have sprung, and it is the first plain announcement in modern history of a program for a new type of Christian society in the modern world, especially in America and England, . . . an absolutely free and independent religious society, and a state in which every man counts as a man, and has his share in shaping both church and state."[22] The most recent Baptist history is that of Robert G. Torbet of the American Baptist Board of Education and Publication. Kenneth Scott Latourette writes the foreword, saying that "nowhere else is there to be found in so nearly inclusive and up-to-date fashion a summary of the people who bear the name Baptist."[23] Torbet concludes that "with respect to the relationship between Anabaptists and Baptists, it is safe to say that the latter are the spiritual descendants of *some* of the former."[24]

In summary, it appears that the position of Walter Rauschenbusch still has very serious support in scholarly opinion despite the rejection of Winthrop Hudson. In any case, his kinship with both continental and Anglo-Saxon left wing Protestantism is real, and his discovery of their relationship to social and political forces is very important.

21 Ernest A. Payne, *The Anabaptists of the 16th Century* (London, 1949) 5 ff.; Payne's critique of Hudson's view in "Who Were the Baptists?" *The Baptist Quarterly* (October 1956) 16:339-42. See also Harold S. Bender, "The Anabaptists and Religious Liberty in the 16th Century," *Archiv für Reformationsgeschichte* (1953) 44:32-50, reprinted in *MQR* (April 1955) 29:83-100, in which the foregoing material is effectively utilized.

22 Rufus M. Jones, *Studies in Mystical Religion* (London, 1923) 369.

23 Quoted in Robert G. Torbet, *A History of the Baptists* (Philadelphia, 1950) 7.

24 *Ibid.*, 54. See also J. G. de Hoop Scheffer, *History of the Free Churchmen Called the Brownists, Pilgrim Fathers, and Baptists in the Dutch Republic 1581-1701* (Ithaca, 1922) for important evidence on the relationship between Baptists and Anabaptists. The most recent research into this problem is now being carried on by Irvin B. Horst in connection with a doctoral dissertation at the University of Amsterdam.

A more valid criticism of Rauschenbusch in the light of recent historiography is his inadequate classification of the different types of Anabaptists. Newman's *A Manual of Church History,* for example, has a very suggestive and, in many ways, still sound classification of five Anabaptist types: 1) chiliastic: Melchiorites and Münsterites; 2) soundly Biblical: Swiss Brethren and followers in South Germany, Moravian Hutterites, and Mennonites; 3) pantheistic: David Joris; 4) mystical: Hans Denk and Ludwig Haetzer; 5) anti-Trinitarian: Socinianism.[25]

Bainton's well-known article in the *Journal of Religion* defines the left wing as follows: "The left wing is composed of those who separated church and state and rejected the civil arm in matters of religion. These groups are commonly on the left also with regard to church organization, sacraments, and creeds."[26] In addition, Bainton would stress the left wing as emphasizing ethical reality, restitution of the apostolic church in place of a fallen church, and the eschatology which was revived by Joachim of Flora in the twelfth century. Robert Friedmann's excellent summary, "Conception of the Anabaptists" in *Church History,* is one of the most solid surveys available. The usefulness of the article is enhanced by the inclusion of charts showing the complexities of Anabaptist historiography.

A second criticism of Rauschenbusch is his failure to utilize Troeltsch with adequate sharpness. In defense of Rauschenbusch, it should be pointed out that *Die Soziallehren der christlichen Kirchen und Gruppen* was published in 1911, hence it was not available for *Christianity and the Social Crisis* (1907); and perhaps not really available for *Christianizing the Social Order* (1913). However, in his last great book, *A Theology for the Social Gospel* (1917), Rauschenbusch definitely mentions Troeltsch: "The monumental

25 A. H. Newman, *A Manual of Church History* (Philadelphia, 1945) 2:156 ff.

26 "The Left Wing of the Reformation," *The Journal of Religion* (April 1941) 21:125. Robert Friedmann, "Conception of the Anabaptists," *Church History* (December 1940) 9:341-65.

work of Troeltsch, 'Die Soziallehren der christlichen Kirchen und Gruppen,' is the first and chief attempt to apply methods of the history of doctrine to the social convictions and hopes of the Churches."[27] To be sure many dimensions of the sectarian view of the church do occur in Rauschenbusch. But the full use of Troeltsch would have sharpened his own formulation. What is more, he might well have adopted Troeltsch's creative concept of "ascetic Protestantism" which represents a fusion of Calvinism, spiritualism, and the sects in a neo-Calvinism. It is what James Hastings Nichols prefers to call Puritan Protestantism.[28]

This is not to say that the Troeltschian typology is perfect. As Robert Kreider points out: "First, the two terms 'church' and 'sect,' which are theoretical types, seldom characterize with precision actual religious bodies, which are invariably a blending of the two types. Second, the definition is a static structural one and fails to account for the genesis and continuing dynamic of religious bodies. Third, this distinction is on a sociological level. . . . The neglect of the spiritual and participationist dimension has left the studies of some sociologists of religion ultimately unconvincing."[29] Nevertheless, Kreider still accepts the rugged usefulness of the basic Troeltschian insights and typology although he feels that the term *brotherhood* would be preferable to *sect*. For Rauschenbusch, too, the Troeltschian typology would have added more clarity.

Finally, a deeper look into origins would have helped Rauschenbusch to go beyond the sociological perspective whereby he saw the left wing of the Reformation as a movement of socio-religious emancipation for oppressed peasants and other disenfranchised groups, the view popularized by Bax in his *Rise and Fall of the Anabaptists*[30] and also affirmed

27 Walter Rauschenbusch, *A Theology for the Social Gospel* (New York, 1917) 28.
28 James Hastings Nichols, *Democracy and the Churches* (Philadelphia, 1951) 10.
29 Robert Kreider, "The Anabaptist Conception of the Church in the Russian Mennonite Environment," *MQR* (January 1951) 25:18.
30 E. Belfort Bax, *Rise and Fall of the Anabaptists* (London, 1903).

in Niebuhr's *Social Sources of Denominationalism*.[31] In addition to the Bax-Rauschenbusch-Niebuhr views the present writer has suggested nine other views, according to which the Anabaptists have been regarded as:[32] (1) forerunners of modern socialism and the culminating effort of medieval communism: Kautsky; (2) a continuation of the third order of St. Francis: Ritschl; (3) a link in the chain of dissenters beginning with the apostolic church and continuing through the Donatists, Paulicians, Cathari, Bogomili, and Waldensians: Ludwig Keller stressing role of Waldensians; Baptist historians stressing continuity; (4) a continuation of medieval mysticism: Rufus M. Jones; (5) heirs of Erasmus: Walther Köhler and Winthrop Hudson; (6) forerunners of modern civilization (divided into evangelical and aggressive wings): Troeltsch; (7) rediscoverers of the theology of marytrdom: Ethelbert Stauffer; (8) *Schwärmer* and heretics: Luther; (9) the culmination of the Reformation, fulfilling the original vision of Luther and Zwingli: Max Göbel, C. A. Cornelius, Johann Loserth, Karl Rembert, Ernst Correll, John Horsch, Fritz Blanke, and H. S. Bender.

These criticisms of Rauschenbusch's limited typology, his inability to utilize Troeltsch, and his inadequate study of origins do not mean to imply that Rauschenbusch lagged behind the scholarship of his day. He possessed a knowledge which was unquestionably better than that of most historians in America who still persisted in ignoring or caricaturing the Anabaptists. In terms of Europe, with men like Loserth and Rembert, he probably lagged behind somewhat because of the inherent limitations of an American location (at that time) for continental research. But, his left wing consciousness proved to be decisive in many respects.

[31] H. Richard Niebuhr, *The Social Sources of Denominationalism* (New York, 1929).

[32] Donovan E. Smucker, "The Anabaptist Historiography in the Scholarship of Today," *MQR* (April 1948) 22:116-27.

✠ ERNEST A. PAYNE ✠

The Anabaptist Impact on
Western Christendom [1]

The present generation, which has at long last had placed before it the documentary material for a just appraisal of the Anabaptist movement, finds itself strangely enough faced again with many of the questions which produced that movement in the sixteenth century. Among theologians and ecclesiastics of many lands interest centers once more on the nature of the church, on the rite of baptism, on the relationship of church and state, on the obligations to discipleship and witness-bearing—all of them matters anxiously debated in the circles from which came that "congeries of sects" which made up the left wing of the Reformation. Moreover, the answers that many are now constrained to give to these questions often approximate closely those offered by the Anabaptists four hundred years ago.

Why was it, then, that the original movement provoked so sharp a reaction on the part of both Catholics and Protestants? How did it come about that "it can safely be said that no other movement for spiritual freedom in the history of the church has such an enormous martyrology"?[2] Why did the very name Anabaptist become one of infamy and reproach? How is it that, even yet, so many seem reluctant to do justice to the little fellowships of believers which sprang up swiftly in

* Ernest A. Payne, formerly Senior Tutor, Regent's Park College, Oxford, is General Secretary of the Baptist Union of Great Britain and Ireland, Vice-Chairman of the Central Committee of the World Council of Churches, and author of *The Free Church Tradition in the Life of England* (London, 1944).

1 In this paper the writer has made use of two pamphlets of his, now out of print, *The Baptist Movement in the Reformation and Onwards* (London, 1947) and *The Anabaptists of the 16th Century and Their Influence in the Modern World* (London, 1949).

2 Rufus M. Jones, *Studies in Mystical Religion* (London, 1909) 392.

so many parts of western Europe in the early decades of the sixteenth century?

A number of reasons may be suggested. The Swiss Brethren who in 1525, as a result of their study of the New Testament, reintroduced believers' baptism, constituted themselves a gathered community of disciples, and began an eager evangelistic movement, did so at the very time when the peasants of Germany revolted against the hardships of their lot. But for the excitement caused in Wittenberg in 1520-22 by the Zwickau "prophets" and the subsequent encouragement of the peasants by Thomas Müntzer, Luther's final decision about baptism might have been different. But with social upheaval and revolution the great German reformer had no sympathy. The Lutherans allied themselves with the princes, as the Zwinglians and Calvinists did with the magistrates. Anabaptism appeared to them to be linked with a dangerous challenge to the accepted order of society. Nor, at a time when many parts of Europe were threatened by the Turks, were most people ready to face the challenge of the doctrine of nonresistance which many Anabaptists adopted.

Moreover, although the main streams of the Reformation were carried forward by a strong current of religious feeling, there was a widespread suspicion of what Luther called *Schwärmerei*—an enthusiasm and fanaticism, impatient of historic forms and ceremonies and all too ready to make extravagant claims to immediate inspiration. Here again, whether or not there was any real contact between Müntzer and the Swiss Brethren, the latter suffered through association, not only at the beginning of their movement but in subsequent generations. Even Reinhold Seeberg in his *Lehrbuch der Dogmengeschichte*,[3] after noting the obvious differences between the "Anabaptists" of Wittenberg and those of Zürich, is able to say that they possessed one principle in common—"Schwarmgeisterei oder Spiritualismus." A sympathetic account of this aspect of the sixteenth-century move-

---

3 Reinhold Seeberg, *Lehrbuch der Dogmengeschichte* (Leipzig, 1917) 4:28.

ment as a whole, with a tracing of its links back to the days of primitive Christianity and forward into the seventeenth century, may be found in the writings of Rufus M. Jones. But distrust of it continues. Anabaptists of all kinds have been in constant danger of dismissal and condemnation as Schwärmer.

From the mid-seventeenth century comes the epigram: "Anabaptista indoctus Socinianus; Socinianus autem doctus Anabaptista." It is true, of course, that some Anabaptists did hold unorthodox or heretical views. It is also true that some anti-Trinitarians rejected infant baptism. Michael Servetus described infant baptism as "a detestable abomination." Refugees from Switzerland carried the views of the Swiss Brethren into northern Italy where they were mingled with the type of thought of which Laelius and Faustus Socinus were the outstanding exponents, and which later established itself in Poland. Melchior Hofmann, whose courage and evangelistic power helped to create gathered fellowships in many parts of northern Europe, combined apocalyptic hopes with an unorthodox Christology, which he seems to have derived directly or indirectly from Caspar Schwenckfeld. In the sixteenth century, due to aberrations of this type, the Anabaptist movement as a whole was charged with departure from the apostolic faith, and the charge was perpetuated through the centuries. Besides the published court records and the proceedings of the Täufer disputations, the *Rechenschaft* of Peter Riedemann (1506-56) and the old Anabaptist hymnbook, the *Ausbund*,[4] are among the works now available to prove how far removed from the truth is such a verdict.

Without doubt it was the happenings in Münster in 1533-35 which were the main cause of Anabaptism's passing under a cloud of obloquy and shame, thus preventing any honest facing of the basic issues raised by the Swiss Brethren and their more responsible followers. It must be remem-

---

4 The earliest known edition of the *Ausbund*, containing 53 hymns, was published in 1564. There are 11 known European and about 20 American editions, the latest published in 1949. Some editions contain as many as 140 hymns, many of them written in prison.

bered, however, that the Münster kingdom was preceded by a steadily mounting horror of beheading and burnings in the Low Countries and elsewhere, and that the "Kingdom of the Saints" was the work of a handful of desperate and deluded men. The researches of C. A. Cornelius, Ludwig Keller, and H. Detmer have helped to set the incident in its true perspective. Professor A. J. Toynbee quotes with approval the verdict of Carew Hunt: "The Münster revolt was really a caricature of the [Anabaptist] movement, which was essentially pacific."[5] Unfortunately, however, the episode brought fresh disasters on Anabaptists of every kind everywhere and made the name one to be feared and hated for generations. Amid so much abuse it was possible for the majority of Christians to forget or to ignore the challenge presented by the Anabaptists in regard to the nature of the church and of baptism, the demands of practical brotherliness and charity, and the principle of toleration.

In any case, there were comparatively few in the sixteenth century who were prepared for radical challenge at these points. By their concern for the *koinonia* and the *ecclesia* portrayed in the New Testament, the Anabaptists were challenging what had been the basis of ecclesiastical theory and practice since the time of Constantine. For them the church had become a fellowship of believing people, entered by baptism on personal profession of repentance and faith, its members committed to aid one another in their discipleship, and called to a life of suffering like their Lord. What must surprise us is not that the Anabaptist movement suffered so grievously at the hands of both Catholics and Protestants, but that its essential insights continued to find expression. Hubmaier's brave claim, "Die Wahrheit ist unsterblich," has been vindicated. A chain of living communities links the Anabaptists of the sixteenth century with the modern world, and the importance of the truths for which they contended has been recognized by ever-widening circles.

5 A. J. Toynbee, *A Study of History* (London, 1947 f.) 5:171 n.

Of the living communities which can trace their descent directly back to the sixteenth-century Anabaptists, the oldest is that of the Hutterites or Hutterian Brethren, who owe their name to Jacob Huter, the chief organizer of the remarkable community life in Moravia. Surviving recurrent waves of persecution, which made frequent migration necessary, the occupants of the Bruderhofs continued to practice a strict religious discipline and preserved their old traditions, as well as their skilled craftsmanship. From 1770 to 1874 a small remnant found asylum in the Ukraine. Then, in the face of renewed difficulties, they secured permission to cross the Atlantic, so that small Hutterite colonies are now to be found in the United States and in Canada, still maintaining their old ways and practicing the kind of communal life which became characteristic of them in Moravia. In the years immediately after the first World War, Eberhard Arnold, stirred by the Christian pacifism and Christian communism of the Hutterian Brethren, established in Germany a little Bruderhof on similar principles and began the careful study of the older communities. Arnold's death and the rise of National Socialism caused the migration of his followers to England. On the outbreak of the second World War many of the members of the colonies established at Ashton Keynes and Oaksey migrated to Paraguay, though a small settlement continues in England at Wheathill.

Neither the Bruderhofs in Alberta and South Dakota nor the independent foundations in England and Paraguay can be regarded as influential, though it is from the former that important historical material has recently come to light by way of A. J. F. Zieglschmid's editions of *Die älteste Chronik der Hutterischen Brüder* (Philadelphia, 1943), which contains records from about 1542 to 1665, and *Das Klein-Geschichtsbuch der Hutterischen Brüder* (Philadelphia, 1947), a compilation begun by Johannes Waldner at the end of the eighteenth century and carrying the story down to modern times. Moreover, the Wheathill community has provided both German and English editions of Ridemann's *Rechenschaft*.[6]

More important for the direct transmission of Anabaptist ideas to the modern world have been the Mennonites. In the twenty-five years after the fall of Münster, Menno Simons gathered and built up from the ruins of the once strong Anabaptism of the Low Countries and Friesland, churches which returned to the outlook and practice of the Swiss Brethren. In the seventeenth and eighteenth centuries Dutch Mennonites were numerous and influential, and the community spread into Germany and Russia. At the end of the seventeenth century a Mennonite settlement was established in Pennsylvania. From this beginning—largely as a result of the influx of varied new groups from the continent of Europe—the community in the United States has grown into a number of separate bodies with minor variations in religious doctrine and practice, their total membership not large, but their influence as a historic peace church very considerable.

According to one of their leading modern scholars, all the Mennonite groups agree "that the New Testament prohibits participation in warfare and in litigation; that the Christian shall not swear an oath but make a solemn declaration of the truth; that the church consists of those who have voluntarily turned from sin and accepted Jesus Christ as their Saviour; that the Christian life involves separation from the sin of the world, and positively the living of the 'simple life'; that Christians shall not unite with secret orders; that baptism shall be administered only to those who accept Christ, not to infants (who are saved without baptism); and that the Christian congregation shall maintain a Scriptural discipline, excluding from its membership impenitent sinners."[7] In all of these beliefs and practices, the Mennonites maintain the witness of their spiritual forebears in the sixteenth century.

---

6 Peter Rideman, *Rechenschaft unserer Religion, Lehr und Glaubens* (Ashton Keynes, 1938); English translation, *Account of Our Religion, Doctrine, and Faith* (London, 1950).

7 J. C. Wenger, *Glimpses of Mennonite History and Doctrine* (Scottdale, 1947) 129-30.

Side by side with these two streams of continuing Anabaptist witness there must be placed what is now known in the United States as the Church of the Brethren. This movement had its origin in Germany in 1708 as a result of a revival of religion led by Alexander Mack; but there seems little doubt that it drew to itself older Anabaptist elements, and a similarity of witness has continued. Peter Becker led a small settlement from Crefeld to Pennsylvania in 1719 and they were long known as Taufers or Dunkers. Though subdivided into a number of groups, they total in all more than 200,000 communicants. They are recognized as a peace church and have engaged, like the Mennonites, in notable missionary and relief activities.

Even when put together, however, these communities of Hutterites, Mennonites, and Brethren are not numerous when compared with the larger churches of Christendom. Were this all that had to be said, it might seem that the Anabaptist movement of the sixteenth century had petered out, save for a few residual groups largely cut off from the main stream of Christian witness. The General Mennonite Society (*Algemeene Doopsgezinde Societeit*) of Holland, and the Church of the Brethren in the United States, are in membership with the World Council of Churches. The other groups, however, still live—as is almost inevitable on the basis of certain principles which they maintain—a more isolated life, some of them like the Hutterites and the Old Order Amish Mennonites consciously reproducing the customs of a vanished age. Many of the basic principles for which the Anabaptists stood, however, were destined to find other outlets.

In estimating the results of the Anabaptist movement and its influence on Christendom as a whole, one has to remember that the Swiss Brethren can be claimed as "the first forerunners of the free church conception." "In Zollikon," Professor Fritz Blanke has said, " a new form of church constitution began to show itself—that of the free church. Zollikon is the cradle of this idea, from whence it set out on its triumphal march through four centuries and through the whole world."[8] This is a bold claim, but it can be substantiated. The English Separatist movement, which proved the main source of the older free churches, has often been regarded as a spontaneous development out of English Puritanism. Its connections with the left wing of the continental Reformation, however, were probably far closer than has been recognized. There was undoubtedly the same basic attitude in regard to the nature of the church. Those Separatists who became Baptists exhibit an even closer similarity by virtue of their adoption of believers' baptism, their eager evangelism, and their passion for religious freedom. The background and origin of the Quaker movement also have relevance in this connection. The early history of the Mennonites, the Baptists, and the Quakers is curiously intertwined, as Robert Barclay showed eighty years ago in his unfinished but still unsurpassed book *The Inner Life of the Religious Societies of the Commonwealth* (London, 1877).

How early Anabaptism reached England, how widespread it was, how soon it passed outside the circles of the Dutch refugees—these are intricate and vexed questions. At the beginning of the sixteenth century there was in England what G. M. Trevelyan has called "a revival of Wycliffism."[9] The Lollardy that had continued as an underground movement emerged into the light again. There must have been some individuals at least as sympathetic to the ideas of the continental radicals as they were to those of the great Reformers. As early as 1534 the name Anabaptist occurs in an English statute. It may be that at first few besides foreign exiles professed the dangerous doctrines associated with this term. The nervousness of the authorities, however, suggests otherwise. There were representatives from England at an Anabaptist

8 Fritz Blanke, "Zollikon 1525," *The Baptist Quarterly* (October 1953) 15:165, English translation by W. M. S. West of an article by Dr. Blanke in the *Theologische Zeitschrift* (Basel, July-August 1952) 8:241 ff.

9 G. M. Trevelyan, *England in the Age of Wycliffe* (London, 1904) 347-49. Cf. E. G. Rupp, *The Making of the English Protestant Tradition* (Cambridge, 1947).

synod in Bockholt, Westphalia, in 1536. By 1549 books against Anabaptists by Calvin and Bullinger had been translated into English. Several of the Anglican *Articles of Religion* are aimed directly at Anabaptist teaching: especially those on baptism, civil magistrates, Christian men's goods, and Christian men's oaths. When, in the seventeenth year of her reign, Elizabeth relighted the fires of Smithfield, the victims were Dutch Anabaptists. By then there were thousands of Dutch refugees in England, in flight from the fury of the Duke of Alva. There were certainly many Anabaptists among them and they were not in character if they refrained from propaganda. One of the radical groups which emerged in Holland in the middle of the sixteenth century from an Anabaptist milieu was the Family of Love, a small perfectionist brotherhood. Its leader, Hendrik Nicklaes, on at least one occasion was in England. In the eighth and ninth decades of the century a number of English books against the Familists appeared, and in 1604 London Familists were bold enough to present their own petition to James I.

There is a persistent tradition that Robert Browne, the father of English Separatism, was influenced by Anabaptists in and around Norwich. In the years which link Elizabethan and Stuart England there were a number of radical religious groups both in London and the provinces, besides those which have received the attention of free church historians. Ideas have wings as well as legs, and that generation had become adept at smuggling in forbidden books and letters. But even if it could be proved—as some have tried to do—that none of the English religious refugees who sought asylum in Holland during the closing years of Elizabeth's reign had prior knowledge of, or contact with Anabaptism, they certainly met it in one or more of its many forms when they reached Middelburg, Amsterdam, and Leyden. The contacts of John Smyth with the Mennonites are well known, and the earliest English Baptist churches maintained friendly contact with the Mennonites of Holland for several decades, even though they differed from them on certain matters. More-over, it is significant that the older Baptist historians—Crosby, Rippon, Ivimey, and Evans—accepted without question the connection between the continental and the English move-ments.[10]

The early English Baptists, however, provided only one of the many bridges by which the ideas of the continental radicals passed over into Britain and into the new lands across the Atlantic. Many of the Commonwealth sects were but giv-ing new and vigorous expression to opinions put forward two or three generations earlier. Behind the Quakers, for exam-ple, stand the English representatives of the Seekers and Familists, groups whose spiritual ancestry carries us back to Schwenckfeld, Denk, and Müntzer. Even the Fifth Monarchy men, the Levellers, and the Diggers represented ideas which had their counterparts in the earlier continental movement. Cornelius Plockhoy van Zierichzee, who visited Cromwell in 1658, called the attention of Englishmen to the Hutterite communities in Moravia and Hungary,[11] and in these com-munities Samuel Hartlib and others took a keen interest. After the Restoration the Baptist, Thomas Tillam, assisted several hundred English people to join the Anabaptists in the Palatinate.

No doubt these were minor incidents which affected only a few persons. It is more important to recognize the main streams of influence. All the English free churches were re-producing many of the basic features of the Anabaptist wit-ness. Congregationalism cannot be understood simply in terms of Geneva or of the Act of Uniformity of 1662, though some recent apologists would have us so believe. The Arian and Socinian movements of the seventeenth and eighteenth centuries, which delivered all the churches from the grosser

10 There seems to have been no disposition to question the connection until the later writings of W. T. Whitley, e.g., his *History of the British Baptists* (London, 1923) 17 ff. In 1909, however, Dr. Whitley had written: "The General Baptists are an English outgrowth of the Continental Anabaptists acting upon the Lollards" (*Minutes of the General Assembly of the General Baptists*, 1:ix).

11 L. and M. Harder, *Plockhoy from Zurik-zee* (Newton, Kans., 1952) 38, 44, and 172.

evils of creedal subscription, undoubtedly drew inspiration from certain of the Anabaptist pioneers of earlier days.

The older free churches have become great world-wide communions. The Baptists alone now claim a membership of over 21,000,000, and beside them, sharing their witness to believers' baptism and their basic doctrine of the church, have emerged the Disciples of Christ and a number of other Christian communities. The doctrine of the church as a fellowship of believers, free from the control of the state or of a separated hierarchy; emphasis on the spirit of man as the candle of the Lord; the claim for toleration and freedom of conscience; the recognition of the obligations resting on all Christians to charity, community, and evangelism; these ideas, with varying degrees of emphasis, have become influential in all parts of the world. They are no longer the monopoly of separately organized church groups, but a study of their history leads us back inevitably to the Anabaptists of the sixteenth century. Even though Christian pacifism is no longer confined to the historic peace churches, nevertheless in modern times its challenge has been most effectively presented by Mennonites, Quakers, and kindred groups.

In recent years, Christians of many different traditions have found themselves compelled to consider again the ordinance of baptism. Is it wise or right that it be administered to infants? Is it then in accord with the New Testament and able to be in a full sense a sacrament of the Gospel, particularly if the parents of the children have themselves no vital connection with the church? Reformed theologians of the eminence of Karl Barth and Emil Brunner have felt compelled to ask these questions,[12] and what they have said has caused anxious debate far beyond the borders of their own churches. Even within the Anglican Church, distinguished scholars like the late Dom Gregory Dix and Dr. Kenneth

12 See, e.g., Karl Barth, *Die Kirchliche Lehre von der Taufe* (Zollikon-Zürich, 1943), English translation, *The Teaching of the Church Regarding Baptism* (London, 1948); and Emil Brunner, *Wahrheit als Begegnung*, English translation, *The Divine-Human Encounter* (Philadelphia, 1943).

Kirk have come to feel that the rites of baptism and confirmation must be brought more closely together again.[13] All this is but further evidence of the significance of the witness offered by the persecuted and maligned Anabaptists of the sixteenth century.

"It would have been quite intelligible," wrote Schleiermacher in 1821, "if, to recover touch with Christ's institution, infant baptism had been abolished at the Reformation." That did not happen, for reasons some of which have already been indicated. Schleiermacher continued: "We ought to make it known that in regard to this point we cancel the sentence of condemnation passed on the Anabaptists."[14] It is time that in regard to other matters as well there be a reappraisal and a recognition of all that western Christendom owes to the left wing of the Reformation.

13 See G. Dix, *The Theology of Confirmation in Relation to Baptism* (London, 1946) and K. Kirk, *Oxford Diocesan Magazine* (1946).

14 Schleiermacher, *The Christian Faith* (English translation of the second German edition, Edinburgh, 1928) 634-38.

✠ ROLAND H. BAINTON ✠

The Anabaptist Contribution to History

The Anabaptist contribution to history is comparable to that of the Norsemen who visited America prior to Columbus. They found what he found and they found it first. Their intrepidity was no less and possibly greater than his. But they do not occupy the same place in history because their deed was without sequel. Not they, but he opened up the trek from Europe to the new world. Similarly, the Anabaptists anticipated all other religious bodies in the proclamation and exemplification of three principles which are on the North American continent among those truths which we hold to be self-evident: the voluntary church, the separation of church and state, and religious liberty. From the days of Constantine to the Anabaptists these principles, to us so cardinal, had been in abeyance. They were not, however, transmitted to us by the Anabaptists, but rather by the Puritan revolution and the French revolution.

The possibility of Anabaptist influence hinges on the question whether the English free churchmen in exile in Holland learned from the Mennonites. The question is worthy of fuller investigation. But this is plain, that as to the voluntary church the English sectaries had already made up their minds before ever they went to Holland, and the other two principles were bound to follow. In the present state of research it appears most likely that the English Puritans and the Anabaptists grew from the same sources. One was Zwingli. Anabaptism, as we well know originated in his circle; and

* Roland H. Bainton is Titus Street Professor of Ecclesiastical History in the Yale University Divinity School and author of *David Joris, Wiedertäufer und Kämpfer für Toleranz im 16. Jahrhundert* (Leipzig, 1937); *Here I Stand, a Life of Martin Luther* (New York, 1950); *The Travail of Religious Liberty* (Philadelphia, 1951); and *The Reformation of the Sixteenth Century* (Boston, 1952).

English Puritanism was in close touch with Zürich. The other source was the New Testament. A minute examination of its contents, with the resolve to restore its pattern, led the Anabaptists to diverge from Zwingli; and this may well have had a like effect in England. On the whole Anabaptism appears to have been an amazingly clear-cut and heroic anticipation of what with us has come to be axiomatic; but the line is not direct. The discovery had to be made over again.

This is not to say that Anabaptism made no contribution to the rise of religious liberty. The Anabaptists in the sixteenth century were the party *par excellence* of suffering. Their pleas for liberty might be discounted as intended only to relieve their own situation. But pleas on their behalf were made by the champions of religious liberty who were not of their party. Sebastian Franck wrote in his *Chronica, Zeytbuch und Geschychtbibel* a most discriminating account of the Anabaptists and pleaded that they be accorded the freedom of their faith. Only those guilty of overt revolution should be constrained and from none did he fear it so little as from the Anabaptists. To be sure Hans Hut was a revolutionary, but he had been repudiated by the Anabaptists. More on this score, according to Franck, was to be feared from the Pope, the Kaiser, and the Turks. Not everything indeed in Anabaptism was to be approved. There was among the Anabaptists a sectarian spirit and too much concern for outward ceremonies. "I have listed them," says Franck, "among the heretics that they may perceive that their church is not the true church, that they may turn to genuine unity in spirit and in truth, but I warn their persecutors not to play the part of Caiaphas and Pilate. The Anabaptists are not entirely right nor is anyone else and from each we should take the best."[1]

Sebastian Castellio likewise, in his *De Haereticis* composed for the immediate purpose of excoriating the execution of Servetus, contained also a protest against the persecution of the Anabaptists. "They were miserably slain," says he,

---

[1] Sebastian Franck, *Chronica, Zeytbuch und Geschychtbibel* (Strasbourg, 1531) ccccxlix-ccccii.

"even those who were not in arms and, what is still more cruel, the suppression was carried on not only by the sword but also in books which reach farther and last longer, or rather forever perpetuate this savagery."[2] At the end of his life Castellio penned a still more poignant plea. It lay in manuscript until discovered in our own day by Professor Bruno Becker of Amsterdam. The whole has not yet been published. The portions were edited by Etienne Giran in *L'Esprit et la Vie*. Although this defense of the Anabaptists cannot be said to have influenced history, it is worth citing because such thoughts lay behind what Castellio committed to the printed page. In this manuscript, addressing Beza, Castellio says:

"With regard to the Anabaptists I would like to know how you know that they condemn legitimate marriages and the magistracy and condone murders. Certainly it is not in their books and much less in their words. You have heard it from their enemies, but if enemies are to be trusted, then in France it was rumored that Zwingli preached to trees, stones, and beasts, because of the text 'Preach the Gospel to all creatures.' And it was said that Farel had as many devils in his beard as hairs, and that whenever he ate he fed the devils. Beza, would you have us believe such things? I do not believe what you say about the Anabaptists. Those at Münster did not reject the magistrate and they retained Knipperdollinck as magistrate. As for marriage, their enemies say that each had more than one wife. Very well, but that is not having wives in common. There are some persons who certainly are not Anabaptists who testify that in Bohemia the Anabaptists hold marriage in such reverence that if any among them is guilty of adultery he is rigorously excluded from their community. Neither should people be held responsible for a position which they have themselves repudiated, any more than you, Beza, should be reproached for the amatory verses of your youth."[3]

2 Sebastian Castellio, "Concerning Heretics," translated and edited by Roland H. Bainton, Columbia University *Records of Civilization* (New York, 1935) 218.
3 *L'Esprit et la Vie*, IV, No. 6 (May 1939).

In England Adriaan van Haemstede, pastor of the Dutch congregation in London in the days of Elizabeth, undertook a defense of the Anabaptists when in 1560 the Queen ordered that they should all leave the realm within twenty days. Haemstede protested on the grounds that the Anabaptist doctrine of the flesh of Christ touched only the nonessentials and not the fundamentals of the Christian religion, and ought therefore to be tolerated. When Haemstede himself in consequence was in trouble, a lance on his behalf was broken by the great champion of religious liberty, Jacob Acontius.[4]

These examples are cited to show that the advocates of religious liberty found their prime examples of persecution in the treatment meted out to the Anabaptists. And therefore by their sufferings it may be said that they contributed directly to the ultimate achievement of freedom in religion. Their most direct contribution, however, lies in another area. It is a demonstration of the power of the segregated church to maintain its identity and continuity over the course of four centuries. This involves three phases. First came the resolve to become a segregated church. Secondly arose the problem of finding a refuge from extermination; and third was the achievement of internal cohesion.

The resolve to be a segregated community came about largely as a result of circumstance. There is at the outset in early Anabaptist literature an ambiguity, not to say a sharp dichotomy, between the concept of the church as a remnant and the Great Commission, binding upon every member, to proclaim the faith to all creatures. What was the purpose of the Great Commission? If the church must always be a remnant the conclusion appears inevitable that the Great Commission was bound to fail. Was this clearly envisaged by those who embarked upon it? Were they not trying to convert, but merely shaking off the dust from their feet as a testimony to increase the condemnation of those who rejected the message? One does not have the feeling in reading the documents that

---

4 Bainton, *op. cit.*, 113-14.

this was the point. There seems rather to have been a genuine hope of conversion. Nor was it fatuous at the time. Anabaptism spread in Switzerland, down the Rhine Valley, and in the Netherlands. The documents now in process of publication reveal an amazing dissemination and indicate a real possibility that Anabaptism, if unimpeded by the sword of the magistrate, might have become the prevailing form of the church in Germany. If that had happened, an infinitude of problems would have confronted the Anabaptists. What then would have happened to the state? Would there have been a theocratic community, with church and state united, and coercion reduced to the ban and avoidance? But we need not pursue these questions because the dilemmas were never raised. The Great Commission did not succeed. Persecution turned the Anabaptists into the Church of the Remnant.

Then came the problem of survival. There were only two ways: one was the way of accommodation and this way was taken by those of the Mennonites who remained in the Netherlands and by those Hutterites in Austria who accepted the mass in return for liberty in every other respect to retain their pattern of life. The other way of survival was that of migration to a frontier, whether that of the eastern fringe of Europe where feudalism still prevailed and some well-disposed nobleman could grant an asylum without interference from the central government, or else the frontier of the forest primeval in Canada, the Dakotas, or Paraguay. Even here survival was conditioned upon participation in the common life of the entire community at one point, namely, the economic. The immigrants were such good farmers that the ruler viewed them as a department of public economy and as contributing to the common effort even in wartime. He could get other people to fight. These pacifists he could use to feed the populace. This observation is not made in scorn. It is part of the dilemma of all pacifism. There is no survival in wartime unless one is prepared to do something which can be regarded as a service useful to those engaged in the conflict.

The next question was that of internal cohesion. Nothing is more amazing than the way these sixteenth-century dissenters learned to live with each other. Their genius and their experience lay in opposition. They were masters in the art of obstruction. They would shock the community by baptizing adults in the public fountain or by marching in procession through the streets of Zürich crying "Woe, Woe," and proclaiming that Zwingli was the dragon of the Apocalypse. Some in Holland like the later Quakers went naked as a sign in imitation of the prophet Isaiah. Some like Blaurock would interrupt public worship, and attempt to supplant the minister in his own pulpit. Summoned before a court, they might refuse to answer a word or they might wax denunciatory and call their examiners idolaters and heathen. Banished, the Anabaptists refused to stay away. Tortured, they endured without flinching. Executed, they died with a song. Even among themselves there were clashes because rival prophets claimed divergent inspirations from the Lord. And the ideal of perfection led not only to scrupulous self-criticism but also to censoriousness in regard to others. That people with such a temper should have been able to establish a stable community is indeed an amazing achievement.

Their squabbles often appear petty unless one bears in mind all they had endured and all they were striving to attain. In the Hutterian colony at Austerlitz quarrels at once commenced when Jacob Wiedemann selected husbands for the girls. The maidens murmured in spite of his remonstrance that if they did not consent the men would have to marry heathen girls. There were complaints that the children were being too severely disciplined. Positive schisms occurred because of personal rivalries. Räbel could not endure the leadership of Wiedemann and led a seceding group to Auschwitz. This group had as its head Simon Schützinger, when Jacob Huter arrived. He too was a shepherd and now the community had two shepherds. The confusion was adjusted by making Simon a "shepherd" and Jacob an "apostle" with differentiation of function. But this arrangement was upset when it was rumored that the Schützingers had violated the rule of absolutely no property. Search was made and in their possession were discovered some extra shirts and four pieces of money. Frau Schützinger was consequently a Sapphira and her husband an Ananias. They had to do penance and he was, of course, deposed from the leadership of the community. But a certain Philip suspected that Jacob Huter had engineered this *coup* and therefore seceded. Then Huter received a call from the Lord to go out on the Great Commission which for him ended in martyrdom. Reconciliation was eventually achieved between the Hutterites and the Philipists and under the leadership of Peter Ridemann a spirit of healing prevailed.[5] Such examples are cited not to stigmatize the movement as contentious and petty, but only to show how difficult and how remarkable was the taming of those very qualities which had made the first generation of Anabaptists so stalwart in their opposition to the world.

The subsequent history centers on the efforts of the community to retain its children, and this was done by fencing them off from the corrupting influences of the world round about. Persecution at this point is of real assistance, provided it stops short of extermination, and nothing is so disruptive of the pattern of the segregated church as friendliness from the outside. Therefore, in our own day the Hutterites and the most extreme of the Mennonites, notably the Amish, have sought in every way to make themselves a peculiar people uncontaminated by the ways of the evil world. They object, not so much to mechanization, and are willing to employ whatever is needful in order to compete with neighboring farmers; but they deliberately choose those forms of mechanization which entail the least contact with the world beyond. Gasoline is preferable to electricity because electricity affords the possibility of introducing so many appliances and gadgets

---

5 A. J. F. Zieglschmid (Ed.), *Die älteste Chronik der Hutterischen Brüder* (Ithaca, 1943). The relevant portions can be found through the index of names.

like the radio and television which bring the outside world into the very parlor. Riding in automobiles is not forbidden, but only the owning of automobiles, because in that case there will be altogether too much running around and the young people will be hard to retain within the confines of the community. The telephone for obvious reasons is taboo, and without it these people are well able to relay news in an incredibly short time. The most acute area of conflict is education because in this land of the free we require that everyone should be free in precisely the same fashion.

One cannot but admire the loyalty of these groups to their tradition which they believe to be the very will of God. They have demonstrated astoundingly the ability of groups despised and rejected by the world to triumph over opposition from without and disintegration from within and to hold their own children. Yet one may question whether such a way of life is to be deliberately chosen in our present culture. Recently there has been a revival of the Hutterite *Bruderhofs* in England, Paraguay, and the United States. A number of our most idealistic and best-trained young people are throwing in their lot with these communities. Such a course appears to me to be justified only on one or two assumptions. The first is that our society is utterly hopeless, that it can never be Christianized nor even ameliorated in a Christian direction. This is an assumption which for myself I am not prepared to make. The very fact that three Anabaptist principles have come to be cardinal for our way of life is itself the demonstration that the world is affected by the church and that some problems do admit of solution on a large scale and in a Christian way. Much indeed remains, and only with qualification can we speak of our country as a Christian land, yet this example should expel the spirit of utter hopelessness.

The second assumption is that a withdrawal may exert an influence upon society as a whole. This is always possible. Catholic monasticism in the Middle Ages undoubtedly exerted an impact on the whole social fabric. The Hutterites and the Amish in our day, however, do not in my judgment exert such an influence. They arouse interest because they are quaint, and in this our stereotyped culture we are glad to discover anything at all different. But this does not mean that we have the least disposition to apply the pattern to ourselves. I greatly question then whether the new *Bruderhofs* will evoke anything more than the interest excited by oddities. If this be true, then the withdrawal in this fashion from the common life, even though the discipline in the societies is rigorous, appears to me to be taking an easy way out of the complexities and dilemmas of our modern society. Living in the midst of the American culture in a world bristling with projectiles is no light assignment for a Christian, but we are not to assume that we are more Christian by disdaining it.

Thus far I have accepted the assignment to speak of the Anabaptists' contribution to history. Let it now be said that the worth of their endeavor is not to be judged in the light of their contribution to history. They took their stand in the light of eternity regardless of what might or might not happen in history. They did not fall into the error of those who treat the way of the cross as if it were a weapon, a political strategy by which to put over a program on the assumption that suffering will melt the persecutor and make him ready to adopt the way of his victim. The persecutor may be melted, but on the other hand he may be hardened, and the cross is not a strategy. It is a witness before God, no matter whether there may or may not be any historical consequences.

For multitudes of the Anabaptists there was not enough of a consequence to let us know even whether they did or did not suffer. We have for example the following list of names of men and women arrested at Augsburg (1528):

"Sebastian Vischgatter, hucker; Jorg Gietler, weber; Mang Betz, ringmacher; Wolf Coderus, schlosser; Hans Schlund, Hans Heises, Wilhalm Echsen; Jorg Schweitzer, wallschlager; Jakob Heises; Hans Hertlin, hucker; Hans

325

Butz, weber; Jos Thoman, ferber; Hans Fesenmair, weber; Eloi Forster, weber; Thoman Paur, tagwerker. . . .

"Getraut Heisesin, Afra Schleichin, Anna Berchtold-mairin, Magdalena Seitzin, Anna Kochin, Elisabeth Woll-schlagerin, Margareth Berchtoldin, Martha Beckin, Max-encia Wisingerin. . . ."[6]

Names, just names! Back of every one lay a history and after every one came a sequel, but we do not know what. Were they imprisoned, banished, beheaded, burned, drowned? The record does not say. Before God they stand with no notice in the annals of man.

There is in these same documents a letter which I found profoundly moving. It is from a wife to the town council of Regensburg in November or December 1539. She writes:

"Most noble lords, I beg you to look upon my petition with favor. Gabriel Weinperger was arrested because of *misglauben*. His case has dragged on for a long time. I am left with my little children without the help of their father and I find it very difficult to provide daily bread. We would like to live together again and I believe that if I can be permitted to speak to my husband I could persuade him for my sake and the children to give up these ideas because he never was a leader and never persuaded any others to take up these errors, but he simply listened to others. That my children may be supported I beg you to let me talk with him and I will not cease to pray God that your government may have long life and good fortune."

At the bottom of the letter is simply written the word "endorsed."[7] If Gabriel Weinperger listened to his wife and renounced his conviction, he would eat out his heart for the rest of his days as a renegade; if he rejected her plea and held firm to his confession, he would eat out his heart with concern for his wife and for his children. What he did we do not know. If he was faithful to his conviction, his deed stands not in the annals of history but in the eternal book of God.

6 Karl Schornbaum (Ed.), *Quellen zur Geschichte der Täufer V: Bayern, II Abteilung* (Gütersloh, 1951) 19.   7 *Ibid.*, 82-83.

✠ PAUL PEACHEY ✠

The Modern Recovery of the Anabaptist Vision

The modern recovery of the Anabaptist vision is a rich chapter in contemporary thought. As an intellectual and spiritual development, it has received contributions from the whole range of modern social and theological inquiry. Among those who have tried their hand at a fresh interpretation of this phase of Reformation history, some with very dubious success, one finds Marxists, socialists, liberals, humanists, mystics, proponents of the social gospel and of Christian socialism, confessionalists, evangelical Christians, and the cultural descendants of the sixteenth-century continental Anabaptist groups. The basic contribution has come, however, not from a particular school of interpretation, but from the modern science of history which has made available to scholars records of the actual words and witness of the little understood Christians of the sixteenth century known as Anabaptists.

This modern rediscovery of the sixteenth-century vision is instructive, however, not only because of the spiritual insights which it mediates, but also because such an attempt has certain lessons of its own to impart. The fact, for example, that men in the twentieth century should become seriously interested in a minority movement of the sixteenth century demonstrates once more the perennial fertility and relevance of any ideas which are genuinely rooted in basic human experience. For whether one approves or disapproves of the course taken by these hardy sixteenth-century Christians, one cannot escape the fact that they grappled earnestly with problems which today are as crucial to the human spirit as they were then.

*Paul Peachey is Associate Professor of Church History and Sociology in Eastern Mennonite College, and author of *Die soziale Herkunft der Schweizer Täufer in der Reformationszeit* (Karlsruhe, 1954).

On the other hand, however, this attempted recovery of the sixteenth-century vision demonstrates also the irreproducibility of certain historical situations or achievements. However faithfully the scholar may retrace the life and faith of these people, this in itself cannot rekindle the sixteenth-century fire. Indeed this may become a trap to him, for in giving intellectual assent, he may fail to see that this is not yet life commitment. For to arrive at a position by an academic tracing of another's steps can never be the same as arriving there, perhaps unpremeditatedly, in the real life struggle. Even if it can be shown that a Luther or a Menno Simons was influenced by earlier Christians, the factors in the creative movements which they led were for them, as they must be for us, "existential" rather than theological.

Does this apparent contradiction—the relevance of the idea, and yet the irreproducibility of the movement—render our preoccupation with Anabaptist research futile? Could this mean that we cannot even comprehend the vision because we cannot reproduce it? Or if the ideas are valid and fertile, may they yet have life meaning for us though in a form completely other than the sixteenth-century form? These are the questions that are to occupy this essay.

As a point of departure we can perhaps do no better than to call up one of the sixteenth-century witnesses, namely, Hans Denk, recognizing, however, that he may not represent fully the main Anabaptist stream. Said Denk in an oft-quoted statement: "No one can truly know Christ, except he follow Him in life." (*Christum vermag niemand wahrlich zu erkennen, es sei denn, dass er ihm nachfolge im Leben.*) This would make us bold to say that no one can comprehend the Anabaptist vision unless he follows it, but also to ask, can we follow it unless we know it? This latter question makes it necessary for us to separate knowing and doing the Anabaptist vision (two operations which, we submit, in the ultimate sense are inseparable). We shall address ourselves to the content of the vision first, and then to the question of its relevance.

I

The term "Anabaptist Vision," dramatized by Harold S. Bender's incisive presidential address before the American Society of Church History in 1943, is a happy one. The concept came as the fruit, not only of his own two decades of creative study in the field, but also of the whole modern Anabaptist research effort. In this paper he proposed that Anabaptism can be understood in terms of three foci of interest: (1) a new understanding of Christianity as discipleship; (2) a new concept of the church "as a body of committed and practicing Christians . . ."; and (3) as an ethic of love and nonresistance in all human relationships. In the discussion which followed the publication of this paper,[1] Bender pointed out further that probably the first of these concepts should be regarded as basic, while the other two might be regarded as derivative. This led him to state still later that the decisive question is our view of Christ: Is He primarily a prophet or moral teacher; or is He a being to be worshiped; or is He a savior; or is He with all this, also Lord? The latter, says Bender, "is the Anabaptist answer to Christ."[2]

Over against this approach stand other lines of interpretation, which, while not necessarily contradictory, nonetheless place the accent on other aspects of the movement. Most prominent among these are the search for the true church as emphasized by Krahn[3] and Littell,[4] Biblicism,[5] and existential Christianity as formulated by Friedmann,[6] but in some sense similar to Bender's theology of discipleship. The list

---

1 Harold S. Bender, "The Anabaptist Vision," *Church History* (March 1944) 13:3-24; in slightly revised form, *MQR* (April 1944) 18:67-88.

2 Bender, "The Anabaptist Theology of Discipleship," *MQR* (January 1950) 24:29.

3 Cornelius Krahn, *Menno Simons* (Karlsruhe, 1936); also his "Prolegomena to an Anabaptist Theology," *MQR* (January 1950) 24:5-11.

4 Franklin H. Littell, *The Anabaptist View of the Church* (Philadelphia, 1952).

5 Cf. Robert Friedmann, "Recent Interpretations of Anabaptism," *Church History* (June 1955) 24:138.

6 *Ibid.*, 24:144.

could be extended. At this juncture one cannot yet say that a conclusion has been reached. The prediction may even be hazarded that no simple formula will ever be forthcoming, for Anabaptism was probably too dynamic a movement to be reduced to a simple definition.

If we recognize this limitation, however, a characterization such as entailed in the term "Anabaptist Vision" can be most fruitful, and indeed has been. Not only has this formula stimulated the world of scholarship, but in some measure it has leaped across library and archive walls to catch the imagination of people in other walks of life. Among American Mennonites in particular, the Anabaptist vision has done much to awaken a sense of historic destiny, and in a measure this is also occurring in other countries as well. To evaluate this development properly, we should note some of the recurrent themes and lasting insights associated with it. This list does not pretend to be new or exhaustive, nor does it seek to define the theological content of the Anabaptist vision. This last is still one of the major tasks to be fulfilled.[7]

1. Today Reformation history is being rewritten. A merely polemical treatment of the conflict between Anabaptism and the great *Volkskirche* traditions is today inexcusable, and indeed increasingly rare. This does not mean that scholars personally reject the latter for the former, but rather that they recognize that under the exigencies of the sixteenth-century church culture the fundamental facts and needs of religious experience were often ignored and violated, and that Anabaptism flourished precisely for this reason. Without necessarily pronouncing upon the wisdom of the one position as over against the other, the genuineness of the latter is now recognized.

2. Not only is the religious concern of the Anabaptists now recognized, but a new estimate of their roots and origin now obtains. Where earlier their impulses were attributed

---

7 See the special Anabaptist theology number of the *MQR* (January 1950) 24:1-98, also Albert D. Klassen, Jr., "Did Our Forefathers Have a Theology?" *Mennonite Life* (October 1956) 11:189 ff.

to social or economic interests or, perhaps with more reason, to vestiges of late medieval sects and protest movements, it is now generally held that Anabaptists were actually the off-spring of the Reformation. The thesis of Waldensian descent in one particular area has been restated recently by a competent historian,[8] but this can only serve to underscore the possibility that such influences may have prepared the soil indirectly for the Anabaptist seed. Then, too, the varied character of Dutch Anabaptism would lend support to the view that earlier influences must certainly have played an important role. But in so far as the movement achieved an outer identity and continuity as an historic group, the roots in the Zwinglian Reformation in Zürich are beyond dispute.

3. In contrast to the emphasis which developed in both the Lutheran and the Reformed traditions, Anabaptism was built on the new life in Christ rather than on (mere) justification by faith. At every juncture the accent fell on the believer's identification with Christ rather than on an objective forensic transaction which had little or no effect on the actual character of the believer.

4. It is generally recognized that the Anabaptists sought the restitution rather than the mere reformation of the church, which was the aim of the major Reformers. This meant a general disregard for historical continuity, based on the conviction that God called men to act immediately through His work in their midst rather than through existent historical structures. This approach has sometimes been called "Christian primitivism," a term readily misunderstood if it is taken to mean an (attempted) external reduplication of apostolic Christianity rather than action in the immediacy of the Spirit.

5. Today there is recognized within the left wing of the Reformation a distinction between the Bible-centered and the community-centered Anabaptists on the one hand, and the spiritualists or individualistic mystics on the other. The

8 Delbert Gratz, *Bernese Anabaptists* (Goshen, 1953) 3-7.

failure to make this distinction has been the cause of some of the difficulty in earlier scholarship. Ernst Troeltsch set forth this distinction by contrasting the mystic (individual) and the sect down through Christian history, a distinction that empirical Anabaptist research has confirmed. This distinction, however, is easier in theory than in practice, and has most certainly been overstressed in some instances.

6. "Classical Anabaptism" is now viewed as essentially nonresistant or pacifist, rather than violently revolutionary. This is stressed, not only against the view that it was innately violent (Münster), but also against the view that its supposed original violence was excised by the moderating hand of Menno Simons. Yet here too, while it is clear that the original movement of 1525 was innately nonresistant, the distinction between this and other violent expressions is not alike clear in all parts of Europe.

7. Anabaptism can be viewed as a synthesis between Christian freedom and discipline rare in history. The fact that one and the same group could be variously accused of legalism and libertinism, as was the case in the sixteenth century, would illustrate the pronounced presence of both impulses. This fact is also illustrated by the modern controversy between Horsch and Kühler over the essence of Anabaptism.[9] Actually, as has been so well said recently: "In the Anabaptist tradition, the freedom of the Christian is combined with the utmost discipline in community."[10]

8. Anabaptism is now widely acclaimed as the pioneer effort in the modern world to achieve the great twin principles of religious voluntarism and of the separation of church and state.

9. Some scholars now recognize that the Anabaptists raised the perennial problem of Christianity in its relation to

9 John Horsch, "Is Dr. Kühler's Conception of Early Dutch Anabaptism Historically Sound?" *MQR* (January and April 1933) 7:48-60, 97-126: a reply to W. J. Kühler, *Geschiedenis der Nederlandsche Doopsgezinden in de Zestiende Eeuw* (Haarlem, 1932).

10 John Dillenberger and Claude Welch, *Protestant Christianity* (New York, 1954) 67.

culture at a time when the distinction was obscure in general thought and practice. For any state church or *Volkskirche* system tends to "baptize" its culture rather indiscriminately, and such was indeed the case in medieval Christendom. That this aspect of Anabaptism leaves us with unsolved problems we shall note presently.

II

Despite these basic achievements, some very crucial problems remain. The first of these has to do with our general view of Anabaptism or the attempt to delineate its essence. Again and again the question of an Anabaptist theology has arisen, and some efforts toward such a formulation have already been made.[11] Certainly it seems both possible and desirable that we should possess a kind of Anabaptist theological compendium. One could, for example, take all the sixteenth-century writings, and from them compile a systematic arrangement, by topics, of all theological utterances. Or one could go further to write a theology based upon such a compilation, and could thereupon conclude with some confidence that an Anabaptist theology had been formulated. It is indeed not too much to hope that in due time both tasks will be done. And yet I am filled with misgivings at the thought. Can Anabaptism be comprehended in this way? Is this the proper method with which to approach these Christians? Can a practical Christianity such as this be grasped by or reduced to a theological system? Would it truly advance the cause of the Anabaptist vision to seek to do so?

A second question deserving further study is that of Anabaptist Biblicism. As Friedmann rightly implies,[12] Anabaptist Biblicism in modern times has become widely identified with the Fundamentalist view of Scripture. It is the view of the present writer that few outside influences have so adversely affected modern Mennonites as this confusion. Quite apart

11 See above, note 7; cf. John C. Wenger, *The Doctrines of the Mennonites* (Scottdale, 1950).

12 Robert Friedmann, "Anabaptism and Protestantism," *MQR* (January 1950) 24:12-24.

from the spiritualists to whom we have already alluded, and the Anabaptists of South Germany who were more spiritualistically colored than the Swiss, the Swiss Brethren as well as Menno Simons are never quite the literalists they are today often made out to be. Menno for example repeatedly refers to the living Word of God to which the Scriptures testify, though there are also times when he identifies the Bible with the Word of God. At a time when great uncertainty and controversy with regard to Bible authority obtain, one can only hope that from this source continued study will shed additional light.

A third major question not yet adequately clarified is the relationship of Anabaptism to culture. A pessimistic view of world culture and the demand for a Christian separation from it is clearly a major Anabaptist tenet. Any attempts to evade this would certainly misconstrue the movement. Because of the early acute persecution, however, it is hard to discern the full scope or content of that nonconformity. One could ask whether persecution may have served the constructive role of sharpening the opposition of church and culture, otherwise the distinction might never have become clear. On the other hand, the early death of the outstanding leaders, especially among the Swiss Brethren, most certainly precluded their working out more fully their attitude toward the state, for example, or their attitude toward the guilds. In practice, great uncertainty regarding the Christian's relation to the general culture obtains among Mennonites today. In the Menno Simons lectures at Bethel College, Roland H. Bainton dealt with one aspect of this problem in a most perceptive way. In discussing the world mission of Christianity, he said: "If there is no accommodation [to culture], Christianity is unintelligible and cannot spread. If there is too much accommodation it will spread, but will no longer be Christianity."[13]

13 Roland H. Bainton, "The Enduring Witness," *Mennonite Life* (April 1954) 9:89.

III

The second phase of our task is more difficult. If today we can look with confidence toward the accomplishment of an adequate historical and theological treatment of Anabaptism, is the same optimism possible with regard to the basic re-activation of the vision in practice? We ask therefore, was Anabaptism merely a movement in the bosom of Christianity which has fulfilled its historic mission and whose contributions have been assimilated by the ongoing stream of the Christian heritage? And is it therefore our task today to study the sixteenth-century Anabaptist movement in order to understand better such great modern concepts as religious liberty or to draw inspiration from the heroic Christian living of other days? Or does the Anabaptist vision still call today toward a different kind of Christian living, as it did four centuries ago? Does it still mean radical dissent from predominant religious patterns of the age?

One is led on the surface to suspect that the out-group scholar would incline toward the former viewpoint, namely, that Anabaptism is one of the rich tributaries to the stream of modern culture.[14] The in-group scholar could be expected to incline toward the latter viewpoint, namely, that there is still a distinct mission for an Anabaptist movement in its own right, though not denying the importance of the other. Certainly the effort of modern Mennonites to revitalize their life and communities by appeal to the Anabaptist ideal gives expression to this latter view. Closer examination, however, will probably show that such a distinction is a dubious one to make, for it is likely to underestimate the seriousness of the one type of study and to overestimate the seriousness of the other. One finds among out-group writers sentiments like those of Walther Köhler who is said to have remarked that

14 For example, it is frequently pointed out today that the concepts of religious voluntarism and separation of church and state find their pioneer advocates in the sixteenth-century Anabaptists. Cf. Fritz Blanke, *Brüder in Christo* (Zürich, 1955) 81 ff.

he "would like to die a Mennonite,"[15] while among in-group writers the case is by no means clear as to the contemporary meaning of Anabaptism. Without identifying the two views regarding the relevance of Anabaptist research with the out-group and in-group writers respectively, it is here that we come to the really crucial issue in our evaluation of the Anabaptist vision. Is this vision relevant because of the light it sheds upon our heritage, or does it rather confront Christendom ever anew with the call to radical discipleship?

It is primarily the latter viewpoint that is represented by the *Mennonite Quarterly Review* and by Dean Bender who has so ably led it through three decades of fruitful work. This does not mean that the former viewpoint is not worth while in its own right, and Bender would probably be the last to deny that that is the case. Precisely in the former sense one can undoubtedly say with Franklin Littell that "the true importance of the churches of the Restitution goes far beyond those communities which today admit lineal descent from the Anabaptist movements."[16] And yet these sixteenth-century Christians would hardly have seen in this secondary contribution the fulfillment of their ideal. Precisely because they rejected the concept of staying in the *Volkskirche* to improve it gradually, to evaluate them only in such terms does not seem to do them justice.

To choose the second viewpoint, however, namely, that there is still a mission for Anabaptism in its own right, confronts us with far greater difficulty. Because we must then decide whether we refer to those communions who stand in the line of direct cultural and even biological descent from the sixteenth-century Anabaptists, or whether we intend a movement in some sense radically discontinuous with the past. To understand this question we must turn our attention to the original constitutive act of the Swiss Brethren and of other early groups. We here see the Zwinglians and the

15 Franklin H. Littell, "New Approach to Anabaptist Research," *Mennonite Life* (October 1953) 8:167.
16 Littell, *Anabaptist View of the Church,* 112.

Grebel party drawn up in juxtaposition. Zwingli has espoused a program of compromise, while Grebel demands Biblical action. Finally this compromise seems so serious that the latter group takes steps sufficiently radical to eventuate in a total break between the two. To affirm their action is to say that apostasy may become so serious as to necessitate and justify religious revolution. The Anabaptists are thus credited with spiritual insight to have assessed the situation properly, and with courage to have acted accordingly.

This evaluation seems correct, but does it go far enough? The ensuing struggle between the several state churches and the believers' *Gemeinden* gives occasion to conclude that the significance of the Anabaptist course of action lay much deeper. For in the court hearings and the disputations held against and with the Anabaptists up and down through western Europe, the duly constituted authorities of church and state again and again challenged these recalcitrants to produce evidence that they were authorized to preach and to act in things religious. Obviously they could not appeal to either the pope or the magistracy since both were precisely what they had repudiated as religious authority. What claims could they make? Usually, of course, they appealed to the personal inner call of the Spirit, but beyond this they also appealed to the church. But what church? Simply to that people in whose midst the Word of God had been proclaimed, and in whom repentance and new life were brought forth and a new gathering of God's people had occurred. This meant that the work of the Spirit as He gathers a people is self-authenticating, not bound or determined by ecclesiastical institutions.

The real import of this radical action by these people lay not merely in their repudiation of apostate or compromised *Volkskirche* traditions, but in the rediscovery that the church is ever the continuously created fellowship of the people of God in Christ through the Spirit. Thus the assembly is vested with the attributes of the church not merely in the exceptional case when occasion for revolution arises, but by her basic nature her authority to act stems from the immediacy of Christ in the midst of His people. Anabaptism means that the living fellowship by its very nature can never be transformed into objectified ecclesiastical structure, for fellowship with Christ and the brother is, in the full-orbed sense, the essence of the church.

This conclusion may at first thought spell pure anarchy; and it must indeed be recognized that this insight does not solve the whole problem. Our real difficulty, however, is one of understanding. Accustomed as we are to conceive the church largely in institutional terms, and to conceive church unity in terms of common theologies, traditions, and unified institutions of government, we are ill-equipped to understand the reality of unity in Christ. Admittedly a church conceived in more spiritual terms is also more dangerous, but the adventures of the Spirit are never "safe." For while reliance on culture and ecclesiastical structure can insure greater uniformity (though not necessarily unity) among a group of like-traditioned and like-minded assemblies, those very unifying entities weigh heavily on the true spiritual creativity of the assembly, and throttle the experience of fellowship with those standing outside the communion in question.

It is on these scales, it seems to me, that the reactivation of the Anabaptist vision among the cultural descendants of the sixteenth-century vision must be weighed. And it is on these scales finally that these groups are found wanting. It cannot be denied that, while there may be genuine spiritual vitality among many, theirs is still in great measure an ethnic cohesion. But in so far as we build upon a carefully guarded cultural continuity, on objectively formulated creeds or theology, on uniform social institutions and culture traits, where is the valiant leap of faith, the eschatological expectancy, and the radical walk of discipleship in the new aeon? It was Menno Simons who insisted not only theologically, but also existentially, that no other foundation can be laid than Jesus

Christ. It was Menno Simons who soundly rebuked the Reformed Gellius Faber for holding that the church is still the church, despite the absence of the true fruit of the Spirit, because Faber thought the church could be inherited outwardly from generation to generation. And as late as 1660 so great a conservative as T. J. van Braght still manifested a fundamental distrust for the idea of external (i.e., apostolic) succession, for he wrote: "By the particular succession is understood the succession of teachers, from person to person, in a particular church. . . . But concerning this there is no promise, law, or commandment to be found in the whole Gospel, and we, therefore, pass on."[17]

As long as Mennonites are tied existentially to their culture as supposedly infused with a spiritual quality (and the same must be said of any other denomination or tradition), the hope that the vision will break forth to become once more a mighty missionary movement will be largely illusory. Other creative movements as Quakerism and Methodism have had similar experiences. As long as their genius had not crystallized into cultural tradition they were creative, but their prophetic impact waned when they developed externally transmissible sub-culture systems. It will be objected that such an analysis is unrealistic, that as Richard Niebuhr so aptly points out, the sect (believers' church) can keep its distinct character only during the first generation. Admittedly, the mere fact that Christian parents seek to throw a Christian influence about their children, may well limit the "chances" that theirs will be a daring, heroic faith. Even one's personal experience of yesterday may militate, as tradition does in the group, against the decision of today! But do these fundamental facts of life justify our transformation of the church of Christ into something which she essentially cannot be and was never intended to be?

17 T. J. van Braght, *Martyrs' Mirror* (Scottdale, 1951) 26. For Menno's statement see *The Complete Writings of Menno Simons* (Scottdale, 1956) 754. For this entire discussion compare the author's "Anabaptism and Church Organization," *MQR* (July 1956) 30:213-28.

I would therefore propose that the genius of the Anabaptist vision lies not merely in the heroic act of men who dared to abandon the apostate *Volkskirche* culture inherited and developed by medieval Christendom, but above all in the reassertion of the fact that the church is always truly the church in the living existential community. It is this vision that calls us to throw off the swaddling clothes of a cultural continuum, and once more to follow Christ only as He dwells in the midst of His people. "No one can truly know Christ, except he follow Him in life." If our study of the Anabaptist vision can serve as a schoolmaster to lead us to Christ, if the Anabaptist heritage can decrease that Christ may increase, Harold S. Bender's noble labor of love can mean much to troubled men in a troubled world. If instead we transform the vision into a terminal cultural value we shall all go down with the other Pharisaisms of history. "Other foundation can no man lay than that is laid, which is Jesus Christ."

Index

342

*mation des Schweitzerland-
es,* 2
Beza, Theodore, 319
Bible Christians, Anabaptists
as, 120, 168, 169, 302
Bible only authority in faith
(see *Sola scriptura*)
Bible study among the Ana-
baptists, 167
Bible translations by Anabap-
tists, 170
Biblicism of the Anabaptists,
38, 57, 67, 69, 70, 79, 84, 85,
88, 95, 96, 102, 103, 106,
137, 155, 156, 157, 167-169,
193, 284, 331, 333
Bibliography on Anabaptism,
1-10, 29n
*Bibliotheca Reformatoria Ne-
erlandica* (B.R.N.), 3, 69n,
70n, 277n
*Biblische Lehre von der
Wehrlosigkeit,* 10
Bidloo, Lambert, 235
Bidloo, Nicolaas, 229
Biestkens Bible, 170
Bigamy of Philip, 179
Bilder und Führergestalten, 6
Bishop, Anabaptist office of,
72
Blanke, Fritz, 4, 37, 57, 120,
194, 195n, 304, 311, 312n
Blaupot ten Cate (see Cate,
Blaupot ten)
Blaurock, George, 62, 66, 237,
322
Bluffton College, 9, 19, 180
Blutgericht in Rottenburg, 5
Bockholt, Westphalia, 313
Bogenitz, Moravia, 164
Bogomiles, 36, 304
Bolt, Eberle, martyr, 64n
Bossert, Gustav, 4, 5, 6, 15,
47n, 125n, 215n
Bouwens, Leonard, 161
Braght, T. J. van, 146n, 175n,
339
Braidl, Claus, 85
Braitmichel, Caspar, 85
Bredero, Gerbrandt A., 278
Brenz, Johannes, 174

Brethren, Church of, 263, 266,
269, 270, 311
Brethren in Christ, 270
Brethren of the Common
Life, 70
Brethren Service Committee,
269
Brinckmann, Heinrich, 281
British treatment of pacifists,
272
Bröske school, 244
Brotherhood character of the
Anabaptist Church 49, 116,
123, 195-201, 223, 253, 303
Brotherhoods, 112
Brotherly love, 255
Brotkasse, 257
Brötli, Johannes, 61, 62, 63n,
237
Browne, Robert, 313
Brüder in Christo, 4, 57n, 62n
Bruin, Claas, 230
Brunner, Emil, 315n
Brüsewitz, C. F., 28
Bucer, Martin, 101n, 102, 199
Bullinger, Heinrich, 30, 44,
46, 59, 163, 198, 202-209,
313
Burkholder, J. Lawrence, 135
Burrage, Henry S., 7
Bussfertigkeit, 39
Busskampf, 116, 241
Butler, Samuel, 278

Calling, Luther's concept of,
139
Calvin, John, 139, 154, 200,
276, 297, 300, 313
Calvinism, 115, 219, 224, 225,
306
Calvinism and the social order, 53
Camerarius, 210n
Canada, Mennonites in, 249,
257, 321
Canadian Alternative Service
program, 268
Capital punishment, Divergent Anabaptist views on,
192

343

346

358

The Contributors

ROLAND H. BAINTON, Titus Street Professor of Ecclesiastical History, Yale University

MARY ELEANOR BENDER, Assistant Professor of English, Goshen College

FRITZ BLANKE, Professor of Church History, University of Zürich

J. LAWRENCE BURKHOLDER, Associate Professor of Bible and Philosophy, Goshen College

ERNST H. CORRELL, Professor of Economic History, American University

ERNST CROUS, Director, Mennonite Research Center, Göttingen

E. K. FRANCIS, Professor of Sociology, University of Notre Dame

J. WINFIELD FRETZ, Professor of Sociology, Bethel College

ROBERT FRIEDMANN, Professor of History and Philosophy, Western Michigan University

MELVIN GINGERICH, Director, Mennonite Research Foundation

J. D. GRABER, Executive Secretary, Mennonite Board of Missions and Charities and Assistant Professor of Missions, Goshen College

GUY F. HERSHBERGER, Professor of History and Sociology, Goshen College

CORNELIUS KRAHN, Professor of Church History, Bethel College; Editor of *Mennonite Life*

ROBERT KREIDER, Dean and Professor of History, Bluffton College

FRANKLIN H. LITTELL, Representative in Germany of the Franz Lieber Foundation

JOHN S. OYER, Assistant Professor of History, Goshen College

ERNEST A. PAYNE, General Secretary of Baptist Union of Great Britain and Ireland, formerly Senior Tutor at Regent's Park College, Oxford

PAUL PEACHEY, Associate Professor of Church History and Sociology, Eastern Mennonite College

DON E. SMUCKER, Professor of Biblical Theology and Christian Ethics, Mennonite Biblical Seminary

JOHN C. WENGER, Professor of Theology, Goshen College Biblical Seminary

JOHN H. YODER, doctoral candidate, University of Basel

N. VAN DER ZIJPP, Professor of Church History, Mennonite Theological Seminary, Amsterdam